Studies in Marxism and Social Theory

Analytical Marxism

Studies in Marxism and Social Theory

Edited by G. A. COHEN, JON ELSTER AND JOHN ROEMER

The series is jointly published by the Cambridge University Press and the Editions de la Maison des Sciences de l'Homme, as part of the joint publishing agreement established in 1977 between the Fondation de la Maison des Sciences de l'Homme and the Syndics of the Cambridge University Press.

The books in the series are intended to exemplify a new paradigm in the study of Marxist social theory. They will not be dogmatic or purely exegetical in approach. Rather, they will examine and develop the theory pioneered by Marx, in the light of the intervening history, and with the tools of non-Marxist social science and philosophy. It is hoped that Marxist thought will thereby be freed from the increasingly discredited methods and presuppositions which are still widely regarded as essential to it, and that what is true and important in Marxism will be more firmly established.

Also in the series

JON ELSTER *Making Sense of Marx*
ADAM PRZEWORSKI *Capitalism and Social Democracy*

Analytical Marxism

Edited by

John Roemer

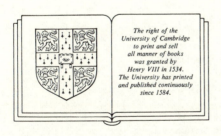

The right of the
University of Cambridge
to print and sell
all manner of books
was granted by
Henry VIII in 1534.
The University has printed
and published continuously
since 1584.

Cambridge University Press

Cambridge

London   New York   New Rochelle

Melbourne   Sydney

Editions de la Maison des Sciences de l'Homme

Paris

Published by the Press Syndicate of the University of Cambridge
The Pitt Building, Trumpington Street, Cambridge CB2 IRP
32 East 57th Street, New York, NY 10022, USA
10 Stamford Road, Oakleigh, Melbourne 3166, Australia
and Editions de la Maison des Sciences de l'Homme
54 Boulevard Raspail, 75270 Paris Cedex 06

© Maison des Sciences de l'Homme and Cambridge University Press 1986

First published 1986

Printed in Great Britain by the University Press, Cambridge

British Library cataloguing in publication data
Analytical Marxism. – (Studies in Marxism and
social theory)
1. Communism 2. Socialism
I. Roemer, John E. II. Series
335.4   HX73

Library of Congress cataloguing in publication data
Analytical Marxism.
(Studies in Marxism and social theory)
Bibliography: p.
1. Marxism economics – Addresses, essays, lectures.
2. Communism – Addresses, essays, lectures.
I. Roemer, John E. II. Series.
HB97.5.A487 1985   335.4   85-11697

ISBN 0 521 30025 8 hard cover
ISBN 0 521 31731 2 paperback
ISBN 2 7351 0118 5 hard covers (France)
ISBN 2 7351 0117 7 paperback (France)

Contents

page

About the authors — vii

Introduction — I

I Historical materialism — 9

1 *G. A. Cohen*, Forces and relations of production — 11

2 *Robert Brenner*, The social basis of economic development — 23

3 *Jon Elster*, The theory of combined and uneven development: a critique — 54

4 *Pranab Bardhan*, Marxist ideas in development economics: an evaluation — 64

II Class — 79

5 *John Roemer*, New directions in the Marxian theory of exploitation and class — 81

6 *Erik Olin Wright*, What is middle about the middle class? — 114

7 *Jon Elster*, Three challenges to class — 141

8 *Adam Przeworski*, Material interests, class compromise, and the transition to socialism — 162

III Method — 189

9 *John Roemer*, 'Rational choice' Marxism: some issues of method and substance — 191

10 *Jon Elster*, Further thoughts on Marxism, functionalism, and game theory — 202

11 *G. A. Cohen*, Marxism and functional explanation — 221

IV Justice — 235

12 *G. A. Cohen*, The structure of proletarian unfreedom — 237

13 *John Roemer*, Should Marxists be interested in exploitation? — 260

14 *Allen Wood*, Marx and equality — 283

Bibliography — 304

v

About the authors

Pranab Bardhan is Professor of Economics at the University of California, Berkeley. He is the author of *Land, Labour and Rural Poverty* (Columbia University Press, 1984), *The Political Economy of Development in India* (Oxford, Basil Blackwell, 1984) and *Economic Growth, Development and Foreign Trade: A Study in Pure Theory* (New York, John Wiley, 1970). His current research interests include the economics of agrarian institutions and the role of the state and social structures in the process of development.

Robert Brenner teaches in the history department at the University of California, Los Angeles. Two of his recent essays on the transition from feudalism to capitalism, which originally appeared in *Past and Present*, will appear in *The Brenner Debate: Agrarian Class Structure and Economic Development in Preindustrial Europe*, ed. T. H. Aston and C. H. E. Philpin (Cambridge University Press, 1985). His book *Merchants and Revolution* will be published by Princeton University Press, in 1985. He is an activist in the labour movement in Los Angeles and an editor of *Against the Current*, a socialist quarterly magazine.

Having taught for twenty-one years in the Philosophy Department at University College, London, *G. A. Cohen* is now Chichele Professor of Social and Political Theory and Fellow of All Souls, Oxford. He is the author of *Karl Marx's Theory of History: A Defence* (Oxford and Princeton, 1978), and of articles on social and political philosophy in academic journals. His principal current interest is in freedom and justice with respect to capitalism and socialism.

Jon Elster (b. 1940) is Professor of Political Science at the University of Chicago and Research Director at the Institute for Social Research, Oslo. His publications include *Making Sense of Marx* (Cambridge University Press, 1985), *Sour Grapes* (Cambridge University Press, 1983), *Explaining Technical Change* (Cambridge University Press, 1983), *Ulysses and the Sirens* (Cambridge University Press, 1979, rev. ed. 1984) and *Logic and Society* (Chichester, John Wiley, 1978). He is currently working on problems related to bargaining, collective action and social justice.

Adam Przeworski is the Martin A. Ryerson Distinguished Service Professor of Political Science at the University of Chicago. His recent publications include *Capitalism and Social Democracy* (Cambridge University Press, 1985) and, as a co-author, *Paper Stones: A History of Electoral Socialism*. Currently (when not engaged in utopian musings), he is working on a project concerning the relation between governments and private economic actors.

After teaching mathematics for five years in San Francisco secondary schools and organizing in a rank-and-file caucus in the teacher's union, *John Roemer* began teaching at the University of California at Davis in 1974, where he is now Professor of Economics. His recent publications include *Analytical Foundations of Marxian Economic Theory* (Cambridge University Press, 1981), *A General Theory of Exploitation and Class* (Harvard University Press, 1982), 'Equality of Talent' (*Economics and Philosophy*, 1985), and other articles which have appeared in journals of economics, philosophy and politics. He is currently working on questions of egalitarianism, distributive justice, and preference formation.

Allen W. Wood has been Professor of Philosophy at Cornell University since 1980. He is author of *Kant's Moral Religion* (Cornell University Press, 1970), *Kant's Rational Theology* (Cornell University Press, 1978), and *Karl Marx* (London, Routledge and Kegan Paul, 1981). His current research interests include Hegel's moral philosophy.

Erik Olin Wright is Professor of Sociology at the University of Wisconsin, Madison, and director of the Havens Center for the Study of Social Structure and Social Change. He is currently working on a large-scale, cross-national study of class structure and class consciousness. His most recent publications include *Classes* (London, New Left Books/Verso, 1985), 'Capitalism's futures' (*Socialist Review*, no. 68, 1983), and 'Giddens's critique of Marxism' (*New Left Review*, no. 138, 1983).

Introduction

During the past decade, what now appears as a new species in social theory has been forming: analytically sophisticated Marxism. Its practitioners are largely inspired by Marxian questions, which they pursue with contemporary tools of logic, mathematics, and model building. Their methodological posture is conventional. These writers are, self-consciously, products of both the Marxian and non-Marxian traditions.

What are the aspects of method by which 'analytical Marxism' differentiates itself from conventional Marxism? First, an unabashed commitment to the necessity for abstraction. Conventional Marxism is, for the most part, hesitant to distance itself too far from actual history. Marxism's deep anchor is a certain view of history – as the progression of class societies in which a small class of non-workers appropriates or expropriates the economic surplus from a large class of workers. If one cuts loose from that anchor, what is there to keep one from being beached on the shoals of bourgeois scholasticism? But abstraction is necessary if one is ever properly to focus on, and reveal, the moving parts of any theory and analytical Marxists are not loath to practise it.

Perhaps the commitment to abstraction follows from another characterizing feature of analytical Marxism, the search for foundations. Thus, many of the essays in this book ask questions that conventional Marxism sees no need to raise. For example: Why do classes emerge as important collective actors (or do they) (Essay 7)? Why is exploitation, the systematic transfer of surplus labour, wrong (or is it) (Essay 13)? Is socialism in the interest of workers in modern capitalism (Essay 8)? Is socialist revolution or transformation possible (Essay 3)? Is the proletariat unfree (Essay 12)? Is equality a goal of Marxian ethics (Essay 14)? The effort to answer these questions, and others like them, follows from the need to understand what more primitive or basic principles underlie Marxian judgments. And the search for basic principles leads naturally to schematizing, simplifying, and modelling.

What produced this search for foundations, which led to asking these perhaps heretical questions, and using state-of-the-art methods of analytical

I

philosophy and 'positivist' social science to study them? I think two phenomena of our era are responsible: the chequered success of socialism and the dubious failure of capitalism. These two events are unquestionably *the* serious challenges to Marxism, as it was inherited from the nineteenth century. One response is to retreat to a Talmudic defence of the Word, and to find an interpretation which conforms with history as it has come to pass. Another is to deny what appear to be the historical facts. A third response is to reject Marxism as fundamentally wrong. The fourth response is to recognize that Marxism is nineteenth-century social science. As such, it is bound to be primitive by modern standards, wrong in detail, and perhaps even in some basic claims. Yet its power in explaining certain historical periods and events seems so strong that one feels there must be a valid core, which needs to be clarified and elucidated. One does not throw away a good tool because it fails in certain applications, especially if one lacks a better one. Instead, one asks: Why does this tool work well sometimes and not other times? Why does this edge cut sometimes and not others? This is the intellectual foundation of the trend I am calling analytical Marxism.

It follows, and hardly needs mentioning, that a third characteristic of the writers represented here is a non-dogmatic approach to Marxism. This is reflected, often, in lack of Marxian exegesis. For the most part, workers in the new tradition are not particularly concerned with what Marx wrote or said. What matters is the coherence of the idea.

But why should this kind of work be called Marxist? I am not sure that it should; but the label does convey at least that certain fundamental insights are viewed as coming from Marx. Historical materialism, class, and exploitation are treated as central organizing categories. There is a belief that some kind of socialism is superior to existing capitalism, and that the alienation and injustice of actually existing capitalism can be overcome. Indeed, perhaps the greatest task for Marxism today is to construct a modern theory of socialism. Such a theory must include an explanation of the inefficiencies and injustices of modern capitalism, and a theoretical blueprint for an alleviation of these flaws in a feasible socialist society. I think the methods and tools of analytical Marxism are what is needed for such a theory.

Each of the four parts in this book presents a significant re-working of classical Marxian concepts. In the first essay, G. A. Cohen presents a summary of his interpretation of the theory of historical materialism, in which the nature of the economic structure (including property relations) depends upon the development of the productive forces. A natural question which arises, given Cohen's 'determinist' conception of historical materialism, concerns the role of class struggle in history. How can the economic structure be determined by the productive forces and yet, at the same time, all history be the history of class struggle? Cohen addresses this apparent contradiction in historical materialism in his essay. Robert Brenner, in the second essay, takes a position almost diametrically opposed to Cohen, as he maintains that changes in property relations must precede economic development (or development of the productive forces), not follow from that development, as Cohen would have it. For Brenner, the behaviour of historical actors is conditioned by their material circumstances, but the outcome of class struggle is very much a consequence of the historically particular balance of class forces. Unlike Cohen, Brenner asserts no general materialist determination of economic transformation. In Cohen's historical materialism, the development of the productive forces is an exogenous datum, while in Brenner's exogeneity is assigned to the relative power of the collective combatants, which determines property relations.

Essays 3 and 4 concentrate on the validity or usefulness of historical materialism in understanding economic development. Jon Elster claims that two conditions must hold for a revolutionary socialist transformation to be successful: there must be a class which is objectively and subjectively capable of making the revolution, and the productive forces must already be sufficiently developed that socialism would dominate capitalism as an economic structure for further developing them. He shows that there are several ways of specifying these two conditions, and then argues that it is likely that the appropriate necessary conditions for successful socialist transformation do not typically (or ever) hold at the same time in one country. The law of combined and uneven development is the claim that successful socialist revolution is still possible if one of the conditions holds in one country and another condition in another country. Elster goes on to claim that even this is unlikely, and that the so-called law is therefore a product of wishful thinking. In Essay 4, Pranab Bardhan discusses in greater detail some of the influence, for good and bad, that historical materialism, and Marxism more generally, has had on development economics. He emphasizes that historical materialism is useful in thinking about long-run trends, but that particular countries can be stuck with institutional rigidities which would often render judgments derived from a schematic model of historical materialism too facile. For instance, the absence of competitive markets characterizes many instances of underdevelopment. In place of markets, other institutions, of perhaps a feudal character, exist (share-cropping is an example of such an institution). It would, however, be a mistake to abolish these institutions before the conditions for markets, which may be more progressive and efficient in their welfare consequences, exist. Bardhan calls for the recognition of 'the economics of second-best reformism'. He concludes with a discussion of the importance of the state in development, and calls for further work on the theory of the state, based on conceiving of the state not simply as a representative of client coalitions, but as an agent in a game of mixed conflict and cooperation with other coalitions.

The second part of the book discusses class, and, to some extent, exploitation. In Essay 5, I outline an economic model in which the class position and the exploitation status of agents emerge from their optimizing behaviour, given the specification of the initial property rights of a capitalist economy. The central point is that the concepts of class and exploitation are not essentially determined with reference to a labour market, but are intimately related to property rights. The labour market is just one particular way, of overwhelming historical importance, of implementing the distributional consequences of an initial unequal distribution of property in the means of production. Here, then, class and exploitation status are not taken to be defining characteristics of agents, but emerge from more basic information. Agents begin with preferences and property endowments, and under given market institutions, their class position and exploitation status emerge endogenously from their optimizing behaviour. Class position and exploitation, and the relationship between the two, are thereby, in a certain manner, 'explained'. Near the end of the essay, I allude to a generalization of the theory of Marxian exploitation which uses ideas of cooperative game theory and which allows discussion of exploitation based on inequality in regimes other than capitalist ones.

In Essay 6, Erik Olin Wright develops further the general conception of exploitation based on inequality associated with various kinds of property, which I propose in the previous essay. He applies it to the problem of the apparent anomaly of the middle class in advanced capitalist countries. Wright shows that the middle class need not be thought of as an anomaly for Marxian class analysis. It is, rather, a class in which different kinds of exploitation overlap in subtle ways. For example: members of the middle class are often exploited with respect to their less-than-average property rights in the conventional means of production, but are exploiters with respect to their more-than-average ownership of inalienable property, such as skills, and organizational assets, these last being positions in hierarchies which give them power over others. Wright presents some empirical work comparing the United States to Sweden, which shows that his conjectured explanation for the behaviour of the middle class works well. In particular, he demonstrates that 'class consciousness', in both Sweden and the United States, correlates well with the total amount of exploitation a person undergoes on the basis of his relative position in the ownership of alienable, inalienable, and organizational assets. One accomplishment, then, of Wright's empirical study is to relate the property-relation conception of exploitation to agents' attitudes, which might in turn help to explain collective class action.

While the first two essays in this section reinforce classical Marxian conceptions of class, the last two are critical. Elster presents various challenges to the contention that classes are the important collective actors in history, maintaining that coalitions organized around other foci such as language, nationality and religion (which are not themselves determined by class) can be equally or more important. He doubts not that classes exist, but whether they are the central collectivities for understanding history. Adam Przeworski maintains that the transition to socialism is not necessarily in the material interest of the working classes of advanced capitalist countries, due to the costs of transition from one regime to another, even if socialism would eventually make them better off than capitalism. Workers, therefore, may be rational in choosing the social democratic compromise, which allows capitalists to retain a certain portion of profits in return for an agreement that they will invest another portion for the continued improvement of working-class welfare. If workers choose the optimal degree of militancy, given their preferences, and if that degree of militancy is consistent with only the social democratic compromise, then the argument for socialism must be made on grounds of freedom, rather than material interest. Przeworski argues that socialism (definitionally) dominates capitalism on grounds of freedom, but not necessarily on grounds of properly calculated material interest. There is a similarity to be noted between Przeworski's argument and Elster's view (Essay 3) that revolution may not be possible in advanced capitalist countries.

The section on method focuses on the importance of methodological individualism as a postulate in modelling Marxian concerns. 'Rational Choice' Marxism has been viewed by many as a contradiction in terms. If Marxism emphasizes the importance of class struggle and collective action, on the one hand, and the social formation of the individual on the other, how could it conceivably use a method which postulates the individual as an agent with given preferences and objectives, determined outside the model, who maximizes individually subject to constraints? In Essay 9, I argue for the importance of methodological individualism for Marxism, and indicate how class action and the social formation of the individual can be studied by means of rational choice models. Jon Elster argues strongly for the application of game theory to Marxian questions, and maintains that the weak explanations in Marxism are its functional ones, which must be repaired by providing micro-foundations for the phenomena studied. Functional explanations are teleological, and teleology is not explanation. Game theory is rich in the interactions between strategy, behaviour, and consequence, which it is able to model, and Elster gives five examples of the efficacy of applying game theory to Marxian questions. In the next essay, which is taken from a chapter of his book (Cohen, 1978), Cohen argues that the only way to make sense of the theory of historical materialism is as functional explanation, and he defines the type of functional explanation he claims historical materialism is. Some further comments on Elster's attack on functional explanation are contained in Cohen's first essay in this book. The difference between Elster and Cohen regarding the validity of functional explanations is not about the importance of basing mechanisms of historical change in the rational behaviour of individuals. It is, rather, a difference of opinion about whether one must understand the micro-mechanisms before an event can be considered explained.

In the fourth section, three essays indicate the kind of work being done by analytical Marxists in political philosophy. Cohen addresses the question: How can it be that proletarians are unfree, as Marxism claims, when any proletarian can escape the working class? He admits the importance of this liberal criticism of Marxism, but argues that even in modern capitalism the proletariat is collectively unfree. I argue in the next essay that exploitation, defined as the unequal exchange of social labour, embodied in goods, for live labour expended by the worker, is not a good statistic for any of the things Marxism is interested in. It is, at best, a proxy for the unequal ownership of the means of production, and I show that it is not even a good proxy for that inequality, in general. It becomes possible for the poor to 'exploit' the rich on the conventional definition of 'exploitation' (if we admit that agents can have preferences for income and leisure which are somewhat less restricted than is assumed in the conventional Marxian model). The classical concept of exploitation should therefore be abandoned, and replaced by a definition of exploitation phrased directly in terms of an unjust distribution of property in the means of production. Finally, Allen Wood challenges the claim that Marxism calls for a thoroughgoing egalitarianism. Egalitarianism, for Marxism, is only a means to an end, the abolition of class society and oppression. He thus reverses what might be the more conventional interpretation, that the abolition of classes is simply a means to the achievement of equality.

The essays collected here are a sample of the work being done by many writers, around the world and in many disciplines. They view Marx as an important intellectual ancestor, but they also acknowledge that he died over a century ago. It is no longer clear what characterizes Marxian scholarly work, nor that it should be characterizable. A particular viewpoint in social theory becomes enduring only if it is able to borrow willingly and easily from other viewpoints, and insofar as they are similarly disposed to borrow from it. The editors of this new Cambridge University Press series hope its existence will encourage this point of view.

J.E.R.

Part I
Historical materialism

1 Forces and relations of production[1]

G. A. Cohen

In Section 1 of this essay I present, in summary form, the interpretation of historical materialism which I offered in Cohen (1978a). I define and relate the concepts of forces and relations of production and I defend the thesis that the basic explanations of historical materialism are what have been called *functional* explanations. Section II places the idea that all history is the history of class struggle in the framework of the theory expounded in section I.

I. An outline of historical materialism

My book says, and it says that Marx says, that history is, fundamentally, the growth of human productive power, and that forms of society rise and fall according as they enable and promote, or prevent and discourage, that growth.

The canonical text for this interpretation is the famous 1859 Preface to *A Contribution to the Critique of Political Economy*, some sentences of which we shall look at shortly. I argue (in section (3) of Cohen (1978a)) that the Preface makes explicit the standpoint on society and history to be found throughout Marx's mature writings, on any reasonable view of the date at which he attained theoretical maturity. In attending to the Preface, we are not looking at just one text among many, but at that text which gives the clearest statement of the theory of historical materialism.

The presentation of the theory in the Preface begins as follows:

In the social production of their life men enter into definite relations that are indispensable and independent of their will, relations of production which *correspond* to a definite stage of development of their material productive forces. The sum total of these relations constitutes the economic structure of society, the real *basis, on which arises* a legal and political superstructure...[2]

These sentences mention three ensembles, the productive forces, the relations of production, and the superstructure, among which certain explanatory

---

[1] This essay originally appeared in *Marx: A Hundred Years On*, edited by Betty Matthews (London, Lawrence and Wishart, 1983). Reprinted with permission.

[2] Marx (1859), italics added.

connections (here indicated by italics) are asserted. I shall first say what I think the ensembles are, and I shall then describe the explanatory connections among them. (All of what follows is argued for in Cohen (1978a), but not all of the argument is given in what follows, which may therefore wrongly impress the reader as dogmatic.)

The productive forces are those facilities and devices which are used in the process of production: means of production on the one hand, and labour power on the other. Means of production are physical productive resources: tools, machinery, raw materials, premises and so forth. Labour power includes not only the strength of producers, but also their skills, and the technical knowledge (which they need not understand) they apply when labouring. Marx says, and I agree, that this subjective dimension of the productive forces is more important than the objective or means of production dimension; and within the more important dimension the part most capable of development is knowledge. Hence, in its later stages, the development of the productive forces is largely a function of the development of productively useful science.

Note that Marx takes for granted in the Preface, what elsewhere he asserts outright, that 'there is a continual movement of growth in productive forces',[3] I argue (in section (6) of Chapter II of Cohen (1978a)) that the relevant standard for measuring that growth in power is how much (or, rather, how little) labour must be spent with given forces to produce what is required to satisfy the inescapable physical needs of the immediate producers.[4] This criterion of social productivity is less equivocal than others which may come to mind, but the decisive reason for choosing it is not its relative clarity but its theoretical appropriateness: if relations of production correspond, as the theory says they do, to levels of development of productive power, then this way of measuring productive power makes the theory's correspondence thesis more plausible.[5]

I do not say that the only explanatory feature of productive power is how much there is of it: qualitative features of productive forces also help to explain the character of relations of production. My claim is that insofar as quantity of productive power is what matters, the key quantity is how much time it takes to (re)produce the producers, that is to say, to produce what they must consume to be able to continue working (as opposed to what they actually consume, which generally, and in contemporary capitalist society considerably, exceeds what they must consume). It is the amount of time

<hr />

[3] Marx (1847a), p. 166.

[4] As opposed, for example, to their socially developed needs, reference to which would be inappropriate here (though not, of course, everywhere).

[5] For a set of correspondences of relations to forces of production, see Cohen (1978a), p. 198.

available beyond, or surplus[6] to, that historically dwindling requirement that is so fateful for the form of the second ensemble we need to describe, the relations of production.

Relations of production are relations of economic power, of the economic power[7] people enjoy or lack over labour power and means of production. In a capitalist society relations of production include the economic power capitalists have over means of production, the economic power workers (unlike slaves) have over their own labour power, and the lack of economic power workers have over means of production. Immediate producers may have no economic power, some economic power, or total economic power over each of their own labour power and the means of production they use. If we permit ourselves a measure of idealization we can construct a table which rather neatly distinguishes the relations of production of historically important immediate producers:

Amount of economic power over

	His labour power	The means of production he uses
Slave	None	None
Serf	Some	Some
Proletarian	All	None
Independent	All	All

The table gives three subordinate producers, and one independent. Since one may have no, some, or total economic power over each of one's labour power and means of production, there is a total of nine cases to consider. I think it is diagnostically valuable to inquire which of the remaining five cases are logically or otherwise possible, and which in turn of those are actual, but I shall not enter on that discussion here.[8]

Now the sum total of relations of production in a given society is said to constitute the economic structure of that society, which is also called – in relation to the superstructure – the basis, or base, or foundation. The economic structure or base therefore consists of relations of production only:

[6] This is not the only important concept of surplus in Marxism, but I invoke it here because it is a concept of something purely material, and I conceive historical materialism as an attempt to explain the social by reference to the material: See Cohen (1978a), pp. 61, 98 and Chapter IV, *passim*, for a defence of the distinction between material and social properties of society.

[7] I call such power 'economic' in virtue of what it is power over, and irrespective of the means of gaining, sustaining, or exercising the power, which need not be economic. See Cohen (1978a), pp. 223–4.

[8] The discussion is pursued at pp. 66–9 of Cohen (1978a).

it does not include the productive forces. It is true that to exclude the productive forces from the economic structure runs against the usual construal of Marx,[9] but he actually said that the economic structure is constituted of relations of production, and he had systematic reasons for saying so.[10] People mistakenly suppose that the productive forces belong to the economic base because they wrongly think that the explanatory importance of the forces ensures their membership in it. But while the forces indeed possess that importance, they are not part of the economic base, since they are not economic phenomena.[11] To stay with the spatial metaphor, they are below the economic foundation, the ground on which it rests.[12]

The Preface describes the superstructure as legal and political. So it at any rate includes the legal and state institutions of society. It is customary to locate other institutions within it too, and it is controversial what its correct demarcation is: my own view is that there are strong textual and systematic reasons for supposing that the superstructure is a lot smaller than many commentators think it is.[13] It is certainly false that every non-economic social phenomenon is superstructural: artistic creation, for example, is demonstrably not, as such, superstructural for Marx. In these remarks I shall discuss the legal order only, which is uncontroversially a part of the superstructure.

So much for the identity of three ensembles mentioned in the Preface. Now relations of production are said to *correspond* to the level of development of the productive forces, and in turn to be a *foundation* on which a superstructure rises. I think these are ways of saying that the level of development of the productive forces explains the nature of the production relations, and that they in turn explain the character of the superstructure co-present with them. But what kind of explanation is ventured here? I argue that in each case what we have is a species of functional explanation.

What is functional explanation? Here are two examples of it: 'Birds have hollow bones because hollow bones facilitate flight', 'Shoe factories operate on a large scale because of the economies large scale brings'. In each case something (birds having hollow bones, shoe factories operating on a large scale) which has a certain effect (flight facilitation, economies of scale) is explained by the fact that it has that effect.

[9] See Cohen (1978a), p. 29, footnote 2, for a list – which could easily be expanded – of authors who take for granted that productive forces belong to the economic structure.
[10] See Cohen (1978a), pp. 28–9.
[11] See *ibid.*, Chapter IV, section (1).
[12] See *ibid.*, p. 30, for a distinction between the material and the economic bases of society: the productive forces belong to the former and are therefore not part of the latter.
[13] I criticize the common practice of overpopulating the superstructure in Cohen (1981c).

But now let me be somewhat more precise.[14] Suppose that e is a cause and f is its effect, and that we are offered a functional explanation of e in terms of its possession of that effect. Note first that the form of the explanation is not: e occurred because f occurred. If that were its form, functional explanation would be the exact opposite of ordinary causal explanation, and it would have the fatal defect that it represented a later occurrence as explaining an earlier one. Nor may we say that the form of the explanation is 'e occurred because it caused f'. Similar constraints on explanation and time order rule that candidate out: by the time e has caused f, e has occurred, so that the fact that it caused f could not explain its occurrence. The only remaining candidate, which I therefore elect, is: e occurred because it would cause f, or, less tersely but more properly: e occurred because the situation was such that an event like e would cause an event like f.

Now if this account of what functional explanations are is correct, then the main explanatory theses of historical materialism are functional explanations, for the following reason: Marx never denied, and sometimes asserted, that superstructures hold foundations together, and that relations of production control the development of the productive forces. Yet he held that the character of the superstructure is explained by the nature of the base, and that the latter is explained by the nature of the productive forces. If the intended explanations are functional ones, we have consistency between the effect of A on B and the explanation of A by B, *and I do not know any other way of rendering historical materialism consistent.*

I shall now expound in greater detail one of the two functional explanatory theses, that which concerns base and superstructure.

The base, it will be recalled, is the sum total of production relations, these being relations of economic power over labour power and means of production. The capitalist's control of means of production is an illustration. And the superstructure, we saw, has more than one part, exactly what its parts are being somewhat uncertain, but certainly one *bona fide* part of it is the legal system, which will occupy us here.

In a capitalist society capitalists have effective power over means of production. What confers that power on a given capitalist, say an owner of a factory? On what can he rely if others attempt to take control of the factory away from him? An important part of the answer is this: he can rely on the law of the land, which is enforced by the might of the state. It is his legal

---

[14] But not as precise as in sections (4) and (7) of Chapter IX of Cohen (1978a) and section (2) of Chapter X of *ibid.*, reprinted at pp. 223–5 below, where the structure of functional explanation is described in greater detail.

right which causes him to have his economic power. What he is effectively able to do depends on what he is legally entitled to do. And this is in general true in law-abiding society with respect to all economic powers and all economic agents. We can therefore say: in law-abiding society people have the economic powers they do because they have the legal rights they do.

That seems to refute the doctrine of base and superstructure, since here superstructural conditions – what legal rights people have – determine basic ones – what their economic powers are. But though it seems to refute the doctrine of base and superstructure, it cannot be denied. And it would not only seem to refute it, but actually would refute it, were it not possible, *and therefore mandatory* (for historical materialists), to present the doctrine of base and superstructure as an instance of functional explanation. For we can add, to the undeniable truth emphasized above, the further thesis that the given capitalist enjoys the stated right because it belongs to a structure of rights, a structure which obtains because it sustains an analogous structure of economic power. The content of the legal system is explained by its function, which is to help sustain an economy of particular kind. People do usually get their powers from their rights, but in a manner which is not only allowed but demanded by the way historical materialism explains superstructural rights by reference to basic powers. Hence the effect of the law of property on the economy is not, as is often supposed, an embarrassment to historical materialism. It is something which historical materialism is committed to emphasizing, because of the particular way it explains law in terms of economic conditions.

Legal structures rise and fall according as they sustain or frustrate forms of economy which, I now add, advance the development of the productive forces. The addition implies an explanation why whatever economic structure obtains at a given time does obtain at that time. Once more the explanation is a functional one: the prevailing production relations prevail *because* they are relations which advance the development of the productive forces. The existing level of productive power determines what relations of production would raise its level, and relations of that type consequently obtain. In other words: if production relations of kind R obtain, then that is because R-type relations are suitable to the development of the forces, in virtue of their existing level of development: that is the canonical form of the explanation in the standard case. But I should also mention the transitional case, in which the relations are not suitable to the development of the forces but, on the contrary, fetter them. In transitional cases the prevailing relations obtain because they recently *were* suitable to the development of the forces, and the class they empower has managed to maintain control despite their no longer being so: it is because ruling classes have an interest in the maintenance of obsolete relations that their *immediate* replacement by freshly suitable relations is not to be expected. People do not rush towards the dustbin of history just as soon as they have played out their historical role.

Now since

(1) the level of development of productive power determines what relations (that is, what sort of economic structure) would advance productive power,

and

(2) relations which advance productive power obtain because they advance productive power,

it follows that

(3) the level of development of productive power explains the nature of the economic structure.

(3) assigns explanatory primacy to the productive forces. (2) does not by itself ensure that primacy, since it is consistent with, e.g.,

(4) the dominant ideology determines what relations would advance productive power,

and if (4) is true, (3) is false.

Now to say that *A* explains *B* is not necessarily to indicate *how A* explains *B*. The child who knows that the match burst into flame because it was struck may not know how the latter event explains the former, because he is ignorant of the relationship between friction and heat, the contribution of oxygen to combustion, and so on. In a widely favoured idiom, he may not know the *mechanism* linking cause and effect, or, as I prefer to say, he may be unable to *elaborate* the explanation. In the relevant sense of 'how', we require an answer to the questions: *how does the fact that the economic structure promotes the development of the productive forces explain the character of the economic structure?* and *how does the fact that the superstructure protects the base explain the character of the superstructure?* Recall the functional explanation of the hollow bones of birds: to say, correctly, that birds have hollow bones because the feature is useful for flight is not to say how its usefulness accounts for its emergence and/or persistence. To that question Lamarck gave an unacceptable answer and Darwin an excellent one. To corresponding questions about explanations of large scale in terms of economies of scale one may answer by referring to conscious human purposes, or to an economic analogue of chance variation and natural selection, or to some mix of the two.[15] But no one has given good answers to the similar questions (italicized above) about historical materialism. I offer some not very satisfactory answers in Chapter X of Cohen (1978a) (part of which appears at pp. 221–34 of this volume). This seems to me an important area of future research for historical

[15] See Cohen (1978a), pp. 287–9, reprinted here at pp. 228–9.

materialists, since the functional construal of their doctrine cannot be avoided.[16]

Let me now summarize my argument for the thesis that the chief explanatory claims of historical materialism are functional in form. Those claims are that

(3) the level of development of productive power explains the nature of the economic structure

and

(5) the economic structure explains the nature of the superstructure.

I take (3) and (5) to be functional explanations because I cannot otherwise reconcile them with two further Marxian theses, namely that

(6) the economic structure promotes the development of the productive forces

and

(7) the superstructure stabilizes the economic structure.

(6) and (7) entail that the economic structure is functional for the development of the productive forces, and that the superstructure is functional for the stability of the economic structure. These claims do not by themselves entail that economic structures and superstructures are *explained* by the stated functions: A may be functional for B even though it is false that A exists *because* it is functional for B. But (6) and (7), *in conjunction with (3) and (5)*, do force us to treat historical materialist explanation as functional. No other treatment preserves consistency between the explanatory primacy of the productive forces over the economic structure and the massive control of the latter over the former, or between the explanatory primacy of the economic structure over the superstructure and the latter's regulation of the former.

I hold that the central explanations of historical materialism are functional explanations, and I defend functional explanation as an explanatory device, but I do not defend the sloppy functional explanatory theorizing in which so many Marxists engage.[17]

Many Marxist exercises in functional explanation fail to satisfy even the preliminary requirement of showing that *A is* functional for B (whether or not it is also *explained* by its function(s)). Take, for example, the claim that the contemporary capitalist state functions to protect and sustain the capitalist system. Legislation and policy in the direct interest of the capitalist class can reasonably be regarded as confirming it. But what about putative counter-examples, such as social welfare provision and legal immunities enjoyed by

---

[16] For recent valuable work on the problem of the mechanism in functional explanation, see Van Parijs (1981).

[17] For an impressive catalogue of methodologically lax uses of functional explanation, see Elster (1982).

trade unions? These too might be functional for capitalism, in an indirect way, but that is something which needs to be argued with care, not just asserted. But those who propound the general claim about the state rarely trouble to say what sort of evidence would falsify or weaken it, and therefore every action of the state is treated as confirmatory, since there is always some way, legitimate or spurious, in which the action can be made to look functional.

Methodological indiscipline is then compounded when, having satisfied himself that state policy is functional, the theorist treats it, without further argument, as also functionally explained. He proceeds from '*A* is functional for *B*' to '*B* functionally explains *A*' without experiencing any need to justify the step, if, indeed, he notices that he has taken a step from one position to a distinct and stronger one.

II. How class struggles fit in

'The history of all hitherto existing society', says *The Communist Manifesto*, 'is the history of class struggles.'[18] Yet class struggle was hardly mentioned in the foregoing outline of historical materialism. Therefore, a critic might say, either Marx had more than one theory of history, or I have misrepresented his views.

One response would be to deflate the theoretical value of the quoted remark by emphasizing its political role as the first sentence of the main body of an insurrectionary text. But I prefer to leave the sentence intact and accommodate it. I do not want to deny that all history is the history of class struggle.

Why, then, did class struggle receive so little attention in section I of this paper? Because that section was devoted to the fundamental explanations of the course of history and the structure of society, not to the main events of that course and the surface relief of society, where class struggle looms large.

There are two ways of accepting the *Manifesto* sentence without sacrificing the theory of section I. The first, and less interesting, way is to take it as saying that *there is always a class struggle going on*. One may claim, in that spirit, that all history is the history of class struggle, without implying that that is all that history is, or even that that is what history most fundamentally is.

In the second way of taking the sentence all history is the history of class struggle in the more important sense that *major historical changes are brought about by class struggle*. Yet that is consistent with the doctrine of section I, since (so historical materialism says) if we want to know why class struggle effects this change rather than that, we must turn to the dialectic of forces and

[18] Marx and Engels (1848), p. 482.

relations of production which governs class behaviour and is not explicable in terms of it, and which determines what the long-term outcome of class struggle will be.

Things other than forces and relations of production, such as the inter-actional structures studied by game theory,[19] help to explain the vicissitudes of class struggle and the strategies pursued in it, but they cannot give a Marxist answer to the question why class wars (as opposed to battles) are settled one way rather than another. *Marx finds the answer in the character of the productive forces*: 'The conditions under which definite productive forces can be applied are the conditions of the rule of a definite class of society'. The class which rules through a period, or emerges triumphant from epochal conflict, is the class best suited, most able and disposed, to preside over the development of the productive forces at the given time.[20] That answer may be untenable, but I cannot envisage an alternative to it which would qualify as historical materialist. It is, moreover, an answer which Marx did not merely give when generalizing about history, but which he applied to cases, as, for example, when he said that

If the proletariat overthrows the political rule of the bourgeoisie, its victory will only be temporary...as long as the material conditions have not yet been created which make necessary the abolition of the bourgeois mode of production.[21]

Note that Marx writes not 'make possible', but 'make necessary', a phrase which limits what can be independently decided by class struggle more than the former one would. *The Communist Manifesto* contains similar phrases,[22] and therefore cannot be recruited to the non-Marxist view that all history is, in the final analysis, *explained* by class struggle.

Prosecuting his contention that Marxism should abandon functional explanation and contract a liaison with game theory, Jon Elster remarks that 'game theory is invaluable to any analysis of the historical process that centres on exploitation, struggle, alliances and revolution'.[23] But for Marxian analysis those phenomena are not primary but, as it were, immediately secondary, on the periphery of the centre: they are among the 'forms in which

[19] Jon Elster has persuaded me that game theory is supremely relevant to certain Marxist concerns. But I would deny that it can replace, or even supplement, functional explanation at the very heart of historical materialism: See Elster (1982) and Cohen (1982).

[20] The quotation is from Marx and Engels (1846), p. 85, and the sentences preceding and following it are from p. 149 of Cohen (1978), which contains further discussion and more textual references.

[21] Marx (1847b). p. 319, and see Wood (1981), p. 250 (41) for a list of texts which carry a similar message.

[22] According to the *Manifesto*, the 'economic and political dominion of the bourgeois class' was an outcome of the fact that feudal relations of production had become fetters on productive progress and therefore '*had* to be burst asunder', Marx and Engels (1848), p. 489.

[23] Elster (1982), p. 453.

men become conscious of the conflict [between forces and relations of production] and fight it out'.[24] To put the point differently, we may say that the items on Elster's list are the actions at the centre of the historical process, but for Marxism there are also items more basic than actions at its centre.

By 'revolution' Elster must mean the political phenomenon of transfer of state power, as opposed to the transformation of economic structure political revolution initiates or reflects. Many facts about political revolutions are accessible to game theoretical explanation, but not the world-historical facts that there was a bourgeois revolution and that there will be a proletarian one.

While realizing that I insist on a 'fundamentalist' reading of historical materialism, Richard Miller notes that 'Cohen...allows that political and ideological struggle may be essential to the destruction of the old social relations'.[25] Indeed, and I am prepared to go further. I do not wish to deny that class struggle is always essential for social transformation. My position does not prevent me from accepting Marx and Engels' statement that 'the class struggle is the immediate driving power of history'.[26] On the contrary: it is the doctrine expounded in Part I of this paper which illuminates the otherwise puzzling occurrence of the word 'immediate' in this important sentence. 'Immediate' is opposed to 'underlying'.

The reader might now agree that the following characterization of my views distorts them:

Cohen...seems committed to the view that the kind of human activity capable of effecting social change would have to be not consciously political activity but technical and scientific activity: the invention of new technology, having as its unconscious byproduct the emergence of new social relations.[27]

I do not see how one can wring out of my book a denial that consciously political activity effects social change. How could an explanation why politics effects this social change rather than that entail a denial that politics effects social change? Marx was not being untrue to what I claim was his theory when he called on workers, rather than scientists and technicians, to revolutionize society. In encouraging workers to bring about social change

[24] Marx (1859).
[25] Miller (1981), p. 94. But Miller appears to think that this view of mine is an optional and rather arbitrarily added extra, 'readily detachable' from a theory assigning primacy to the development of the productive forces, since such a theory would 'suggest the effectiveness of an alternative to revolution, in which change is brought about by appeals to material desires common to all classes' (Miller (1984), p. 68). This rather astonishingly presupposes that the material interest of humanity could not conflict with the material interest of ruling class persons. For my part, I expect no one under socialism to be as rich as Rockefeller, and I therefore expect Rockefeller to be hostile to the idea of socialism.
[26] It comes from their letter of 17–18/9, 1879 to Bebel, Liebknecht and Bracke: see Marx and Engels (1975), p. 307. (The word translated 'immediate' is 'nächste'.)
[27] Norman (1980), p. 6.

he was not asking them to bring about what would explain their doing so: the exhaustion of the progressive capacity of the capitalist order, and the availability of enough productive power to install a socialist one.

I admitted on p. 17 that I do not have a good answer to the question how productive forces select economic structures which promote their development. To be sure, we can say that the adjustment of relations to forces occurs through class struggle. But that is not a fully satisfying answer to the question of p. 17, since it does not specify the filiation, or filiations, from contradiction between forces and relations of production to the class struggle supposed to resolve it. What activates the prospective new class? What ensures its victory? These are the questions that need attention, and not only for the sake of good theory.[28]

---

[28] For good criticisms of my failure to deal well with these questions, see Elster (1980), p. 124; Levine and Wright (1980), pp. 58ff.; J. Cohen (1982), pp. 266ff. Part of the object of their criticism appears on pp. 233–4 of this volume.

2 The social basis of economic development

Robert Brenner

1. Adam Smith and the explanation of modern economic growth

In a consideration of the explanation of economic growth in the very long run, the work of Adam Smith traditionally has been the place to start. Even today, the Smithian paradigm provides the foundations for most theories of economic development, and for economic historiography in general. That this should be the case, is, in my view, quite proper; for Smith, I would argue, both captured the essence of modern economic growth and discovered what might be called the key mechanism responsible for its taking place – or at least provided the basis for doing these things. Nevertheless, Smith failed to explain the conditions under which his key mechanism does and does not operate; indeed he seemed not to realize that there *are* conditions under which it does not operate. This essay seeks to provide the basis for a general theory of economic development, firstly, by extracting from Smith's argument what I take to be the defining feature of modern economic growth and the fundamental mechanism behind such growth, and, secondly, by specifying the particular conditions under which this mechanism can and cannot be expected to operate.

As is well-known, Smith thought that the pursuit of rational self-interest leads individual producers to try to make use of the specialized productive capacities of other producers. They do this, Smith believed, by specializing themselves and by offering their output for exchange to their prospective trading partners, who can then be expected to do the same. Individual rational self-interest thus leads to generalized, specialized production for exchange. Of course, producers who specialize for the market must buy their means of production and means of subsistence on the market; specialization entails dependence on the market. But producers who must buy what they need on the market in order to continue in production must also be able to sell their product on the market; and they must be able to do this *competitively*. To sell competitively, producers must be able to produce what is demanded and to do so with a minimum of cost – i.e. to produce at 'the socially necessary rate' or to 'maximize the price/cost ratio' of their output. But in order to be able to produce at the socially necessary rate, producers must seek, continually and systematically, to cut costs by further specializing, accumulating their surpluses, and adopting the best available production techniques (innovating). Thus, for Smith, the pursuit of individual rational self-interest leads to ongoing economy-wide development.

What I take to be Smith's two indispensable conclusions are captured in the foregoing sketch of the operation of the invisible hand. The first conclusion is that what constitutes the *differentia specifica* of modern economic growth is not this or that once-and-for-all improvement in the productive forces – this or that specialization, this or that allocation of the surplus, this or that innovation. It is not, *per se*, the spread of international trade, nor the rise of cooperation, nor the growth of manufacture, nor the extension of machinofacture – although all of these things do, of course, contribute to economic growth. What distinguishes modern economic growth is something more general and abstract: it is the presence in the economy of a *systematic* and *continuous* tendency or drive to transform production in the direction of greater efficiency. This is expressed in the more or less continuous growth of *per capita* output. Smith's second indispensable conclusion is that the reason modern economic growth actually takes place is because the individual economic actors find it in their self-interest to undertake patterns of productive activity which correspond, more or less systematically, to the requirements for economic growth of the economy as a whole. It just so happens that what individuals find it rational to do is to carry out full-scale production for exchange by means of systematic cutting of costs through specialization, accumulation and innovation, and these turn out to be the very things the economy requires for ongoing growth. What's good for every individual economic actor is good for aggregate economic growth.

Paradoxically, despite his invaluable insights, Smith's theory as actually presented turns out to be rather unhelpful, indeed positively misleading, for explaining the appearance of modern economic growth; for he ends up assuming the extraordinary phenomenon that needs to be explained: namely the correspondence between what is required for the economic growth of the system as a whole and the self-interested actions of the individual economic actors. This is because, by taking for granted the now famous 'natural tendency of men to truck and barter', Smith takes for granted precisely what needs to be demonstrated: namely, that the producers will commoditize all or most of their output. It is the producers' commoditizing of their output and their *consequent dependence* upon the market which results in their subjection to the creative pressures of competition. Smith also assumes without explanation that the producers are able to allocate their resources as they see fit and to appropriate the full returns on their investments, free from the exactions or controls of 'political' powers.[1] Implicit are a whole series of choices on the part of the economic actors which can by no means be taken for granted. Smith thus assumes, first, that the producers' rational self-interest will require them to maximize exchange values and to produce all or most of their output for the market *rather than* to produce the full range of their subsistence needs so as directly to insure their maintenance, while marketing only physical surpluses beyond subsistence. He assumes, secondly, that the direct producers will find it in their rational self-interest to direct their resources toward improving their capacities to produce competitively, *rather than* toward improving their capacities to transfer the product from others by force. Smith assumes, thirdly, that to the extent that the direct producers do find it in their rational self-interest to try to cut productive costs, they will find that the most effective way of doing so is by improving the process of production (getting more output from the same inputs, or the same outputs from fewer inputs), *rather than* by squeezing the direct producers (possibly themselves) via cutting the level of subsistence, increasing the length of the working day, or intensifying labour. Smith assumes, finally, that whatever the individuals ultimately decide is the most rational way to allocate their resources, they will be free to pursue their choice and, moreover, that they will receive the full fruits of their economic activity. But this is to take for granted a society of free economic actors, *rather than* one of economic actors subject to non-economic constraints.

In sum, by assuming that, as a rule, the individual economic actors can and will do what's necessary for economic growth in the aggregate, Smith begged the fundamental question: *under what conditions* will or will not the patterns of economic action pursued by individuals correspond to the requirements of economic growth of the economy as a whole? The remainder of this essay will be concerned with confronting this question by clarifying, arguing for, and enlarging upon the following four fundamental theses:

(i) The prevalence of certain quite specific, historically-developed *property relations* (to be understood, as we shall see, as *relations of reproduction*) provides the fundamental condition under which individual economic actors will find it rational and possible to follow patterns of economic action supportive of modern

---

[1] This is not really fair to Adam Smith, since in Book III of *The Wealth of Nations* he devotes considerable attention to the barriers to economic growth constituted by feudal lordship. Nevertheless, Smith also implies that the rise of exchange will, more or less directly, dissolve these barriers; so one is entitled to ask just how seriously he takes them (see Brenner, 1985). In any case, my intention here is not so much to explicate Smith's real meaning, as to make certain arguments about the conditions for economic development. My apologies to Adam Smith, if, in the process, I have failed to do him justice.

economic growth *à la* Adam Smith. I will call these *capitalist* property relations. On the other hand, through most of world history, from the appearance of settled agriculture till the early modern period (and in most places well beyond that time), economies have been characterized by forms of property relations which impose on the individual economic actors patterns of economic action which, although individually rational, are nonetheless systematically subversive, in the long run, of economic development. At minimum, the result of their action for the economy as a whole has been to preclude the appearance of those trends which distinguish modern economic growth.

(ii) As a rule, the transition from pre-capitalist to capitalist property relations cannot occur as the intended result of the rationally self-interested actions of *individual* pre-capitalist economic actors, even given the appearance of new opportunities for exchange or of new technologies or new demographic trends. On the contrary, their rationally self-interested activity will, as a rule, have as one of its goals *maintaining* those pre-capitalist property relations, which structure non-development.

(iii) The rationally self-interested action of social *classes* in pre-capitalist economies generally had the intention of maintaining and strengthening pre-capitalist property relations and rarely, if ever, had the goal of transforming these relations.

(iv) The original onset of modern economic growth depended upon the transition from pre-capitalist to capitalist property relations. But this outcome is inexplicable in terms of the rationally self-interested actions of pre-capitalist individual economic actors or classes; it must be understood as an *unintended consequence* of the actions of individual pre-capitalist actors and especially the conflicts between pre-capitalist classes.

2. Property relations, rules for reproduction, and economic development

By property relations, I mean the relationships among the direct producers, among the class of exploiters (if any exists), and between the exploiters and producers, which specify and determine the regular and systematic access of the individual economic actors (or families) to the means of production *and* to the economic product. In every social economy, such property relations will exist, and make it possible for the direct producers and exploiters (if any) to continue to maintain themselves as they were – i.e. in the class position they already held, as producers or exploiters. But more to the point, these property relations, once established, will determine the economic course of action which is rational for the direct producers and the exploiters. Since this is so, the property relations will, to a large degree, determine the pattern of economic development of any society; for that pattern is, to a very great extent, merely the *aggregate* result of the carrying out of the rules for reproduction of the direct producers and exploiters. So, the causal sequence runs roughly as follows: form of property relations→rules for reproduction of the individual economic actors→long-term pattern of economic development/non-development. Using these basic propositions as our point of departure, we can move to consider the four fundamental theses listed above.[2]

i. Why pre-capitalist property relations prevent development and why capitalist property relations condition modern economic growth
Pre-capitalist property relations

More or less from the origins of settled agriculture until the early modern period (and in many places well beyond that time) agricultural societies, with few if any exceptions, have been predominantly characterized by property relations of a single broad type, imposing rules of reproduction quite inimical to the requirements of modern economic growth. In all of these societies, the property relations had two defining traits:

First: the direct producers held direct (i.e. non-market) access to their full means of subsistence, that is the tools and land needed to maintain themselves. In some instances they possessed this individually. In other cases they held it as a usufruct from the community of producers which was the formal owner. There were, moreover, many intermediate forms between these poles. But the point is that in every case *they did possess it.* The communities of producers organized themselves in a variety of ways, under different conditions, to protect this possession, a point to which we shall return. But however this was, the peasants – the term we shall use for all direct producers who have full access to their means of subsistence, whether individually or via membership in a community – *were not expropriable.*

Second: in consequence of the direct producers' possession, the members of the class of exploiters (if one existed) were obliged to reproduce themselves through appropriating a part of the product of the direct producers *by means of extra-economic coercion.* In other words, because the direct producers were economically independent by virtue of their possession of the means of subsistence, the exploiters' ownership of other means of production, notably land, did not *in itself* allow them to realize a part of the product (unless of course they worked themselves). Indeed, because there was no class of economic actors devoid of the means of reproduction (subsistence) to take up the lords' land as exploited tenants or to work the lords' land as exploited wage workers, *the individual lords did not, as a rule, find it in their self-interest to expropriate their own peasants.*[3] But, finally, even if the lords did desire to

---

[2] In the remainder of this essay, each of the sections headed by small roman numerals (i, ii, iii, iv) considers the corresponding one of the aforementioned four fundamental theses.

[3] Of course, the lords might come to have an interest in expropriating their peasants, when and if there emerged a class of economic actors who had no access to their full means of

expropriate their peasants, they generally could not do so, because they were prevented by the peasant community/communities which stood as the ultimate guardian of the peasants' land.

Because of this *merger* of the direct producers with their means of reproduction, the lords depended for their maintenance upon institutionalized relationships with their peasants which enabled them to appropriate by force part of the peasants' product. In some instances, the exploiters applied force to extract their product *directly*, that is *as individuals*. In this case, the individual exploiters might either appropriate the product from each individual direct producer, or they might appropriate it from the community of producers as a whole (in which instance, the community would be responsible for collecting the rent from each of its members). In other instances, the exploiters applied force *collectively*, as a class, and appropriated their product indirectly: thus, they received their income by virtue of holding a position or office which was, in turn, supported by the collectivity of exploiters' levying a tax on the direct producers. In this case, the collectivity of exploiters, again, could either levy this tax on each individual producer; or, alternatively, they might levy it on communities (which would have to collect the tax from each of their members). But whatever the specific form of the levy, all pre-capitalist exploiters, whom we shall henceforth refer to as lords, found the application of extra-economic coercion to be indispensable to their establishment and reproduction as an exploiting class, and participation in the institutionalized structures through which force was applied and surplus extracted to be indispensable to their membership, as individuals, within it.

Pre-capitalist property relations, in societies which had achieved settled agriculture, imposed upon the economic actors, producers and exploiters alike, rules of reproduction which were, in the end, antithetical to the requirements for the development of the economy as a whole. Under these relations, both direct producers and exploiters found it rational to adopt patterns of economic action which, in the long run, prevented increases in aggregate *per capita* output. Why was this so?

First, and perhaps *ultimately* most critical, in allowing both exploiters and producers direct access to their means of reproduction, pre-capitalist property forms (as 'patriarchal' forms) freed both exploiters and producers from the *necessity to buy* on the market what they needed to reproduce, thus of the necessity to produce for exchange, thus of the necessity to sell competitively on the market their output, and thus of the necessity to produce at the socially necessary rate (or so as to maximize the price/cost ratio of their output). In

reproduction and who therefore had to lease the land or work it for a wage in order to survive. But the emergence of such a class would signal the emergence of, or transition to, a new set of property relations, thus a new set of requirements for the reproduction of the economic actors.

consequence, both producers and exploiters were relieved of the necessity to cut costs so as to maintain themselves, and so of the necessity constantly to improve production through specialization and/or accumulation and/or innovation. The property relations, in themselves, failed to *impose* that relentless pressure on the individual producers to improve which, as we shall argue, is an indispensable condition for economic development.

Without the *necessity* to maximize exchange values, the direct producers, as individuals and as members of communities of cultivators, tended to find it most sensible to deploy their resources so as to ensure their maintenance by producing directly the full range of their necessities (i.e. to produce for subsistence). *Given* the low level of agricultural productivity which perforce prevailed, harvests and therefore food supplies were highly uncertain. Since food constituted so large a part of total consumption, the uncertainty of the food market brought with it highly uncertain markets for other commercial crops. It was therefore sensible for the peasants to avoid dependence upon the market – above all dependence upon purchases of subsistence goods, but also to avoid dependence upon sales of commercial crops. To avoid this dependence, the peasants had to diversify, so as to produce directly all they needed, and to market only physical surpluses[3a]. The resulting tendency to production for subsistence naturally constituted a powerful barrier to commercial specialization and ultimately the transformation of production. This barrier was especially difficult to surmount, since its transcendence appeared to require nothing less than the *previous* transformation of the reproductive patterns (i.e. rules for reproduction) of the individual producers. Thus, so long as the direct producers retained direct access to their means of reproduction, they would not voluntarily turn to specialization, unless there *previously* had been massive improvements in the security of the food supply; yet, massive improvements in the security of the food supply seemed to require the peasants' specialization.[4]

The effects of the tendency of the peasant producers to treat their means of production (land, tools, labour power) as the means directly to maintain their subsistence affected not only their own output, but that of others in the economy. Thus, the peasants' refusal to part with their plots – which they could not afford to regard as abstract commercial investments and had to

---

[3a] Indeed, it is likely that the peasants would have sought to avoid specialization and dependence on exchange simply to avoid becoming subject to the dictates of the market and the whole transformation of life which that entailed.

[4] Naturally, the pressure on peasants to diversify and 'produce for subsistence' would decrease to the extent that the growth of food production elsewhere (and the improvement of transportation) allowed for increasingly secure food imports and thereby decreased the riskiness of specialization. Once capitalism had developed in some places, what constituted the rational economic self-interest, and thus the rules for reproduction, of the pre-capitalist economic actors was subject to change.

regard as the concrete and indispensable bases for their existence – limited the extension of the market in land. Potential accumulators were thus hindered in acquiring the land they needed to build up the units of production required to make improvements which depended upon scale and cooperation. In turn, because they possessed the means to maintain themselves, the peasants were not compelled to sell their labour power. In consequence the labour market was restricted and thereby (again) the potential for cooperation and scale in production.

Moreover, in those (many) cases where the community as a whole either constituted the ultimate owner of the peasants' land or in other ways controlled its allocation, it almost always wielded this ownership or control so as to restrict the individual cultivators' ability to alienate their plots. On the other hand, where the individual peasants did directly control the allocation of their land, they tended to make sure that it was passed on to their children, so as to provide the basis for the maintenance of future generations. Meanwhile, they tended to find it rational to have a large number of children so as to ensure themselves support in their old age. This naturally tended to intensify the subdivision of plots resulting from inheritance. The outcome was not merely to limit the land market and the build-up of holdings, but actually to increase the break-up and dispersion of the land and other productive resources.

Nor, given the prevalence of precapitalist property relations, were the exploiting lords much better-situated to pursue a pattern of economic action supportive of development. As noted, the lords' patriarchal position as possessors of the requirements for their reproduction as lords freed them of any need to increase their income for the purpose of increasing their *productive capacities*, since they were shielded from the necessity of selling competitively on the market. All else being equal, this same freedom would manifest itself in a tendency to allocate what resources were necessary to *directly* insure maintenance (without recourse to market purchases) and to devote to market production only surplus resources beyond that. It is true, of course, that there were often *other* reasons (beside the desire to improve production so as to compete) that the lords might wish to increase their income, perhaps the most common being to improve their capacity for politico-military competition with other lords. But insofar as the lords did try to raise their income for this or any other purpose, they were *by and large* prevented from doing so by means of improving the productiveness of their men and land. Thus, to the extent that pre-capitalist property relations prevailed, if they wished to organize production themselves, the lords had to depend on labourers who possessed their means of subsistence. This being the case, the exploiters could get them to work only by directly coercing them. For the same reason, they could not 'fire' them, and the consequences of this were extremely far-reaching, since the lords were thereby deprived of perhaps the most effective means yet discovered to impose labour discipline in class-divided societies. Because the peasant labourers had no *economic* incentive to work diligently or efficiently, the lords found it extremely difficult to get them to use more advanced means of production in an effective manner. They could force them to do so, only at the cost of major unproductive investments in supervision. Under such conditions, it made little sense for the lords to allocate their income toward investment in the means of production. They found it rational instead to direct their resources toward various forms of unproductive (though reproductively effective) *consumption*.

It might be objected that the lords could circumvent this problem by offering their labourers *economic incentives* to work harder and more efficiently, but this is by no means obviously the case. Since the producers possessed their means of subsistence, they could be assumed to have no incentive to work harder or more efficiently, *unless* they were paid the full equivalent of their additional labour. This was because they had the alternative precisely of applying any extra energy or time to their own plots and getting the full return for this input. In consequence, they could not be assumed to be exploitable through the exchange of labour power for a wage. The lords through offering an incentive could get exactly what they paid for and no more, so had little obvious motive for pursuing this tactic.[5]

In view of the difficulty, in the presence of pre-capitalist property relations, of raising returns from investment in the means of production (via increases in productive efficiency), the lords found that if they wished to increase their income, they had little choice but to do so by *redistributing* wealth and income away from their peasants or from other members of the exploiting class. This meant they had to deploy their resources toward building up their *means of coercion* – by investment in military men and equipment. Speaking broadly, they were obliged to invest in their politico-military apparatuses. To the extent they had to do this effectively enough to compete with other lords who were

---

[5] On the other hand, if the lords could apply on their land means of production which were more efficient than those available to the peasants, they would have the potential of being able to use economic incentives to overcome the problem of motivating the peasants to do decent work. Specifically, if the lords could apply on their own land techniques which were so productive as to allow them to pay the peasants more per unit of labour (time × energy) than the peasant could get by applying that amount of labour on their own plots and still have a profit left over, then the lords were in a position to use economic incentives to elicit more effective labour from the peasants. Naturally, the *actual* viability of such a course would depend on the *de facto* availability of (relatively) highly productive techniques which were available to the lords and not to the peasants. I wish to thank G. A. Cohen and Jon Elster for bringing this point to my attention.

doing the same thing, they would have had to maximize both their military investments and the efficiency of these investments. They would have had, in fact, to attempt, continually and systematically, to improve their methods of war. Indeed, we can say the drive to *political accumulation*, to *state building*, is the *pre-capitalist* analogue to the capitalist drive to *accumulate capital*.

Now to the extent that the lords followed such a pattern of allocation, they could only diminish the resources potentially available for 'productive' production, and that is what actually occurred when they were successful. They applied their increased income to investments in the means of war, specifically to provisioning and supplying with tools (directly or indirectly) the *producers* of arms and luxuries, as well as to supporting the warriors themselves. They thereby reduced the means of consumption and production available to the peasant producers, and, in consequence, undermined the economy's fundamental productiveness.

In sum, so long as non-capitalist property relations prevail, we can expect the following rules for reproduction for the individual economic actors to obtain:

(a) in general, the economic actors will direct their resources toward making possible certain specific *forms of consumption*;
(b) the direct producers, possessing their means of subsistence, will deploy their resources so as to produce the full complement of their subsistence requirements, and so as to maintain the productive base to continue to do so;
(c) the exploiters will direct their resources toward strengthening the means of coercion whereby they can re-distribute the product from the direct producers and other exploiters in order to acquire the military equipment and luxury goods needed to strengthen their means of coercion and so on. More broadly, they will build states.

On the basis of the foregoing rules for individual reproduction, we can expect the following economy-wide developmental trends:

(a) economic growth in agriculture will, by and large, take the form of the multiplication of units of production on already-existing lines;
(b) industrial production, to the extent it develops, will take non-productive forms (military and luxury production);
(c) the long-term developmental trend will be toward stagnation, if not crisis – depending on the available land, rate of demographic growth (itself a function of the form of possession and the form of coercive extraction), and the degree and manner in which the direct producers' output is appropriated by the exploiters.

A pattern of ongoing growth via the regular improvement of the productive forces is out of the question.[6]

---

[6] It might be thought that pre-capitalist slave economies would have had such very different forms of operation and development from those discussed here as to require separate

Capitalist property relations

Under what conditions, then, will the economic actors adopt patterns of economic action conducive, in the aggregate, to modern economic growth? In my view, they can be *expected* to do so, only where all the direct producers are separated from their means of subsistence, *above all the land*, and where no exploiters are able to maintain themselves through surplus extraction by extra-economic coercion. It is only where the organizers of production and the direct producers (sometimes the same person) have been separated from direct access to the means of subsistence, that they *must* buy on the market the tools and means of subsistence they need to reproduce themselves. It is only where the producers must buy on the market their means of reproduction, that they must be able to sell *competitively* on the market, i.e. at the socially necessary rate. It is only in the presence of the necessity of competitive production – and the correlative absence of the possibility of cutting costs, or otherwise raising income, by forcefully squeezing the direct producers – that we can expect the systematic and continual pressure to increase the efficiency of production which is the *sine qua non* of modern economic growth.

Naturally, in an economy where the direct producers have been separated from their means of subsistence, it will be somewhat difficult to develop productive efficiency through the familiar methods requiring *cooperative labour* unless it is possible to purchase on the market not only tools and means of subsistence, but also labour power. It is a good question, moreover, whether or not the availability of labour power depends upon the separating of some economic actors not only from their full means of subsistence, but also from their means of production – i.e. leaving some economic actors with *only* their labour power to sell in order to reproduce themselves. But however this may

treatment. I do not believe this is so – at least, given the level of generality and the specific concerns of this essay. First of all, it seems that even where pre-capitalist slavery was most developed, it always existed alongside a substantial sector of patriarchal peasant possessors. Indeed, the peasant possessors sometimes used slaves themselves. Second, the lordly slave-owners were also patriarchal in that, via their land and their slaves, they had direct (non-market) access to their full means of reproduction, so were (like the peasants) freed from the requirements of competition on the market and thus the need to produce for exchange. Thirdly, although the slaves themselves did not of course possess their means of reproduction, as property of the lords they were in their own way effectively *merged* with their means of subsistence. In consequence, the lords could not fire the slaves and had to coerce them to get them to work, with the result that they experienced some of the same difficulties in developing production on the basis of skilled and careful labour as did the feudal lords with respect to their coerced peasant possessors. Finally, given the patriarchal character of all of the economic actors, all were faced with the same sorts of problems in amassing land and labour power as faced the economic actors in feudal societies. Naturally, I am not contending that slave-based societies were precisely the same as more purely peasant-based economies, or denying that there were developmental patterns specific to slave society and absent in purely peasant-based societies. Nonetheless, what allows me, I believe, to assimilate them for present purposes, is that the economic actors in both sorts of society were subject to roughly similar rules for reproduction – rules for reproduction which put modern economic development or any smooth transition to capitalist property relations out of the question.

be, in an economy of producers deprived of their full means of subsistence, we can expect that the entailed processes of competitive accumulation and innovation will *themselves* lead to the *differentiation* of the economy into those with means of production (as well as labour power) and those possessing only labour power. This is because these processes give a competitive advantage to those who can deploy relatively large, and ever larger masses of means of production. To put it succinctly, in a capitalist economy, the process of capital accumulation creates its own labour force of proletarians.

In sum, it is only where capitalist property relations prevail, that all the economic actors have no choice but to adopt as their rule for reproduction the putting on the market of their product (whatever it is) at the competitive, i.e. lowest, price. It is only in such an economy that all economic actors are perpetually *motivated* to cut costs. It is only in such an economy that there exists a *mechanism of natural selection* (i.e. competition on the market) to eliminate those producers who are not effectively cutting costs. It is for these reasons that only under capitalist property relations can we expect a pattern of modern economic growth.

Pre-capitalist economies, capitalist economies, and Adam Smith
We may briefly conclude this section by placing its results in the context of Adam Smith's theory, where we began. To the extent that Smith was right that men are systematically truckers and barterers, i.e. systematic producers for exchange, he was right to expect a pattern of economic growth. An economy of producers for exchange is necessarily also a competitive economy and can be expected, in turn, to be a developing economy, all else being equal. Nevertheless, Smith was quite wrong to believe that systematic production for exchange was itself the simple and direct expression of rational self-interest, specifically the producers' rational self-interest in the gains which might be gotten from participation in a nexus of complementary specializers. Smith thought people specialized for exchange *because* this was the way they could induce and take advantage of the specialization for exchange of others. He may have derived this conclusion from his quite correct understanding that, *given* the existence of such a nexus of specialized producers for exchange, those who participate in it are better off than they would have been had they not participated in it and produced all their requirements by themselves (all else, e.g. risk, being equal). But we have tried to show that (abstractly correct analyses of the 'gains from trade' notwithstanding), so long as pre-capitalist property relations prevail, the economic actors cannot be expected to find it in their rational self-interest systematically to specialize, to make themselves dependent on the market, so they will not produce for exchange. On the

contrary, producers will find it in their rational self-interest to specialize only under capitalist property relations, and then only *because they have no choice* but to produce competitively for the market. To put it as simply as possible: it is not that people exchange so as to specialize, or specialize so as to exchange; they specialize because they *must* exchange.[7] Since this occurs only in the presence of capitalist property relations, to understand the onset of modern economic growth is to understand how capitalist property relations come to prevail.

ii. The growth of trade, the development of the productive forces, and economic development: a critique of modified Smithianism

It is possible that most of today's development economists and economic historians are no longer pure and simple Smithians. But even if this were true (and it is by no means obvious) the fact remains that the overwhelming majority remain Smithians at heart. They would not perhaps contend that the mere application of individual economic rationality will, directly and automatically, bring about aggregate economic development. But they *would* argue, that, *given* the appearance of certain specific, *quite-reasonable-to-expect* exogenous economic stimuli, rational self-interested individual economic activity can indeed be expected to detonate a pattern of growth. It is their hypothesis, that in responding to these external stimuli and the opportunities they create, rational self-interested individuals will in fact come to adopt capitalist rules for reproduction – act like capitalists – and, in so doing, will bring about the transformation of pre-capitalist to capitalist property relations. The outcome will be the inauguration of a pattern of modern economic growth. Depending on the theorist, one of three external stimuli will be chosen as the key determinant of development – the rise of trade, the appearance of new productive forces, the growth of population.[8] But what marks off each of these approaches as Smithian are three defining characteristics common to them all. First, *given* the appearance of the specified key factor, each

[7] To put the point in still another way: where specialized production already exists, the economic actors are, by that fact, dependent on sales and purchases, so must compete and therefore must specialize further, accumulate, and innovate. But this is not to say that specialization and exchange emerge as an immediate expression of economic rationality or can set off a process of economic development. On the contrary, both the specialization and the exchange which lead to economic development are the result of *the necessity to exchange*, which itself initially arises only where the direct producers are separated from their means of reproduction. 'Production for exchange' properly defined is thus the necessity of producing for exchange.

[8] In this essay, I will consider only the first two of these stimuli and, because of considerations of space, will leave aside population growth. For some consideration of the demographic factor in the sort of analytical framework developed here, see Brenner, 1976; Brenner, 1982; Brenner, 1985.

approach ascribes to the pre-capitalist economic actors capitalist motivations and capitalist rules for reproduction. Second, each treats property relations as if they were, in essence, techniques or organizations of production, *constituted within the individual productive units*, which are adopted or discarded by individual economic actors according to their effectiveness in developing production in those individual units. Finally, each ends up, implicitly and illegitimately, taking for granted the prevalence of capitalist property relations, both within the individual unit and beyond, so as to give the appearance of rationality to the economic strategy which is (mis)attributed to the economic actors. The result, in each case, is that capitalism is assumed in order to explain the onset of modern economic growth, while pre-capitalist property relations somehow magically disappear.

Historicized Smithianism: the rise of trade
Beginning with Adam Smith himself, many historically-sensitive theorists of economic development have understood it to depend on the growth of trade, specifically the rise of exchange *between* two previously separate and self-subsisting economies. Although beginning their analyses from different historical starting points and thus from somewhat different initial systems of property relations, Smith and his very many followers all make arguments which follow the same fundamental progression. First, merchants with their merchant capital offer previously unobtainable products to hitherto self-subsistent economic actors. This is understood as an epoch-making historical event, an original rise of trade. Next, the opportunity to purchase these commodities induces the individual economic actors to relinquish production for subsistence and to adopt the economic strategy of capitalists-in-embryo – i.e. production for exchange so as to maximize returns (the price/cost ratio) by way of cost cutting. Third, since pre-capitalist property relations marked by the direct producers' possession of the means of subsistence and the exploiters' extraction of a surplus by means of extra-economic coercion prevent the individual productive units from most effectively deploying their resources, the individual economic actors *within* each unit, both producers and exploiters, move to transform these property relations in the direction of capitalist property relations. On this transformed basis, they are able to pursue more effectively their drive to cut costs via specialization, accumulation, and innovation. The causal sequence can thus be summarized as follows: rise of trade → adoption of capitalist rules (or strategies) of reproduction by individual economic actors, specifically production for exchange → installation of capitalist property relations within each unit of production → tendency to

specialization, accumulation, and innovation within each unit → onset of modern economic growth. Let us follow this argument, step-by-step.

As for merchant capital, it does indeed appear as the original form of 'abstract wealth' and, as such, it is, in a sense, a precondition for economic development. Moreover, merchants do tend to be systematic profit maximizers, *to the extent they are able.* They are, as a rule, cut off from direct access to their means of reproduction. Therefore, in so far as they wish to maintain themselves as merchants, they have little choice but to attempt to employ their merchants' capital to buy cheap and sell dear on the market so as to make a profit. Nevertheless, the question remains: Can merchant capital, by itself, bring about the adoption of capitalist rules for reproduction on the part of the pre-capitalist economic actors and, in turn, the rise of capitalist property relations leading to economic development?

In the first place, despite his possession of money and/or commodities, the merchant can in no way ensure by his own selling and buying efforts that the pre-capitalist economic actors will even put the products they produce on the market. The merchant may carry commodities from one part of the globe to another, from one region to another, but the mere offer of these commodities does not at all automatically call forth the appearance on the market of products for exchange. For the exploiters and direct producers already have what is necessary to reproduce themselves. The appearance of new goods leads to the *potential* for increased consumption and therefore the potential for exchange, but it may nonetheless call forth no response.

Secondly, even to the extent that the appearance of new goods brought by merchants does lead the surplus extracting or exploiting class and direct producers to try to orient their production toward exchange, this process may be strictly limited to *immediate surpluses.* In other words (until reasons to expect the contrary are provided) one may reasonably assume that the surplus extractors and direct producers will make sure that they can carry out the diversified production needed to assure the fulfilment of their basic economic needs prior to allocating resources to commercialized, specialized production. In other words, only what might be called surplus resources will be devoted to commercialized, specialized production. To the degree this is so, masses, of labour power and land, devoted to production for immediate reproduction, remain strictly separated from the sphere of commodity production. Despite trade, *these* factors of production are entirely immune to tendencies toward specialization, accumulation, and innovation. In such a situation, there *is*, of course, a 'surplus' commercial-specialized sector (alongside the subsistence sector) and thus a rudimentary division of labour – different producers or regions selling specialized products to one another. Still, it should not be forgotten that neither the individual exploiters nor producers are economically dependent on this specialized, commercialized production – so that neither the exploiters nor producers must treat the resources of this sector in accord with capitalist rules for reproduction (maximizing the price/cost ratio, etc.). In consequence, the degree to which the productive system as a whole partakes of the distinctively modern developmental tendencies toward systematic and increasing specialization, accumulation, and innovation is at best sharply restricted.

Thirdly, even to the degree that, in response to market opportunities, the individual exploiters or direct producers or the merchants themselves do seek to specialize as much as is possible in the aforementioned 'surplus' commercial sector, and, beyond that, to accumulate and innovate, there are, as already emphasized, barriers to their doing so built into the environment structured by pre-capitalist property relations. Precisely because of the prevalence of property relations characterized by the merger of the economic actors with their means of reproduction, it will be difficult or impossible for potential accumulators to acquire the greater amounts of land and labour power needed to facilitate cooperative and scale production and other improvements, and in that way to increase output for the market. This is because the *other* exploiters and direct producers cannot be counted on to part with the land and labour power which constitute the immediate basis of their reproduction. Moreover, even to the extent that any given exploiter already disposes over his own direct producers (as in feudalism or patriarchal slavery), he will find it difficult to use this labour effectively to improve production by means of the adoption of new, more effective tools and techniques, for reasons already stated.

So long as pre-capitalist property relations persist, then, trade appears powerless to set off a process of development. Recognizing this, historicized Smithians – including Adam Smith (1776), H. Pirenne (1937), P. Sweezy (1950) – have seen the growth of exchange as leading the individual pre-capitalist actors to find it in their rational self-interest to dismantle, in piecemeal fashion, the existing pre-capitalist property relations and to constitute capitalist property relations so as to achieve greater productive efficiency. Thus, they envision a process whereby the individual pre-capitalist exploiters respond to the new opportunities originating with the growth of exchange by seeking to introduce more effective productive techniques. In order to accomplish this, they dispense with their (unproductive) military followers and military-luxury expenditures; they free their hitherto-dominated peasant producers; they expropriate these peasants from the land; then, finally, they enter into contractual relations with these peasants. This gives rise, *within each unit*, to the installation of a free necessarily commercialized (market-dependent) tenant on an economic lease who (ultimately) hires wage labourers. The end result is the establishment of capitalist property relations in the economy as a whole and the onset of economic development.

Unfortunately, this analysis takes into account pre-capitalist property relations only to end up by ignoring their significance. Under pre-capitalist property relations, *pace* the historicized Smithians, the individual exploiter can hardly find it in his rational self-interest to free his peasants, for he would lose thereby his ability to exploit them. Once freed from the lord's extra-economic domination, his *possessing* peasants would have no need to pay *any* levy to him, let alone increase the quality and quantity of their work for him. Moreover, even if the lord could at the same time free *and* expropriate his peasants, he would still lose by the resulting transformation of his unfree peasant possessors into free landless tenants and wage labourers; for the newly created landless tenants or wage labourers would have no reason to stay and work for their former lord or take up a lease from him. The error, therefore, is two-fold: first, the distinctively pre-capitalist rationality and rules for reproduction imposed by pre-capitalist property relations are ignored; second, the property relations characterizing the (ill-defined) 'productive unit' are viewed as, in essence, technical relations, to be altered by the exploiters as conditions change – specifically, when the appearance of trade transforms their self-interest. To make the same point from a slightly different angle: the historicized Smithians take for granted the existence of capitalist property relations in order to account for their appearance: in the presence of trade, they see the productive units as subject to capitalist rules for reproduction while (unjustifiably) assuming that the economy, both internal and external to the units, is (already) composed of the capitalist actors necessary to fully reconstitute these units – specifically tenants (and workers) separated from their means of subsistence (and production).

In fact, precisely because pre-capitalist exploiters find it difficult to adopt more efficient productive techniques and irrational to install new property relations within their units, if they wish to respond to new opportunities created by trade, they have little alternative but to try to do so within the constraints imposed by pre-capitalist property relations – by increasing their levies on the direct producers in money, kind, or labour. To make this possible, they have no choice but to try to build up their relations of domination over them. They cannot, of course, be sure they will succeed, for the peasants might resist. But this is their most promising route.

Finally, what is most likely to stimulate the exploiters actually to *try* to increase their returns is the appearance on the market of goods which 'fit' their specific reproductive needs. As emphasized, these are not producer goods, but, on the contrary, means of consumption – specifically materials helpful to the exploiters' political and military strength. These are certainly not luxury goods in the ordinary sense of superfluities, for they are, in a way, necessities for the exploiters. But they are luxuries in that their production involves a subtraction from the means available to the economy to expand its fundamental productive base.

Paradoxically, then, to the extent that the rise of trade can be expected to affect pre-capitalist economies, it is likely to bring about not the loosening, but the tightening, of pre-capitalist property forms, and the quickening not of economic growth, but of stagnation and decline.

The problem with the historicized version of Smithianism thus turns out to be pretty much the same as with Smithianism pure and simple. In pure and simple Smithianism, exchange is seen as natural; in historicized Smithianism, it has an historical origin. But in both cases, the process foreseen is essentially the same: rationally self-interested individuals with the opportunity to exchange cannot but exploit exchange, and they will inevitably do so by acting like capitalists – whatever the existing property relations and rules for reproduction apparently entail. Capitalists *in potential* are assumed to exist; and it is a foregone conclusion that they will promote growth if given the chance to do so, if necessary by transforming piecemeal the relations of property.

Marxist Smithianism: the development of the productive forces

The theory that the growth of the productive forces is the key to economic development over the long run is today associated with Marxism. But, in my view, its original conceptual source is, once again, Adam Smith. The theory can be stated briefly, but not without considerable ambiguity. It says, I think, that (1) the productive forces (broadly conceived, as including not just tools, but the organization of production) potentially adoptable by the economic actors – namely the level of available technique – will increase; (2) up to a certain point, the existing property relations will allow for the adoption of the available productive forces, and thus for increases in productive efficiency; (3) but, after a certain point, in order to allow for the further adoption of the available productive forces (which are assumed to continue to develop), and thus increases in productive efficiency, it is necessary to have new property relations; (4) new property relations will emerge, and facilitate the further adoption of the productive forces, and thus the growth of productiveness.

Now, what one regards as the actual content of this theory depends upon how one interprets property relations, or what Marx called the relations of production.[9] In my view, the theory can be made to work only on the basis of a certain construal of property relations, indeed a distinctively Smithian mis-construal. But if the theory is formulated in such Smithian terms, it becomes useless for explaining economic development. As we shall see, this is for the same reasons that Smithian approaches are generally useless for explaining economic development.

Thus, if we start from the account I have presented here of property relations as relations of reproduction which dictate the adoption of certain specific rules for reproduction, it is hard to see how the theory of the development of the productive forces could function at all. We begin where we must begin, namely with the prevalence of pre-capitalist property relations. We can agree that it is reasonable to expect, even in pre-capitalist economies, significant, though varying, amounts of technical progress: thus, the productive forces potentially useable, i.e. available, will increase. The question, however, is whether or not such increases will set off a process of economic development.

First, and once again, given the presence of the patriarchal property relations which structure pre-capitalist economies, none of the individual economic actors is compelled to adopt the new techniques in order to increase their efficiency in production, for they do not have to produce for exchange and compete on the market.

Secondly, those economic actors who may wish to adopt new techniques will encounter the already specified barriers to their doing so, which are built into the pre-capitalist property relations. The direct producers (peasants) will be reluctant to adopt new techniques which require much specialization. (Yet, it should perhaps be mentioned in passing that, historically, powerful, productivity-raising advances in agriculture almost always have been bound up with increased specialization.) The exploiters will find it difficult to adopt new techniques which require the application of careful, highly motivated labour. Those economic actors who do not dispose directly – i.e. by ownership or domination – of large masses of land and labour power, will tend to find

---

[9] This formulation is derived from Marx's famous Preface to *The Critique of Political Economy* (1859) and, more especially, from the techno-determinist interpretation of Marx presented by G. A. Cohen (see Cohen, 1978a). Cohen's account is, however, based on the explicitly *functionalist* argument that the property relations which facilitate the development of the productive forces emerge precisely because they function to, or have the consequence of, facilitating the development of the productive forces. As an alternative – and to supply the defect of and avoid dependence upon questionable functionalist arguments – the techno-determinist interpretation presented here includes a causal mechanism which can account for the appearance of the new productive relations which facilitate the development of the productive forces. As will be seen, however, this account has its own problems.

it difficult to adopt technical advances requiring scale and/or cooperative labour, due to limitations of land and labour markets.

Thirdly, those with resources to invest – most often the exploiters – are likely to find that they will get the best return by investing in the means of coercion, rather than the means of production. Indeed, in pre-capitalist economies, we are likely to find a general tendency to the development of the means of coercion at the expense of developing the means of production.

Fourthly, even if some economic actors do adopt a new technique, we have no reason to expect that that technique will be generally adopted – as we would in an economy structured by capitalist property relations.

Fifthly, let us consider the case where some technical advance is, somehow, widely adopted in a pre-capitalist setting. Even this will not, as a rule, bring about economic development properly understood. For the positive effect on the growth of productiveness which may be achieved through even a universally adopted once-and-for-all advance generally is not at all comparable to that which is normally achieved as a consequence of the continual pressure to cut costs and improve which can be expected in economies structured by capitalist property relations.[10] In other words, it is the capitalist property relations *per se* which account for the distinctive productiveness of modern economies – not any particular advance in the productive forces – and this is because capitalist property relations impose the requirement to specialize, accumulate, and innovate or go out of business.

Finally, for reasons stated above, given the presence of pre-capitalist property relations, the individual economic actors – both exploiters and producers – will find it irrational to attempt to install capitalist property relations within the individual productive unit.[11]

---

[10] Of course, it is possible to think up examples where the generalized adoption of a once-and-for-all advance in technique in a pre-capitalist economy would be very significant indeed – say, the generalized adoption of cotton machinofacture in an economy of serf estates. This would still not amount to a tendency to *ongoing* transformation, but it would probably be question-begging to deny that this is an example of economic development. Nevertheless, the question which must be asked is whether or not such a process actually could come about. It is not easy to answer this question in a definitive way. What it amounts to is whether a process of development of the productive forces of the sort which could issue, for example, in the widespread capacity to make and operate cotton factories could take place within a pre-capitalist context if modern economic growth was not already occurring elsewhere. If the framework advanced here is valid, it would seem unlikely that this could happen. Since in pre-capitalist economies, investment is likely to be directed towards developing the means of coercion, not the means of production, we should perhaps expect that to the extent resources are consistently devoted to innovation, it would be to innovation in politico-military techniques and organization. Correlatively, it would seem to require a capitalist process of development, to elicit the sort of *sustained* and *cumulative* process of technical advance required for the emergence of, say, cotton machinofacture. Nonetheless, this question of whether incremental, cumulative processes of technical innovation could ultimately amount to economic development within the pre-capitalist framework remains an open one.   [11] See above, pp. 38–39.

In sum, if we take the prevalence of pre-capitalist property relations as our point of departure – and accept the account here presented of property relations as relations of reproduction – it is difficult to see how the growth of the productive forces could be seen to bring about economic development, in particular by means of bringing about the transformation of property relations in a capitalist direction. As it happens, the theory that the growth of the productive forces will bring about economic development by means of bringing about changes in the property relations has, classically, depended upon a construal of property relations very different from the one offered here – in particular, a reading of property relations as 'relations of production' and a reduction of relations of production to socio-technical relations within the unit of production. In this rendering of the theory, so-called relations of production are constituted by the division of labour within the unit of production (the labour process). The division of labour within the unit of production directly expresses the functional requirements of the particular techniques there in use. The arrangement of managerial/supervisory labour, skilled labour, and unskilled labour of specific sorts is thus technically determined. As a result, the so-called relations of production are merely a reflection of the technical relations within the unit. Finally, to complete the picture, in the classical, and internally consistent, texts where this theory is propounded – notably Marx's *German Ideology* – the relations of production are also what are understood in that context to be relations of property because they determine the distribution of product among the social classes. In fact, the relations of production constitute the social classes, since classes, on this view, are defined by their position/function within the immediate process of production – classically, the position in the structure of authority (managers/managed, organizers/organized). Reward thus follows contribution or function.

Now, if one thus views *property* relations (relations of distribution) as expressing the so-called relations of production and one understands the relations of production as determined by the technique in use, it certainly makes sense to see the growth of the productive forces – i.e. the improvement in the available techniques – as leading to economic development by means of leading to the rise of new productive relations. As new techniques become available, we can naturally expect the (rational) economic actors to try to adopt them. Why shouldn't they? In turn, since adopting the new techniques generally requires constituting a new division of labour within the unit in order to put the new technique into effect, there is every reason to expect that the economic actors will reorganize their units. In so doing, they will have to change the relations of production and, in turn, the property relations. The

new relations of production and new property relations will then facilitate
the adoption of the new productive forces, leading to economic development.
The causal sequence foreseen runs as follows: (autonomous) appearance
(new availability) of new productive forces → adoption of new division of
labour, an aspect of which is new relations of production within the
productive units (an aspect of which is new relations of property and
class) → adoption of new forces of production.

Now, in the *German Ideology*, Marx exemplified this theory by laying out
the following progression, in which each successive stage in the development
of the productive forces gave rise to new relations of production which
allowed for the adoption of the new techniques peculiar to that stage: (1)
(autonomous rise of) craft technology → production relations of master
craftsmen and journeymen (to facilitate craft production); (2) (autonomous
rise of) machinofacturing technology → production relations of merchant
entrepreneurs and detail labourers (to facilitate manufacture); (3) (autonomous rise of) machinofacturing technology → production relations of capitalist-
managers and unskilled workers (to facilitate machinofacture). The increase
in the level of technique thus gives rise to new relations of production which
facilitate the adoption of the new techniques and thus the growth of
productiveness.[12]

Nevertheless, it does not take much probing to see that the foregoing
construction requires at once leaving out any consideration of property
relations (i.e. the relations of reproduction) and the smuggling in of capitalist
property relations as premises.

In the first place, the foregoing theory assumes (without explanation) that
the functional positioning of the economic actors within the productive
unit – especially their positioning as manager versus managed or organizer
versus organized, as in Marx's *German Ideology* – will bring with it a distribution
of income among classes, defined according to productive function or,
perhaps more precisely, according to type of labour contributed. But it is
difficult to see how this can happen, unless some system of property relations
is specified; for there is no reason simply to assume that the distribution of
people in different productive roles (even managerial versus managed or
authority versus subordinate roles) will, in itself, determine a particular
distribution of income. Of course, if capitalist property relations (relations of
reproduction) are assumed – i.e. it is assumed that the producers are deprived
of their means of subsistence (not necessarily their means of production) and
that no one can reproduce himself by appropriating a product by extra-
economic coercion – it is reasonable to expect that the reward for labour will

[12] See Brenner (1985).

be commensurate with the qualification of the labour (assuming equal quantity and quality of labour). For under capitalist property relations, reproduction must be organized through the exchange of commodities and specifically the exchange of labour power for commodities (assuming that there is some cooperative labour), and presumably no one would work unless he was paid commensurately with what he contributed (and vice versa). Returns will be according to socially necessary labour, allowing for qualification, as well as amount and quality. Of course, to say even this does not get us very far, for the whole question of 'returns to ownership' of property in the means of production – the key aspect of distribution and, thus, of reproduction under capitalism – is simply left aside.

Far more germane to our present purposes, however, is that the progression foreseen by the theory whereby individual economic actors adopt more effective techniques by bringing in new relations of production simply because the techniques are more productively effective, obviously depends upon the existence of capitalist property relations. Only under capitalism, as we have argued *ad infinitum*, will the individual economic actors necessarily have the motivation (survival) to adopt new techniques; only under capitalism will there obtain a process of natural selection to weed out those who do not. But to assume the existence of capitalism in order to explain modern economic growth is, of course, to beg the question.

To make the same point from a different angle, the theory of economic development as a function of the growth of the productive forces involves all of the classic Smithian assumptions. First, justifying the expectation that the mere appearance of a new technique will as a rule induce the economic actors to try to adopt it, requires ascribing to (pre-capitalist) economic actors capitalist motivations and capitalist rules for reproduction – assuming that they will act like capitalists. Secondly, justifying the expectation that the economic actors can and will reconstitute the division of labour inside the unit of production so as to be able to bring in the new technique and, in the process, reconstitute the property relations within the unit, requires treating property relations as if they were, in essence, techniques of production, constituted within the individual productive units, which can be adopted or discarded by individual economic actors according to their effectiveness in developing production in those individual units. Finally, justifying the expectation that the appearance of new techniques will, in itself, bring about the adoption of those techniques, requires taking it for granted that capitalist property relations obtain both inside and outside the unit, for this is the only condition under which it is economically rational for the economic actors to adopt the new technique, where it is generally possible for the economic actors to do so, and where their failure to do so will as a rule lead to their going out of business.

The point can be brought home, finally, by referring once again to what we mean by property relations. These are not, in any useful sense, understandable as relations of production *per se*, but must be seen as relations of reproduction. Property relations specify the relationships of possession and coercion among the economic actors – the producers and producers, the exploiters and exploiters, the producers and exploiters – which make it possible for them to have the regular access to the means of production and/or the economic product which is necessary for their maintenance (reproduction) as they were. Now, since (by the argument I have been presenting) the property relations determine the economic actors' rule for (best strategy for) reproduction, they can also be seen to determine their capacity for innovation and thus the general pattern of development or non-development of the productive forces.

But the converse obviously is not true: the mere appearance of new productive forces simply cannot call into being/determine the property relations which would have to exist if they were to be put into effect. It cannot do so, first of all, because, as I have argued, under pre-capitalist property relations, the economic actors, as individuals, cannot be expected systematically to adopt new and better productive techniques, let alone find it in their rational self-interest to adopt new property relations in order to do so. But it cannot do so for a more specific reason: the key to the productiveness of capitalism, it will be remembered, is not its association with any particular technique or form of productive organization, however efficient, but the drive to cut costs by way of specialization, accumulation and innovation which it imposes on the economic actors. But this means that for the individual pre-capitalist economic actors conceivably to 'choose capitalism' in order to benefit from its productiveness: (1) they would have to understand the connection between capitalist property relations *per se* and capitalist productiveness; (2) on that basis, they would have to find it in their own individual, rational self-interest to carry through a change to capitalist property relations; (3) finally, they would have to be able, in practice, to reconstitute the new structure of property relations, i.e. eliminate the pre-capitalist property relations and install capitalist property relations. Merely to specify these conditions is, I think, to rule out the possibility of such a process – at least until ongoing capitalist relations already existed somewhere else.[13] Of course

[13] It should perhaps be noted, in passing, that if one accepts the analysis presented here of the theory of the productive forces, it becomes very difficult to see how a functionalist account along the lines of G. A. Cohen's in his *Karl Marx's Theory of History. A Defense* can be made

to say this is merely to state, in still another way, a thesis of this paper: that individual economic actors will not find it in their rational self-interest to bring about the rise of capitalist property relations. Whether the individual pre-capitalist actors might bring about the installation of capitalist property relations either unintentionally, or by acting collectively, organized as classes, are problems to which we must now turn.

to work. Cohen thinks it is legitimate to say that the growth of the productive forces explains the transformation of productive relations (property relations) required to put those productive forces into effect, even if one cannot always specify the causal mechanism by which this takes place. But, if I understand him properly, Cohen believes this, in part, because he also believes that there *will be* such a mechanism, i.e. that the new productive forces will, by *some* mechanism, call into existence the productive relations (property relations) requisite to their adoption. But why should such a mechanism be supplied? Cohen seems to think that precisely because the new productive forces increase productive efficiency, that some economic actors will, sooner or later, find it in their rational self-interest to adopt them and will find a way to transform the property relations to make this possible.

Now, it has, of course, been the burden of this paper, particularly of the previous section, to show that making this assumption is unwarranted. I have argued, therefore, that, given the prevalence of pre-capitalist property relations, economic actors simply cannot be assumed to find it in their self-interest to adopt new, more effective techniques and, above all, that they cannot be assumed to find it in their self-interest or their capacity to make the necessary changes in the property relations required to adopt the new techniques. But, even more to the point, if one believes, as I have contended, that the unprecedented productiveness of capitalism derives not from any particular productive force or technique, but is a consequence of the property relations themselves, it becomes just about impossible to see how the sort of argument Cohen makes for the primacy of the productive forces can be sustained. This is, most simply, because, on this premise, no particular advance in technique – no increase in the productive forces – is necessary to bring about either capitalist property relations or the tremendous increases in productiveness associated with them. Thus, capitalism could appear at a point when no new techniques beyond those already available to the economic actors under feudalism had yet come into existence; in this case, it would still yield a tremendous increase in productiveness, because, minimally, it would tend to bring about the generalized adoption of all those techniques only partially adopted under feudalism and because, more generally, it would constitute an economy in which all the economic actors find it rational to try to cut costs and increase efficiency as much as possible by specializing, accumulating, and innovating (and one in which those actors who failed to do this tended to go out of business). So, it might, just conceivably, be possible to argue (as Cohen might) that, all else being equal, individual economic actors might, on occasion, even under pre-capitalist property relations, find it sensible to *attempt* to adopt certain new techniques and, in turn, at least *try* to transform the property relationships within their individual units to make it possible to adopt such techniques; but it does not seem reasonable to argue that those same individual economic actors might find it both sensible and possible to seek to adopt, not individually but on an economy-wide basis, a system of property relations which had the merit not of facilitating the productiveness of any specific one of the economic actors, but of bringing about a general increase in productiveness for the whole system – above all, when such a system had never previously existed. So, one could not, I think, conceivably argue that individual pre-capitalist economic actors would seek to separate the pre-capitalist producers from their means of subsistence and break up the lords' institutionalized relationships with the producers which allowed them to extract a surplus by extraeconomic compulsion in order to install a system where the individual actors had, as their rule for reproduction, the maximization of profits (saw accumulate, accumulate as the moses and the prophets)...especially when such a system had never previously existed. Nevertheless, only if we could conceive of the economic actors as making such an unlikely move, could we accept the theory that the growth of the

iii. *The reproduction of property relations: stability and transformation*

Up to this point, I have taken the property relations as given, and as constraining on individual economic actors, but have provided no explanation as to what actually maintains the property relations, keeps them going. How are the property relations themselves reproduced? This problem is too complex to be treated fully here. I shall consider what I believe to be one fundamental aspect, with the purpose of bringing to a conclusion my general argument concerning the social basis for economic development.

The single point I wish to develop is that the critical condition for the reproduction of the property relations is the existence of a community of economic actors which sees the reproduction of these relations as its *conscious* purpose. The community's members will seek to maintain them, simply because one of its main, explicit functions is to reproduce the property relations, and specifically to protect the access of its individual members to their means of reproduction. The community will thus see its goal to be, above all, protecting the ongoing access of its members to their means of reproduction against threats posed to this by outsiders, other members of the community, and, especially, opposing classes. To do this, the members of the community have to organize themselves into various sorts of regulative and coordinating bodies – i.e. *political* institutions.

Thus, the pre-capitalist *producers* are organized into communities, the fundamental purpose of which is to protect their members' *individual possession*

productive forces was primary in the march of history – that history was driven forward, in the last analysis, by the growth of technical knowledge and its application.

Now, a defender of the primacy of the productive forces might perhaps grant that capitalism's unique productiveness is not tied to any particular development of the productive forces which it facilitates, but is rooted in its property relations themselves, as I have argued. Possibly, he might still defend the primacy of the productive forces thesis by arguing that, as a matter of fact (or hypothesis), capitalist property relations do facilitate the adoption of certain particular techniques (for example, those involving cooperation in the labour process), and that, in fact, when these techniques become available, they are (would be) adopted precisely by means of adopting capitalist property relations. In consequence, it could still presumably be said that the appearance of new techniques calls into being capitalist property relations and thus, indirectly, the systematic growth of productiveness which is associated with these property relations. Nevertheless, this would be, I think, a fairly paradoxical defence of the thesis of the primacy of the productive forces. For it would admit that developments of the productive forces were crucial to economic development not because they themselves brought increased productiveness (and called into existence the property relations requisite to their own use), but because they brought into existence the capitalist property relations which were in *themselves* critical for economic development. The new techniques would, by this argument, be critical to the growth of the productive forces only accidentally – only because they had the accidental effect of bringing into being capitalist property relations. On the basis of such an argument we would have no reason to look to the appearance of new techniques, in particular, to bring about economic development, but could look to *any* phenomenon which could have the accidental consequence of bringing into existence capitalist property relations. Plagues, earthquakes, or the previous evolution of property relations might, on this view, be equally good candidates for the position of primacy.

of the means of subsistence. The communities of direct producers function, therefore, to counteract the threats from foreigners, the tendencies to conflict and mutual expropriation among their own members, and, especially, the pressures from the exploiters or potential exploiters. The pre-capitalist *exploiters*, similarly, will be able to establish and maintain themselves as exploiters only on the condition that they are organized into a self-conscious group (or groups) which is (are) capable, by virtue of its self-organization and resources, to impose, on a continuing basis, a levy on the communities of direct producers, as well as to protect itself against other groups of exploiters and to regulate the internal conflicts among its own members, especially over property. For example, the class of feudal lords was able to establish itself as a dominant class only when the groups of lords which came to compose it were able to organize themselves *as groups* through the feudal bond – by which the overlords brought together the underlords around them on the basis of the grant of land (with peasants) for military-political service. They required, further, as a condition of their establishment and reproduction, certain crucial resources, specifically, castles and the equipment needed by mounted knights. Based in castles, the collectivities of lords and mounted knights were able to impose taxes on the peasants sufficient for their reproduction as feudal exploiters.

If it is accepted that the main classes of pre-capitalist economies are self-organized into communities which have as one of their conscious goals maintaining the established access of the economic actors to their means of reproduction, then it seems reasonable to propose that neither the direct producers nor the exploiters are likely, *as collectivities*, to take action which has the conscious purpose of creating the social conditions required for economic development – i.e. of bringing about the transformation from pre-capitalist to capitalist property relations. This is perhaps easiest to see with respect to the direct producers. The goal of the communities of peasants is to maintain its members in possession of their means of reproduction. In so far as they find it necessary to enter into conflict with the lords, because the lords' levies threaten what they perceive to be their reproductive requirements, they will naturally seek, so far as they are able, to reduce the lords' capacities to levy taxes/rents. But even if the direct producers should succeed fully, and reduce to zero the levies of the lords, they will still exist as communities of producers in possession of their full means of subsistence. The barriers to economic development entailed by this set of property relations will thus remain intact, and it is not easy to think of conditions in which the community of peasant producers would intentionally remove them, by breaking up their members' direct, non-market access to the means of reproduction.

The case of the pre-capitalist exploiters is somewhat more complicated. Still, given the fact that the lords reproduce themselves precisely by means of asserting and maintaining their domination over the direct producers, it does not seem far-fetched to assert that, *as a rule*, to the extent they wish to improve their position by increasing their income and resources, they will do so by strengthening their domination. This means increasing their capacity to levy exactions upon the direct producers by means of extra-economic compulsion – and thereby intensifying the barriers to the emergence of the conditions necessary for economic development.

Can we conceive of *any* conditions in which the pre-capitalist exploiters *as a collectivity* would move, not to strengthen pre-capitalist property relations, but to transform them in a capitalist direction? This is a difficult question. We have already explained that individual exploiters could not find it in their interest to move *individually* to free their direct producers and expropriate them, because such a transformation, taking place in the individual unit, would actually reduce their ability to take an income by exploiting the direct producers. Are there conditions under which the exploiters could *increase* their income by carrying out the change *collectively* and *all at once* through the economy as a whole? For the change to be advantageous to them, the lords would have to be able to expect to collect a higher rent from direct producers now reduced to free (landless) commercial tenants, than they could from the same producers when they were unfree possessors of the means of subsistence. Nevertheless, it is not easy to see why this result would obtain, unless additional hypotheses were introduced about the differential capacity – either in general or under particular conditions – of the producing class to resist levies in each situation.[14]

If we reject, for purposes of the argument, the idea that unfree peasant possessors are necessarily less exploitable than free landless tenants, we can argue that the situation in which the pre-capitalist exploiters are most likely to find it in their rational self-interest to transform the property relations in the direction of capitalism is where, upon making the transition they consciously *expect* to be able to use the new property relations so as to be better able to make specific improvements (for example, in order to install forms of production requiring careful cooperative labour using advanced means of production), or, more generally, to benefit from the system-wide productiveness of capitalist property relations. Nevertheless, it is difficult to see how this situation could arise, unless the existence of capitalist property relations accompanied by modern economic growth *elsewhere* had already shown them the advantages which might be gained through making the transformation.

[14] This is not to rule out that such convincing hypotheses could be adduced.

But to account for economic development by positing the existence of modern economic growth is once again to finesse the fundamental problem: that is, how modern economic growth came to occur at all.

3. Routes of transition?

Modern economic growth requires the break-up of pre-capitalist property relations characterized by the producers' possession and the exploiters' surplus extraction by extra-economic coercion. Nevertheless, unless capitalist property relations have *already* made for ongoing economic growth *elsewhere*, neither producers nor exploiters in the pre-capitalist context will find it in their rational self-interest to move, either individually or collectively, to adopt capitalist property relations. How then can these pre-capitalist property relations be transcended? How were they, in fact, transcended? Obviously, this is not the place for an extended historical discussion. I will confine myself to two very preliminary sets of observations to indicate further implications of the general approach adopted here, and to set out possible lines of historical investigation.

iv. The rise of capitalist property relations as an unintended consequence
Firstly, given that pre-capitalist property relations normally impose upon the economic actors – both exploiters and producers, as individuals and as organized into classes – strategies for reproduction which lead them, in one way or another, to seek to *strengthen* these relations, we can put forward the following basic hypothesis, which follows from our overall approach: the rise of capitalist property relations occurs as an *unintended consequence* of the operation of the rules for reproduction of individual pre-capitalist actors and/or of the conflicts between pre-capitalist classes.

Secondly, under what general conditions are these unintended processes most likely to occur? Pre-capitalist societies, as noted, may be constituted on the basis of either individual or collective possession by the direct producers and either individual or collective surplus extraction by extra-economic coercion by the exploiters. From this fact, we can set out four possible general types of pre-capitalist economies, corresponding to the four possible combinations of peasant possession and lordly surplus extraction: collective possession/collective surplus extraction; collective possession/individual surplus extraction; individual possession/collective surplus extraction; individual possession/individual surplus extraction.

Now, from what has already been said, it may be reasonable to argue that those pre-capitalist economies in which the peasants possess *collectively*, as communities, their means of reproduction will be the least likely to transform themselves in a capitalist direction. First of all, such communities are constituted, in part, precisely to retain and regulate the allocation and use of the peasants' land. Functioning so as to ensure the maintenance of their individual members, these communities are at once unlikely to allow individual members to lose entirely their access to their means of reproduction or, correspondingly, to allow individual members to dispose of the land in a way which would separate it from the community. Since the community itself directly possesses the land it is in an unsurpassed position to insure individual and community access to the means of reproduction and can hardly take action which separates the peasants from their means of subsistence.

Correlatively, where peasants possess their means of reproduction collectively through their communities, the exploiters, too, would seem unlikely to follow paths leading to the separation of the producers from their means of subsistence, whether they themselves extracted collectively or individually. As extractors of the surplus from the whole peasant communities, the lords would, it seems, find it in their interest *consciously* to support (at least up to a point) the authority and coherence of the communities. Moreover, given the need to deal with the communities on a regular basis in collecting taxes or rents, the exploiters would be relatively unlikely, it seems, to take *unintentional* actions which would undermine the communities. Finally, at least in those cases where the lords extracted the surplus as a collective, in the unlikely instance where they somehow undermined the community and began to separate its members from their means of subsistence, they would find it in their interest, due to their collective dependence upon tax revenues, actually to reconstitute the community and thereby the peasants' possession.

By the same sort of reasoning, it seems reasonable to hypothesize that where historical developments issued in economies in which the peasants possessed *individually* their means of subsistence, an ulterior evolution toward capitalism was most likely.

First, where the peasants possessed individually, the peasants' own actions could, quite clearly, have the unintended effect of separating them from their means of subsistence. Such an outcome could result not only from decisions to specialize or sell land leading to permanent losses of land (which, from the vantage point of this essay would be irrational, though presumably possible). More to the point, the peasants could, relatively easily, find themselves without access to the land required for their reproduction simply as a result of the demographic growth and parcelization of holdings which were the unintended outcomes of previous generations of peasants pursuing their individually rational patterns of reproduction and inheritance.

Secondly, where the peasants possessed individually, the lords' surplus extraction by extra-economic compulsion could more easily have the unintended effect of leaving the peasants unable to pay their rent and/or with incomes insufficient for subsistence, thus forcing the peasants to give up their plots. Here the community could not be counted on to mediate between the exploiters and possessors with the same degree of effectiveness as it could when it directly possessed the land. Moreover, especially in those instances where the lords extracted a surplus collectively through taxation, the mere fact that over-taxation leading to expropriation might be unintended and undesired could not be counted upon to prevent this from happening. Mutual adjustment between the tax state and the whole population of *individual peasants* could be, in practice, rather difficult.

Thirdly, where the peasants possessed individually, the lords who extracted individually might, in extreme cases, find it in their self-interest to evict their peasants – or at least deprive them of possession. Thus, where peasant resistance reduced rents so much as to threaten the reality of lordly domination – i.e. the lords' very right and capacity to extract a surplus by extra-economic compulsion – the peasants would, in effect, be asserting full property in the land. In this instance, the lords might be led to 'expropriate' the peasants by asserting their own ownership of the land and thereby their right to raise rent *in the future*, even while leaving the actual current levy pretty much as before.

In light of the foregoing discussion, two overriding speculative conclusions may suggest themselves. The first is that pre-capitalist economies have an internal logic and solidity which should not be underestimated. The second is that capitalist economic development is perhaps an historically more limited, surprising and peculiar phenomenon than is often appreciated.

3 The theory of combined and uneven development: a critique*

Jon Elster

World history may be studied from two points of view: as the rise and decline of nations or as the rise and fall of institutions. The former approach is that of Thorstein Veblen and, more recently, of Mancur Olson.[1] It involves a consideration of the process whereby a nation gains dominance and momentum and then, as a result of ossification and accumulation of special-interest groups, loses them again. The latter perspective is that of Marx and, more recently, of Douglass North.[2] They consider the evolution of institutional forms of surplus-extraction, according to their ability to maximize technical change or the tax revenues of the rulers. The typical Veblen–Olson question would be: why was England first ahead of Germany in the process of industrialization only to fall behind later on? The typical Marx–North question would be: why did feudal property relations give way to capitalist ones? In neither case does the answer to the chosen question involve a consideration of the other.

Trotsky's theory of combined and uneven development says that these questions are interrelated.[3] The rise and fall of economic institutions can only be explained by considering the presence of several, competing, unequally developed nation-states. New property structures do not emerge endogenously within a single nation. Rather, they are the outcome of a complex interaction between several nations at different stages of economic development. The central explanatory concept is what Veblen called 'the advantages of backwardness', with the concomitant notion of 'the penalty for taking the lead'.[4] In Veblen's application these notions explain relative rates of advance within a given institutional framework, not the changes that occur in the framework itself. Trotsky addressed himself to the latter question. More

---

* This article draws heavily on Elster (1985a), Ch. 5.

[1] Veblen (1915); Olson (1982). For a more detailed comparison, see Elster (1984a).

[2] North (1981).

[3] The present essay does not reflect a high level of Trotsky scholarship. I hope that I have correctly identified his central views, on the basis mainly of Trotsky (1969, 1977) and Keni-Paz (1977), but there may well be other writings which, had I known them, would have suggested some additions and modifications.   [4] Veblen (1915).

specifically, he argued that the coming transition from capitalism to communism was crucially dependent on the existence within capitalism of an advanced centre and a backward periphery. My task in this essay is to assess the validity of this argument.

The classical statement of the 'law' of combined and uneven development is the following:

> The laws of history have nothing in common with a pedantic schematism. Unevenness, the most general law of the historic process, reveals itself most sharply and complexly in the destiny of the backward countries. Under the whip of external necessity, their backward culture is compelled to make leaps. From the universal law of unevenness thus derives another law which, for the lack of a better name, we may call the law of *combined development* – by which we mean a drawing together of the different stages of the journey, a combining of separate steps, an amalgam of archaic with more contemporary forms. Without this law, to be taken of course in its whole material content, it is impossible to understand the history of Russia, and indeed of any country of the second, third or tenth cultural class.[5]

As laws go, even in the social and historical sciences, this is rather vapid. It amounts to a denial of the theory of unilinear development, but does not make any positive contribution. Elsewhere Trotsky makes it clear that the key explanatory notion is that of the 'privilege of historic backwardness'.[6] The latecomers can adopt the achievements of the pioneers, without having to go through the suffering and birth pains that accompanied their first emergence. Yet even with this specification, there might not appear to be much that differs from Veblen, or from the earlier, nineteenth-century Russian tradition that also emphasized the advantages to Russia of staying behind the main European development.[7] It is clear, however, that the main thrust of Trotsky's argument is that the epochal transition from a capitalist to a communist property regime can only come about through the privilege of backwardness.

As far as I know, Trotsky did not make a similar argument with respect to the transition from feudalism to capitalism, or from slavery to feudalism. Although he refers to unevenness as 'the most general law of the historic process', he does not say in so many words that it is at work in all transitions from one mode of production to another. In any case, I shall mainly discuss his argument as it applies to the transition from capitalism to communism. Before I proceed, however, I ought to mention that others have applied his conceptual scheme to earlier transitions. In a recent exchange on the passage from feudalism to capitalism, Robert Brenner and Guy Bois both rely on the notion of uneven and combined development to support quite different

---

[5] Trotsky (1977), pp. 27–18.
[6] *Ibid.*, p. 26.   [7] Gerschenkron (1962), Chs. 1 and 7.

accounts of that transition.[8] Neither writer, however, states the theory with sufficient precision and generality to allow one to assess its power. The 'combined and uneven development', like the 'contradiction between productive forces and relations of production' that will also occupy us below, belongs to a class of Marxist notions whose suggestiveness is equalled only by their elusiveness.

In my discussion I shall draw upon Marx as well as Trotsky. On two occasions in his life Marx was concerned with the revolutionary division of labour between the various European countries. Around 1850 the focus was on the relation between England on the one hand, France and Germany on the other. Towards 1880, his attention shifted towards the relation between Western Europe and Russia. (In between there was a period of approximately 20 years in which there was near-exclusive emphasis on the internal developments of the capitalist countries, culminating in a famous passage from the Preface to the first volume of *Capital* in which Marx tells his German readers that they are doomed to repeat the English experience.[9]) We shall see that the specific forms of interaction also differ in the writings from these two periods.

One obvious objection should be met at the outset. The historian will be understandably reluctant to consider a theory that addresses itself exclusively to the future – a transition from capitalism to communism that arguably has not taken place anywhere. Indeed, I do not believe that the theory of uneven and combined development can explain any actual transitions. It can, however, help us to locate conflicts and dilemmas that are permanent features of modernizing and developing countries. Trotsky believed that by a suitable combination of circumstances it was possible to get the best of both worlds – the revolutionary potential of the backward countries and the high developed technology of the advanced. He believed, in other words, that there existed a viable path between premature revolutions and revolutions preempted by reform. Although I shall argue that his argument fails, it represents a belief that has been and still is politically efficacious. Briefly: the lesson we need to learn today is that of the disadvantages of backwardness.

The transition from capitalism to communism requires two conditions. First, the productive forces must be developed to a level at which communism is objectively viable, in a sense to be defined later. Secondly, the workers (and possibly their allies) must take the political power and set up communist relations of production. The second condition in turn subdivides into two. The workers must have an opportunity to take the power, i.e. the ruling class must

[8] Bois (1978), p. 66; Brenner (1982), p. 52.   [9] Marx (1867), p. 8.

not be able to repress them by force. Also, they must be motivated to a bid for power. The last, finally, can be further split into two conditions. The workers must be frustrated or unhappy with their life under capitalism, and they must believe that communism is a viable superior alternative. For the purposes of the present essay, I shall disregard the question of opportunity, important though it is in other contexts. I shall focus instead on the first, objective condition and the two subjective, motivational conditions.

Historical materialism asserts that the transition will occur 'when and because' there arises a 'contradiction between the productive forces and the relations of production'.[10] This in itself ensures that the objective condition is met, as will be shown shortly. The big question is whether the contradiction can plausibly generate the necessary subjective conditions. The theory of uneven and combined development finds its *raison d'être* in the fact that it is unlikely that the subjective conditions will be satisfied as long as we restrict ourselves to a single country.

To substantiate these assertions, I first sketch an interpretation of the 'contradiction between productive forces and relations of production', again limiting myself to the case of capitalism.[11] I understand this contradiction as a *suboptimal rate of change of the productive forces* – a lower rate of change than would have been feasible under communist relations of production. This contradiction does not imply technical stagnation. On the contrary, Marx almost certainly believed that capitalism would exhibit uninterrupted and in fact increasingly rapid technical progress. In spite of this, it would at some point become inferior to communism. These statements assume that the following time trajectories can be defined. First, we need to know the level of the productive forces under capitalism as a function of time. This function, $f(t)$, must be defined both for the actual capitalist past and for a – possibly hypothetical – capitalist future. If the communist revolution occurs because capitalism has become suboptimal for the development of the productive forces, we must be able to say something about how they would have developed under a continued capitalist regime. Next, assuming that a communist revolution occurs at time s, let $f_s(t)$ denote the level of productivity that would then obtain at time t. The notions of correspondence and contradiction between the forces and relations of production can be made precise by considering various possible relations between such time profiles. They are subject to two constraints. First, we must assume the *initial indispensability of capitalism*: there exists a time s and a number A such that

---

[10] Marx (1859), pp. 20–1 is the classical statement.
[11] For a fuller exposition, see Elster (1983), Appendix 2 and Elster (1985a), Ch. 5.

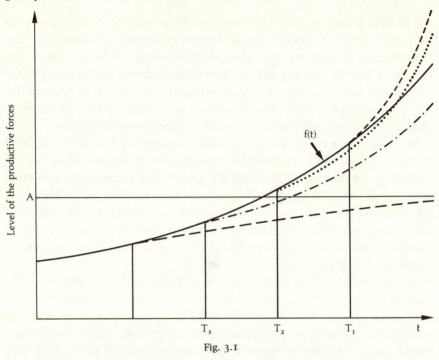

Fig. 3.1

for all t, $f_s(t) < A$. Secondly, we assume as a postulate the *ultimate superiority of communism*: there exists a time s such that for all $t > s$, $f_s(t) > f(t)$. This is a highly speculative assumption,[12] made here for the sake of argument.

To say that the revolution will occur when and because the capitalist relations become suboptimal, implies that it will occur at the earliest time s satisfying the last-mentioned condition. Let us call this time T_1. It represents, I believe, what Marxists have most frequently had in mind when referring to the danger of premature revolution. I discuss below whether T_1 is a plausible date with respect to the subjective conditions for revolution. Here I want to note that while sufficient for the objective condition, it is not necessary. That condition would also be met if the revolution occurred earlier than T_1, if the development of the productive forces would ultimately overtake that which would have occurred under capitalism. Formally, we ask whether there is a time $s < T_1$ and a time $s' > s$ such that for all $t > s'$, $f_s(t) > f(t)$, even if by construction $f_s(s) < f(s)$. If this is the case, we define T_2 as the earliest such s. Clearly, for any s between T_2 and T_1, $f_s(T_1) < f_s(T_1)$: preferring an earlier

---

[12] Marx believed that communism would be superior both with respect to the *intensity of search* for new techniques and with respect to the *efficiency of selection* among the techniques uncovered by the search. While he had at least a sketch of an argument for the second part of this view, the first was largely Utopian. Cp. Elster (1985a), Chs. 3 and 5.

transition time will postpone the time at which communism becomes superior to capitalism. Note that the objective condition would not be met by letting the revolution occur at a still earlier time, T_3, defined as the earliest time at which capitalism is no longer indispensable for the development of the productive forces. Although communism introduced at this time would not be condemned to stagnation, it would never overtake capitalism – a condition that Marx, rightly or wrongly, believed to be essential. Hence only the dates after T_2 represent acceptable transition times. Between T_2 and T_1 there is a trade-off to be considered: should the material conditions for communism be developed by capitalism, which is the more rapid way, or should one prefer the slower development whereby communism itself creates the conditions for its future blossoming?

The comments in the preceding paragraph embody abstract, welfare-theoretic considerations about what course of development would be optimal, given the feasibility. Not all trajectories, however, are feasible, in the sense of satisfying the subjective conditions. Consider again the assertion that the revolution will occur 'when and because' the productive forces enter into contradiction with the relations of production, i.e. when and because the rate of technical change, while high and in fact increasing, becomes lower than what it could be under communism. I submit that it is highly unlikely that a revolution could occur *because* of this suboptimality. Given a satisfactory performance of the capitalist system, the abstract possibility that communism could do even better would not motivate the workers to take the plunge. Both uncertainty and the costs of transition would deter them. If one could point to a declining performance over time, this might provide an incentive to change the system; similarly if one could compare the existing capitalist system in one country with an existing, superior communist system in another. But the first argument rests on a premise denied by Marx, and the second is of no avail in explaining the transition in the crucial first country to set up communist relations of production. Without an internal crisis or an external example, the appeal to the superiority of communism is condemned to be inefficacious.

It might still be true, however, that the revolution can be expected to occur *when* the contradiction emerges. The subjective motive for revolution, that is, might be causally correlated with the development of the productive forces up to the point at which communism is or will be superior for their further development, even if that superiority does not itself provide the motive. One version of this argument – a version found in many of Marx's writings – is that the revolution will occur because of the increasingly suboptimal *use* that capitalism makes of the productive forces it has developed. Specifically, because of lack of coordination in the market, capitalism generates unemployment, unused productive capacities and goods that meet no effective demand. Also, the productive forces under capitalism are used in an inhuman way – because the workers do not fully exercise their creative capacities and because production caters only to their baser needs. In other words, *market failures* and *alienation* provide the subjective levers for revolution.

This would provide a satisfactory theory if one could expect these subjective conditions to emerge simultaneously with the objective ones. 'But societies are not so rational in building that the dates for proletarian dictatorship arrive exactly at that moment when the economic and cultural conditions are ripe for socialism.'[13] In this succinct observation Trotsky stated one premise for the theory of combined and uneven development. The other premise, that the gap between the subjective and the objective conditions may be bridged by international diffusion, is discussed below.

To flesh out Trotsky's insight, we may observe that the subjective conditions for a communist revolution can only be expected to be present within a certain time interval. On the one hand we may define T_4 as the earliest time in the development of capitalism at which these conditions are present. In particular, there must obtain 'the very first prerequisite of a proletarian revolution... namely the existence of an *industrial* proletariat on a national scale'.[14] On the other hand we may define T_5 as the latest time at which the subjective conditions are united. Why should there be any such upper limit? Generally speaking: because capitalism simply is not so perverse that it will generate universal misery while developing productive forces that allow for universal self-fulfilment. In his discussion of the Factory Acts, Marx himself argued that these came into being because intelligent capitalists, paternalistic landowners and statesmen acting on behalf of 'society', saw the writing on the wall. Whenever the social wealth makes it possible to preempt revolution by reform, i.e. by buying off the workers, the ruling class may be expected to do so. In retrospect, it is possible to see the reasons for the massive historical experience that revolution has tended to occur in backward countries.

We may now consider various possibilities and problems. First, the time between T_5 and T_6 might be very short, even vanishingly so. The emergence of a nation-wide proletariat could occur *pari passu* with the improvement of its living conditions, so that the working class would be first too small and then too affluent to make a revolution. Next, consider the possibility that the revolution might occur prematurely. If $T_4 < T_1 < T_5$, the revolution might occur too early according to the criterion of instantaneous superiority, if

[13] Trotsky (1977), p. 334.   [14] Marx (1860), p. 91.

$T_4 < T_2 < T_5$, too early according to the criterion of ultimate superiority. It might, but it need not. Under these conditions, the task of the proletarian leadership would be to prevent a premature revolution. It may be worth while spelling out why the attempt is unlikely to succeed.

In backward countries the development of working-class organizations will invariably be in advance of the development of capitalism. The implantation of socialist ideas can proceed more rapidly than the accumulation of capital, because the dissemination of ideas is essentially costless. Also, in backward nations like Russia the employment of the most recent, large-scale methods of production concentrates a huge number of workers and facilitates class-consciousness.[15] Under such conditions, there will typically be a great deal of impatience among the workers. Their leaders, assuming them to understand the danger of a premature revolution, have the choice between two alternatives. One is to stave off the revolution at least to T_2. The other is to speed up the economic development, to bring T_2 closer to T_4. For easily understood reasons, Marxists have usually chosen the second, less quietist alternative. This was Marx's policy (or one of his policies) in 1848; that of the Mensheviks before 1917 and that of the Chinese Communists up to the Shanghai massacre. For equally obvious reasons, it has invariably failed. For one thing, once the workers have engaged in a successful struggle against the feudal-absolutist-colonial regime, it is hard to stop them from turning – prematurely – against their former ally, the bourgeoisie. For another, the bourgeoisie will recognize this danger, and therefore be quite circumspect about entering into an alliance with their future enemies. The only scenario that would satisfy the Marxist is one in which the workers successfully help the bourgeoisie to power, and then unsuccessfully try to replace them. This defeat will provide time for capitalist development, and harden the class-consciousness of the workers for later struggles. A delicate balance is needed. The workers must be strong, yet not too powerful. The bourgeoisie must be so weak that they need the help of the workers, yet not so weak that they cannot resist them. In practice, it has not worked out.

There is, however, also the possibility that premature revolutions have occurred because $T_5 < T_2$. This, I believe, is what Trotsky referred to in his comment on the irrational building of societies. The subjective and objective conditions are not just partly, but wholly non-overlapping in time. At least this holds with respect to a given country. The theory of combined and uneven development tries to overcome the difficulty by suggesting that the subjective and objective conditions might emerge simultaneously, but in different countries. Specifically, the objective conditions would emerge in the advanced

[15] Trotsky (1977), p. 33.

industrial nations, the subjective conditions in the backward ones. Moreover, by a suitable process of diffusion the communist revolution and the conditions for a viable communism might be brought together, thus creating the synthesis that neither the capitalist centrum nor its periphery could have achieved on their own.

The theory postulates two forms of interaction between the advanced and the backward countries – one prior to the revolution, one posterior to it. Before the revolution, the interaction ensures that a revolution will indeed occur in the backward countries. Economically as well as politically, the backward countries experience the impact of the advanced ones. Both Marx and Trotsky argued that the economic crises that were generated in the centre of the capitalist world, were most deeply felt in the periphery.[16] Trotsky, moreover, argued that the revolutionary class-consciousness of the workers in the backward countries was far more developed than in the advanced countries, for the reasons that I have indicated. True, the interaction also causes the revolution to occur prematurely, but this is supposed to be corrected in the post-revolutionary interaction.

After the revolution, the advanced and the backward countries will interact in a way that brings together the objective and the subjective conditions. In Marx's writings there are two suggestions about the precise form of interaction. Around 1850, he believed in the diffusion of revolution from East to West – from the European Continent to England. 'A European war will be the first result of a successful workers' revolution in France. England will head the counterrevolutionary armies, just as it did during the Napoleonic period, but through the war itself will be thrown to the head of the revolutionary movement.'[17] It is not clear why England would be thrown to the head of the revolution if she engaged in a counterrevolutionary war, nor why she should do so if it was clear that this would be the outcome. Marx, irrationally, hoped for his adversary to be less rational than himself.[18] Similarly, Trotsky put his faith in an international revolutionary conflagration, ignited by the revolution in Russia.[19]

Around 1880, in his writings on the development of Russia, Marx suggested a different mechanism: the diffusion of technology from West to East. Although post-revolutionary Russia would not by herself be able to develop into a viable communism, she could do so by borrowing Western technology.[20] He underestimated the difficulties, of which we know much more today, that a backward country will experience in trying to apply

---

[16] Marx (1850), p. 134.   [17] *Neue Rheinische Zeitung*, 1.1.1849.
[18] Cp. the discussion of the principle of mutual rationality in this volume, pp. 207–8.
[19] Trotsky (1969), Ch. IX.   [20] See notably Marx (1880).

techniques far ahead of its own stage of economic development. Successful learning and borrowing requires that the backward country be just a little behind, since otherwise the prerequisites for making good use of the advanced technology will be lacking.

The final verdict, of course, is not yet in. Marx might still be vindicated, in one of several ways. Revolution in the West could erupt, as a result of economic and ecological crises or of wars between capitalist nations. More plausibly, economic development in the East might overtake that of the West. It might turn out, that is, that $T_2 < 1917 < T_1$, rather than $1917 < T_2$. Yet I cannot see any rational grounds for holding either view. The experience of the last century does not confirm the view that there is a compensatory justice in history, which ensures that the last shall be the first. Rather it indicates that the principle of justice is that of St Matthew: to him that hath, unto him shall be given.

Let me summarize the argument. I have been concerned to argue against all the following propositions:

(1) Within at least one capitalist country the communist revolution will occur when and because the relations of production become suboptimal for the further development of the productive forces.

(2) Within at least one capitalist country the communist revolution will occur when the relations of production have become suboptimal.

(3) The communist revolution will occur in one country when the relations of production have become suboptimal in another country. A viable communism will emerge by diffusion of the revolution from the former to the latter.

(4) The communist revolution will occur in one country when the relations of production have become suboptimal in another country. A viable communism will emerge by diffusion of technology from the latter to the former.

Of these, (1) is the traditional, undiluted Marxist argument and (2) a diluted, yet also traditional position. (3) and (4) embody different versions of the theory of combined and uneven development. (3) is the view held by Marx at one time and by Trotsky, (4) the position held at another time by Marx. Both (3) and (4) suffer, essentially, from wishful thinking. There are no reasons to think that the proletariat in the advanced countries will make common cause with a revolution occurring in a backward country, even in the unlikely event that the advanced countries should engage in a counter-revolutionary war. Nor can we assume that diffusion of technology will take place when the conditions for accepting and using it are absent. The 'advantages of backwardness' should be relegated to their proper place – a mechanism of secondary importance that affects the pace of economic development, but not its fundamental forms.

4 Marxist ideas in development economics: an evaluation

Pranab Bardhan

I

Development economics is the only major branch of economics where elements of Marxist and Marx-inspired ideas have had a significant impact on the mainstream. Concerns for unequal exchange and exploitation, generation and appropriation of surplus, institutional barriers to accumulation and innovation, the ubiquity of market failures and more generally the market as a historical category being inapplicable to some social formations, transition from one mode of production to another, planning for industrialization – these issues, relegated to the periphery of much of mainline economics, are central to the subject matter of development economics. The extreme heterogeneity of social formations of developing countries, in contrast with the developed capitalist countries, while it contributes to the exasperating amorphousness of development economics, makes the ahistorical narrowness and insularity of standard neo-classical economics particularly palpable. Yet, as we shall point out later, at some risk of blasphemy, the methodology of neo-classical economics is quite often useful in sharpening the analysis of questions of Marxist concern. It should also be noted that many of the central issues of development economics noted above draw more profitably upon Marxian historical studies and political sociology than upon traditional Marxian economic theory as such (having, for example, very little of essence to do with Marxian theory of value and prices, theory of crises or with theory of technical change); even within Marxist economics, some of the development issues as articulated owe more to Lenin, Luxemburg, Bukharin and Preobrazhensky than to Marx himself.

A major point of apparent conflict between neo-classical (or classical) and Marxist views that looms large in development economics centres around the idea of gains from trade and specialization. Liberal economists never tire of emphasizing the benefits of voluntary exchange based on comparative advantage (with appropriate qualifications for learning by doing, externalities, diversification as insurance against market risks and so on). At the other end

64

there is a large number of development economists, some, though certainly not all, of whom are associated with the Latin American dependency school (both Marxist and non-Marxist), who are deeply suspicious of trade contacts and foreign economic 'intrusions', based on the historical experience of oppressive relationships between the 'centre' and the 'periphery'. Some of the heat generated in the debates between the two sides is, of course, attributable to misunderstanding of each other's position and talking at cross-purposes. For example, it is quite consistent for the 'periphery' to gain from trade with the 'centre' (in the Samuelsonian sense of having the opportunity to trade as better than being denied that opportunity), and yet for the former to be exploited by the latter in the Marxian sense (that the former would have been better off in the counterfactual world of a more egalitarian international distribution of assets),[1] just as in a capitalist society the assetless worker gains from trading his labour power (as opposed to not working for the capitalist), and yet is exploited in the Marxian sense. There is also often an elementary confusion about the meaning of a nation's 'gain' that the liberal economist imputes to trade: he means *potential* gain with appropriate inter-group redistribution. In the absence of such redistribution, the gain may accrue only to a 'comprador' class with the majority of people actually losing from trade. To the extent the idea of unequal exchange[2] refers to a transfer of value from the capital-poor periphery to the capital-rich centre in the process of international trade, it thus does not negate the neo-classical idea of potential gains from trade. To the extent unequal exchange refers to the real possibility of unfavourable terms of trade for the periphery, this has long been recognized in standard trade theory, given the high income elasticity of import demand in the periphery, relatively low world demand for many of its exportables and the monopoly power of giant trading companies of the centre.

But Marxist theory goes beyond static distribution effects of trade and other transactions with foreign countries. The theory of imperialism emphasizes the dynamic effects (some positive, some negative) of foreign capitalist penetration of underdeveloped economies. Marx and Engels primarily stressed (though with some reservations in their later years) the historically progressive role of colonialism and trade, with their 'brutal but necessary' function of destroying pre-capitalist structures. Marxist writers on imperialism at the turn of the century (Lenin, Luxemburg and others) pointed to the ambiguous role of foreign capital, the weak and dependent nature of local bourgeoisie and the tendency of the international division of labour to confine colonial

---

[1] For a rigorous exposition of this idea, see Roemer (1983b).
[2] Emmanuel (1972).

production to mineral and agricultural primary products. In more recent years writers like Baran (1957) and many of his direct or indirect followers in the dependency school[3] have gone farther and seriously questioned the viability of capitalist development in underdeveloped countries integrated into the world economy, in view of surplus expropriation by foreign capital in alliance with domestic pre-capitalist oligarchies. Ironically, pessimism about prospects of peripheral capitalism reached new heights among these writers of the dependency school precisely in the decades when many of these less developed countries were experiencing a substantial expansion in capitalist growth and trade. As Cardoso (1977) remarks, 'history had prepared a trap for pessimists'. Foreign capital and transnational enterprise have led to a rapid capitalist transformation of some of these economies (examples: Brazil, Mexico, Malaysia); on the other hand, industrial growth was very slow in countries like Burma which adopted a policy of virtual delinking with foreign trade and investment interests, or like India which compared to most other major non-socialist developing countries followed a substantially autarchic policy. The dramatic cases of growth in some of the East Asian 'open' economies (like South Korea or Taiwan) have even started posing a competitive challenge to the industrially advanced economies in many sectors. Much of this growth cannot be described as 'dependent' development. In this process, as in the earlier phase of nationalization of foreign investment in the extractive industries and public utilities in most countries, the state along with the domestic capitalist class has played the decisive role. Even in Brazil, where the military regime has had a strong commitment to the internationalization of the domestic market with a substantial involvement of the transnationals, a tight integration of state and local private capital has transformed some of the leading sectors in Brazilian growth, most notably the petrochemical sector.[4] Of course, many Marxists have elaborately commented on the negative consequences of the uneven, lopsided, 'disarticulated' pattern of growth in these countries, but what else should one expect of capitalist growth? The issue of unpleasant aspects of capitalist growth should surely be kept separate from that of viability of capitalism.

While in the development literature the negative dynamic effects of foreign connections are emphasized, orthodox Marxism often shares with classical economics a general presumption of the positive effects on accumulation and innovation following from the pressures and opportunities of market expansion (foreign or domestic). Let me illustrate this from the sphere of domestic economy, particularly with reference to the labour market. Marxists often

---

[3] Palma (1978) has traced the Marxist origin of the main ideas of this school to the Sixth Congress of the Communist International in 1928.   [4] See Evans (1982).

presume an automatic relation between proletarianization (i.e. development of the labour market where a labourer is free to trade his labour power as a commodity) and capitalist progress. Cohen (1978a) even asserts a logical proposition: 'if the producers are free labourers, production is for the sake of accumulating capital'. In spelling out the steps in this argument he writes: 'If labour is free and commodity production is well-established, there is competition between producing units. Competition between producing units imposes a policy of capital accumulation: a unit not disposed to increase the exchange-value at its disposal will lack the resources to prevail in competition.' Thus free trade in the labour market must serve the cause of capital accumulation. Yet there are numerous instances in many countries today, as well as in history, where proletarianization of the labour force is not associated with capitalist development. In Bardhan (1982) I have cited statistical evidence from Indian agriculture: comparing across a large number of agro-climatic regions in India, one finds that the areas of a high degree of proletarianization (usually the more densely populated areas) are not necessarily technologically more progressive, and capitalist accumulation has been more impressive in areas where the proportion of wage labour (as opposed to family labour) on the farm is relatively low. I think the problem with Cohen's argument is the presumption of competitive markets. If there is territorial monopoly of landlords and village markets are isolated and fragmented, a system of surplus extraction from local wage labour may survive for long without being forced by competition to serve the accumulation of capital. Similarly, with reference to land, credit or product markets in a backward agrarian economy, Bhaduri (1983) has emphasized how surplus extraction by rentier, merchant or money-lending interests may drive the poor peasants into exchange relations[5] (like distress sales of grains or land and incurring of consumption debt), raising the index of commercialization of the economy without any necessary positive effects on accumulation. This is related to Marx's idea, in the third volume of *Capital*, of two alternative historical paths that may be taken by merchant's capital, in developing or retarding the growth of industrial capitalism.

When we depart from the presumption of competitive markets, either of

[5] Bhaduri (1983) describes these exchange relationships as 'forced commerce' and comments: 'they do not arise from voluntary market participation guided by the motive of "gains from trade"'. Yet they are not any more forced than the peasant dispossessed of his land selling his labour power in the free labour market. In either case there need not be any extra-economic coercion, and the peasant, *given* his zero or low asset situation, may still be gaining from trade in the neo-classical sense that he is better off compared to the situation where he is denied the opportunity to borrow or sell, other things remaining the same. Of course, he is worse off compared to the situation where he had more assets enabling him to avoid the clutches of the rapacious money-lender or trader.

the neo-classical or the basic Marxian model of capitalism, an important methodological issue concerning rational choice arises. Rational choice methodology is usually associated with neo-classical economics. Marxists often emphasize the overwhelming importance of structural constraints, leaving little scope for freedom of action or rational choice. As Elster (1979a) comments, clearly they mean this to apply with some asymmetry, members of ruling classes, for example, having more choice and less hemmed in by structural constraints than the subordinate classes. And in their choice, even if not all members of the former classes are maximizers, the competitive process will tend to weed out the non-maximizers. This biological model of the survival of profit maximizers is, for example, implicit in the Marxian assumption of equality of profit rates through competition of capital. But when competition is lacking, when markets are 'thin' or highly segmented or inadequately formed, non-maximizers (like large landowners wastefully using their land) can survive for a prolonged period. Similarly, patron-client relationships, in which transactions are marked by reciprocity and mutual help particularly at times of emergency but not by any precise accounting of the balance of payments between the two sides (qualitatively similar to the case of gift and counter-gift giving of traditional societies described by anthropologists), can be remarkably durable. It should also be noted that economists usually interpret rational choice in very narrow economic terms. It may be quite rational for a landlord or an industrial monopolist to 'waste' some resources in activities and rituals enhancing his social status or political power, which (in terms of current industrial organization theory) may often be regarded as investment in entry barriers to particular markets. In spite of all this, I believe that the presumption of rationality is a good starting hypothesis to work from, even if one ends up by finding it to be violated in many particular cases. As Elster (1979a) comments: 'This presumption is a "principle of charity" similar to the one often used in textual interpretation. One should never take textual contradictions at their face value, but consider whether the context might not give a clue to consistency. Similarly, one should always look very closely at apparently irrational behaviour to see whether there could not be some pattern there after all.' Development economics is full of examples of how apparently irrational behaviour may be successfully explained as an outcome of more complex exercises in rationality, particularly with deeper probes into the nature of the feasibility constraints (especially in the face of various kinds of risks and uncertainty) or the preference patterns.

II

A persistent theme in Marxist writings in development economics is how certain institutions or production relations act as 'fetters' on the development of forces of production. The most frequent examples here are drawn from the retarding effects of agrarian institutions in many poor countries, like the elaborate hierarchy of rent-extracting land rights, sharecropping, usury, speculative trading and so on. The nature of these effects, however, needs to be clearly spelled out. It is easy to see that the direct cultivator, squeezed by layers of landlords in the subinfeudation process, has limited incentive to fully utilize or develop the forces of production. But the primary question is why the landlord does not use his surplus in productive accumulation. To answer this by showing that the rate of return to rentier activities or usury or speculation is high is somewhat circular; one still has to show (a) why the rate return to productive investment is low, and (b) why and how yield-increasing innovations, potentially raising the latter rate of return, will be blocked by the unproductive landlord, money-lender or trader interests. In large parts of the world where some of the poorest people live (for example in regions of monsoon paddy or unirrigated dryland cultivation) the basic technology has remained extremely backward and ecologically fragile, not always because easily available technological improvements have been undercut by vested interests, but often because prerequisites for such improvements involve massive public investment in irrigation and flood-control, research and extension and the privately inappropriable externalities they generate. In areas or crops where high-yielding (and disease-resistant) seeds are available, along with a public network of irrigation and drainage, the merchant–money-lender resistance to adoption of innovation has not been significant and even rentier landlords have often converted themselves, in the style of later Prussian junkers, into enterprising farmers.[6]

Even when economic betterment following from adoption of innovations is to increase the general bargaining power of agricultural workers or reduce the political control of landlords over them, in an environment of competition no individual landlord will be rationally deterred from such adoption. But in a situation of market segmentation and territorial monopoly, a local landlord

---

[6] In this context I do not find Bhaduri's (1983) predator–prey model (with antagonistic relationship between merchant–money-lender class and the class of rich farmers) very plausible, either on theoretical or empirical grounds. Theoretically, he has not shown why and how entry from one of these classes to the other is restricted; empirically, he ignores the substantial evidence of portfolio diversification of the rural rich in farming, lending, trading and other businesses and services, nor does he cite any evidence that in recent years productive investment by rich farmers has been resisted by professional money-lenders or traders.

can get away with delaying adoption. Similarly, it is not enough to point out that land-saving bio-chemical technology (as in the case of much of the so-called green revolution) may reduce the scarcity rent of land, unlike labour-saving mechanical innovations, and hence the landlords will adopt the latter over the former. An individual landlord will economize both on land and labour costs. But agricultural technology is often primarily generated in public research institutions and its diffusion is seriously dependent on public extension, credit and hydraulic works. If the landed oligarchy, sufficiently small and cohesive (overcoming the collective action problem), can influence state policies regarding research and diffusion, the nature of technological development may be affected, as has been claimed in the case of Argentine agriculture by de Janvry (1978).

Marxist development economics often refer to certain institutional constraints, taken as frozen data from history, and concentrate on their adverse effects on the use and development of the forces of production, overlooking the economic rationale of the formation of these institutions as well as how in the historical-evolutionary process the underlying rationale changes and the same institutional forms adapt and mutate in response to the changed circumstances. I shall give two examples from peasant agriculture, one from the profuse literature on land tenure and the other from that on labour transactions. Take the case of sharecropping, which is often cited as an institutional obstacle to development. The neo-classical property rights school, on the other hand, emphasizes how, given well-defined property rights, efficient resource allocation is independent of the choice of land tenure. This school often ignores the serious cases of market failures, incomplete markets and information asymmetry (which falsify the presumption of efficiency of resource allocation) that give rise to sharecropping as an imperfect economic response.[7] But the Marxists often ignore the origin and nature of this economic response: under a set of constraints (like market failure), sharecropping does serve a real economic function, and its simple abolition without taking care of the factors that gave rise to this institution in the first place may not necessarily improve the conditions of the intended beneficiaries of the abolition programme.[8] There are some important political lessons here

---

[7] For a review of the literature relating sharecropping to market failures and imperfections in credit, risk and human and animal labour markets and costly monitoring of worker effort, see Newbery and Stiglitz (1979) and Bardhan (1984a).

[8] Marx himself was, however, aware how the share tenancy system also acted as a credit system. In considering the institution of metayage he remarks in *Capital*: 'On the one hand, the farmer here lacks sufficient capital required for complete capitalist management. On the other hand, the share here appropriated by the landlord does not bear the pure form of rent. On the one hand, the sharecropper...is to lay claim to a portion of the product...as possessor of part of the instruments of labour, as his own capitalist. On the other hand, the landlord claims his share not exclusively on the basis of his land ownership, but also as lender of capital.'

from what may be called the economics of second-best reformism. Marxists have also a tendency to equate sharecropping tenancy mechanically with the 'feudal' or 'semi-feudal' mode of production, thus ignoring how in the real world the same institution adapts itself to the development of the forces of production, with numerous cases of capitalist share-tenant farmers (as, for example, in Punjab) or more widespread cases of cost-sharing and other forms of landlord–tenant partnership in adoption of the new technology of high-yielding varieties in agriculture. Thus while Marxists have been most vocal in raising the issue of agrarian institutions and their interaction with technological development, the more substantive contributions in development theory in this respect have been carried out with neo-classical methodology looking into the micro-foundatioins of their rationale, drawing upon the growing literature on imperfect information, uncertainty, incentives and principal-agent games.

My other example relates to the case of labour-tying arrangements in agriculture. Historically, agrarian labour-tying brings to mind the blatant cases of obligatory service by the tenant-serf to the lord of the manor (as in the classic instances of European feudalism) or those of debt-peonage to money-lender-cum-landlord as prevailed in many parts of the world. These are clearly cases where tying involves a continuing lack of freedom on the part of the labourer and the sanctions underlying the employer's authority are based primarily on social or legal coercion. This is to be distinguished from the case where the labourer voluntarily enters long-duration contracts with his employer and reserves the right to leave unconditionally at the end of the specified period. This latter type of (implicit) labour-tying contracts is quite significant in agriculture in many areas. Neo-classical methodology has been quite useful in exploring their rationale[9] (in terms of 'labour-hoarding' for tight peak seasons, risk-sharing, productivity effects of continued relationships, etc.), and in some cases it is not difficult to show why such contracts may even increase in importance with yield-increasing improvements and capitalist development in agriculture at least in the early phases. Yet most Marxists continue to identify all forms of labour-tying as 'bonded labour' and characterize them as symptoms of economic stagnation.

Many such implicit futures contracts in labour or land-lease markets of poor agrarian economies are cemented by credit relationships. By their very nature such interlocking transactions are often highly personalized.[10] Such personal ties between transacting agents are automatically described as pre-capitalist in the Marxist development literature, while in contrast the literature on implicit contracts and imperfect information in the context of industrially

[9] See Bardhan (1983).
[10] For a review of the literature on this see Bardhan (1980).

advanced economies often emphasizes the importance of 'customer' (as opposed to 'auction') markets.[11] Neo-classical economists who discuss the rationale of personalized interlinked contracts in these terms often, in their turn, overlook that the elaborate labour market segmentation which such personalization involves in poor economies frequently leaves the weaker partner in these transactions with virtually all-or-nothing choices. Also, that some of these contractual arrangements may turn out to be locally efficient ('second-best') under the existing set of constraints should not divert our attention from the basic issue of removing these constraints.

On the question of institutional obstacles to agricultural progress, the Marxist literature emphasizing the retarding effects of rent, usury or speculation or wasteful cultivation under *latifundia* domination is large, compared to that on the constraint posed by petty peasant proprietorship. Both Lenin and Luxemburg pointed to the tenacity of peasant survival delaying capitalist take-over in European agriculture. In the much more densely populated agriculture of Asia, this delay has often been prolonged enough to raise doubts about the transitional nature of the mode of peasant proprietorship. While Marxists often see in this tenacity peasants' astonishing capacity to take punishment or 'self-exploitation', writers like Boserup (1965) have pointed to many cases of improvement in traditional agricultural practices on peasant farms induced by population growth (Marxists usually ignore such effects of demography on the development of the forces of production) and Geertz (1963) has pointed to the related demographic-ecological processes of 'agricultural involution' providing a surprising elasticity to the system. While orthodox Marxists usually associate capitalist agriculture with large-scale capital-intensive methods of production, more recent advances in bio-chemical technology associated with the so-called green revolution have shown possibilities of successful adoption on small farms. The main constraint here is not the small-scale nature of production as such but more the availability of public infrastructural facilities like irrigation, power, extension services, and credit and the acute problem of externalities generated by a crazy quilt of petty private property rights, underlining the need for community cooperation in land consolidation, water allocation, soil conservation and so on. In parts of East Asia (Japan, Taiwan, etc.) where the public infrastructure and cooperative organizations have provided these services, small-scale labour-intensive peasant farms have thrived for a long time. In densely populated countries the Japanese road to agriculture development may be a historical alternative to Lenin's oft-quoted 'Prussian' or 'American' roads.

A different kind of example of production relations blocking development,

[11] See Okun (1981).

quite common in the Marxist literature in Latin America and India, relates to the underconsumptionist constraint on industrial growth. Existing production relations perpetuating mass poverty in the countryside are found to pose severe limits to the expansion of home market for manufactured goods. As Lustig (1980) points out, this market insufficiency theory is quite different from Marxist realization crisis theories, and is more akin to the underconsumption thesis of Sismondi and later some Russian Populists (like Nicolai-on and Vorontsov). At the empirical level this argument does not explain why, even with unequal distribution of income and wealth, capitalist industrial growth sustained by expansion of exports and of the home market for consumer durables largely demanded by the wealthy is not feasible.

Finally, discussion in Marxist development economics on relations of production fettering the use and development of the forces of production needs to be linked up with the recent methodological discussion in Western Marxism on the question of 'primacy' of forces of production and class capacities.[12] Historians and economists studying underdevelopment implicitly or explicitly tend to attribute primacy to relations of production and point to different historically specific ways in which the conflict involved in the fettering issue does or does not get resolved. As Roemer (1982f) suggests, historical materialism, even in its logically clearest exposition as in Cohen (1978a), often does not go much beyond providing a grand theory of long-run equilibria (where relations of production correspond to forces of production), without a satisfactory theory of disequilibrium dynamics, of how one moves from one equilibrium to another and the disturbances in the path of such convergence (even in the well-documented case of transition from feudalism to capitalism in Britain, the literature, including that on the so-called Dobb–Sweezy controversy, remains to date highly inconclusive). In an incisive analysis of European history, Brenner (1977) focuses on different paths of transition (the contrasting experiences of Western and Eastern Europe, of British agricultural capitalism and French small peasant proprietorship even within Western Europe) in which specific historical processes of class capacity for resistance and struggle play the crucial role. There is no grand theory here, the determinants of the balance of class forces are left hanging in the air, but economists impressed by the heterogeneity of development experience will feel less uncomfortable with this than with the technological certainties of the laws of historical materialism. Some of them may even claim that capitalism of the West itself is a historically specific phenomenon (like the specificity of European feudalism as Perry Anderson and others have claimed), to which a false generality is ascribed in both Marxist and

[12] See, for example, the review article by Levine and Wright (1980) of Cohen's book (1978a).

neo-classical literature; in their study of development they find the frequent quotation[13] from the preface to *Capital*, that 'the industrially most developed country does nothing but hold up to those who follow it on the industrial ladder the image of their own future' just as unacceptable as the Rostovian stages of growth. Similarly, attempts to understand pre-capitalist social formations in terms of capitalist teleology or concepts (like that of class) essentially formulated and shaped in the context of capitalist societies (to take, in Marx's words, 'man' as the clue to the anatomy of 'the ape') have not always succeeded in rising above a certain ethno-centric narrowness of outlook.

III

The preceding section concentrated on the constraints posed by pre-capitalist production relations in the path of transition to capitalist development. Another major area of Marxist contributions to development economics has to do more with problems originating in the transition process towards socialism and state-led industrialization. The Soviet industrialization controversies of the 1920s anticipated in rich details some of the central issues in debates on development planning that raged in the 1950s and 1960s. The stylized dual-economy models of this literature, with an industrial sector largely under the control of the state, the agricultural sector in private hands and the industrial work force spending most of their wage on food marketed by the latter sector, have clear Soviet parentage in the N.E.P. and the immediate period thereafter. The problems of what Preobrazhensky (1926) called 'primitive socialist accumulation' and his disputes with Bukharin on appropriate policies for mobilizing marketable surplus of food from the peasantry, and their diverse response to the sharp inter-sectoral terms-of-trade movements (picturesquely called 'the scissors crisis') reverberate in the development literature of mixed economies to this day.

Some critics of industrialization programmes in developing economies trace an alleged bias towards 'squeezing' the agricultural sector to the net effects of this Soviet legacy on the early planning literature and of the more general Marxian distrust of peasants. But at an analytical level the price or tax policies (of Preobrazhensky and his latter-day followers among development

---

[13] It should be noted, however, as Hirschman (1981) draws our attention, this passage of Marx is followed in the next paragraph by the prediction of a very different path for Germany and continental Europe in relation to England because of the absence of factory laws and in general because of a variety of social and political residues from feudalism that did not exist in England. It is quite characteristic of Marx's writings to oscillate between the grand generalization and the richly textured specificities of particular countries or periods.

economists) aimed at mobilizing agricultural surplus essentially incorporate not an anti-peasant bias as such, but the imputation of a relatively large social weight to investment as compared to current consumption.[14] The same imputation of a low social rate of time discount calls for the choice of relatively capital-intensive techniques in industrial production even in the face of a large supply of underemployed labour (which may look like the working of an anti-worker bias), as has been shown in Dobb (1960), Sen (1960) and Marglin (1967); or in investment allocation with sectoral non-shiftability of capital for an emphasis on basic capital goods industries as opposed to consumer goods industries, as is suggested in the planning models of Fel'dman (1928) and Mahalanobis (1953). The presumption of a low social rate of time discount and also of a general emphasis on national self-sufficiency and autarchy in these models of development planning may be viewed as a direct or indirect Soviet legacy. The rationale provided by the economic and particularly military exigencies of Soviet industrialization in the period preceding the Second World War does not carry over very well to the case of many developing countries in recent years. Consumption sacrifices on the part of workers and peasants for the sake of investment in capital-intensive industrialization programmes have been hard to justify[15] in the face of increasing inequality, unemployment and the government's frequent inability to control conspicuous consumption of the rich and wastage and graft in the public bureaucracy and the white elephants in the state-run industrial sector. Export pessimism as a rationale for the autarchic policies in countries like India has also been hard to justify at a time when some of the more 'open' developing countries were expanding their exports at a rapid rate.

Most Marxist writers in the literature on development planning presume and urge an active role of the state in industrialization (in some contrast to Marx himself who largely shared the anti-étatist views of nineteenth-century liberals and made the Asiatic state with its monopoly of economic initiative responsible for the backwardness of the East) without spelling out their underlying theory of the state.[16] In some cases faith in planning for taking over the 'commanding heights' of the economy has coexisted with a crude instrumentalist theory of the state (as a direct tool of the dominant class) popularized by the official Marxism of the Communist Parties or with a vision of the historically progressive role of the 'national bourgeoisie'. Even those Marxists who recognize the state as a largely autonomous actor in goal

[14] For a lucid demonstration of this see Sah and Stiglitz (1984).
[15] For an analysis of the sub-optimality of collective savings and the 'prisoners' dilemma' aspect of the social rate of time discount, see Sen (1961) and (1967).
[16] For a brief discussion of the Marxist theories of the state from the point of view of state-led industrialization, see Bardhan (1984b), Ch. 5.

formulation, agenda setting and policy execution subject to some very general constraints (posed by dominant class interests) do not have a satisfactory theory explaining how different interventionist states with command over roughly similar instruments of control end up being a developmental state in some cases (example: South Korea) as opposed to a primarily regulatory one in some others (example: India), or for the same country (say, South Korea) pass from a preoccupation with zero-sum rent-seeking (in the Rhee regime) to a dynamic entrepreneurial state (as in the Park regime). While Marxist theories of the state remain largely functionalist and teleological, the slowly growing literature on rent-seeking in a clientelist polity and attempts[17] to explain cases of stagnation in terms of the difficulty of taking collective action in large lobbying coalitions, coming from largely neo-classical sources, may some day provide useful building blocks to a more satisfactory political economy of the state,[18] once they go beyond their assumption of the state as merely an arena of group competition and include the state itself as a strategic actor in a game of mixed conflict and cooperation with other groups. Yet there is no doubt that more than anybody else Marxists are most insistent in raising the basic questions here, on state policies and their interaction with class coalitions, even though their answers may not always be adequate.

Overall, in development economics, as in much of social science in general, the most valuable contribution of the Marxist approach is the sense of history with which it is imbued, its focus on the tension between property relations and productive potential in a given social formation, and on the importance of collective action and power in enhancing or thwarting processes of institutional change to resolve that tension, its insistence on bringing to the forefront of public policy debates an analysis of the nature of the state and the constellation of power groupings in civil society, and, of course, its abiding commitment to certain normative ideas on questions of exploitation and injustice. Its processes of reasoning, however, leave much to be desired, with its frequent substitution of convenient teleology for explanatory mechanisms and of a kind of murky institutionalism for rigorous rationale of contractual arrangements, and its failure to base aggregative results firmly on consistent actions of economic agents at the micro-level, ignoring as a consequence incentive compatibility problems, issues of contract enforcement and repetitive transactions, strategic interaction of agents (even with commonality of class interests), the free rider problem in class formation and action, and the disequilibrium dynamics of adjustment paths. Some versions

---

[17] See, for example, Olson (1982).

[18] For an oversimplified exercise in explaining slow growth in India in terms of the politics of log-rolling in an heterogeneous coalition of proprietary classes, see Bardhan (1984b).

of it also claim too much in the generality of its laws of motion of history, overlooking important historical specificities and localized contexts of culture, geography and demography not always reflecting the technological base. In the development planning literature it also brings a certain legacy of single-minded pursuit of accumulation (along with an autarchic zeal), often slighting acute problems of present consumption, incentives, adjustments, managerial and administrative capacities, ecological balance, and ways of expanding human capabilities beyond improvements on the technological frontier.

Part II
Class

5 New directions in the Marxian theory of exploitation and class*

John Roemer

An important problem confronting Marxists today is to explain adequately the political and economic developments of modern socialist societies. Another problem is to explain clearly why workers in modern capitalist societies should be considered exploited: Marxists insist that a certain share of the workers' labour is 'unpaid', and workers are thereby exploited; non-Marxists point out that everyone gains from the trade of labour, and therefore workers are not exploited. The link between these problems is the failure of Marxian economics to state precisely what are the causes of exploitation under capitalism; from that might follow an understanding of which of those causes remain under socialism.

To clarify these problems, I propose in the following a general theory of exploitation. The proposed theory of exploitation is general in the sense that 'Marxian exploitation' (the type of inequality that Marxists consider exploitative) is one special case of it. Other special cases are feudal exploitation, socialist exploitation, status exploitation, and 'neo-classical exploitation' (the type of inequality that neo-classical economists consider exploitative). By embedding both Marxian and neo-classical exploitations in a more general setting, we are able to contrast the ethical principles that lie behind the two ideologies. By embedding socialist exploitation in the same general model, we gain greater understanding of the types of inequality and perhaps class formation that exist in modern socialism.

My approach to developing a general theory of exploitation is similar to that of Marx in his study of capitalism. The economic problem for Marx was to explain the persistent accumulation of wealth by one class and the persistent impoverishment of another, in an economic system characterized by voluntary trade. Under feudalism, it was no surprise that the lords became rich from serf labour, since the institution of labour exchange was a coercive one, characterized by bondage and requiring the serf to perform corvée and demesne labour. It was, then, perfectly clear where the locus of surplus

* This essay originally appeared in *Politics and Society*, vol. 11, no. 3, 1982. Reprinted with permission.

expropriation was. Obviously, the same is true of societies where the institution of labour exchange was slavery. Capitalism, however, rendered labour exchange noncoercive: wage workers voluntarily trade labour power on the labour market. Perhaps the bargaining power of the two sides is not in balance, but the institution itself remains noncoercive. The riddle for Marx was how to explain the systematic expropriation of the surplus product (beyond subsistence requirements of the workers) by one class, that is by one side of the market, when the institution for labour exchange is not coercive. To answer this riddle, Marx constructed his theory of value and exploitation. According to this theory, exchanges under capitalism are not coercive but competitive, and all commodities exchange 'at their values'. (Coercive exchange would, on the contrary, involve one side being forced to exchange its service for less than its value.) Despite these competitive exchanges in the labour market (and elsewhere), Marx maintained, a systematic expropriation of surplus value emerges, and upon this understanding, he based his theory of exploitation.

The institutional culprit in the Marxist idea of exploitation was private ownership of the means of production or, more accurately, the concentration of such ownership in the hands of a small class. Accordingly, if the means of production were socialized and put in the control of the working class, then capitalist exploitation would cease. Although this recipe was shared by many socialists of the period, Marx and Engels took it a step further by claiming that such a development was possible, perhaps inevitable, and by displaying the mechanism by which the transformation would occur.

We face a parallel problem in the study of modern socialism. We understand the locus of surplus expropriation under capitalism, as Marx did for feudalism. In the transition to socialist society, the institutional culprit responsible for capitalist exploitation, that is, private ownership of the means of production, has been eliminated. Nevertheless, we observe certain systematic types of inequality and certain political behaviour that are less than ideal – we might wish to think of them as an indication of exploitation (which, of course, is an undefined term in this context). The institutional dimension that we are now required to vary is the one labelled 'ownership locus of the means of production' and not the one with which Marx was concerned, labelled 'coerciveness of the institution of labour exchange'. The formal problem, however, has the same abstract structure for us as for Marx. He required a theory of exploitation that was robust even without a coercive institution of labour exchange; we require a theory of exploitation that is robust even without private ownership of the means of production.

Which institutions and characteristics of an economy are essential for a conception of exploitation to make sense, and which are incidental? Can we conceive of a theory of exploitation sufficiently general to permit definition even under conditions of considerable institutional variation? Such a theory should apply not only to Marxian exploitation, when the institutions are capitalist, but to neoclassical exploitation, when, roughly speaking, labour is not paid its marginal product, and to socialist exploitation, when the institutions of the economy are socialist.

I have arrived at such a theory only after experimenting with many models that were designed to study Marxian exploitation. My approach to these models was to change the institutional environment in which Marxian exploitation resides and then to ask if Marxian exploitation continues to exist. How robust is the Marxian phenomenon with respect to changes in its usual institutional habitat? The models that discuss the variants of Marxian exploitation are presented in sections 1 to 4. Through these institutional experiments with Marxian exploitation, I have been able to develop an endogenous theory of class formation and to demonstrate the relationship between exploitation and class.

Moreover, this approach resolves several classical questions in the Marxian theory of value by showing that, in a general setting, labour value depends on equilibrium prices (sections 5 and 6). This dependence is exactly the reverse of the orthodox Marxian view of the relation between price and labour value. I also present a new argument supporting labour as the value numeraire in the Marxian system (section 7). Indeed, the corollaries of the approach for classical issues in the Marxian theory of value and exploitation constitute the major part of this essay. My general theory of exploitation is outlined in section 8.

In the final section, I offer a defence of my methodology. Here, however, I would like to mention also that while the models I use employ two techniques of modern mathematical economics – general equilibrium theory and cooperative game theory – I have, nevertheless, presented the material in a nontechnical fashion in this paper. A more thorough and rigorous treatment of this material will be found in my book, *A General Theory of Exploitation and Class*.[1] In addition, various parts of the theory have been expanded in other articles.[2] A very slight amount of formalism is introduced in this essay, which will be clarifying to some readers. These passages may be skipped without loss of comprehension by those readers who are unaccustomed to mathematical notation.

Although two problems are referred to in the first paragraph, I will deal only superficially with how the theory applies to the problem of understanding

[1] Roemer (1982a).   [2] Roemer (1982g); Roemer (1982e); Roemer (1983b).

socialist society.[3] Here I will concentrate on what the theory has to say concerning Marxian exploitation and on how that concept compares to the prevailing neo-classical notion of exploitation.

I. Exploitation without a labour market

What economic institutions appear to be necessary for one producer to appropriate the labour of another? As has been discussed, Marx's task was to construct a theory of exploitation that was operative even when a coercive institution of labour exchange was absent. Our task will be to propose a theory of exploitation that is operative even when private property in the means of production is absent. Our first step, however, is not to abstract from private property, but to investigate models of pre-capitalist, subsistence, private ownership, and exchange economies. In the first of these models there is no accumulation and no labour market or institution for labour exchange. Yet, surprisingly perhaps, Marxian exploitation does emerge. This suggests that there is a theory of exploitation considerably more general, in terms of the institutional variation permitted, than the Marxian theory.

The pre-capitalist economy without a labour market is defined as follows. There are N producers, each holding an initial endowment of produced goods and his own labour power. Although each producer has one unit of labour power to dispose of, they possess, in general, different vectors of produced goods. The goal of each producer will be to produce goods with sufficient exchange value, net of replacing what he used up in production, that can meet his subsistence needs at going prices. Subject to producing goods that can be traded for his subsistence, each producer *minimizes the labour he expends* on production.

All producers have the same subsistence needs and face the same technology. They differ only in their initial endowments of produced goods. These enter into the problem in the following way. Production takes time, and a producer must lay out the costs of production today, while not receiving revenues until the end of the period. The current costs of production must be financed out of current holdings. A producer's endowment thus becomes finance capital, valued at the given prices, and this finance capital limits the production activities he can engage in. A wealthy producer will, therefore, have more production options than a poor one and hence will be able to produce goods worth the market value of his subsistence needs by working less time than the poorer producer. (He can, essentially, choose capital intensive activities to operate.)

---

[3] See Roemer (1982a, Chapter 8) for a more thorough discussion of this problem.

Formally, the model is represented as follows. Let:

A = the $n \times n$ Leontief input matrix describing production
L = the $1 \times n$ vector of direct labour inputs into production
b = the $n \times 1$ vector of subsistence needs for a producer
ω^v = the $n \times 1$ vector of produced endowments of the vth producer

Facing a price vector p for produced goods, a $1 \times n$ vector, producer v chooses

x^v, an activity vector in R^n, to min Lx^v

subject to

$$p(I-A)x^v \geq pb \qquad\qquad (\text{1.1})$$

$$pAx^v \leq p\omega^v \qquad\qquad (\text{1.2})$$

$$Lx^v \leq 1 \qquad\qquad (\text{1.3})$$

$$x^v \geq 0$$

(P)

Inequality (1.1) states that v must operate the technology at activity levels x^v so that the net exchange value he produces at going prices p is sufficient to purchase subsistence bundle b. Inequality (1.2) is the capital constraint. Producer v is constrained to choose a vector of activity levels that he can afford to operate; pAx^v are the costs of inputs at activity levels x^v; and $p\omega^v$ is the producer's wealth, his finance capital. Inequality (1.3) is simply the labour constraint. Subject to the constraints, the producer minimizes labour expended. This is the form the assumption of a subsistence economy takes.

The equilibrium in this model is a vector of commodity prices p, which allows all markets to clear while every producer optimizes. There are two sets of markets. First, producers come to the market to trade their particular endowments of produced goods for what they need to operate their chosen production plan; then, at the end of the period, they return to the market to trade what they produce for their subsistence needs. An equilibrium price vector must clear both markets, while allowing all stocks used up in production to be replaced as well. Since all stocks are replaced at equilibrium and since each producer subsists, I call the equilibrium a *reproducible solution*.

Formally, a reproducible solution is a price vector (p) for which the following hold:

(1) Each producer possesses an optimal solution x^v to his programme (P)
(2) Let $x = \Sigma x^v$. Then, $Ax \leq \omega = \Sigma \omega^v$ (production feasibility)
(3) $(I-A)x \geq Nb$ (reproducibility)

Equation (2) states that the total demand for production inputs can be satisfied with existing capital stock, and equation (3) states that the aggregate net output is sufficient to satisfy total consumption demand.

It is important to reiterate that no producer works for any other producer in this economy. All producers operate their own shops. That they choose to operate different processes, and hence work different amounts of time, is a consequence of their different financial constraints, which determine the scope of production possibilities open to each.

It is well known that the vector of labour values for produced commodities in this economy is $\Lambda = L(I-A)^{-1}$. It is not surprising that one can prove that at a reproducible solution in the pre-capitalist subsistence economy total time worked is precisely $N\Lambda b$; that is precisely *socially necessary labour time* in the Marxian sense. (Λb is the labour embodied in subsistence needs and is defined as socially necessary labour.) This is because there is no surplus produced.

The following is a dichotomous description of reproducible solutions that occur. Either such a solution is *egalitarian*, when each producer works exactly time Λb at the equilibrium, or the solution is *inegalitarian*, when some work less than Λb and others must, therefore, work longer than Λb.

Consider an inegalitarian solution in an economy with two producers. At the solution, Mr i works more than Λb, and Ms j works less than Λb. Then j is exploiting i, in the sense that she is able to work less than socially necessary labour time because i is working more; somehow, i is working 'for' j, and i's surplus labour time is transferred to j through the market. Suppose j killed i and took i's endowment and then tried to reproduce herself in the economy where only she existed; she would then have to work time Λb to reproduce herself. Thus, j is able to work less than socially necessary labour time (when i is present) because is is there; she is somehow expropriating labour from i. Thus this exploitation can exist even though there is no surplus and no institution for labour exchange. The institutions of the model that produce exploitation are competitive markets and differential private ownership of the means of production, which is to say, differential financial capital. While Marx could produce a theory of exploitation appropriate when the institution of labour exchange was noncoercive, we can produce a theory of exploitation, defined as the expropriation of labour, even in the absence of an institution for labour exchange. Exploitation can be mediated entirely through the markets for produced commodities.

This forces a reconsideration of the classical Marxist claim that exploitation takes place primarily in the labour market and in the extraction of surplus labour at the point of production. Indeed, the chief culprits seem to be competitive markets and private property in the means of production. The advent of a labour market does enrich our understanding of exploitation, however, since it brings about a decomposition of society into classes, which do not exist in the model described thus far.

II. The labour market and the emergence of class

It is not intended that the foregoing model describe actual pre-capitalist history; it is a hypothetical inquiry into the logical prerequisites for a general theory of exploitation. I continue by introducing next a labour market. On Labour Market Island, producers are still operating a subsistence economy, availing themselves of a common technology, and working only long enough to provide the funds to purchase their common subsistence requirement b, after replacing materials used up. They have, however, one more option than the inhabitants of the economy in section 1 : they can hire or sell labour power. Another market has opened, which increases the opportunities of the producers. Now a producer must decide what vector of activities to operate himself, what vector of activities to hire others to operate on his funds, and what amount of labour power to sell on the labour market.

Let:

x^v = the n-vector of activity levels that producer v operates himself (there are n processes in the Leontief matrix)

y^v = the n-vector of activity levels he hires others to operate

z^v = the amount of labour time he sells

The producer's optimization problem is now to choose a production plan that will minimize the total labour he expends (in his own shop plus on the labour market), subject to the financial constraint that the production inputs he requires to operate activities himself and to equip those whom he hires can be paid for out of his current wealth. The structure of the problem is the same as in the first economy (without labour market) except now there is a labour market.

Formally, the programme for producer v is represented thus. Facing a price-wage vector (p,w), producer v chooses

$(x^v,\ y^v,\ z^v)$ to min $(Lx^v + z^v)$

subject to

$$p(I-A)x^v + (p-(pA+wL))y^v + wz^v \geq pb \qquad (2.1)$$

$$pAx^v + pAy^v \leq p\omega^v \qquad (2.2)$$

$$Lx^v + z^v \leq 1 \qquad (2.3)$$

The three terms on the left-hand side of inequality (2.1) are the net incomes from operating activities oneself in one's own shop at activity levels x^v, hiring others to operate activities at levels y^v, and selling labour power in amount z^v. The inequality states that this total net income must be sufficient to purchase subsistence b at going prices. Inequality (2.1) is the capital constraint. (Note wages are paid at the end of the period, by convention, and need not be advanced from capital.) The programme directs the producer to minimize the time he works, subject to the constraints.

The definition of a reproducible solution, an equilibrium for this model, is analogous to before. A price and wage vector equilibrates the system if, when all producers optimize, aggregate production is feasible, global reproducibility is achieved, and the labour market clears. That is, the markets for inputs and consumption goods all clear. Formally, a reproducible solution is a price vector (p,w), and an optimal solution (x^v, y^v, z^v) for each producer, such that when $x = \Sigma x^v$, $y = \Sigma y^v$, and $z = \Sigma z^v$:

(1) $A(x+y) \leqq \omega \leqq \Sigma\omega^v$ (production feasibility)
(2) $(I-A)(x+y) \geqq Nb$ (reproducibility)
(3) $Ly = z$ (labour market equilibrium)

Inequality (1) states that total production input demand can be satisfied from existing aggregate stock; inequality (2) states that total net output is sufficient to satisfy all consumption demand; and equation (3) states that the demand for labour equals the supply of labour so that every producer is able to realize his desired offer of labour power on the labour market.

At a reproducible solution, society works, as before, precisely $N\Lambda b$ labour time in total, just aggregate socially necessary labour time. Thus, at an inegalitarian solution, society is divided into two groups of agents: the exploited, who work longer than Λb and the exploiters, who work less than Λb. (There may also be some agents who are neither exploiters nor exploited, but work precisely Λb, socially necessary labour time.)

But there is a second decomposition of producers in this economy, a decomposition into *classes*. In the model of section 1, all producers are of the same class and relate to the means of production in the same way. In this model, however, producers can relate to the means of production in different ways; they can work in their own shop, hire labour, sell labour, or do some combination of these. Indeed, how he relates to the buying and selling of labour power defines an agent's class position. Schematically, this is represented as follows. To optimize, a producer chooses a long vector of the form $\langle x^v, y^v, z^v \rangle$ where x^v, y^v, and z^v are defined as above. We may represent a producer's optimal solution as a sequence of plus and zero symbols, such as

Table 1. *Class structure on Labour Market Island*

		$\langle x^v$	y^v	$z^v \rangle$	
(landlord)	1.	$\langle 0$	$+$	$0 \rangle$	pure capitalist
(kulak)	2.	$\langle +$	$+$	$0 \rangle$	small capitalist
(middle peasant)	3.	$\langle +$	0	$0 \rangle$	petit bourgeois
(poor peasant)	4.	$\langle +$	0	$+ \rangle$	mixed proletarian
(landless labourer)	5.	$\langle 0$	0	$+ \rangle$	proletarian

$\langle 0, +, 0 \rangle$. If a producer has an optimal solution of the form $\langle 0, +, 0 \rangle$, that means he optimizes by making $x^v = 0$ and $z^v = 0$, but $y^v > 0$; that is, he optimizes by only hiring labour power, but not by working for himself or by selling labour power on the market. The particular sequence of pluses and zeroes defines the producer's *class position*. Thus, we might call a producer possessing an optimal solution of the form $\langle 0, +, 0 \rangle$ a pure capitalist, as he optimizes by only hiring others.

There are, altogether, eight possible class positions, as there are eight ways of arranging pluses and zeroes in the three places in $\langle , , \rangle$. It can be proved, however, that every producer, at an equilibrium, is a member of precisely one of five classes (see Table 1). The reader should check back against the definitions x^v, y^v, and z^v to see the motivation for the names. The agricultural labelling is provided as well, because it coincides with the analysis Mao Zedong gave of the class structure of the Chinese countryside in his 1925 pamphlet.[4]

By optimizing against a wealth constraint, each producer has placed himself in one of these classes. Class position is endogenous to the model; we are not told before the action begins who is a capitalist and who is a proletarian. That emerges as a consequence of the individual's behaviour facing competitive markets.

The first theorem relates a producer's class position to his wealth. It asserts that if we list all agents from richest to poorest, then they will fall into classes in precisely the order indicated in Table 1. The richest are pure capitalists, then come small capitalists, the petite bourgeoisie, the mixed proletarians, and, at the bottom of the wealth hierarchy, the proletarians. In fact, the proletarians are precisely those with no produced assets (zero wealth), those who have nothing to trade but their labour power (and nothing to lose but their chains). Thus, the classical ordering of classes by wealth is a theorem of this analysis, not a postulate or a definition.

The second theorem, which I call the Class-Exploitation Correspondence

[4] Mao Zedong (1964).

Principle (CECP), relates the two decompositions of society: the decomposition of society into exploiters and exploited and the decomposition of society into classes. The CECP states that *every agent who is in a labour-hiring class* (classes 1 or 2) *is an exploiter, and every agent who is in a labour-selling class* (classes 4 or 5) *is exploited*. The exploitation status of members of the petite bourgeoisie is ambiguous. (This turns out to be equivalent to the transformation problem, but that topic is beyond the scope of this survey.) Thus, we prove another classical Marxian idea – that the selling of labour power is associated with being exploited and the hiring of labour power with being an exploiter.

The CECP may strike some as obvious or trivial, but I must insist this is not the case. We are used to defining exploiters as those who hire labour power and the exploited as those who sell it. But in this analysis, both exploitation status and class status emerge endogenously from agents' optimizing behaviour, given their differential wealths. An individual is exploited if at the equilibrium he works more time than is socially necessary, Λb, and he is an exploiter if he works less than Λb. An individual's class position is defined by the relation to the labour market he has chosen in his labour-minimizing optimization. It is not a trivial statement to demonstrate a relationship between the two endogenously determined classifications. In this sense, the present analysis provides a foundation for the Marxian theory of exploitation and class, as it produces our intuitive conclusions about those concepts from prior institutional and behavioural specifications of the agents.

It is important to note that producers choose their own class position. Their problem is to optimize, in this case a labour-minimizing programme of production choices, subject to a capital constraint. All that is specified a priori is the optimizing behaviour of agents and their differential initial endowments of capital stock. Given this, some producers must hire labour power to optimize (the two top classes) and some must sell labour power to optimize (the two bottom classes). Compulsory labour hirers necessarily emerge as exploiters and compulsory labour sellers as exploited. This result is derived entirely from the differential distribution of endowments and therefore of wealths. (In particular, if all producers had the same wealth at a reproducible solution (p,w) then there would be no exploitation, and they would all be members of the petite bourgeoisie.) Optimization on competitive markets and differential ownership of the means of production result in producers sorting themselves into classes, with the classical association between exploitation and class.

In the economy described in section 1, I showed that exploitation emerges logically prior to the production of a surplus and prior to any institution for labour exchange. When a labour market is introduced, we generate not only exploitation but a class structure that relates to exploitation and wealth in the way it should, still without any surplus production. Although an institution for labour exchange was not necessary to produce exploitation, it does appear necessary to generate classes. In this sense, perhaps, the labour market *is* central to Marxian analysis. I next extend the heresy of section 1 by showing that even the Marxian class structure can be produced without any institution for labour exchange.

III. The functional equivalence of labour and credit markets

Imagine that instead of opening a labour market as a way of broadening choices in the original subsistence economy of section 1, a credit market is opened. On Credit Market Island, we have the subsistence economy, with markets in all produced goods, plus one more market, whose price is an interest rate and on which agents can borrow or lend finance capital. On Credit Market Island, there is, however, no labour market. Thus, a poor producer, who has few production options open to him because of his limited finance capital, can borrow more capital at the going interest rate to expand his production possibilities. As before, the goal of our typical agent is to minimize the labour he performs, subject to the constraint that he produce net exchange value sufficient to purchase his subsistence needs and that he finance production out of his capital plus loans. The poor agent who borrows capital will have to pay back interest, too, of course.

An equilibrium price vector now consists of commodity prices and an interest rate that clear all markets: the market for production inputs, the market for trades in final output against subsistence needs, and the credit market. As before, it can be proved that at an equilibrium, a reproducible solution, total labour time expended is just $N\Lambda b$. Thus, either a solution is egalitarian, when each worker works just socially necessary labour time Λb, or it is inegalitarian, when society is decomposed into exploiters working less than Λb and exploited working more than Λb.

There is also a class structure in this model. On Credit Market Island, there are several ways a producer can relate to the means of production: he can work borrowed capital, work his own capital, or lend his capital to others, or he can do some combination of these three things. Let, at given prices:

x^v = the vector or production activities that producer v operates using his own capital

y^v = the amount of capital (a number) that v chooses to lend others

z^v = the vector of activities that v operates on borrowed capital.

An optimal solution for producer v, facing prices p and interest rate r, is some

92   *John Roemer*

Table 2. *Class structure on Credit Market Island*

	x^v	y^v	z^v	
1.	$\langle$ 0	+	0 $\rangle$	big lender
2.	$\langle$ +	+	0 $\rangle$	mixed lender
3.	$\langle$ +	0	0 $\rangle$	neither borrower nor lender
4.	$\langle$ +	0	+ $\rangle$	mixed borrower
5.	$\langle$ 0	0	+ $\rangle$	pure borrower

long vector $\langle x^v, y^v, z^v \rangle$. We can schematically denote a solution as a sequence of pluses and zeroes. For example, producer v may optimize by choosing a solution of the form $\langle$ 0, +, 0 $\rangle$, which means he is a pure lender, since $x^v = z^v = $ 0 and $y^v > $ 0.

It is proved that each producer, at a reproducible solution, belongs to precisely one of five classes (see Table 2). Comparing Table 2 to Table 1, we find that the class structure appears formally identical. As on Labour Market Island, the ordering of the five classes on Credit Market Island, as presented in Table 2, is faithful to the wealth ordering. Moreover, the Class-Exploitation Correspondence Principle holds on Credit Market Island in that any member of a lending class (class 1 or 2) is necessarily an exploiter, and any member of a borrowing class (class 4 or 5) is exploited.

But a stronger statement can be made. The economies on the two islands are isomorphic. Suppose the inhabitants of Credit Market Island and Labour Market Island are identical, and their technologies and subsistence needs are identical. Each agent on one island has a twin on the other with the same endowment as himself. The only difference between the islands is that on one the labour market operates and on the other the credit market operates, in addition to the markets for produced goods. Let there be a reproducible solution on Labour Market Island, entailing a price-wage vector (p,w). Then there is a companion reproducible solution (p,r) on Credit Market Island, such that every agent on one island works precisely as long as his twin on the other island and is, therefore, exploited or exploiting to the same degree. Also, each pair of twins occupies identical class positions on the two islands, according to the class definitions of Tables 1 and 2. In class and exploitation properties, the two solutions are isomorphic; the credit market and the labour market are functionally equivalent. We can thus produce the highly articulated class structure usually associated with a labour market, with no institution for labour exchange, and using just a credit market. The heresy is complete. Not only does exploitation emerge logically prior to accumulation and an institution for labour exchange, but so does the articulation of exploitation into class.

It is worth modifying a venerable neoclassical adage at this point. On Labour Market Island, capital hires labour. On Credit Market Island, labour hires capital. The adage in question states, 'it doesn't matter whether labour hires capital or capital hires labour in a competitive model'. Truly, this is so, but it is our modification that the wealthy exploit and the poor are exploited in either case. The neo-classical adage is often interpreted as implying there is nothing nasty about capital hiring labour, since labour could just as well hire capital. My conclusion, on the contrary, is that labour can be just as exploited if it hires capital as it is if it is hired by capital. The key question is the wealth position of the labourer and not which market is used.

IV. Summary: exploitation versus alienation

The models thus far show that if producers have differential ownership of the means of production then a regime of competitive markets is sufficient to produce the exploitation and class characteristics of capitalism as predicted by classical Marxism. It is more enlightening, perhaps, to emphasize what is *not* necessary to produce this result, namely, an institution for the exchange of labour. Exploitation can be mediated entirely through the exchange of produced commodities, and classes can exist with respect to a credit market instead of a labour market – at least at this level of abstraction.

In this analysis, coercion is still necessary to produce Marxian exploitation and class. However, it suffices for the coercion to be at the point of maintaining property relations and not at the point of extracting surplus labour directly from the worker. Although coercion in the work place exists also in capitalism, such coercion is of secondary importance in understanding exploitation and class. It is a mistake to elevate the struggle between worker and capitalist in the process of production to a more privileged position in the theory than the differential ownership of productive assets.

These results thus force a re-evaluation of the classical belief that the labour process is at the centre of the Marxian analysis of exploitation and class, a belief that has become even more prominent since the pioneering work of Braverman.[5] I have demonstrated that the entire constellation of Marxian 'welfare' concepts can be generated with no institution for the exchange of labour. Furthermore, this has been done at the level of abstraction at which Marxian value theory is customarily performed. Just as Marx wanted to

[5] Braverman (1974).

explain as much as possible about exploitation and class with the assumption of competitive markets, so I have tried to explain as much as possible without invoking the necessary existence of labour exchange.

To put the matter more sharply, this analysis challenges those who believe that the process of labour exchange is the critical moment in the genesis of capitalist exploitation. Such a position cannot be maintained at the usual level of abstraction at which Marxian value theory is done. In particular, such a position would have to invoke critical differences between labour and credit markets. Certainly there are such differences; labour markets require supervision on the factory floor, while credit markets require collateral, and these two enforcement costs may differ. Furthermore, economies of scale enter differently in the two markets, for one capitalist can hire many workers and expand production indefinitely, but one worker cannot expand production indefinitely by borrowing a lot of capital.[6] Informational constraints enter differently, also, in a less abstract picture of Credit Market Island and Labour Market Island. In short, there may well be reasons to focus on the labour market as a key moment in the genesis of capitalist exploitation and class. However, these reasons do not exist at the level of abstraction of classical Marxian value theory. A Marxian theory of class that gives priority to the labour market depends on the existence of transactions costs, economies of scale, information, risk.

A misplaced emphasis on the labour process can lead to a faulty, or at least a nonmaterialist, analysis. If, for instance, we observe that the labour process appears much the same in existing socialism as it does in capitalism, we might conclude that the exploitation of workers in existing socialist countries is essentially the same as in capitalist countries. This is, indeed, the inference of many Marxists who see the labour process and industrial democracy, rather than property relations, as the defining characteristics of the mode of production. A distinction needs to be made between *alienation* and *exploitation*. Workers may always feel alienated, to some extent, in a labour process that employs the detailed division of labour, one-man management, and so on, but whether exploitation exists (or whether, more precisely, it is capitalist exploitation) is another matter. There is not a one-to-one correspondence between regimes of property relations and organizational forms of work. When two different regimes give rise to similar organizational work forms, it is the property relations that define the nature of exploitation and surplus extraction, not the organization work forms, which define the nature of

---

[6] However, many workers could get together and take out a loan to run a factory, thus availing themselves of economies of scale by using the credit market. Why are there not more worker-owned firms under capitalism?

alienation. The labour process approach, however, takes the organization of work as the touchstone for passing judgment on a form of economic organization. It thereby elevates alienation in work to a higher analytical plane than the relations of exploitation.

Capitalist exploitation is the appropriation of the labour of one class by another class, realized because of their differential ownership of or access to the nonhuman means of production. This can be accomplished, in principle, with or without any direct relationship between the exploiters and the exploited in the process of work. One might argue that there is exploitation without alienation in the economy of section 1, since each producer is in control of the labour process in that economy, that is, each producer works for himself in his own shop. Conversely, as we know, capitalist exploitation can be eliminated, with or without eliminating relations of authority (and thereby alienation?) in the process of work. Given this muddy relationship between the organization of work (alienation) and property relations (exploitation), is one of these two criteria more relevant than the other for understanding the laws of motion of society? Historical materialism directs us to emphasize property relations (exploitation) as the more relevant. Historical materialism may be incorrect in so doing, but one must at least understand the implications of taking the other approach.

V. Exploitation in an accumulation economy

Thus far, the analysis has been of subsistence economies. The next task is to consider an economy in which accumulation is the goal. In this section, I summarize briefly the treatment of exploitation in the model with accumulation, for it provides a definition of exploitation that is not only independent of any subsistence concept but is also independent of the subjective preferences of agents. This last I take as a requirement of a Marxian theory of exploitation, for whether a worker is exploited or not should not depend on what he chooses to do, if he has some choice, but should rather be an objective feature of his situation. The definition of exploitation provided here is more realistic for advanced capitalism, where workers in fact do choose to consume different bundles and are not limited to subsistence in any meaningful sense.

In the accumulation economy, all agents want to maximize their revenues. As in the subsistence economies, agents differ only in their endowment of produced goods and hence, their wealths. An agent's wealth constrains his choice of production activities, as he must finance the costs of production from his initial wealth. Assume there is a labour market. (We could just as well use a credit market.) At an equilibrium, producers choose to be in one of various classes, as before, defined by their relationship to the hiring or selling of labour power. How do we define exploitation? Look at the revenues of a particular producer, which we shall call Π^v. These revenues come from various sources – profits and wages. Consider all possible bundles of goods that producer v can purchase with Π^v and evaluate the embodied labour time of each of these bundles. If the maximum of these embodied labour times is less than the amount of time producer v worked, then I shall call him exploited. If the minimum of these embodied labour times is greater than the amount of time he worked, then he is an exploiter. To put the case generally, an exploited producer is one who cannot possibly command as much labour value, through the purchase of goods with his revenues, as the labour he contributed in production, and an exploiter is one who unambiguously commands more labour time through goods purchased no matter how he dispenses his revenues. This is a generalization of the classical Marxian definition that the worker is exploited because the labour he expends is greater than the labour embodied in the only bundle he can feasibly purchase (and stay alive), his subsistence bundle.

Notice this definition is independent of any subsistence concept and also is independent of what bundle a worker actually chooses to consume. We do not call a producer exploited if he happens to like cantaloupes, which have a low embodied labour time but a high price (let us say); he is only exploited if there is no way he can possibly command, through his purchases of goods, labour value equal to his contributed labour.

Because an agent is only classified as exploited if he necessarily commands less labour power through purchases than he worked, and an agent is only classified as an exploiter if he necessarily commands more labour power through his purchases than he worked, there will in general be a large 'grey area' of agents, who are neither exploiters nor exploited. If an agent can purchase some bundle embodying more labour than he worked and another bundle embodying less labour than he worked, then he is in the grey area, and if equilibrium prices are not proportional to labour values, there will be an interval of wealths corresponding to agents in the grey area. Because of the grey area, the Class-Exploitation Correspondence Principle for this model is a more delicate question than in the subsistence model. Will it necessarily be true that every member of a labour-hiring class is an exploiter and every labour-seller is exploited? Equivalently, will the grey area of agents be entirely contained in the class $(+, 0, 0)$ of petite bourgeoisie? It is a remarkable fact that this theorem is true.

The definition that has been proposed for exploiters and exploited in the accumulation model makes the group of exploited and the group of exploiters as small as possible. Nevertheless, every agent who optimizes by hiring labour power is in the (small) group of exploiters. Alternatively, one could define the exploitation status of an agent by examining the labour embodied in the bundle he actually chooses to purchase. An exploited agent is one who chooses a bundle embodying less labour than he worked, an exploiter is one who chooses a bundle embodying more labour than he worked. I have already noted my objections to this more subjective definition of exploitation status. But for those who prefer it, notice that under this definition a fortiori the Class-Exploitation Correspondence Principle is true as well, for the group of exploiters and exploited will each be strictly larger than under the more objective definition. Thus, the verification of the Class-Exploitation Correspondence Principle based on the definition of exploitation that is independent of subjective preferences is the strongest possible verification we could ask for, as it gives rise to the largest possible grey area.

Notice the role the CECP now plays. Although its formal appearance is a theorem, its epistemological role is as a postulate. We seek to construct models that allow us to prove this principle. The deep theory of Marxism says the correspondence between exploitation and class should hold, and this directs our choice of models to allow the theory to be verified.[7] In the next section, we see the CECP again plays a role in directing our choice of model.

VI. The dependence of labour value on price

Until this point, it has been assumed that the technology producers face is a Leontief input-output matrix. This enables an unambiguous definition of the vector of embodied labour times Λ, hence of socially necessary labour time Λb, and hence of exploitation. A generalization is now in order to allow production sets to be more general than Leontief matrices. This can be accomplished but with some startling results for the venerable debate on the relationship between labour values and prices.

Marxian value theory has been generalized to a production environment of the von Neumann activity analysis by Morishima[8] and to a general convex production set (constant or decreasing returns to scale) by myself.[9] The importance of these generalizations is that they show the Marxian concepts of embodied labour time and exploitation are robust in technologies that are sufficiently general to include fixed capital, differential turnover times, and the like. Marxian value theory can be done in production models as general as the usual neo-classical analysis uses. The question posed by the previous sections is: Does the Class-Exploitation Correspondence Principle hold in an economy with one of these more general production sets? This is not a

---

[7] For more on the relationship between a theory and its models, see Roemer (1981).
[8] Morishima (1974). [9] Roemer (1981, Chapter 2).

question of generalization for its own sake. The Leontief technology is terribly special, and a theory that is only true for that technology is a fragile theory.

To answer this, I study an economy where the production set is simply defined as constant returns to scale (a convex cone). This includes the von Neumann model as a special case; it also includes production with substitution, such as the neo-classical production function (Cobb–Douglas, for example). To define exploitation, we require first a definition of embodied labour time, for it is by looking at the embodied labour time of the bundle of goods that the producer can purchase that we can decide his exploitation status.

The standard definition of embodied labour time for general production sets is as follows.[10] We start by defining the labour embodied in a given bundle of commodities, c. To do this, scan the entire production set for all possible ways of producing c as a net output. Among all these ways, choose the one that minimizes direct labour used. Define that amount of labour as the embodied labour of c. Once labour embodied is defined, exploitation can be defined as in section 5. An agent is exploited if the labour embodied in the bundles of goods he can purchase is unambiguously less than the labour he expends in production. In the various sources cited, it is shown that if this definition of embodied labour time is chosen, then the so-called Fundamental Marxian Theorem is true, the equivalence of positive exploitation and positive profits. Epistemologically, this has been taken by many (including myself) to indicate the 'correct' nature of the definition of embodied labour time in the general model.

Here is the rub. *If we adopt the Morishima definition of labour value for the general technology, then the Class-Exploitation Correspondence Principle is, in general, false.* Are we to conclude that the CECP is so frail that it holds only for one very special technology, the Leontief one? In particular, does the CECP fail with fixed capital? This would, indeed, be a blow to the Marxian theory of exploitation and class.

There is a way out, which entails choosing a different definition of embodied labour time. Assume we are at an equilibrium, which is to say, we know prices. To calculate the labour embodied in the given bundle c, do not scan the entire production set for ways of producing c as net output. Instead, limit the scan to those processes that produce c as net output and that achieve the maximal profit rate, at going prices. (Recall, for instance, that many processes in the von Neumann model will not be profitable at a particular price vector and hence would be ineligible in our evaluation of the labour content of c.) Define the labour value of c as the minimum amount of direct labour used in producing c, minimized over the set of maximally profitable processes.

[10] This definition is presented in detail in Morishima (1981) and in Roemer (1981).

This generates a definition of exploitation for which the CECP is true in the general constant returns to scale model of production.

Now for the heresy. Notice that in this definition of labour value, that labour value depends on price. We can only decide which processes are maximally profitable if we first know equilibrium prices. In particular, the same economy (that is, one set of data) may support different equilibrium price vectors, each one generating different embodied labour values of commodities, as they each pick out different processes as maximally profitable.

Orthodox Marxism sees labour value as existing logically prior to price. A recent revisionist position states that labour value does not exist logically prior to price but that prices and labour values have a common ancestor.[11] Now I am forced to claim that prices emerge logically prior to labour values. If we wish to preserve the CECP, we must adopt the definition of embodied labour time that depends on price. The Fundamental Marxian Theorem was not a sufficiently discriminating tool to enable us to see this, but the Class-Exploitation Correspondence Principle is.

With hindsight, we can observe that the new price-dependent definition of embodied labour corresponds quite nicely to some ideas of Marx. Value, he claimed, was a concept that depended on the market and on commodity production. While the Morishima definition of value is a purely technological one, the new definition is market dependent. Socially necessary labour time is the time required to produce commodities by capitalists, who will only employ profitable processes, not time that is simply technologically feasible for the production of the commodities. Labour value thus adheres specifically to capitalist commodity production under this definition, not to an abstract concept of technological production feasibility.

The epistemological role of the Class-Exploitation Correspondence Principle must again be emphasized. In trying to preserve this principle in a general model of production, we are led to a new definition of labour embodied in commodities, which necessarily depends on equilibrium prices. If we wish to preserve the fundamental relation between exploitation and class status, there is no choice but to make labour value depend on price. Although the formal appearance of the CECP is as a theorem, its informal role is the other way around – to direct us to choose definitions that will preserve it as a theorem. To use Lakatos's term, the dependence of labour value on prices is a 'proof-generated definition'.[12] Furthermore, the ability of the CECP to discriminate between the two definitions of embodied labour time increases our understanding of the theory of price and value. For this very reason, the

[11] See Steedman (1977); Morishima (1973); Roemer (1981).
[12] Lakatos (1976).

CECP is a much more powerful concept than the so-called Fundamental Marxian Theorem with respect to the theory of value.

The implication of this result for those who continue to insist on the logical priority of labour values over equilibrium prices is, I think, devastating. Value is a concept useful in a theory of exploitation, but irrelevant as a theory of price, at any level of abstraction.[13]

VII. Why a labour theory of exploitation?

Why do Marxists choose labour power as the numeraire commodity for defining value and exploitation? This is another venerable question in Marxian economics, and one upon which the CECP can again offer some insight. Neo-classical economists, for example, frequently ask why not choose corn or oil as the value numeraire?

First, it must be pointed out that Marx was completely wrong about one thing. Labour power as a commodity is not unique in its magical property of producing more value than it embodies. Indeed, in an economy capable of producing a surplus, any commodity has this magical property. If we choose corn as the value numeraire and calculate embodied corn values of commodities and the embodied corn value of corn, we can prove that the economy is capable of producing a surplus if and only if corn is exploited, in the sense that the corn value of a unit of corn is less than one.[14] There is absolutely nothing special about labour power in this regard.

A second reason for choosing labour power as the value numeraire might be our interest in studying the history of people and not of corn. But this reason is superficial, because we could study the relations among people by studying their relation to corn. For instance, we could classify producers as corn exploited if the amount of corn value they can command through goods they purchase is less than the amount of corn they contributed to production, analogous to the definition of labour exploitation. This will provide a decomposition of society into exploiters and exploited. Thus our interest in the history of society or labour is not sufficient to mandate a labour theory of value.

Consider this modification of the model employed thus far. Assume producers differ not only in their endowments of produced goods but in their endowments of labour power as well. All labour is homogeneous, but some producers have the capacity to deliver more of it than others. (This is a crude

---

[13] This point is pursued in Roemer (1981, Chapter 7).
[14] A proof of this appears in Roemer (1982a, Appendix to Chapter 6); and in Bowles and Gintis (1981).

way of capturing skill differentials.) Is the CECP true in this model? Yes. Labour sellers are exploited and labour hirers are exploited. What fails, however, is the correlation between exploitation status and wealth. There may be very wealthy and skilled producers who sell labour power and are exploited, and there may be poor, unskilled producers who hire labour and are exploiters. A skilled, wealthy architect or a rich surgeon may be exploited in this model.

What is needed to produce a 'proper' theory of exploitation, by which I mean a theory that classifies the poor as exploited and the rich as exploiters, is a commodity that is uniformly distributed among the population. Now, according to the Marxian theory of capitalism, there is just one such commodity, and that is labour power. No produced commodity is uniformly distributed, since proletarians are dispossessed of all produced productive assets. Furthermore, labour power is indeed uniformly distributed, at least it may be appropriate to assume so for the study of capitalism at one level of abstraction. We assume, in other words, that agents differ only in their endowments of produced assets and not in their skills or labour power. (Workers are exploited under capitalism not because capitalists are especially skilled and endowed with entrepreneurial talent, but in spite of the fact that they are not.)

To complete the story, one need observe what the purpose of a theory of exploitation is. I take it as a theory that intends to explain class struggle. As Marxists, we look at history and see poor workers fighting rich capitalists. To explain this, or to justify it, or to direct it and provide it with ideological ammunition, we construct a theory of exploitation in which the two antagonistic sides become classified as the exploiters and exploited. I have explained why labour power is uniquely suited as the numeraire for this task. If one believed that history was most fruitfully interpreted as the struggle of man against scarcity, rather than that of class against class, then another theory of value would be mandated, perhaps an energy theory of value in 1980 or a corn theory of value in 1800, whatever the scarce commodity is. Thus, different theories of history imply their respective theories of value, from which it follows that we would do better to debate our underlying theories of history than their corollary theories of value. There is nothing objectively correct about the labour theory of exploitation, in the sense of its being deducible from economic data. It is rather a particular theory of exploitation that corresponds to the interpretation of capitalism as a class struggle between poor workers and rich capitalists, which, according to historical materialism, is the most informative historical interpretation of capitalism.

In contrast, the choice of a *labour* theory of exploitation cannot be to explain the accumulation of capital, as is sometimes maintained. Such a claim would be sound if labour power were the only exploited commodity under capitalism. But as mentioned above, every commodity is exploited in a surplus-producing economy – labour power is not special in this regard, contrary to what Marx implied. The accumulation of capital can therefore be explained, as a technical fact, by choosing any commodity as value numeraire. But class struggle between proletarians and capitalists can only be explained by choosing labour as the value numeraire.

VIII. A general theory of exploitation

In the previous section I claimed that the labour theory of value is the one to be adopted if one wishes to produce the decomposition of society into exploiters and exploited that corresponds to the class struggles of capitalism. In this section I characterize Marxian exploitation in another way, a way that makes clear what the ethical imperative of the theory is. That is, why do we choose, pejoratively, to call workers exploited? Why should the inability to command labour value in goods in an amount equal to the labour a producer expends be considered an exploitative transfer? The bourgeois thinker argues that the proletarian is gaining from trade, and his trade of labour power is voluntary, and so the transfer of 'surplus' labour time should not be considered exploitative. The quid pro quo is surplus labour in exchange for access to the means of production. This is a serious objection, and it is useful to clarify what one means by exploitation in general terms to understand the difference between Marxian and neo-classical views of exploitation. I shall outline below a general theory of exploitation that has various special cases of interest: feudal exploitation, neoclassical exploitation, Marxian exploitation, socialist exploitation, and status exploitation. Only the first three will be discussed in detail here, as the analysis of socialism is beyond the scope of this paper.

In virtually every society or economy, there is inequality. Yet not all inequality is viewed by a society as exploitative, or unjust. Certainly, however, the notion of exploitation involves inequality in some way. What forms of inequality does a particular society view as exploitative, and what forms does it not? The inequality of master and slave was viewed as nonexploitative in ancient society, as was the inequality of lord and serf in feudal society, although most inhabitants of the twentieth century consider both of these relationships exploitative. Similarly, Marxists view the inequality in the capitalist–worker relationship as exploitative, although this inequality is conceived of as nonexploitative by many people in capitalist society today.

What device can be proposed that distinguishes accurately exploitative from nonexploitative inequality, according to the norms of a particular society?

To capture what is meant when it is said that a particular person or group is exploited, I propose that a group be conceived of as exploited if it has some *conditionally feasible alternative* under which its members would be better off. Precisely what is the alternative is left unspecified for the moment. The idea is that this device can be applied whenever people use the word 'exploit' referring to the human condition. If two people disagree on whether a particular group is exploited in some situation, then our device leads us to ask if they are specifying the alternative for the group differently. I wish to propose different specifications of the alternative that will generate different definitions of exploitation.

Formally, this amounts to specifying a game played by coalitions of agents in the economy. A coalition can either participate in or withdraw from the economy. To define the game, I specify what any particular coalition can achieve on its own if it withdraws from the economy. Given these specifications, if a coalition can do better for its members by 'withdrawing', then it is exploited.

This idea can be formalized using the idea of the core of a game, from the theory of cooperative games. We can specify the payoff or reward that each coalition would receive by 'withdrawing' under hypothetical conditions. Under the conditions hypothesized, call this payoff to coalition S in game v the amount $v(S)$. Now, in the economy as it exists, there is a certain distribution of income (or utility or whatever). We say that a coalition S is exploited if its payoff $v(S)$ is greater than what it currently receives in the actual income distribution. The *core* of a game is that set of income distributions for which no coalition is exploited; that is, an income distribution is in the core of game v if each coalition S, by taking its payoff $v(S)$, can do no better than it is currently doing. In game theory, we say S can 'block' a distribution of income if it does better with payoff $v(S)$ than with its current income. A blocking coalition is an exploited coalition.[15]

[15] More precisely, a coalition S is said to be exploited at an allocation if two conditions hold: (1) that S does better than at the current allocation by taking its payoff as specified by the characteristic function of the game; (2) that the complement of S (called S') does worse than at the current allocation by taking its payoff. If the game is super-additive and the allocation under investigation is Pareto optimal, then condition (2) can be shown to follow from (1); hence, in the text above, I have mentioned only condition (1). What condition (2) does is to assure us that if a coalition is exploited, then it is exploited by some other coalition; that is, S' is gaining (in the present allocation) at the expense of S. Without (2), this statement could not be made, and we would not have the exploitation of man by man, but (for example) of man by nature.
  There are some situations where conditions (1) and (2) hold for a coalition S, but we do not wish to view S as exploited or S' as exploiting. For instance, let S' be a set of invalids,

As an example, consider the notion of the core of a private-ownership exchange economy. The private-ownership core is the set of allocations (say, of goods or income) upon which no coalition can improve should it refuse to participate in the society as a whole and given that it can take with it the original, private endowments of its members. Under these particular withdrawal rules, there is a certain class of distributions of goods available to any coalition. I say a coalition is exploited if it receives goods that can be dominated by some distribution that it could achieve after withdrawing with its own assets. If we adopt a different rule of withdrawal, that is, a different specification concerning the achievable rewards of the various coalitions on their own, we will have a different game and a different core.

This device captures the idea of exploitation as the possibility of a better alternative. Our proposal for what constitutes feudal exploitation and capitalist exploitation (and socialist exploitation) amounts to naming different specifications of withdrawal rules. We can then compare different concepts of exploitation by comparing the different rule specifications that define their respective games.

Feudal exploitation

For a feudal economy, think of agents with various endowments, who are engaged in production and consumption under feudal relations. We say a coalition is feudally exploited if it can improve its lot by withdrawing from the economy and taking its own endowments. Thus, feudally nonexploitative allocations are the private-ownership core of the exchange game, as discussed above. This withdrawal specification correctly captures feudal exploitation because it gives the result that serfs are exploited and lords are exploiters. Moreover, non-serf proletarians, for instance, will not be a feudally exploited coalition, under these rules, and so the definition captures only feudal exploitation.

To support this conclusion, I will assume first that feudal serfs owned their own land. Feudal law required them to work the corvée and demesne not in order that they have access to the family plot, but in spite of this access. Thus, were a group of serfs to be allowed to withdraw from feudal society with their endowments, in which we shall include the family plots, they would have been

or of the aged, or of children, supported by S. According to the definition, one would consider the coalition of socially supported invalids to be exploiting the rest of society, under most rules of withdrawal. I will not pursue this problem here, but simply note the game-theoretic definition should be thought of as applicable in situations of arms-length economic transactions. One way to preempt the invalid example might be to require a third condition for exploitation, namely, (3) that S′ be in a relation of dominance to S. Since dominance is undefined, and is as elusive a concept as exploitation, the addition of (3) is ad hoc, it seems, and reduces the sharpness of the game-theoretic characterization. (With respect to our earlier discussion domination exists at the point of maintaining property relations.)

better off, having the same consumption, but providing no labour for the lord. Withdrawal, under these rules, amounts to withdrawal from feudal bondage. It has also been argued that many serfs would have been better off withdrawing from bondage even without their land; surveillance of serfs was necessary to prevent them from running away to the towns, to which they could presumably carry only their nonland endowments. Indeed, one way capitalism improved over feudalism was to make such surveillance unnecessary; proletarians could not survive simply on their own endowments and so were forced to participate in a voluntary labour market.

A feudal ideologue might argue that serfs would not be better off by withdrawing with their own endowments, because they receive various benefits from the lord that they could not produce on their own. The most obvious of these is military protection. Also, he might argue, the lord possessed certain skills or abilities of organization of manor life, without which the serfs would be worse off. (Indeed, the story has a familiar ring.) I will not attempt here to rebut this argument.[16] Let me simply observe that even were military protection necessary, the serfs' corvée labour produced a good deal more than that – witness the castles and extravaganzas of the lords. (One aspect of extravaganza was military adventure.) Furthermore, it can be maintained that large groups of serfs themselves possessed the requisite skills to organize military protection and to take advantage of other externalities and economies of scale accompanying manor life.

Capitalist exploitation

To test whether a coalition of agents is capitalistically exploited, I specify a different set of withdrawal rules to define a different game. When a coalition 'withdraws', it is allowed to take with it its *per capita* share of society's alienable productive assets, not its own private assets, as in the previous game. While the test for feudal exploitation amounts to eliminating feudal bonds in constructing the hypothetical alternative against which the current allocation is judged, the test for capitalist exploitation amounts to equalizing every agent's access to society's alienable property (means of production). For feudalism, we asked how well agents would do if relations of feudal bondage were abolished; under capitalism, we ask how they would fare if relations of alienable property were abolished. Given this phrasing of the alternative, it is not surprising that capitalist exploitation, as here defined, is equivalent to the usual Marxist definition of exploitation, which is in terms of socially necessary labour time and surplus value.

That, indeed, is the main theorem: capitalist exploitation is equivalent to

---

[16] See North and Thomas (1973), who maintain that serfs were not feudally exploited, in my sense; and Brenner (1976), for a rebuttal.

Marxian exploitation, at least for simple models. Any producer or group of producers who is Marxian exploited, according to usual definition of surplus-value transfer, is capitalistically exploited, in that the producer or group in question could improve its income by withdrawing with its *per capita* share of society's alienable productive assets; conversely, any group or individual who is capitalistically exploited is Marxian exploited. To characterize capitalist exploitation in terms of an alternative egalitarian distribution of private property in the means of production captures precisely what Marxists mean by exploitation.[17]

I would further argue that to characterize Marxian exploitation in terms of property relations is superior to doing so in terms of surplus value. The idea of property relations makes clear what is the ethical imperative when one speaks of exploitation in that it allows us to conceive of an alternative in which the proletariat (or the exploited coalition) has access to its *per capita* share of society's productive assets. We shall see shortly, in contrast, what the ethical imperative for a neo-classical economist is when he speaks of exploitation.

Just as the feudal ideologue argued that serfs would not have been better off had they withdrawn with their own endowments, so a bourgeois ideologue might argue that those who are Marxian exploited (that is, whose surplus value is appropriated by others) would not be better off were they to withdraw with their *per capita* share of society's produced goods. He claims, in other words, that the proletariat is not capitalistically exploited. He might argue that the surplus value workers contribute to the capitalist is traded in return for a scarce skill that the capitalist possesses and that is necessary for organizing production. In the models of Marxian exploitation discussed in this essay, this is not an issue, as capitalists are pictured as simply owning resources and not as the vessels of entrepreneurial talent. Nevertheless, the bourgeois argument is in principle a correct one; if equalization of produced assets would not be sufficient to make Marxian exploited workers better off on their own, then they are not capitalistically exploited. This is an important bone of contention between Marxist and bourgeois thinkers. I will call this the subtle disagreement on the existence of capitalist exploitation under capitalism.

Another disagreement, however, is much less subtle. A common neo-classical position, I believe, is that exploitation cannot be said to exist at a competitive equilibrium, because everyone has gained from trade as much as possible.

---

[17] In the usual models, the game-theoretic and surplus-value characterizations of Marxian exploitation are equivalent. However, there are some important cases where the two definitions render different judgments on whether some groups are exploited. In these cases, I defend the property-relations approach as superior (see Roemer (1982d), and Essay 13 in this book).

How can one say *A* is exploiting *B* if *B* has voluntarily entered into and gained from trade with *A*? Now the models of Marxian exploitation referred to above show that *gains from trade and Marxian exploitation are not mutually exclusive.* The proletarian gains from trading his labour power, since otherwise he starves, but his surplus labour is nevertheless expropriated. What is at issue here is the difference between feudal and capitalist exploitation. The statement that no coalition can gain further from trade amounts to saying that the allocation is in the (feudal) core of the economy; no group of agents, withdrawing with its private endowments, can trade to a superior allocation for its members. Hence, this variant of the neo-classical position says, 'There is no feudal exploitation under capitalism', a statement that is indeed true since competitive equilibria lie in the core of the private ownership game.[18]

It is not always obvious whether objections to the Marxian notion of exploitation are of the subtle form (in which case there is a substantial disagreement about the contribution of agents' inalienable assets to produc- tion), or of the nonsubtle form (in which case there are two different varieties of exploitation under discussion). In the nonsubtle case, the antagonists are posing different specifications for the hypothetical alternative to be used in testing for 'exploitation'. I would argue that the nonsubtle disagreement is quite prevalent. Indeed, if both antagonists agree that the hypothetical agents differ only in their ownership rights of produced goods, then the disagreement must be of the nonsubtle form. When a neo-classical economist says that the proletarian is not exploited by the capitalist because the latter requires a return to his capital (being, we insist, produced goods, not skills), he is also saying that ownership rights of produced means of production must be respected, and, therefore, the test for capitalist exploitation is not appropriate.

To be more precise in discussions of this nature, we should differentiate between the entrepreneurs and the rentiers among 'capitalists'. Entrepreneurs presumably earn a high return for their inalienable endowments, while rentiers earn a return only for their alienable endowments. If the capitalist class is predominantly composed of entrepreneurs, then the statement that 'exploitation does not exist under capitalism' can be consistently interpreted as referring to capitalist exploitation; if the capitalist class is predominantly rentier, then such a statement could only refer to feudal exploitation.

There is, however, one most important piece of circumstantial evidence against the hypothesis that the prevailing disagreement about exploitation under capitalism is of the subtle variety. Prevailing ethical norms of liberal, pluralist social science accept private property in the means of production. (In contrast, they do not accept relations of personal bondage of either the

[18] This is a well-known theorem of neo-classical economics. See, for example, Varian (1978).

slave or the feudal type.) Consequently, prevailing liberal philosophy cannot accept the test for capitalist exploitation just proposed, for that test nullifies property relations. Note that a proponent of the existence of capitalist exploitation would not judge all inequality under capitalism as being of the exploitative type. He would condemn only inequality that has its origins in capitalist exploitation and that could be eliminated by an egalitarian distribution of endowments of alienable resources. Differential reward to skill does not constitute capitalist exploitation.

I will, therefore, tentatively conclude that a fair summary of prevailing liberal opinion, which argues against applying the term *exploitation* to the idealized equilibria of a private-ownership market economy, is: 'There is no feudal exploitation under capitalism.' This is a true statement. Marxists would argue, however, that there is capitalist exploitation under capitalism, although – and this is critical – they would also argue that not all inequality would be eliminated by abolishing private ownership of the means of production.

Thus, the ethical imperative of feudal (or neoclassical) exploitation is to respect private property in the means of production while eliminating barriers to free trade – barriers of bondage, slavery, tariffs, and so on.[19] This is what is implied by the private-ownership game. The ethical imperative of capitalist or Marxian exploitation is to eliminate other barriers to production and to income-generating activity – barriers that producers face as a consequence of their differential access to the alienable means of production.

This section has presented another reason for choosing the labour theory of exploitation: the ensuing characterization of exploitation is equilvalent to the property-relations characterization of capitalist exploitation in that both call for socialization of alienable productive assets. This is so in the sense that the Marxist surplus-value theory of exploitation is equivalent to capitalist exploitation, in which the ethical imperative is the pooling of alienable productive assets. Historical materialists contend, furthermore, that this imperative is not only ethical (some would say not at all ethical) but rather historical.

In this section I have briefly explained how both Marxist and neoclassical notions of exploitation can be seen as special cases of a more general approach to exploitation. A group is considered exploited with respect to a specific conception of alternative property relations. We can develop a formal conception of the alternative by using game-theoretic definitions. Non-exploitative allocations are those in the core of the game, and we vary the

---

[19] Exploitation due to monopoly, however, is not captured by the private-ownership withdrawal rule. That type of exploitation, which is of neo-classical concern, is qualitatively different.

notion of exploitation by varying the payoffs of the game. This characterization of Marxian exploitation, which is in terms of property relations, is superior to the classical definition, which is in terms of surplus value, because it displays explicitly the alternative that Marxists are comparing to capitalism, when they say proletarians are exploited.

Further issues
Socialist exploitation
A coalition is considered capitalistically exploited if it would be better off with access to its *per capita* share of society's alienable assets (means of production, resources). Note, however, that *inalienable* assets (skills) are not pooled in testing for capitalist exploitation. If capitalist exploitation were annihilated inequalities would continue to exist, due to differential inalienable assets possessed by individuals. This inequality I call socialist exploitation. A coalition is socialistically exploited if it could improve its lot by withdrawing with its *per capita* share of society's inalienable assets, once alienable assets are distributed equally. While carrying out such redistribution of skills might be impossible, or at the least would involve formidable incentive problems, as a thought experiment the calculations can be made.

Socialist exploitation is supposed to exist in socialism, where people are to be paid 'according to their work' and thus not in an egalitarian manner. The bourgeois argument is that what Marxists call capitalist exploitation is in reality socialist exploitation, that inequalities under capitalism are a consequence of competitive returns to differential skills.

If all individual endowments are of either the alienable or inalienable type, then a distribution of income is free of socialist exploitation when it is egalitarian. One should note how a certain classical conception of historical materialism is reflected in these definitions. The task of the bourgeois revolution is to eliminate only feudal exploitation, leaving capitalist and socialist exploitation. The task of the socialist revolution is to eliminate only capitalist exploitation. Each revolution eliminates the inequalities associated with its characteristic form of property (the feudal bond, alienable means of production, finally inalienable assets); the scope of assets that are allowed to be private becomes progressively narrower as history proceeds. Historical materialism asserts that forms of exploitation are eliminated in a certain order.

Status exploitation
Yet much inequality in existing socialism is not of the 'socialist' variety. In addition, remuneration is made according to status, where that status is not representative of a special skill. It is difficult to separate status from skill, but

to the extent that special incomes attach themselves to certain positions, entirely independently of the skills necessary to occupy those positions, I call the phenomenon status exploitation. Some people maintain that most inequality in existing socialist societies is of the status variety. Some maintain that it is of the capitalist variety, since bureaucratic status often gives its possessor some control of social capital.

Socially necessary exploitation

The withdrawal criteria proposed for testing the existence of the various forms of exploitation assume that incentives are unaffected by the new distribution of 'property', whether it be alienable or inalienable property or property in position. If proletarians in early capitalism had withdrawn with their *per capita* share of capital, perhaps they would have been worse off than under capitalism, because of the alteration in incentives that would have accompanied socialization of the means of production. (Note, this is an entirely different argument from that of the bourgeois ideologue discussed earlier.) The test for exploitation should therefore be: if the coalition were to work just as hard after its 'withdrawal', would it be better off (have more income)? If so, it is exploited, according to the particular exploitation concept in question. If, however, withdrawal altered incentives to the point that the coalition was worse off in terms of income (if not immediately, then soon), I refer to the exploitation as socially necessary. In general, Marxists believe early capitalist exploitation was socially necessary in this sense, and socialist exploitation is socially necessary in present-day socialism. Most bourgeois opinion maintains that capitalist exploitation is still socially necessary, that is, the abolition of private ownership in the means of production would render workers worse off due to failure of incentives of both capitalist and workers.[20]

Increasing returns to scale

If an economy is characterized by increasing returns to scale, it may be that no individual would be classified as exploited by the game-theoretic test of withdrawal. Were any individual worker to withdraw with his share of the social assets, he would be worse off than at present because of the penalty he would pay for working alone. This problem can be resolved by speaking of the exploitation of suitably large coalitions of agents, not of individuals.

[20] These ideas are pursued more carefully in Roemer (1982a, Chapters 7–9).

On methodology

It is still necessary, within Marxism, to argue for the usefulness of the analytical method, including the use of formal, mathematical models. A fundamentalist quarter continues to maintain that mathematics and models can only reify the essential social insights with which Marxism is concerned. I hope this essay (and its parent book) will not only provide some new insights into the questions of content with which Marxists are concerned but will present a methodological lesson of the usefulness of economic models, including the techniques developed by neoclassical economics. The two major tools that I have used are general equilibrium theory and game theory. Obviously, I do not believe use of these tools condemns my analysis, although it is also clearly true that not all questions of interest in Marxism can be attacked with these tools.

In this essay I have tried to summarize arguments without presenting the formalism, but I must emphasize that the development of these arguments would have been impossible (for me, at least) without formal modelling. Many will agree that formal models are a good language for convincing others of one's intuitions, because they are a language, that is, a commonly agreed upon standard of communication and rigour. What I claim, however, is that formal modelling is also useful in producing ideas. On a number of occasions, formalism led me to conclusions of which I had no prior inkling.

For example, in trying to demonstrate the Class-Exploitation Correspondence Principle for the general constant returns to scale technology, I was initially discouraged to discover the principle was false if one employed the Morishima definition of embodied labour time for the general technology. I eventually noticed, in a purely technical manner, that the crucial break in the proof could be repaired if I defined labour value after equilibrium prices were known. This discovery, then, was due in this instance to formal manipulation, although ex post facto I could find intuitive justification for the result.

More generally as well, the CECP played an important role in developing this theory. We chose models to make the CECP true. In doing so we made a number of discoveries. We found, for example, that labour value depended on price. We found that exploitation depends neither on a subsistence concept nor on subjective preferences of agents. And we found a new argument for why and when labour is a good numeraire for a Marxian theory of exploitation. In each case, it was by examining the CECP and what happened to it when some aspect of the model was altered that led to a conclusion about the deep theory of Marxian economics. While the correspondence between class and exploitation is itself of interest, the point here is rather what we learn by forcing ourselves to construct models in which the correspondence is maintained. The proof of an important theorem completes the circuit, as it were, and convinces us that the component parts are correctly built. It is for this reason that I say the epistemological role of the CECP is as a postulate, even though it appears as a theorem in the formal presentation.

I would like further to emphasize the superiority of the property-relations characterization of Marxian exploitation to the classical surplus-value characterization. The property-relations approach is superior for at least these following reasons.

It makes clear what the ethical imperative of the Marxian theory is, which the surplus-value theory does not. Although surplus value may also be produced under socialism and under feudalism, as well as under capitalism, the classical Marxian theory does not adequately distinguish among the different natures of surplus production in the three modes of production. For instance, because the classical theory does not adequately distinguish the different property relations under capitalism and socialism, some have argued that socialism must entail zero growth. The property-relations game-theory approach makes it completely clear that the production of a surplus under socialist relations of property cannot be construed as capitalist exploitation.

The property-relations approach also makes clear the link between the Marxian idea of exploitation and the idea of 'unequal exchange' between countries. In particular, unequal exchange can be viewed as an instance of capitalist exploitation where the agents are viewed as nations, not individuals.[21]

Furthermore, the game-theory definition of capitalist exploitation generalizes immediately when heterogeneous labour and even many primary factors exist (such as land as well as labour). The test for capitalist exploitation remains identical: evaluate how well an agent or coalition can do if it withdraws with its *per capita* share of the nonhuman alienable assets. The surplus-labour theory of exploitation fails with heterogeneous labour, despite various attempts to save it. (Even if one disagrees with my diagnosis, it is uncontestable that the game-theory approach has the merit of much greater simplicity.) The surplus-labour characterization is useful only when capitalism is seen as a system with one primary factor, labour, which is homogeneous and equally endowed to all. With the property-relations characterization, Marxists are no longer forced to claim that capitalism actually looks like this special case, for the theory applies in a completely general environment. Thus, not only is the

---

[21] The connection between the property-relations approach and unequal exchange is further developed in Roemer (1983b).

labour theory of value irrelevant as a theory of price, but its role in the theory of exploitation is superseded.

Most generally, the property-relations approach focuses on the differential ownership of the means of production as the culprit in capitalist exploitation, while the surplus-value approach focuses on the relations between agents (capitalist and worker) in a particular market and process (the labour market and process). I believe it is the ownership relations that are primary, with the particular markets and processes through which exploitation is mediated being somewhat incidental (as shown in sections 1, 2, and 3). Different regimes (capitalism, feudalism, and so on) are characterized by different property relations, and the kinds of exploitation characteristic of those regimes are best understood by taking the property-relations rather than the surplus-labour approach.

Only one set of conclusions from the general theory of exploitation has been explained in this essay. In *A General Theory of Exploitation and Class* I use the theory to develop a materialist analysis of the structure of inequality and class under socialism. In addition, I cast the major claims of historical materialism into the language of the general theory of exploitation and discuss the ethical posture of historical materialists toward the various kinds of exploitation, each of which in turn becomes important and the focus of class struggle, as history evolves.

6 What is middle about the middle class?*

Erik Olin Wright

At the heart of the recent resurgence of Marxist theorizing on the problem of class has been what might be termed the 'embarrassment' of the middle class. For all of their disagreements, all Marxists share a basic commitment to a polarized abstract concept of class relations, and yet the concrete class structures of contemporary advanced capitalist societies look anything but polarized.

This empirical evidence of a large 'middle class' has provided critics of Marxism with one of their principal arguments against Marxist class theory. Typically, the observation that the class structures of advanced capitalist countries are not violently polarized between two hostile camps is taken as the definitive proof of the failure, or even the irrelevance, of Marxism for understanding contemporary society. While not drawing this same conclusion, Marxists for their part have also seen the expansion of the 'middle class' as a serious theoretical and political problem. Theoretically, some kind of reconstruction of the elements in Marxist class theory is needed to adequately account for these structural features of contemporary capitalist society. Politically, the project for building a viable strategy for socalism must contend with the existence of this relatively large mass of nonpolarized locations within contemporary class relations.

This essay will explore a new approach to understanding the middle class within a broadly Marxist conceptual framework. The pivot of the argument will be an analysis of the specific relationship between the middle class and the problem of exploitation. In section I we will briefly review and then critique alternative strategies for dealing with the middle class in contemporary

* This paper draws heavily from Chapters 3, 4 and 7 of my book, *Classes* (London: New Left Books, 1985), and from a paper, 'A General Framework for the Analysis of Class Structure' *Politics & Society*, vol. 13, no. 4, 1984. The arguments have benefited from comments by Robbie Manchin, Michael Burawoy, John Roemer, Adam Przeworski, Robert Van Der Veen, Phillipe von Parijs, Jon Elster, Andrew Levine, Ron Aminzade, Richard Lachmann, Daniel Bertaux and Perry Anderson. The research was supported in part by grants from the National Science Foundation (SES 82-08238), the German Marshall Fund of the United States and the Wisconsin Alumni Research Committee.

Marxism. Section II will explore the general relation between class and exploitation, using John Roemer's (1982b) approach to exploitation as the point of departure. Section III will then examine the implications of this analysis of class and exploitation for understanding the middle classes, not only in contemporary capitalism but in noncapitalist societies as well. Finally, section IV will bring this reconceptualization of the middle class to bear on a set of empirical problems concerned with the income inequality and class attitudes.

I. The point of departure: neo-Marxist analyses of class structure

Without going into any detail, it is possible to identify four broadly different strategies that Marxists have adopted to deal with the conceptual problem of nonpolarized class positions within a logic of polarized class relations:[1]

(1) The class structure of advanced capitalist societies really *is* polarized; the 'middle class' is strictly an ideological illusion. This position deals with the problem of the middle class by denying the problem itself. Relatively few theorists have adopted this stance.

(2) The middle class should be viewed as a *segment* of some other class, typically a 'new petty bourgeoisie' (e.g. Poulantzas, 1975) or a 'new working class' (e.g. Mallet, 1963). In this strategy the basic polarized class map of capitalism remains intact, but significant internal differentiations within classes are added to the analysis of class structure.

(3) The middle class is really a new class in its own right, completely distinct from either the bourgeoisie, the proletariat or the petty bourgeoisie. Sometimes this class is given a specific name, such as the Professional-Managerial Class (Ehrenreich and Ehrenreich, 1977); sometimes it is simply called 'the New Class' (Gouldner, 1979; Konrad and Szeleyni, 1979). By adding entirely new classes to the class structure, this approach more radically alters the class map of capitalism than the class segment strategy.

(4) The positions aggregated under the popular rubric 'middle class' are not really in *a* class at all. Rather they should be viewed as locations which are simultaneously in more than one class, positions which I have characterized as 'contradictory locations within class relations' (Wright, 1976, 1978; see also Carchedi, 1977). Managers, for example, should be viewed as simultaneously in the working class (in so far as they are wage labourers dominated by capitalists) and in the capitalist class (in so far as they control the operation of production and the labour of workers). This strategy departs most from

[1] For a more detailed review of these alternatives, see Wright (1980).

the traditional Marxist vision of class structure since the very meaning of a 'location' is altered: there is no longer a one-to-one correspondence between structural locations filled by individuals and classes. This is the theoretical position which I have defended in the recent debates on the problem of class structure, arguing that it provided a more coherent conceptualization of the middle classes than any of the available alternatives.

I no longer feel that this fourth solution is satisfactory. In particular, I feel that it suffers from two important problems which it shares with most other neo-Marxist conceptualizations of class structure: first, it tends to shift the analysis of class relations from exploitation to domination; and second, it implicitly regards socialism – a society within which the working class is the 'ruling class' – as the only possible alternative to capitalism.

Domination vs. exploitation

Throughout the development of the concept of contradictory class locations, I insisted that this was a reformulation of a distinctively Marxist class concept. As part of the rhetoric of such an enterprise, I affirmed the relationship between class and exploitation. Nevertheless, in practice the concept of contradictory locations within class relations rested almost exclusively on relations of *domination* rather than exploitation. Reference to exploitation functioned more as a background concept to the discussion of classes than as a constitutive element of the analysis of class structures. Managers, for example, were basically defined as a contradictory location because they were simultaneously dominators and dominated. Domination relations were also decisive in defining the class character of 'semiautonomous employees' – locations which, I argued, were simultaneously petty bourgeois and proletarian by virtue of their self-direction within the labour process – since 'autonomy' defines a condition with respect to domination.[2] This same tendency of substituting domination for exploitation at the core of the concept of class is found in most other neo-Marxist conceptualizations of class structure.

[2] In terms of the development of this critique of contradictory locations within class relations, the semiautonomous employee category has been particularly important. For many critics, autonomy always seemed more of a characteristic of 'working conditions' than a proper dimension of class relations as such, and as a result there was a fair amount of scepticism in my characterization of semiautonomous employees as constituting a distinctive kind of location within the class structure. In my empirical research on class structure, the semiautonomous category has also proved particularly troublesome, generating a number of quite counterintuitive results. For example janitors in schools who also perform a variety of 'handyman' tasks ended up being more autonomous than airline pilots. Of course this could be regarded as a profound discovery – that contrary to appearances, the pilot of a jumbo jet is more proletarianized than a janitor. On the other hand, such results could indicate that autonomy itself should not be treated as a class criterion.

For some people, of course, marginalizing the concept of exploitation is a virtue, not a sin. My own view, however, is that this is a serious weakness for two reasons. First, the shift to a domination-centred concept of class weakens the linkage between the analysis of class locations and the analysis of objective interests. The concept of 'domination' does not in and of itself imply any specific interests of the actors. Parents dominate small children, but this does not imply that they have intrinsically opposed interests to their children. What would make those interests antagonistic is if the relation of parents to children were exploitative as well. Exploitation intrinsically implies a set of opposing material interests. Second, domination-centred concepts of class tend to slide into what can be termed the 'multiple oppressions' approach to understanding society. Societies, in this view, are characterized by a plurality of oppressions each rooted in a different form of domination – sexual, racial, national, economic, etc. – none of which have any explanatory priority over any other. Class, then, becomes just one of many oppressions, with no particular centrality to social and historical analysis.[3] Again, this displacement of class from the centre stage may be viewed as an achievement rather than a problem, but if one wants to retain the traditional centrality Marxism has accorded the concept of class, then the domination-centred concept of class does pose real problems.

Classes in postcapitalist societies
Classical Marxism was absolutely unequivocal about the historical prognosis for capitalism: socialism – and ultimately communism – was the future of capitalist societies. The bearer of that necessary future was the working class. The polarized class structure *within* capitalism between the bourgeoisie and the proletariat thus paralleled the polarized historical alternatives *between* capitalism and socialism.

The actual historical experience of the twentieth century has called into question, although not unambiguously refuted, this historical vision. As I have argued elsewhere (Wright, 1983a), it is necessary to at least entertain the possibility of postcapitalist class structures. The difficulty is that with very few exceptions, the conceptual frameworks adopted by Marxists for analysing capitalist class relations do not contain adequate criteria for understanding postcapitalist classes. In particular, all of the class categories in my analysis of contradictory locations within class relations were either situated firmly

---

[3] This view is characteristic of what is sometimes called 'post-Marxist' radical theory. Some of the leading proponents include Albert and Hahnel (1978, 1981), J. Cohen (1982), Aaronowitz (1981).

within capitalist relations (bourgeoisie, managers, workers) or in contradictory locations involving basically precapitalist relations (semiautonomous employees, the petty bourgeoisie and small employers). There were no elements within this analysis of class relations in capitalist society which could point the direction for the analysis of postcapitalist classes. The result is a tendency for discussions of postcapitalist class structures – the class structures of 'actually existing socialisms' – to have a very ad hoc character to them.

Given these conceptual problems – the shift from exploitation to domination and the lack of a conceptual basis for analysing postcapitalist classes – there are really two theoretical alternatives that could be pursued. One possibility is to celebrate the shift to a domination-centred concept and use this new class concept as the basis for analysing both capitalist and postcapitalist society. This would lead class analysis firmly in the direction of Dahrendorf's (1959) analysis of classes as positions within authority relations. A second alternative is to attempt to restore exploitation to the centre of class analysis in such a way that it can both accommodate the empirical complexities of the 'middle class' within capitalism and the historical reality of postcapitalist class structures. It is this second course of action which I will pursue in the rest of this essay.

The basis for this reconstruction of an exploitation-centred concept of class comes from the recent work on the concept of exploitation by John Roemer (1982a). While Roemer himself has not been particularly concerned with problems of empirical investigation or the elaboration of concrete maps of class structures, nevertheless his work does provide a rich foundation for such endeavours. As I will attempt to show, with suitable modification and extension, his strategy of analysis can provide a rigorous basis for resolving the problems in the concept of contradictory class locations.

II. Class and exploitation

The central message of Roemer's approach to the analysis of exploitation is that the material basis of exploitation is inequalities in distributions of productive assets, or what is usually referred to as property relations. On the one hand, inequalities of assets are sufficient to account for transfers of surplus; on the other hand, different forms of asset inequality specify different systems of exploitation. Classes are then defined as positions within the social relations of production derived from these relations of exploitation.

These conclusions have led Roemer to challenge directly the tendency of Marxists (like myself) to define class relations primarily in terms of domination relations within production. Of course, exploiting classes dominate exploited classes in the sense of preventing the exploited classes from taking the exploiting class's productive assets. But domination *within* production, Roemer insists, is not a central part of defining class relations as such.[4]

In a previous work I have criticized Roemer's position on this issue (Wright, 1982). I argued that class relations intrinsically involved domination *at the point of production*, not simply in the repressive protection of the property relations as such. I now think that Roemer is correct on this point. While the fact that capitalists boss workers around within production is unquestionably an important feature of most historic forms of capitalist production and may play a central role in explaining the forms of class organization and class conflict within production, the basis of the capital–labour relation should be identified with the relations of effective control (i.e. real economic ownership) over productive assets as such.

In Roemer's own explicit formulation, only two kinds of assets are formally considered: physical assets (alienable assets in his terminology) and skill assets (inalienable assets). Inequalities in the first of these generates capitalist exploitation; inequalities in the second, 'socialist' exploitation.

I would like to extend Roemer's analysis by considering two additional productive assets: assets in people and assets in organization. Inequalities in the distribution of assets in people, or perhaps more precisely, labour power assets, constitute the basis for *feudal* exploitation and the accompanying feudal class relations. Labour power is a productive asset.[5] In capitalist societies everyone owns one unit of this asset, namely themselves. In feudalism, on the other hand, ownership rights over labour power are unequally distributed: feudal lords have more than one unit, serfs have less than one unit. To be sure, it is not typical of feudalism for serfs to own no labour power – they are not generally slaves divested of all ownership rights in their own labour power – but they do not have complete effective control over their own persons as productive actors, and this is what it means to 'own' one's own labour power assets.[6] Feudal exploitation is thus exploitation (transfers of labour) which result from inequalities in the distribution of assets in labour power.[7]

---

[4] This is not to imply that domination in the labour process is *institutionally* unimportant, or indeed, that such domination does not in practice intensify capitalist exploitation and reinforce the capital–labour class relation. Roemer's point is simply that it is not the actual criterion for class relations; that criterion is strictly based on property relations as such. For a debate on these specific issues, see Roemer (1982h).

[5] See G. A. Cohen (1978:40–1) for a discussion of why labour power should be considered part of the forces of production (i.e. a productive asset).

[6] In this formulation, slavery should be viewed as a limiting case of feudal exploitation, where the slave has no ownership rights at all in his/her own labour power, while the slave owner has complete ownership rights in slaves.

[7] In Roemer's technical exposition, using a game theory approach to defining exploitation, the distinction between exploitation in feudalism and capitalism revolves around the nature of

The second productive asset which I want to add to Roemer's analysis is more problematic. I will term it 'organization assets'. Inequalities in the distribution of this asset provide the basis for the distinctive forms of exploitation and the accompanying class relations of 'actually existing socialist societies'. The anticapitalist revolutions in Russia and elsewhere resulted in the virtual elimination of private property in the means of production: individuals cannot own means of production, they cannot inherit them or dispose of them on a market, etc. And yet it seems unsatisfactory to characterize such societies simply in terms of skill-based exploitation. Experts do not appear to be the 'ruling class' in those societies, and the dynamic of the societies does not seem to revolve around skill inequalities as such.

Roemer recognized this problem and introduced what he termed 'status exploitation' to deal with it. The exploitation exercised by bureaucrats is the prototypical example. 'If these positions', Roemer (1982a:243) writes, 'required special skills, then one might be justified in calling the differential remuneration to these positions an aspect of socialist [skill-based] exploit-ation...[However] there is some extra remuneration to holders of those positions which accrues solely by virtue of the position and not by virtue of the skill necessary to carry out the tasks associated with it. These special payments to positions give rise to *status exploitation*.'

Roemer's concept of status exploitation may provide a useful descriptive account of the location of exploiters in a state socialist society, but it is unsatisfactory theoretically since it breaks decisively with the logic of the rest of his analysis of exploitation. In each of the other cases, exploitation is rooted in property relations to the forces of production. Each of the other forms of exploitation is 'materialist' not just in the sense that the concept is meant to explain material distribution, but because it is based in the relation to the material conditions of production. 'Status' exploitation has no necessary relationship to production at all.

The problems with the concept of status exploitation can be solved by analysing exploitation based on 'organization assets'. As both Adam Smith and Marx noted, the technical division of labour among producers was itself a source of productivity. The way the process of production is organized is a productive resource independent of the expenditure of labour power, the use of means of production or the skills of the producer. Of course there is

the withdrawal rules with respect to physical assets (withdrawing with one's personal assets to define feudal exploitation vs. withdrawing with one's *per capita* share of total assets to define capitalist exploitation). What is being suggested here is that withdrawing with one's personal physical assets is equivalent to redistributing (equalizing) assets in people. The withdrawal rule which defines feudal exploitation can then be specified as leaving the feudal game with one's *per capita* share of society's assets in labour power, namely one unit.

an interrelationship between organization and these other assets, just as there is an interdependence between means of production and skills. But organization – the conditions of coordinated cooperation among producers in a complex division of labour – is a productive resource in its own right.

How is this asset distributed in different kinds of societies? How should the relations of 'real economic ownership' over this asset be defined? In contemporary capitalism, organization assets are generally controlled by managers and capitalists: managers control the organization assets within specific firms under constraints imposed by the ownership of the capital assets by capitalists. Entrepreneurial capitalists directly own both kinds of assets (and probably skill assets as well); pure rentier capitalists (coupon-clippers) only own capital assets. Because of the anarchy of the capitalist market, no set of actors controls the technical division of labour across firms.

In state bureaucratic socialism, or as it is sometimes called, the 'statist mode of production' (see Wright, 1983a), organization assets assume a much greater importance. Controlling the technical division of labour – the coordination of productive activities within and across labour processes – becomes a societal task organized at the centre. The control over organization assets is no longer simply the task of firm-level managers, but extends into the central organs of planning within the state. When it is said that exploitation in such societies is based on bureaucratic power what is meant is that the control over organization assets defines the material basis for class relations and exploitation.

This notion of organization assets bears a close relation to the problem of authority and hierarchy. The asset is organization. The activity of using that asset is coordinated decision-making over a complex technical division of labour. When that asset is distributed unequally, so some positions have effective control over much more of the asset than others, then the social relation with respect to that asset takes the form of hierarchical authority. Authority, however, is not the asset as such; organization is the asset which is controlled through a hierarchy of authority.

The claim that the effective control over organization assets is a basis of exploitation is equivalent to saying (a) that nonmanagers would be better off and managers/bureaucrats worse off if organization assets were equalized (or, equivalently, if organizational control were democratized); and (b) that by virtue of effectively controlling organization assets managers/bureaucrats control part or all of the socially produced surplus.[8]

---

[8] This 'control of the surplus', it must be noted, is *not* the equivalent of the *actual* personal consumption income of managers and bureaucrats, any more than capitalist profits or feudal rents are the equivalent of the personally consumed income of capitalists and feudal lords.

Table I. *Assets, exploitation and classes*

Type of class structure	Principal asset that is unequally distributed	Mechanism of exploitation	Classes	Central task of revolutionary transformation
Feudalism	Labour power	Coercive extraction of surplus labour	Lords and serfs	Individual liberty
Capitalism	Means of production	Market exchanges of labour power and commodities	Capitalists and workers	Socializing means of production
State bureau-cratic socialism	Organization	Planned appropriation and distribution of surplus based on hierarchy	Managers-bureaucrats and nonmanagement	Democratization of organizational control
Socialism	Skills	Negotiated redistri-bution of surplus from workers to experts	Experts and workers	Substantive equality

If we add organization assets to the list in Roemer's analysis, we generate the more complex typology presented in Table 1.

Let us briefly look at each row of this table and examine its logic. Feudalism is a class system based on unequal distribution of ownership rights in labour power. What 'personal bondage' means is that feudal lords have partial effective economic control over vassals. The empirical manifestation of this unequal distribution of ownership rights over labour power in classical feudalism is the coercive extraction of labour dues from serfs. When corvée labour is commuted to rents in kinds and eventually money rents, the feudal character of the exploitation relation is reflected in the legal prohibitions on the movement of peasants off of the land. The 'flight' of a peasant to the city is, in effect, a form of theft: the peasant is stealing part of the labour power owned by the lord.[9] Feudal lords may also have more means of production than serfs, more organizational assets and more productive skills (although this is unlikely) and thus they may be exploiters with respect to these assets as well. What defines the society as 'feudal', however, is the primacy of the distinctively feudal mechanisms of exploitation, and which, accordingly, means that feudal class relations will be the primary structural basis of class struggle.

The bourgeois revolutions radically redistributed productive assets in people: everyone, at least in principle, owns one unit – themselves. This is precisely what is meant by 'bourgeois freedoms', and it is the sense in which capitalism can be regarded as an historically progressive force. But capitalism raises the second type of exploitation, exploitation based on property relations in means of production, to an unprecedented level.[10]

The typical institutional form of capitalist class relations is capitalists having full ownership rights in the means of production and workers none. Other possibilities, however, have existed historically. Cottage industry in early capitalism involved workers owning some of their means of production,

It is historically variable both within and between types of societies what fraction of the surplus effectively controlled by exploiting classes is used for personal consumption and what portion is used for other purposes (feudal military expenditures, capitalist accumulation, organization growth, etc.). The claim that managers/bureaucrats would be 'worse off' under conditions of a redistribution of organization assets refers to the amount of income they effectively control, and which is therefore potentially available for personal appropriation, not simply the amount they actually personally consume.

[9] In this logic, once peasants are free to move, free to leave the feudal contract, then feudal rents (and thus feudal exploitation) would be in the process of transformation into a form of capitalist exploitation. That transformation would be complete once land itself became 'capital' – that is, it could be freely bought and sold on a market.

[10] It is because capitalism simultaneously largely eliminates one form of exploitation and accentuates another that it is difficult to say whether or not in the transition from feudalism to capitalism overall exploitation increased or decreased.

but not having sufficient assets to actually produce commodities without the assistance of capitalists. Such workers were still being capitalistically exploited even though there was no formal labour markets with wages, etc. In all capitalist exploitation, the mediating mechanism is market exchanges. Unlike in feudalism, surplus is not directly appropriated from workers in the form of coerced labour. Rather, it is appropriated through market exchanges: workers are paid a wage which covers the cost of production of their labour power; capitalists receive an income from the sale of the commodities produced by workers. The difference in these quantities constitutes the exploitative surplus appropriated by capitalists.[11]

Anticapitalist revolutions attempt to eliminate the distinctively capitalist form of exploitation, exploitation based on private ownership of the means of production. The nationalization of the principal means of production is, in effect, a radical equalization of ownership of capital: everyone owns one citizen-share. Such revolutions, however, do not eliminate, and indeed may considerably strengthen and deepen, inequalities of effective control over organization assets. Whereas in capitalism the control over organization assets does not extend beyond the firm, in state bureaucratic socialism the coordinated integration of the division of labour extends to the whole society through institutions of central state planning. The mechanism by which this generates exploitative transfers of surplus involves the centrally planned bureaucratic appropriation and distribution of the surplus along hierarchical principles. The corresponding class relation is therefore between managers/ bureaucrats – people who control organization assets – and nonmanagers.

The historical task of revolutionary transformation of state bureaucratic socialism revolves around the equalization of effective economic control over organization assets, or, equivalently, the democratization of bureaucratic apparatuses.[12] This need not imply total direct democracy, where all decisions of any consequence are directly made in democratic assemblies. There may still be delegated responsibilities, and there certainly can be representative forms of democratic control. But it does mean that the basic parameters of planning and coordination of social production are made through democratic mechanisms and that incumbency within delegated positions of responsibility

[11] It should be noted that this claim is logically independent of the labour theory of value. There is no assumption that commodities exchange in proportions regulated by the amount of socially necessary labour embodied in them. What is claimed is that the income of capitalists constitutes the monetary value of the surplus produced by workers. That is sufficient for their income to be treated as exploitative. See G. A. Cohen (1981d) for a discussion of this treatment of capitalist exploitation and its relation to the labour theory of value.

[12] This, it should be noted, is precisely what leftist critics within 'actually existing socialist societies' say is the core problem on the political agenda of radical change in those countries.

does not give incumbents any personal claims on the social surplus.[13] Such equalization, however, would not necessarily affect exploitation based on skills/credentials. Such exploitation would remain a central feature of socialism.

'Skill' in this context is not a trivial concept. The mere possession of enhanced labouring capabilities acquired through training is not sufficient to generate relations of exploitation, since the income of such trained labour may simply reflect the costs of acquiring the training. In such cases there is neither a transfer of surplus, nor would the untrained be better off under the game-theoretic specification of exploitation if skills were redistributed. For a skill to be the basis of exploitation, therefore, it has to be in some sense scarce relative to its demand, and there must be a mechanism through which individual owners of scarce skills are able to translate that scarcity into higher incomes.

In this conceptualization of socialism, a socialist society is essentially a kind of nonbureaucratic technocracy. Experts control their own skills/knowledge within production, and by virtue of such control are able to appropriate some of the surplus out of production. However, because of the democratization of organization assets, the actual making of planning decisions would not be under the direct control of experts but would be made through some kind of democratic procedure (this is in effect what democratization of organization-assets means: equalizing control over the planning and coordinating of social production). This implies that the actual class power of a socialist technocratic exploiting class will be much weaker than the class power of previous class systems. Their ownership rights extend to only a limited part of the social surplus.[14]

Table 1 represents the general framework for analysing class structure. I

[13] Lenin's original vision of 'Soviet' democracy, in which officials would be paid no more than average workers and would be immediately revocable at any time, and in which the basic contours of social planning would be debated and decided through democratic participation, embodied such principles of equalization of organization assets. Once in power, as we know, the Bolsheviks were either unable or unwilling to seriously attempt the elimination of organization exploitation. For a discussion of these issues in the context of the Russian Revolution and other attempts at workers democracy, see Siriani (1982).

[14] This much more limited basis of *domination* implied by skill-based exploitation is consistent with the spirit, if not the letter, of Marx's claim that socialism is the 'lower stage' of communism since classes are already in a partial state of dissolution in a society with only skill-based exploitation. Communism itself, then, would be understood as a society within which skill-based exploitation itself had 'withered away', i.e., in which ownership rights in skills had been equalized. This does not mean, it must be stressed, that all individuals would actually *possess* the same skills in communism, any more than eliminating property rights in means of production implies that all individuals would actively use the same amount of physical capital. What is equalized is effective control over skills as a productive resource.

would now like to explore the theoretical implications of this framework for the problem of the middle classes. Once this new conceptualization of middle classes has been elaborated, we will then turn to a statistical analysis of certain empirical implications.

III. The middle classes and exploitation

What is middle about the middle class?
The framework in Table 1 enables us to pose the problem of middle classes in a new way. Two different kinds of nonpolarized class locations can be defined in the logic of this framework:

(1) There are class locations that are neither exploiters nor exploited, i.e. people who have precisely the *per capita* level of the relevant asset. A petty bourgeois, self-employed producer with average capital stock, for example, would be neither exploiter nor exploited within capitalist relations.[15] These kinds of positions are what can be called the 'traditional' or 'old' middle class of a particular kind of class system.

(2) Since concrete societies are rarely, if ever, characterized by a single mode of production, the actual class structures of given societies will be characterized by complex patterns of intersecting exploitation relations. There will therefore tend to be some positions which along one dimension of exploitation relations are exploiting, while on another are exploited. Highly skilled wage-earners (e.g. professionals) in capitalism are a good example: they are capitalistically exploited because they lack assets in capital and yet are skill-exploiters. Such positions are what are typically referred to as the 'new middle class' of a given class system.

The 'old middle class' thus consists of positions which are *neither* exploiting nor exploited; the 'new middle class', of positions which are *simultaneously* exploiting and exploited. In both cases, what is 'middle' about the middle class is the distinctiveness of their location within exploitation relations.

Table 2 presents a schematic typology of such complex class locations for capitalism. The typology is divided into two segments: one for owners of the means of production and one for nonowners. Within the wage-earner section of the typology, locations are distinguished by the two subordinate relations of exploitation characteristic of capitalist society – organization assets and skill/credential assets. It is thus possible within this framework to distinguish a whole terrain of class-locations in capitalist *society* that are distinct from

[15] As Roemer points out in his analysis of the Class-Exploitation Correspondence Principle, *some* petty bourgeois, in this formulation, will actually be exploited by capital (through unequal exchange on the market) because they own such minimal means of production, and some will be capitalistic exploiters because they own a great deal of capital even though they may not hire any wage-earners. Exploitation status, therefore, cannot strictly be equated with self-employment/wage-earner status.

Table 2. *Basic typology of exploitation and class*

Assets in the means of production

Owners   Nonowners (wage labourers)

1 Bourgeoisie U.S.　1.8% Sweden 0.7%	4 Expert 　manager U.S.　　3.9% Sweden 4.4%	7 Semi-cre- 　dentialled 　manager U.S.　　6.2% Sweden 4.0%	10 Uncre- 　dentialled 　manager U.S.　　2.3% Sweden 2.5%	+
2 Small 　employer U.S.　　6.0% Sweden 4.8%	5 Expert 　supervisor U.S.　　3.7% Sweden 3.8%	8 Semi-cre- 　dentialled 　supervisor U.S.　　6.8% Sweden 3.2%	11 uncre- 　dentialled 　supervisor U.S.　　6.9% Sweden 3.1%	Organization > 0 assets
3 Petty 　Bourgeoisie U.S.　　6.9% Sweden 5.4%	6 Expert 　nonmanager U.S.　　3.4% Sweden 6.8%	9 Semi-cre- 　dentialled 　worker U.S.　　12.2% Sweden 17.8%	12 Proletarian U.S.　　39.9% Sweden 43.5%	−

　　　　　　+　　　　　　　　> 0　　　　　　−
　　　　　　　　　　　　Skill assets

United States: N = 1,487
Sweden:　　　 N = 1,179
Distributions are of people working in the labour force, thus excluding unemployed, housewives, pensioners, etc.

the polarized class of the capitalist *mode of production*: expert managers, nonmanagerial experts, nonexpert managers, etc.

What is the relationship between this heterogeneous exploitation definition of the middle class and my previous conceptualization of such positions as contradictory locations within class relations? There is still a sense in which such positions could be characterized as 'contradictory locations', for they will typically hold contradictory interests with respect to the primary forms of class struggle in capitalist society, the struggle between labour and capital. On the one hand, they are like workers in being excluded from ownership of the means of production.[16] On the other hand they have interests opposed to workers because of their effective control of organization and skill assets. Within the struggles of capitalism, therefore, these 'new' middle classes do

[16] This is not to deny that many professionals and managers become significant owners of capital assets through savings out of high incomes. To the extent that this happens, however, their class location objectively begins to shift and they move into an objectively bourgeois location. Here I am talking only about those professional and managerial positions which are not vehicles for entry into the bourgeoisie itself.

constitute contradictory locations, or more precisely, contradictory locations within exploitation relations.

The historical trajectory of middle classes

This conceptualization of the middle classes suggests that historically the principal forms of contradictory locations will vary depending upon the particular combinations of exploitation relations in a given society. These principal contradictory locations are presented in Table 3. In feudalism, the critical contradictory location is constituted by the bourgeoisie, the rising class of the successor mode of production.[17] Within capitalism, the central contradictory location within exploitation relations is constituted by managers and state bureaucrats. They embody a principle of class organization which is quite distinct from capitalism and which potentially poses an alternative to capitalist relations. This is particularly true for state managers who, unlike corporate managers, are less likely to have their careers tightly integrated with the interests of the capitalist class. Finally, in state bureaucratic socialism, the 'Intelligentsia' broadly defined constitutes the pivotal contradictory location.[18]

One of the upshots of this reconceptualization of the middle class is that it is no longer axiomatic that the proletariat is the unique, or perhaps even the central, rival to the capitalist class for class power in capitalist society. That classical Marxist assumption depended upon the thesis that there were no other classes within capitalism that could be viewed as the 'bearers' of an historical alternative to capitalism. Socialism (as the transition to communism) was the only possible future to capitalism. What Table 3 suggests is that there are other class forces within capitalism that potentially pose an alternative to capitalism.[19] This does not imply that there is any

[17] The old middle class in feudalism, on the other hand, is defined by the freed peasant (yeoman farmer), the peasant who, within a system of unequally distributed assets in labour power owns his/her *per capita* share of that asset (i.e. they are 'free').
[18] Theorists who have attempted to analyse the class structures of 'actually existing socialism' in terms of a concept of a 'New Class' generally lend to amalgamate state bureaucrats and experts into a single dominant class location, rather than seeing them as essentially vying for class power. Some theorists, such as Konrad and Szelenyi (1979) and Gouldner (1979), do recognize this division, although they do not theorize the problem in precisely the way posed here.
[19] Alvin Gouldner and others have argued that historically the beneficiaries of social revolutions have not been the oppressed classes of the prior mode of production, but 'third classes'. Most notably, it was not the peasantry who became the ruling class with the demise of feudalism, but the bourgeoisie, a class that was located outside of the principal exploitation relation of feudalism. A similar argument could be extended to manager-bureaucrats with respect to capitalism and experts with respect to state bureaucratic socialism: in each case these constitute potential rivals to the existing ruling class.

Table 3. *Basic classes and contradictory locations in successive modes of production*

Mode of production	Basic classes	Principal contradictory location
Feudalism	Lords and serfs	Bourgeoisie
Capitalism	Bourgeoisie and proletariat	Managers/bureaucrats
State bureaucratic socialism	Bureaucrats and workers	Intelligentsia/experts

inevitability to the sequence feudalism–capitalism–state bureaucratic social-ism–socialism–communism; there is nothing which implies that state bureau-crats are destined to be the future ruling class of present-day capitalisms. But it does suggest that the process of class formation and class struggle is considerably more complex and indeterminate than the traditional Marxist story has allowed. There are multiple possible futures to capitalism that can be realized through those struggles, and the particular ways in which alliances are forged between contradictory locations and polarized classes is of crucial importance in understanding the process by which particular historical possibilities become actualities.

Class alliances and the middle class
Individuals in contradictory locations within class relations face three broad strategies in their relationship to class struggle: first, they can try to use their position as an exploiter to gain entry as individuals into the dominant exploiting class itself; second, they can attempt to forge an alliance with the dominant exploiting class; third, they can form some kind of alliance with the principal exploited class.

In general, the immediate class aspiration of people in contradictory locations is to enter the dominant exploiting class by 'cashing in' the fruits of their exploitation location into the dominant asset. Thus, in feudalism, the rising bourgeoisie frequently used part of the surplus acquired through capitalist exploitation to buy land and feudal titles, i.e. to obtain 'feudal assets'. Part of what a bourgeois revolution consists of, then, is preventing the feudalization of capitalist accumulation. Similarly, in capitalism, the exploitative transfers personally available to managers and professionals are often used to buy capital, property, stocks, etc., in order to obtain the 'unearned' income from capital ownership. Finally, in state bureaucratic socialism, experts try to use their control over knowledge as a vehicle for entering the bureaucratic apparatus and acquiring control over organization assets.

Dominant exploiting classes have generally pursued class alliances with contradictory locations, at least when they were financially capable of doing so. Such a strategy attempts to neutralize the potential threat from contradictory locations by tying their interests directly to those of the dominant exploiting class. When such 'hegemonic strategies' are effective, they help to create a stable basis for all exploiting classes to contain struggles by exploited classes. One of the elements of such a strategy is making it easy for people in contradictory locations to enter the dominant class; a second is to reduce the exploitation of contradictory locations by the dominant exploiting class to the point that such positions involve 'net' exploitation. The extremely high salaries paid to upper level managers in large corporations almost certainly means that they are net exploiters. This can have the effect of minimizing any possible conflicts of interests between such positions and those of the dominant exploiting class itself.

Such hegemonic strategies, however, are expensive. They require allowing large segments of contradictory locations access to significant portions of the social surplus. One indicator of the vitality of a particular mode of production is its ability to carry these costs of hegemony; and one of the reasons why stagnation and decline in the long run may engender social and political crises is that such costs become increasingly difficult for ruling classes to bear. It has been argued by some economists (Bowles, Gordon and Weisskopf, 1984) that this corporate hegemonic strategy may be one of the central causes for the general tendency towards stagnation in advanced capitalist economies, and that this in turn may be undermining the viability of the strategy itself.[20] The erosion of the economic foundations of this alliance may generate the emergence of more anticapitalist tendencies among experts and even among managers. Particularly in the state sector where the careers of experts and bureaucrats are less directly tied to the welfare of corporate capital it would be expected that more 'statist' views of how the economy should be managed would gain credence.

The potential class alliances of contradictory locations are not simply with the bourgeoisie. There is, under certain historical situations, the potential for alliances with the 'popular' exploited classes – classes which are not also exploiters (i.e. they are not in contradictory locations within exploitation

[20] The argument is that the growth of managerial costs associated with the growth of the megacorporation is one of the key factors undermining productivity growth in certain capitalist countries.

relations). Such classes, however, generally face a more difficult task in trying to forge an alliance with contradictory locations, since they generally lack the capacity to offer significant bribes to people in those positions. This does not mean, however, that class alliances between workers and some segments of contradictory locations is impossible. Particularly under conditions where contradictory locations are being subjected to a process of 'degradation' – deskilling, proletarianization, routinization of authority, etc. – it may be quite possible for people in those contradictory locations which are clearly net exploited to see the balance of their interests being more in line with the working class.

Where class alliances between workers and various categories of managers and experts occur, the critical political question becomes defining the political and ideological direction of the alliance. If the analysis presented in this essay is correct, these contradictory locations are the 'bearers' of certain futures to capitalism, futures within which the working class would remain an exploited and dominated class. Should workers support such alliances? Is it in their interests to struggle for a society within which they remain exploited, albeit in noncapitalist ways? I do not think that there is a general answer to these questions. The answers depend upon the real historical possibilities facing the working class and other classes in a given society.[21]

IV. Empirical implications

The concept of exploitation is meant to identify situations in which there are intrinsically opposed material interests between actors. The concept of exploitation should thus have considerable explanatory power in accounting for various kinds of overt conflict between those actors. The characterization of a class structure as rooted in a complex pattern of exploitation relations, therefore, is meant to provide insight into the distribution of fundamental material interests across positions in that structure and the corresponding lines of cleavage in class conflicts.

The empirical question is then how this complex typology of class locations is related to a variety of 'dependent' variables. In the present analysis, I will focus on two of these: income and class attitudes. In what follows, I will briefly discuss the rationales for analysing each of these variables, the data sources to be used in the analysis and the construction of the operational variables. Once these preliminaries are completed we will turn to the empirical results themselves.

[21] For a discussion of the problem of class formation and historical possibilities that has influenced the present analysis of these issues, see Adam Przeworski (1977, 1981).

Rationales for variables

While the relationship between the theoretical concept of exploitation and empirical data on personal income is not a simple one, nevertheless, the two should be closely related. If, therefore, ownership/control of productive assets is in fact the basis for exploitation, then incomes should vary systematically across the cells of the class typology in Table 2. More specifically, we can make two basic hypotheses:

> *Hypothesis (1)*. Mean incomes should be polarized in the class structure between the bourgeoisie and the proletariat.
>
> *Hypothesis (2)*. Mean incomes should increase monotonically in every direction from the proletarian corner of the table to the expert manager corner, and from the petty bourgeoisie to the bourgeoisie.

Examining the relationship between class structure and income, therefore, is a way of adding credibility to the theoretical claims underlying the class typology.

The rationale for examining class attitudes is that such attitudes should at least tend to reflect the real interests of incumbents of class positions, and thus will vary systematically across the cells of the class typology. Two objections can be raised against studying attitudes. The first is that class structure is meant to explain class struggle, particularly the organized forms of class actions, not inter-individual variations in mental states. The second is that even if class location shapes individual mental states, responses to an attitude survey are an inappropriate way of tapping those class-determined mental states. Mental states are sufficiently context-dependent that the responses to the artificial context of a survey interview cannot be viewed as indicators of mental states in the real life situations of class relations.

Both of these objections need to be taken seriously. To the first I would say that even if the utlimate object of explanation of class structure is collectively organized class struggles, it is individuals who participate in those struggles, who make the decisions to act in particular ways, and thus individual mental states have to be implicated in the process in one way or another. To the second objection, I would argue that to the extent mental states are context-dependent, then the relationship between class location and class attitudes as measured by a survey should be attenuated, not strengthened. The context of the survey interview should tend to scramble the results, add noise to the real effects of class location. If, therefore, we observe a systematic relationship in spite of this context-distortion, if anything this should add confidence in the meaningfulness of the results.

Data

The data we will examine comes from a large, cross-national project on class structure and class consciousness. Details of the study can be found in Wright *et al.* (1982) and Wright (1985). In the present analysis we will consider the data from only two countries, the United States and Sweden. Within the family of advanced capitalist countries with roughly similar levels of technological development and average standards of living, these two societies represent almost polar cases: the United States has among the highest levels of real income inequality (i.e. after taxes and after transfers) of any developed capitalist society while Sweden has the lowest; Sweden has the highest proportion of its civilian labour force directly employed by the state (over 45 percent) while the United States has the lowest (under 20 percent); Sweden has had the highest level of governance by social democratic parties of any capitalist country; the United States, the lowest. Because of this basic similarity in the levels of economic development combined with these salient political differences, the comparison between Sweden and the United States on the effects of class on income and attitudes should be particularly interesting.

Variables

Complete details on the measures we will use can be found in Wright (1985). The income variable is total personal annual income, before taxes, from all sources. It therefore combines wage income with various sources of nonwage income. The class attitude variable is a scale constructed by combining the responses to six items, each of which has a fairly transparent class content. For example, respondents who agreed with the statement 'Employers should be prohibited by law from hiring strikebreakers during a strike' were classified as having taken the proworking class position, those who disagreed with this statement were classified as having taken the procapitalist position. The scale goes from -6 (the respondent takes the procapitalist position on all six items) to $+6$ (the respondent takes the proworker position on all items).

The ownership of productive assets which underlies the class structure typology is operationalized through the use of a wide range of questions on decision-making, authority, property ownership, occupational skills and educational credentials. There are, needless to say, a host of methodological problems with these measures, particularly the measures of skill/credential assets. For this reason I have trichotomized each of the assets. The two poles of each dimension constitute positions with unambiguous relations to the asset in question. The 'intermediate' position is a combination of cases with marginal assets and cases for which the measures are ambiguous.

Table 4. *Mean annual individual incomes by class location in Sweden and the United States*

Assets in the means of production

Owners   Nonowners (wage labourers)

1 Bourgeoisie
 	
U.S. $52,621
Sweden $28,333
	4 Expert
	   manager
	
	U.S. $28,665
	Sweden $29,952
		7 Semi-cre-
		   dentialled
		   manager
		U.S. $20,701
		Sweden $20,820
			10 Uncre-
			    dentialled
			    manager
			U.S. $12,276
			Sweden $15,475
				+

2 Small
   employer
 	
U.S. $24,828
Sweden $17,237
	5 Expert
	   supervisor
	
	U.S. $23,057
	Sweden $18,859
		8 Semi-cre-
		   dentialled
		   supervisor
		U.S. $18,023
		Sweden $19,711
			11 Uncre-
			    dentialled
			    supervisor
			U.S. $13,045
			Sweden $15,411
				Organization
				> 0 assets

3 Petty
   Bourgeoisie
 	
U.S. $14,496
Sweden $13,503
	6 Expert
	   nonmanager
	
	U.S. $15,251
	Sweden $14,890
		9 Semi-cre-
		   dentialled
		   worker
		U.S. $16,034
		Sweden $14,879
			12 Proletarian
			
			U.S. $11,161
			Sweden $11,876
				−

          +   > 0   −
                          Skill assets

United States: N = 1,282
Sweden: N = 1,049
Entries in cells are the means for gross annual individual income from all sources before taxes. The Swedish incomes were converted to dollars at the 1980 exchange rate.

Empirical results: income

Table 4 presents the data for mean personal income by class for the United States and Sweden. In general, the data in this table is strongly consistent with the theoretical rationale for the exploitation-based conceptualization of class structure.

In the United States, income is strongly polarized between the proletarian cell in the typology and the bourgeoisie: the former earn, on average, just over $11,000 a year, the latter over $52,000. In Sweden, the results are not as clean: the bourgeoisie in the sample has essentially identical income to expert managers. Two things need to be said about this: first, there are only eight respondents in the bourgeoisie category in the Swedish sample, and they are certainly relatively small capitalists. Secondly, because of the very heavy taxation on personal income in Sweden, capitalists take a substantial part of their income in-kind rather than as salary. It is impossible to measure such nonmonetary elements in personal income with the data we have available, so the figure in Table 4 is certainly an underestimate. Hypothesis 1 is thus strongly supported in the United States, and at least provisionally supported in Sweden.

The results for Hypothesis 2 are less equivocal. In both the United States and Sweden incomes increase in a nearly perfectly monotonic manner in every dimension of the table as you move from the proletarian corner in the class structure matrix to the expert-manager corner. The only exceptions are that categories 10 and 11 (uncredentialled managers and uncredentialled supervisors) are essentially identical and categories 6 and 9 (credentialled and semi-credentialled nonmanagerial employees) are essentially identical in both the United States and Sweden. Given the conceptual status of the 'intermediate' categories of 'uncredentialled supervisors' (category 11) and 'semi-credentialled workers' (category 9), these results are not inconsistent with the theoretical model.

What is particularly striking in the pattern in Table 4 is the interaction between the two dimensions of exploitation relations among wage-earners. The increase in average income is relatively modest as you move along either organization assets or credential assets taken separately (i.e. as you move along the bottom of the table and the right hand column). Where the sharp increase in incomes occurs is where you combine these two exploitation mechanisms (i.e moving along the top of the table and the left hand column of among wage-earners). Hypothesis 2 is thus strongly supported.[22]

Empirical results attitudes

Table 5 presents the mean values on the class consciousness scale by class location in the United States and Sweden.

Several generalizations can be drawn from these results:

(1) *The Overall Pattern of Variations.* In Table 5 the overall *pattern* of variations in means (not the actual value of the means, but the patterning of the means) is quite similar in the United States and Sweden. In both countries the table is basically polarized between the capitalist class and the working class (in neither table is there a significant difference between proletarians and semi-credentialled workers).[23] In both countries the values on the scale

[22] In a separate analysis, not reported here, in which nonwage income was the dependent variable, the same monotonic pattern was observed, only with a considerably steeper differential between workers and expert managers. See Wright (1985, Chapter 6).

[23] In the United States, expert managers are slightly more procapitalist than the bourgeoisie itself, but the difference is sufficiently small that they should be treated as essentially equally polarized with respect to the working class. It should be remembered in this context that most respondents in what I am calling the 'bourgeoisie' are still fairly modest capitalists. 83 percent of these capitalists employ less than 50 employees. Only 8 percent of expert-managers, on the other hand, work for business with less than 50 employees. It would be expected that if we had data on a sample of large capitalists, the results would be somewhat different.

Table 5. *Class consciousness by location in the class structure*

I. The United States
Assets in the means of production

Owners	Nonowners (wage labourers)			
1 Bourgeoisie −1.31	4 Expert manager −1.46	7 Semi-cre- dentialled manager −0.34	10 Uncre- dentialled manager −0.29	+
2 Small employer −0.87	5 Expert supervisor −0.78	8 Semi-cre- dentialled supervisor −0.24	11 Uncre- dentialled supervisor +0.54	Organization > o assets
3 Petty Bourgeoisie −0.09	6 Expert nonmanager −0.09	9 Semi-cre- dentialled worker +0.78	12 Proletarian +0.78	−
	+	> o	−	
		Skill assets		

II. Sweden
Assets in the means of production

Owners	Nonowners (wage labourers)			
1 Bourgeoisie −2.00	4 Expert manager −0.70	7 Semi-cre- dentialled manager +1.03	10 Uncre- dentialled manager +1.81	+
2 Small employer −0.98	5 Expert supervisor +0.07	8 Semi-cre- dentialled supervisor +0.74	11 Uncre- dentialled supervisor +1.98	Organization > o assets
3 Petty Bourgeoisie +0.46	6 Expert nonmanager +1.29	9 Semi-cre- dentialled worker +2.81	12 Proletarian +2.60	−
	+	> o	−	
		Skill assets		

Entries in the table are means on the working class consciousness scale. The values on the scale range from +6 (pro-working class on every item) to −6 (pro-capitalist on every item).

become decreasingly proworking class and eventually procapitalist class as one moves from the proletarian corner of the table to the expert-manager corner of the table. As in the results for income, the means on the attitude scale change in a nearly monotonic manner along every dimension of the table. And in both countries, the means become increasingly procapitalist as you move from the petty bourgeoisie to the capitalist class proper among the self-employed.[24]

(2) *The Degree of Polarization.* While the patterning of differences in attitudes is similar in the two countries, the degree of polarization within that common pattern is dramatically different. In the United States the difference between the capitalist class and the working class is just over 2 points on the scale; in Sweden the difference is 4.6 points. The data indicate that there is basically an international consensus within the capitalist class on class-based attitudes, whereas no such consensus exists in the working class: Swedish and American workers differ on this scale by nearly as much as U.S. workers and capitalists.

(3) *Class Alliances.* The patterns of class alliances – the ways in which the terrain of class structure becomes transformed into class formations – suggested by the patterns of consciousness in Table 5 varies considerably in the two countries. In Sweden the only wage-earner category with an emphatically procapitalist position is expert managers; in the United States, procapitalist positions penetrate much further into the wage-earner population. In the United States, only the three cells in the lower right hand corner of the table can be considered part of a working class coalition; in Sweden the coalition extends to all uncredentialled wage-earners and all nonmanagement wage earners, and at least weakly includes semi-credentialled managers and semi-credentialled supervisors as well. Turning these results into proportions of the labour force in Table 2, in the United States the bourgeois coalition encompasses approximately 30 percent of the labour force whereas in Sweden the corresponding figure is only 10 percent. On the other hand, in Sweden the working class coalition includes between 73 percent and 80 percent of the labour force (depending upon whether or not semi-credentialled managers and supervisors are included in the coalition), whereas the working class coalition in the United States includes only 58 percent of the labour force.[25] The working class coalition in the United States is thus not only less ideologically polarized with the bourgeoisie than in Sweden, it is also much smaller.

[24] It might be objected that these results could be artifacts of other variables that are not included in the analysis. The sex composition of class categories, for example, could conceivably explain the observed patterns across the cells in the table. I have analysed the results in Table 5 controlling for a range of possible confounding variables – age, sex, class origin, union membership, income – and while certain details of the patterns are affected by these 'controls', the basic patterns remain intact. For a discussion of this multivariate analysis, see Wright (1985, Chapter 7).

[25] These estimates are based on the following aggregations from Table 5: Swedish bourgeois coalition – cells 1, 2, 4; U.S. bourgeois coalition – cells 1, 2, 4, 5, 7, 8, 10; Swedish working class coalition – cells 6, 9, 10, 11, 12 (low estimate) and also 7, 8 (high estimate); U.S. working class coalition – cells 9, 11, 12. Note that in neither country is the petty bourgeoisie – category 3 – part of either coalition.

Interpretations

Several general conclusions can be drawn from these results:

First, the data are systematically consistent with the proposed reconceptualization of class in terms of relations of exploitation. Both in terms of the relationship between class and income and the analysis of the relationship between class and consciousness, the basically monotonic relationship between both results add credibility to the concept.

Second, the data support the thesis that the underlying structure of class relations shapes the overall pattern of class consciousness. In spite of the dramatic political differences between Sweden and the United States the basic pattern linking class structure to class consciousness is very similar in the two countries: they are both polarized along the three dimensions of exploitation, and the values on the consciousness scale basically vary monotonically as one moves along these dimensions.

Finally, while the overall patterning of consciousness is structurally determined by class relations, the level of working class consciousness in a given society and the nature of the class coalitions that are built upon those class relations are shaped by the organizational and political practices that characterize the history of class struggle. For all of their reformism and their efforts at building a stable class compromise in Swedish society, the Swedish Social Democratic Party and the associated Swedish labour movement have adopted strategies which reinforce certain aspects of working class consciousness. Issues of power and property are frequently at the centre of the political agenda, social democratic state policies tend to reinforce the material interests of capitalistically exploited wage-earners, and at least the radical wing of the labour movement and the Social Democratic Party keep alive the vision of alternatives to the existing structure of society.

In contrast to the Swedish case, political parties and unions in the United States have engaged in practices which, wittingly or unwittingly, have undermined working class consciousness. The Democratic Party has systematically displaced political discourse away from a language of class. While of course there are exceptions, the general tendency has been to organize social conflicts in nonclass ways and to emphasize the extremely limited range of alternatives for dealing with problems of power and property. State welfare policies have tended to heighten rather than reduce class-based divisions among wager-earners. And the ineffectiveness of the labour movement to unionize even a majority of manual industrial workers, let alone white collar employees, has meant that the divisions of exploitation-based interests among wage-earners have tended to be large relative to their common interests *vis-à-vis* capital. As a result, as the rhetoric of the 1984 Presidential Campaign suggests, the labour movement is regarded as a 'special interest' group in the United States rather than a representative of the general economic interests of wage-earners.

The net result of these differences in the political strategies and ideologies of parties and unions in the two countries is that class has considerably greater salience in Sweden than in the United States: class location and class experiences have a bigger impact on class consciousness; classes are more polarized ideologically; and the working class coalition built upon that more polarized ideological terrain is much bigger.

V. Conclusions

The heart of the proposal advanced in this essay is that the concept of class should be systematically rooted in the problem of forms of exploitation. In my previous work, and the work of many Marxists, the concept of class had effectively shifted from an exploitation-centred concept to a domination-centred concept. Although exploitation remained part of the background context for the discussion of class, it did not systematically enter into the elaboration of actual class maps. That shift, I now believe, undermines the coherence of the concept of class and should be replaced by a rigorous exploitation-centred conceptualization.

If the arguments in this essay are persuasive, the specific exploitation-centred class concept which I have elaborated has several significant advantages over alternative approaches:

First, the exploitation-centred concept provides a much more coherent and compelling way of understanding the class location of the 'middle class' than alternative concepts, both in capitalist societies and various kinds of noncapitalist societies. The middle class ceases to be a residual category or a relatively ad hoc amendment to the class map of polarized classes. Rather, middle classes are defined by the same relations that define the polarized classes themselves; the difference lies in the ways those relations are structurally combined in the concrete institutional forms of a given society.

Second, the exploitation-centred concept provides a much more coherent way of describing the qualitative differences among types of class structures than alternative concepts. The abstract criteria for assessing the class relations of a given society are consistent across qualitatively distinct societies, and yet allow for the specificity of any given society's class structures to be investigated. The concept thus avoids the kind of ad hoc quality that plagues most other class concepts as they move across historically distinct types of societies.

Third, the exploitation-centred concept is more systematically *materialist* than domination concepts. Classes are derived from the patterns of effective ownership over aspects of the forces of production. The different kinds of exploitation relations which define different kinds of classes are all linked to the qualitative properties of these different aspects of forces of production.

Fourth, the exploitation-centred concept provides a more *historical* class concept than does domination-centred concepts. It is the development of the forces of production which impart whatever directionality exists to epocal social change.[26] Since in the framework discussed in this essay, the class-exploitation nexus is defined with respect to specific kinds of forces of production, the development of those forces of pro'' iction is what gives an historical trajectory to systems of class relations. The order to the forms of society presented in Table 1 and Table 3, therefore, is not arbitrary, but defines a developmental tendency in class structures.

Fifth, the concept of class elaborated in this essay has a particularly sustained *critical* character. The very definition of exploitation as developed by Roemer contains within itself the notion of alternative forms of society that are immanent within an existing social structure. And the historical character of the analysis of the possible social forms implies that this critical character of the class concept will not have a purely moral or utopian basis. Class, when defined in terms of qualitatively distinct asset-based forms of exploitation, both provides a way of describing the nature of class relations in a given society and of the immanent possibilities for transformation posed by those relations.

Finally, the exploitation-centred concept provides a much clearer linkage to the problem of interests than domination based concepts. And this in turn provides the basis for a more systematic analysis of the relationship between the objective properties of class structures and the problems of class formation, class alliances and class struggle.

---

[26] See Wright (1983b) for a discussion of why the forces of production can plausibly be viewed as giving history a directionality.

7 Three challenges to class*

Jon Elster

I. Introduction

Not all societies contain classes, in the sense used by Marx and defined in section II. Those that do, we may refer to as class societies. That term, however, is misleading in that it suggests that these societies are organized predominantly around class. I want to discuss whether classes are equally central in all societies where they exist. More specifically, I want to ask whether there could not be other, equally important foci of collective action – alternative lines of division that give rise to solidarity and mobilization. Having set out what I take to be Marx's theory, I go on to discuss three challenges to his view. In section III class is contrasted with *estate* or order, that has been taken as the main organizing principle of pre-capitalist societies. In section IV *power* is considered as an alternative source of conflict and loyalty. In section V the challenge to class comes from *cultural identity* – based on language, religion, ethnicity or nationality.

The problem is one of *explaining collective action*. Hence I do not consider the challenges to class that come from the problem of explaining individual-level behaviour. It may be true, for instance, that to explain health differences among individuals it is more fruitful to look at their position in the technical division of labour than to look at their class position. If so, this is not a challenge to traditional Marxism. Marx was little concerned with what we may call the texture of everyday life – health and morbidity, leisure activities, delinquency etc. If challenged, he might well have offered an explanation of such phenomena in terms of the class structure. He does in fact suggest – tongue in cheek – that crime is to be explained by its beneficial function as a spur on capitalist competition;[1] also, in a more serious vein, that upwards social mobility is to be explained by its useful consequences for capitalist rule.[2] Whatever the validity of such arguments, they are not relevant for the present discussion.

* This paper draws extensively on Elster (1985a). I am grateful to G. A. Cohen and John Roemer for many helpful discussions.

[1] Marx (1905–10), vol. 1, pp. 386–7.   [2] Marx (1894), pp. 600–1.

In any given society one may draw two maps. First, there is the map of classes, in the sense defined below. Next, there is the map of empirically observable collective actors. (I define a collective actor as an interest-group that has succeeded in overcoming the free-rider obstacle to concerted action.[3]) The Marxist view is *not* that these two maps coincide or converge towards one another. Rather, it is that the second map can be *explained* in terms of the first. If, for instance, there occurs organized conflict between groups of workers, this is compatible with Marxism if it can be shown that the conflict is explained by its stabilizing effect on the class structure. I return to such 'divide and conquer' arguments in section V below.

II. Marx's theory of class

It is well known that Marx never defined the notion of class, which he used in many of his writings. To reconstruct a definition that can be attributed to him, two types of constraints must be respected. First, the definition must be broadly consistent with Marx's usage. Ideally, it should generate all the groups that he refers to as separate classes, and none of the groups to which he denies that name. (If in addition it generates some groups to which the term is neither applied nor refused, this does not materially affect the proposal.) Secondly, the definition must be consistent with Marx's theoretical purpose – to explain collective action.

In various writings Marx mentions some *fifteen groups* that appear as classes in the various modes of production: bureaucracy and theocracy in the Asiatic mode; slaves, plebeians and patricians under slavery; lord, serf, guild-master and journeyman under feudalism; industrial capitalists, financial capitalists, landlords, peasants, petty bourgeoisie and workers under capitalism.[4] The task is to construct an intensional definition that is consistent both with this enumeration and with the theoretical constraints on the notion. The general explanatory constraint mentioned above has several implications. If the notion of class is to enter into a theory of social conflict, it must be defined in terms that have subjective meaning for the agents. Also, there is a need to define classes so that in any given society the number of classes is relatively small.

Keeping these constraints in mind, I shall discuss *four possible definitions of class* that emphasize, respectively, property, exploitation status, market behaviour and power. We shall not find what we want in any single criterion, but the discussion will allow us to construct a notion that appears fairly adequate, even if also quite complex. Part of the complexity stems from the

[3] Olson (1965).   [4] For detailed references, see Elster (1985a).

need to take account of the difference between market and non-market economies. Also, the distinction between private and corporate ownership of the means of production creates difficulties for any attempt to construct a simple definition.

The view most frequently attributed to Marx is that a class is a group of persons who stand in the same relation of property or non-property to the factors of production, i.e. labour-power and means of production. This proposal comes up against several difficulties. Clearly, property and non-property are too crude as indicators of class membership. They do not, for instance, allow us to distinguish between landlords and capitalists, nor between a small capitalist and a wage labourer who owns some of the means of production (e.g. in the putting-out system). And Marx warns against any attempt to define classes in terms of the *kind* or the *amount* of property owned. The first criterion would have the absurd consequence that 'owners of vineyards, farm owners, mine owners and owners of fisheries'[5] form separate social classes, the second would lead to an 'infinite fragmentation'[6] of classes. A final difficulty is created by corporate property, e.g. church and state land. The managers of such property form a class, but not by virtue of property-ownership, since in a real sense the property belongs to the corporation rather than to any individual or individuals.[7] As further argued below, they form a class by virtue of their power to decide how the factors of production shall be used, i.e. by their ability to issue legitimate orders. Their command over property emerges as a result of attaining a certain class position, and is not a prior fact explaining their class membership.

Next, consider the proposal that classes be defined in terms of exploitation. The main classes of society would then be (i) those who work less than is required to produce what they get, (ii) those who work more and (iii) those who work approximately as many hours as are required to produce what they get. This offers a small and well-defined number of classes. Moreover, by making exploitation constitutive of class it suggests a motivation for class conflict. On closer inspection, however, the proposal is neither extensionally nor theoretically adequate. It does not allow us to define the petty bourgeoisie, since this class does not coincide with group (iii), but comprises exploiters as well as exploited.[8] Nor does it allow us to distinguish between landlords and capitalists, or between slaves and wage labourers in societies where they have coexisted. Moreover, exploitation cannot serve as a motivation for collective action, since no one in a society can know exactly where the dividing line

[5] Marx (1894), p. 886. [6] *Ibid.*
[7] Coleman (1974) insists on this point.
[8] See Roemer (1982a) for the relation between exploitation status and class status.

between exploiters and exploited is to be drawn. The labour-value calculations that would be necessary to determine this line would be horrendously complex.

A third proposal, which will prove more useful, is to define classes in terms of market behaviour. In economies with a labour-market this would give three main classes: those who buy labour-power, those who sell labour-power, and the petty bourgeois who do neither. In economies with credit markets similar classes can be defined with respect to the lending and borrowing of capital. An obvious objection is that the definition is unhelpful in the case of non-market economies. I show in section III that Marx was tempted by the idea of restricting classes to market economies, but his main view was certainly that classes also existed in societies where the extraction of surplus labour took place by extra-economic coercion rather than by market exchange. I shall argue, however, that a broad analogy to the present proposal, or rather to a reconstructed version of the present proposal, also applies to non-market economies.

The need for a reconstruction arises because the proposal overemphasizes actual behaviour and neglects its causal grounding in the endowment structure. Classes should be defined in terms of what people (in some sense) *have* to do, not by what they actually do.[9] Xenophon's gentleman-farmer who works on the farm 'for pleasure and for the sake of the physical and moral benefits such exercise can bestow, and not because economic necessity obliges him to work'[10] does not belong to the same class as someone who *must* work on his land himself. A Rockefeller cannot turn into a worker simply by taking a salaried job, unless he also gives away his fortune. A self-proletarianized student does not become a member of the working class if the option of becoming self-employed remains open. These remarks follow from the constraints that the notion of class is ultimately to be used in a theory of social conflict. We would not expect the agents who have to work or to sell their labour-power to align themselves with non-compulsory workers or sellers of labour-power.

John Roemer has proposed a general theory of classes in terms of compulsory market behaviour.[11] He assumes that the economic agents are endowed with different amounts of non-labour factors of production, and then enter into market transactions in order to maximize their income (at equilibrium prices). As a result of such optimizing behaviour, the agents will spontaneously sort themselves into a small number of classes: those who must

[9] Cohen (1978a), pp. 70ff. and Roemer (1982a), p. 81.
[10] Ste Croix (1981), p. 121.
[11] Roemer (1982a), Chs. 2 and 4. See also Roemer, 'New directions', in this book.

sell their labour-power in order to optimize, those who can only optimize by buying labour-power and those who can optimize by working for themselves. A similar approach also works for credit market economies. On this proposal, the criterion for class membership becomes *endowment-necessitated market behaviour.*

As with the other proposals, we must consider the extensional adequacy of the definition. Once again, the landlord-capitalist distinction offers the most recalcitrant case. The landlord is anomalous from the present point of view, since he earns an income without working *and* without hiring labour. He does not *produce* anything, but lives off the rent from his land. In the models that Roemer uses in his book, this is not conceivable, since here labour is the only non-depreciating asset and agents are not allowed to eat up their capital. In a model with both land and labour as non-produced and non-depreciating assets,[12] landlord behaviour would be feasible, and in fact optimal with a suitability chosen objective function.[13] Hence the presently considered proposal could, if suitably extended, also generate the landlord-capitalist distinction, and no doubt the distinction between independent artisans and independent peasants as well.

In market economies, then, *classes are characterized by the activities in which they are compelled to engage by virtue of the endowment structure.* These are the activities of working, buying and selling labour-power, lending or borrowing capital, hiring and renting land. The notion of compulsion must be taken in the sense that I have explained. For all agents, it means that they must engage in these activities if they are to optimize. For some agents it is also true that they are forced to optimize – notably the workers who are forced to sell their labour-power.[14] The definition makes good sociological sense even for the agents who are not forced to optimize. They may have the option of engaging in activities which other agents are forced to take up, but they do not by taking that option become members of the same class as the latter. The rationale behind these statements is an intuition – to be verified – that what determines coalition behaviour is not what agents can do, or do do, but what they must do to optimize.

If taken in a general sense, the italicized phrase in the last paragraph can also serve to define classes in non-market economies based on private property in the factors of production. Observe, namely, that in such economies the producing agents have no or only partial control over their labour-power. This

---

[12] Roemer (1982b).
[13] Landlord behaviour could be optimal, for instance, if the objective is to minimize working hours subject to a consumption constraint, and then to consume as much as possible if it involves no labour.   [14] Cohen (1983a).

lack of control is part of the property-endowment structure, and by definition is what enables (in fact compels) the controllers to compel them to work for them. Of course, the relation between the property structure and the activities in which the agents engage compulsorily differs fundamentally in the two cases. In market economies the distribution of agents into classes is not immediately given by the endowment structure. It must be derived from that structure by assuming that the agents enter into market transactions.[15] In non-market economies, on the other hand, who compels whom to do what is an institutional fact, given prior to any actual transactions. Also, the compulsion has different meanings in the two cases. The extra-economic coercion of pre-capitalist society must be distinguished from the 'dull compulsion of economic relations'.[16]

These differences notwithstanding, the italicized formula is sufficiently general to cover both cases. It links what agents *do* to what they *have*, by defining classes in terms of what they must do to make the best use of what they have. Neither behaviour nor property endowments by themselves will give a concept that is both extensionally and theoretically adequate. A further generalization of this formula is proposed below.

First, however, we have to consider a final proposal, namely that classes be defined in terms of power relations. I believe that Marx was committed to this definition with respect to classes in pre-capitalist society. In section IV it is argued that he erred in underestimating its importance with respect to classes in capitalism, but here I do not touch upon this issue.

There are two ways in which power may be constitutive of class (as distinct from a relation obtaining between independently defined classes). First, this clearly is true for the classes in non-market economies based on private ownership in the means of production. The endowment structure that gives rise to classes includes the fact that some individuals have full or partial ownership of the labour-power of others. But to own the labour-power of another conceptually implies that one has power over him. Hence in such economies the definition of class in terms of endowment-necessitated behaviour gives the same result as the definition in terms of power. Ownership of persons *is* power.

Secondly, there is the thorny question of the class status of those involved in handling corporate property – the theocrats and bureaucrats in the Asiatic mode of production (and possibly the officials of the Catholic Church in the Middle Ages[17]). Clearly, to characterize the functionaries as *one* class would

---

[15] In addition there is the problem that there may be multiple price equilibria, each of which assigns agents to different class positions. This shows even more dramatically that class status is much more weakly linked to *having* property than to *being* property.

[16] Marx (1867), p. 737.   [17] Marx (1861–2), p. 116 and Marx (1894), p. 601.

obfuscate the difference between hierarchical ranks. A definition of class that has the Vatican's janitor and the Pope become members of the same class does not seem very useful. The lines of cleavage within the bureaucracy could be drawn in several ways, using either exploitation status or power relations as the criterion. The reasons adduced above against exploitation as a criterion also apply here. Hence, adopting the second proposal, we say that those who control the labour-power of others – not by virtue of owning it, but by virtue of hierarchical rank – form a separate class from those that do not. This may also be extended into a trichotomy, distinguishing between those who only control (upper managers), those who only obey (workers) and those who have someone above them as well as someone below them (lower managers).

Once again, however, this is too behavioural. The proposal defines the classes of managers and non-managers in terms of what they actually do, not by what they must do by virtue of what they have. But it still holds that a Rockefeller cannot change his class status by taking a subordinate management job. Clearly, it would be highly desirable to find a structural foundation for domination and subordination, similar to property in the case of buying and selling labour-power. This foundation would presumably include 'cultural capital' as well as innate skills among the endowments that determine what are the optimizing activities of the agents. Unfortunately, we are very far from being able to construct simple, robust models of how this determination takes place. Yet even in the absence of such models, the underlying intuition should be retained, and guide further research.

This, finally, allows us to propose a general definition of classes, in terms of endowments and behaviour. The endowments include tangible property, intangible skills and more subtle cultural traits. The behaviour is defined in such economic terms as working vs not working, selling vs buying labour-power, lending vs borrowing capital, renting vs hiring land, giving vs receiving commands in the management of corporate property. *A class is a group of people who by virtue of what they possess are compelled to engage in the same activities if they want to make the best use of their endowments.*

Now a definition does not give us a theory. Marx's *theory of classes* is implicit in what has been said earlier: classes as thus defined offer the explanation of collective action. The main variety of such explanation simply states that objectively defined classes tend to crystallize into collective actors. Moreover, Marx clearly believed that non-class collective actors tended to lose their importance. Hence, in terms of the two maps of society, Marx did believe that the map of collective actors *largely* tended to coincide with the map of classes. But this is not the full theory. Marx, and even more some of his successors, also attempted to explain the persistence of non-class collective actors by the stabilizing impact on the class structure. I postpone this issue to section V.

In sections III and IV the theory of class is reduced to a simpler form, as a statement about the coincidence or convergence of the two maps. The challenges to class then arise (i) from non-class collective actors, and (ii) from classes that persistently fail to organize as collective actors.

III. Class and estate

Max Weber wrote that 'In contrast to the purely economically determined "class situation", we wish to designate as a *status situation* every typical component of the life of men that is determined by a specific, positive or negative, social estimation of *honour*.'[18] Or again, 'classes are stratified according to their relations to the production and acquisition of goods, whereas status groups are stratified according to the principles of their *consumption* of goods as represented by special styles of life'.[19] His main emphasis was on status groups as closed *Gemeinschaften*, 'based on a subjective feeling of the parties, whether affectual or traditional, that they belong together',[20] with the deliberate exclusion of outsiders as the other side of the coin.[21] On this basis he distinguished between societies based predominantly on class and societies based predominantly on status.[22] Since, unlike Marx, he defined classes exclusively in terms of market behaviour,[23] this contrast follows in a fairly natural way.

There are elements in Marx of a very similar view. Although his main position was that all history up to the present was based on class struggle and hence on classes, he sometimes appears to argue that class is so intimately linked to money and mobility that it only came into being with the modern age. In *The German Ideology*, in the course of a discussion of the modern distinction between the personal and the professional lives of individuals, he writes that

In the estate (and even more in the tribe) this is as yet concealed: for instance, a nobleman always remains a nobleman, a commoner always a commoner, a quality inseparable from his individuality irrespective of his other relations. The difference between the private individual and the class individual, the accidental nature of the conditions of life for the individual, appears only with the emergence of the class, which is itself a product of the bourgeoisie.[24]

Later in the same work there is a reference to the countries 'where the estates have not yet completely developed into classes'.[25] In the somewhat obscure

---

[18] Weber (1968), p. 932.   [19] *Ibid.*, p. 937.   [20] *Ibid.*, p. 40.
[21] *Ibid.*, pp. 341ff.   [22] *Ibid.*, p. 306.
[23] *Ibid.*, p. 928. There is a slight inconsistency in that elsewhere (*ibid.*, p. 305) he refers to the struggle between peasants and manorial lords as a *class* struggle, even though these are not part of a market economy.   [24] Marx (1845–6), p. 78.   [25] *Ibid.*, p. 90.

'Reflections' from 1851 this is also a major theme, as in the following contrast between estate and class:

In the case of the estate system, the consumption of the individual, his material exchange, depends on the particular division of labour to which he is subordinated. In the class system it depends only on the universal medium of exchange which he is able to acquire. In the first case, he as a socially circumscribed person takes part in exchange operations which are circumscribed by his social position. In the second case he as an owner of the universal medium of exchange is able to obtain everything that money can exchange for this token of everything.[26]

These passages show clearly that Marx felt a difficulty in applying the notion of class to pre-capitalist society. Yet in the main, of course, this is exactly what he did. The class–estate contrast is present only as a minor, discordant theme. Let us take leave of this exegetical issue, and turn instead to the substantive question whether class is equally central in pre-capitalist and capitalist societies. Although I do not have the competence to answer the question, I can perhaps contribute to a more useful way of formulating it.

I shall consider social conflicts in classical antiquity. Here we are in the fortunate situation that we can compare the work of an outstanding Weberian historian – Moses Finley – with that of an equally outstanding Marxist historian – G. E. M. de Ste Croix. The former strongly denies, the latter equally vehemently affirms, the centrality of class in the ancient world.

In Finley's *The Ancient Economy* we read the following:

There is little agreement among historians or sociologists about the definition of 'class' or the canons by which to assign anyone to a class. Not even the apparently clearcut, unequivocal Marxist concept of class turns out to be without difficulties. Men are classed according to their relation to the means of production, first between those who do and those who do not own the means of production; second, among the former, between those who work themselves and those who live off the labour of others. Whatever the applicability of that classification in present-day society, for the ancient historian there is an obvious difficulty: the slave and the free wage labourer would then be members of the same class, on a mechanical interpretation, as would the richest senator and the non-working owner of a small pottery. That does not seem a very sensible way to analyse ancient society.[27]

One can certainly agree with the last sentence, while adding that Finley's is not a very sensible way to understand the Marxist concept of class. Since ownership of labour-power is one of the main determinants of class, the slave and the free wage labourer do not belong to the same class. The other example represents a more interesting challenge, and I shall return to it in a moment. First, however, we should note that Finley contrasts class not only with *orders*

[26] Marx (1851), pp. 590–1.　　　　[27] Finley (1973), p. 49.

(or estates), but also with *status groups*. 'An order or estate is a juridically defined group within a population, possessing formalized privileges and disabilities on one or more fields of activity, governmental, military, legal, economic, religious, marital, and *standing in a hierarchical relation to other orders*.'[28] Although Finley does not offer an equally explicit definition of status groups, his gloss on the concept suggests that he has in mind something very similar to Weber's notion – a generalized notion of closed groups that keep intruders out by informal sanctions as well as by legal means. Members of an order or a status group by definition are conscious of their common status. Class, by contrast, is defined by the relations of members to members of other classes, not to members of the same class.[29] Class membership may, but need not, go together with class consciousness.

What does it mean to say that order or status is more central than class? Clearly, we must specify the purpose for which it is central. Assuming that we are only dealing with explanatory purposes, this means that we must *specify the explanandum* for which order, status and class are the competing explanantia. If order or status are to represent a challenge to class, they must address the same explanandum, viz. collective action. To explain individual-level behaviour in terms of these variables does not invalidate Marxist class theory. Pierre Bourdieu, for instance, argues that cultural behaviour can be explained in terms of Weberian status groups, so that the nouveaux riches behave systematically different from 'old wealth'.[30] Finley makes a similar observation à propos Trimalchio in Petronius' *Satyricon*.[31] I fail to see that these plausible views in any way impugn Marx's theory of class. If Finley's senator and pottery-owner differ only in such respects, the contrast is irrelevant for the point he wants to make.

An example of social conflict organized around order rather than class was the struggle between Patricians and Plebeians in Rome. It has often been taken to show the lack of relevance of class in the ancient world,[32] and there certainly is a strong prima facie case to be made for this view. As observed by P. A. Brunt, 'the conflict of the orders is unintelligible unless there were rich plebeians',[33] hence one cannot say in any simple, immediate sense that the struggle was one between economically defined classes. Ste Croix offers, however, the following counterargument:

[The] conflict which was ended in theory in 287 was conducted, so to speak, on two levels. Formally, it was a struggle between the two 'orders'; but it was *also* in a very real political sense a class struggle, the participants in which were on the one side a fairly solid group consisting of a good proportion of the principal landowners and on

[28] *Ibid.*, p. 45.
[29] Weber (1968), p. 930.
[30] Bourdieu (1979).
[31] Finley (1973), pp. 50–1.
[32] See, for instance, Papaioannou (1983), pp. 193ff.
[33] Brunt (1971), p. 47.

the other side a much less unified collection of men with very different interests, but the great majority of whom were concerned to protect themselves against political oppression or economic exploitation or both. The political class struggle, however, was masked – as class struggles so often have been – by the fact that it was formally a struggle between 'orders', and was therefore led on the Plebeian side by men who were qualified to become members of the oligarchy in every respect save the purely technical, legal one, that they were not Patricians but Plebeians. It is legitimate to see the 'conflict of orders' as involving a series of tacit bargains between the two different Plebeian groups: first, the leaders, who had no important economic grievances or demands and whose aims were purely political (and usually, no doubt, selfish), concerned with the removal of a strictly legal disqualification for offices which they were otherwise well qualified to hold; and secondly the mass of Plebeians, who hardly suffered at all *as Plebeians*, because the legal disqualifications of Plebeians as such were for posts the vast majority of them could not hope to fill in any event. Thus it was in the interest of each of the two main groups of Plebeians to join with the other: the mass of the Plebeians would help their leaders to achieve office so that they might be more influential as their protectors, and the leaders would obtain the essential help of the masses for their own advancement by holding out the hope that they could ensure the fulfilment of their aspirations for an improvement in their condition.[34]

I do not think this argument succeeds in showing that the conflict was only 'formally' one between orders, and that in a 'real' sense it was a class struggle. The undisputed fact is that the solidarity within the orders proved stronger than the solidarity within classes, contrary to what Marxist theory leads us to expect. The fact that the solidarity within the Plebeian order was the outcome of bargaining between members of different classes, does not change the matter. The substance of the class theory is precisely that such bargaining will *not* succeed in eclipsing class conflict. Moreover, in the absence of the political grievances of the rich Plebeians there seems to be no reason to think that there would have been any class struggle. Hence it is misleading to say that the struggle between the orders 'masked' the class struggle. Ste Croix's own exposition supports the view that class was not the fundamental explanation of the struggle between the orders – which is not to deny that class affected the modalities of the struggle.

There is another difficulty with the application of Marxist class theory to the ancient world: the absence of class struggles between masters and slaves. Marx's own thoughts on this topic are unclear. In the opening sentences of the Communist Manifesto the struggle between 'freeman and slave' is cited as one form of class struggle in the ancient world. This is puzzling, since 'freemen' were not a class. They included both slaveowners and non-slaveowning free. In any case, the statement is flatly contradicted by a passage from the 1869 Preface to the second edition of the *18th Brumaire:* 'in Rome

[34] Ste Croix (1981), p. 336.

the class struggle mainly took place within a privileged minority, between the free rich and the free poor', with the slaves forming the 'passive pedestal' for the conflict.[35] This suggests the lack of collective actorhood of one central class, adding to the difficulties created by the presence of non-class collective actors.

One can imagine three forms of struggle among the slaves: struggle to improve the slave condition, struggle to escape the slave condition, struggle to abolish the slave condition. The only organized collective action by slaves in Classical Antiquity – the slave revolts – took the second form. Slaves, when they revolted, fought for a freedom that included the right to possess other individuals as slaves.[36] I hesitate calling this class struggle in the Marxist sense. Marx, in his comments on a similar desire for upwards social mobility in capitalism, certainly did not refer to it as a form of class struggle.[37] Of course, the analogy is incomplete, since the slave could escape his condition only by forcible collective action. Yet the fact that the slave revolts shared this feature with genuine revolutionary movements does not qualify them as revolutionary. For a struggle between classes to be a class struggle it has to address itself to the *class conditions*, not to class membership. Such at any rate is my intuition, shaped by reading Marx. It is tempting then to conclude that Marx was right in 1869 and wrong in 1848. There was no overt class struggle involving slaves in Classical Antiquity.

Yet there was 'latent class struggle', in this sense. Any slaveowner knew that his slaves might rise against him, and took care to minimize the probability of this event. This could take the form, for example, of mixing slaves from different nationalities, so as to prevent communication and the emergence of class solidarity.[38] He might also treat the slaves more leniently than he would otherwise have done, or more harshly. It is misleading, therefore, to say that the slaves had a merely passive existence. They were not full-fledged collective actors, but they existed as potential, threatening collectivities for the slaveowner. Class has no explanatory power if it remains totally *an sich*, but this was not the case with the slaves. Although rarely endowed with an existence *für sich*, they existed *für andere* – for the slave-holders. Although the slaves rarely crystallized into collective actors, and then only for the purpose of escaping the slave condition, the known danger that they might do so went into the shaping of that condition itself. It would of course be wrong to say that this effect 'explains' or was 'the real goal' of the revolts.[39] It is only in an indirect, Pickwickian sense that one can say that

[35] Marx (1869), p. 359.   [36] Finley (1981), p. 119.
[37] Marx (1865), p. 1079.
[38] Finley (1981), pp. 109, 171; Ste Croix (1981), pp. 65, 93, 146.
[39] Elster (1978), p. 119.

the class struggle 'was about' the conditions of slave life. Yet I believe that this observation takes some of the bite out of the objection to Marxism that I have raised. Although the slaves did not *qua* collective actors try to change their condition, their potential for collective action had some impact on it.

To summarize, the ancient status societies pose one important problem for the Marxist theory of class – the conflict between non-class collective actors. The importance of status in shaping life styles falls outside the central concerns of Marx, and hence offers no real challenge. Nor does the lack of overt collective action among the slaves, since the ever-present threat of such action was an important factor in shaping social relations.

IV. Class and power

Here is a version of Marxism that probably has widespread acceptance – as a true theory about the world, or at least a correct rendering of Marx. A capitalist economy is characterized by the absence of direct power relations. Exploitation is mediated by the neutral, anonymous market exchanges, whereby some agents emerge as sellers of labour-power and others as buyers. In the background of these exchanges, however, we find the coercive power of the capitalist state. The state guarantees property and the binding character of contracts, without which stable market transactions would be impossible. In addition to these (*ex ante*) class-neutral functions the state also acts in the one-sided interest of the capitalist class. It does so in two main ways: by facilitating collective action among the capitalists, and by preventing collective action among the workers. Hence at the micro level class is dissociated from power, whereas at the macro level there is perfect association between the interests of one class and the actions taken by those who have the political power. I shall argue that neither view is substantively correct. The first is exegetically true, whereas the second corresponds to a view that Marx held up to 1848 and then abandoned.

In section II it was argued that Marx was committed to viewing power relations in the management of corporate property as constitutive of class, at least with respect to the ancient bureaucracies and theocracies. It seems quite clear to me that this also applies to advanced capitalist societies, not only with respect to state functionaries, but also with respect to the class of managers in capitalist firms. True, one might argue that what holds for state and church property does not automatically hold for the business corporation, since in the latter the property is ultimately owned by individual shareholders. Apart from the fact that this rests on an overly simplified view of the modern business corporation,[40] it cannot be relevant for the class status of managers.

[40] Coleman (1974), p. 37.

The manager of the Vatican's bank and of a privately owned bank must belong to the same class, or else the concept loses all significance. Hence within a given firm, the operations of buying and selling labour-power, and the giving and receiving of commands, combine to generate four distinct classes: capitalists, upper managers, lower managers and workers. In addition a capitalist economy at any given time will contain a number of self-employed petty bourgeois. Like the lower managers, they form an intermediate group, but unlike them they do not actually mediate between the classes above and below themselves. This is the revised theory of class developed by Ralf Dahrendorf and others, and generally accepted by many Marxist sociologists.[41] It places power alongside of market behaviour as a central criterion of class membership.

There is a subtly different issue that should also be mentioned here. The importance of power for class relations in capitalism can be asserted on two grounds. First, one might argue that the hierarchical organization of the large capitalist firm creates new classes, defined by the relations of domination and subordination. This is the view set out in the preceding paragraph. One could also argue, however, that even when classes are *defined* by market behaviour, the main *relations* between them are relations of domination and subordination. Even in a small capitalist firm owned and managed by one person who employs a number of workers, 'authority at the point of production must be used to *evince* worker behaviour not guaranteed by the wage labour contract'.[42] I believe this to be incorrect, or at least misleading. For one thing, even in modern capitalism piece-work and other modified putting-out methods abound, with no power relations involved. For another, even when there are such relations, they *are* frequently guaranteed by the wage contract. The use of authority in the production process is often a clause in the contract itself. Be this as it may, I only want to emphasize that when I refer to power as central in the class structure of modern capitalism, I have in mind the role of power in the *constitution* of classes, and not simply the role of power in the *relations* between them.

Consider now class and power at the macro level. I believe that up to 1848 Marx held the view that the power of the state was exclusively a tool of the economically dominant class. The defeat of the French and German revolutions in 1848–9, where the bourgeoisie refused to assume its historical role and destroy the old political fabric, together with the similarly hesitant attitude of the English bourgeoisie made him change his mind. Without changing his basic theory of the state, he had to face the fact that the bourgeoisie was 'la

[41] See, for instance, Wright (1979).   [42] Bowles and Gintis (1978).

première classe possédante à n'être pas gouvernante'.[43] His solution was that the state in these societies has an autonomy that was lent them by the capitalist class, who found it in their interest to abdicate from power, or from abstaining from assuming it even though it was theirs for the taking.

For simplicity of exposition, I focus on the English case. Marx is not the only writer to have been struck by the incongruous political position of the English bourgeoisie in the nineteenth century. It will prove useful to survey some of the other views before I deal with Marx's theory and the lessons to be drawn from it.

An editorial in *The Economist* from 1862 – possibly by Walter Bagehot – was titled 'The advantage to a commercial country of a non-commercial government'. It argued that 'not only for the interest of the country at large, but especially for the interest of its commerce, it is in the highest degree desirable that the Government should stand high above the influence of commercial interest'.[44] This suggests that the aristocratic government of England was a solution to the bourgeoisie's weakness of will. Like Ulysses binding himself to the mast, the bourgeoisie could not trust itself not to succumb to the temptation of short-term greed.

A related argument was offered by Schumpeter, substituting lack of ability for weakness of will. In his words, 'a genius in the business office may be, and often is, utterly unable outside it to say boo to a goose – both in the drawing room and on the platform. Knowing this he wants to be left alone and to leave politics alone.' Hence, 'without protection by some non-bourgeois group, the bourgeoisie is politically helpless and unable not only to lead its nation but even to take care of its particular class interest. Which amounts to saying that it needs a master.'[45]

A more sober explanation is offered by G. D. H. Cole. He argued that the industrial capitalists 'were too occupied with their own affairs to wish to take the exercise of political authority directly into their own hands' – 'provided that the government did not govern too much, and protected their property against levellers from below as well as against extortions in the interest of the old aristocratic class'.[46] I read this as suggesting that to the bourgeoisie the opportunity cost of going into politics exceeded the potential gains, given the knowledge that the government would not go too far in acting against their interests.

Seymour Lipset, citing Engels, argues in a quite different vein from all the preceding writers (and from Marx). Engels had written that 'the English

[43] Veyne (1976), p. 117.
[44] *The Economist*, 4.1.1862.
[45] Schumpeter (1961), p. 138.
[46] Cole (1955), pp. 84–5.

bourgeoisie are, up to the present day, so deeply penetrated by a sense of their social inferiority that they keep up, at their own expense and that of the nation, an ornamental caste of drones to represent the nation worthily at all state functions'. According to Lipset, this 'is a situation in which an old upper class, which had declined in economic power, continued to maintain its control over the governmental machinery because it remained the highest status group in society'.[47] There is no suggestion here that the bourgeoisie derived any advantage from not having power.

Marx, finally, believed that the bourgeoisie kept away from power in order to lead the working class into a war on two fronts, against Government and Capital. The 'social revolution of England' will date from the moment when 'the struggle against capital will no longer be distinct from the struggle against the existing Government'.[48] Moreover, 'it is the instinctive perception of this fact that already fetters the action of [the bourgeoisie] against the aristocracy'.[49] The bourgeoisie used the aristocracy as a lightning-rod 'in order to deflect the indignation of the working classes from their real antagonist'.[50] The following statement about France also applies to English politics: 'As long as the rule of the bourgeois class had not been organised completely, as long as it had not acquired its pure political expression, the antagonism of the other classes, likewise, could not appear in its pure form, and where it did appear could not take the dangerous turn that transforms every struggle against the state power into a struggle against capital.'[51] Following his bent for functional explanation, Marx argues that the beneficial effects for the bourgeoisie of abstaining from power also *explain* its abstention. Hence its abstention was not a sign of weakness, but a form of exercising power. The autonomy of the state was nothing but a fief from the bourgeoisie.

I want to question this conceptualization of power, and to argue that the autonomy of the state was more substantial than Marx allowed for. Observe first that group interest can shape political policies in two ways: by serving as a maximand for the policy choices or as a constraint on them. On first glance, it is tempting to say that if the choice between the feasible political alternatives is always made according to the interest of one specific group, then that group has concentrated all power in its hands. On reflection, however, we see that power also must include the ability to define the set of alternatives, to set constraints on what is feasible.

Imagine, now, that there are two agents, A and B, initially facing a given number of alternatives. B has the formal power of decision to choose among

[47] Lipset (1968), pp. 312–13.
[48] Marx, in the New York Daily Tribune, 25.8.1852.
[49] Ibid., 1.8.1854.
[50] Ibid., 15.11.1853.
[51] Marx (1852b), p. 142.

the feasible alternatives, *A* may have the power to exclude some of the alternatives from being considered. What follows is mainly intended to serve as a framework for discussing nineteenth-century European politics, with *A* as the bourgeoisie and *B* as the government. It can also, however, be read as a story about twentieth-century politics, with the working class either in the role of *B* (in the social democratic countries) or in the role of *A* (in welfare states with right-wing governments).[52]

Assume that in *A*'s judgment, some of the alternatives are very bad, to be avoided at all costs. Among the remaining some are judged better than others, but none is outstandingly superior. If the bad alternatives can somehow be excluded from the feasible set, it might not matter much if *B* within the restricted set chooses an alternative that is not highly ranked by *A*. It might not even be necessary for *A* to exclude the inferior alternatives. *B*, acting on 'the law of anticipated reactions'[53] might abstain from choosing any of these, knowing that if he does, *A* has the power and the motive to dethrone him. Moreover, to the extent that what is bad for *A* is also bad for *B*, perhaps because *B*'s affluence depends to some extent on *A*'s, *B* might not want to choose an inferior alternative even if he could get away with it. On the other hand, *A* might actually welcome the fact that *B* does not choose the alternative top-ranked by *A*, e.g. if *A* does not want to be seen as having power or if he deplores his own ability to defer satisfaction. Or, if he does not welcome it, he might at least tolerate it as a lesser evil compared to the costs involved in *taking* the formal power of decision, as distinct from having it. In either case *B* would be invested with some autonomous power of decision, although its substance might be questioned, since ultimately it can be said to derive from *A*.

Consider, however, the same situation from *B*'s perspective. He will correctly perceive his power as deriving from the cost to *A* of having or taking power. To be sure, *B*'s power is limited by the fact that there are certain bounds that he cannot transgress without provoking *A* into taking power for himself, possibly also by the need to avoid killing the goose that lays the golden eggs. But conversely *A*'s power is limited by his desire not to assume power unless provoked. Both actors, in fact, have power, of an equally substantial nature. They need not, of course, have equal amounts of power. The exact distribution of their powers to shape the outcome depends on the strength of *A*'s aversion to having or taking power, as well as of *B*'s need to avoid harming *A*.

In the light of the various theories of abdication cited earlier, what could *A*'s motive be for not wanting power? One reason might be the existence of

[52] For important work in this direction see Przeworski and Wallerstein (1982).
[53] Friedrich (1950).

some third actor C, who is already involved in a struggle with A and who also tends to oppose whoever has the formal power of decision. For A it might then be better that B have the power so that some of C's attention and energy should be directed towards B, and correspondingly diverted from A. Another reason might be that A knows that if in power he will take decisions motivated by short-term gains to himself, and that he wants to prevent this by letting the power remain safely outside his reach. From the point of view of A's long-term interest it may be better having the decisions taken in accordance with B's interest (although not as good as if B would take them to promote A's long-term interest). A third reason could simply be that if one has to devote some of one's time to making political decisions there is less time left for pursuing private interests. Again, those interests may be harmed by someone else exercising the formal power, but perhaps less so than if one is distracted by having to assume it oneself. As to the reasons for not wanting to *take* power, assuming one would not mind having it, one explanation could be a short time horizon – i.e. a high rate of time discounting. To go into politics is like a costly investment, bearing fruit only after some time, while requiring outlays in the present. If one's interests are reasonably well respected in the present, the prospect of a future in which they might be even better respected need not look very attractive, considering the costs involved in the transition. This also creates an incentive for B to make those costs as large as possible, and to make sure that A's interests are just sufficiently respected to make the costs an effective deterrent.

Why did Marx think that the government held power as a fief from the capitalists? Tentatively, I believe it was because he held a limited, pre-strategic view of what constitutes a political resource. On this view, power grows out of the end of a gun – or, more generally, out of money and manpower. Yet we know today that the power base of a political actor can also be his place in a web of strategic relationships. In three-person games, for instance, the non-cooperative outcome may easily be that the weaker agent comes out on the top, after the other two have destroyed one another.[54] Similarly, in the case I have been discussing the capitalist's fear of the rising working class gives a lever to the aristocratic government that has little to do with the positive resources actually at its disposal.

Marx, I said in section II, argued that classes tend to crystallize into collective actors. Up to a certain point, he saw the bourgeoisie as conforming to this pattern. The Anti-Corn Law League brought it to a level of organization from which the next, obvious step was to assume the political power. Yet, instead of advancing, the bourgeoisie retreated, dismantling the apparatus

[54] For an instructive example see Shubik (1982), pp. 22ff.

they had created. Similar events took place in France and Germany. Instead of drawing the correct lesson from what had happened, and admitting that the political domain creates its own sources of power, he tried to fit the events into the Procrustean framework of his earlier theory. While recognizing that the state was not in any immediate sense the tool of the bourgeoisie, he still argued that it had an instrumental character, but at one remove. Hence he missed a unique chance of formulating a non-reductionist theory of politics, as constrained by economics but not fully explicable in terms of it.

V. Class and cultural identity

A look at the contemporary world shows that social conflict is far from always about class, in a direct sense. Religious feelings are the mainsprings of struggle in the Middle East, Northern Ireland or Sri Lanka. Racial conflicts shape social life in South Africa and the U.S. Linguistic differences mobilize the masses in Belgium or Canada. Nationalistic sentiments remain as potent as ever in most of the world. These feelings of *cultural identity* give rise to non-class collective actors on a vast scale, and create a serious problem indeed for the Marxist theory of class. Frank Parkin argues that 'it becomes increasingly less possible to operate with models of class based predominantly on categories drawn from the division of labour, property ownership, or the productive system, when the political character of collective action is conditioned by the social and cultural make-up of the groups involved'.[55] Is there a plausible Marxist response to this challenge?

A first line of reply could be that the cultural divisions are never class-neutral. Although there are not many cases in which a culturally defined category coincides exactly with a class – American negro slaves would be one instance – it is invariably the case that the classes are non-randomly distributed over the cultural groups. Hence behind the war between Protestants and Catholics, French and Flemish or whites and blacks, there is the class conflict between propertied and unpropertied. The correlation is not perfect, but sufficiently robust to justify the macro-sociological view that collective action tends to form around economically defined classes.

This response is manifestly implausible. For one thing, there *are* cases where culture and class are randomly related. This is true, for instance, when workers and capitalists in the periphery of a nation ally themselves against workers and capitalists in the centre. True, it will typically be the case that the capitalists in the centre are richer than those in the periphery, but wealth alone is not a criterion of class. The undiluted Marxist theory of class says

[55] Parkin (1979), p. 42; see also Cohen (1983b) for a similar view.

that the bond between rich and poor capitalists is stronger than regional bonds between workers and capitalists. To say otherwise, is to fall victim to ad-hoc thinking. For another thing, the response fails to provide any sense in which class is more basic than culture, i.e. it fails to provide a mechanism whereby the former generates or otherwise explains the latter. In the absence of such a mechanism, one could equally well turn the argument around and say that class is the imperfect expression of the more fundamental cultural conflicts.

The proposal has been made that cultural divisions are a form of 'divide and conquer'. The internal cleavages within the exploited class can be explained by the beneficial consequences it has for the exploiters. I discuss this proposal in another contribution to this volume.[56] Here I need only summarize that discussion by saying that the proposal fails by confusing *divide et impera* with *tertius gaudens* – by turning accidental third-party benefits into explanatory ones. The analysis can be related to the problems discussed in section IV. It may be quite useful for the capitalist class not to utilize its full capacity for collective action. Similarly, it is useful for that class if the working class does not form one homogeneous collective actor, but is split by internal cleavages along cultural lines. In both cases we observe (i) that the map of classes differs from the map of collective actors and (ii) that this non-coincidence benefits the capitalist class. The Marxist theory of class would be upheld if one could demonstrate (iii) that the benefits *explain* the formation of non-class collective actors and the non-formation of classes as collective actors. This, of course, requires more than just pointing to the benefits. To offer a satisfactory explanation one would have to provide a *mechanism* – a story that traces the feedback loop from the benefits to the behaviour that creates them.

VI. Summary

It is hard to imagine a society containing classes in which class was not a pervasive source of conflict – one source, at least, among others. Moreover, in any social conflict predominantly organized along non-class issues, class will usually affect the forms in which it is acted out. Black workers and white workers have a common enemy in white capitalists; rich and poor Plebeians a common enemy in the Patricians. Class becomes a terrain on which alliances are formed, even when it is not itself the object of conflict. Class will always constrain power, even when it falls short of being the sole determinant. Arguably, no other issue has the same salience in all societies. Marx, however, claimed more. He believed that in any society class was the most salient issue. This is what I have been concerned to discuss. To do so, it is

[56] Cp. pp. 214ff. in the present volume.

necessary to state the Marxist theory of class in a way that allows us to distinguish between the relevance of class and the centrality of class. I have done so by focusing on the link between class and collective action, taking Marx to be saying that the class structure in all societies provides the main explanation of social conflict between organized groups. The best-known version of this theory is the simple statement that classes tend to become collective actors and non-class collective actors to disappear. A more sophisticated version, that provides a fall-back position if the simple theory fails, is the view that whenever the set of classes differs from the set of collective actors, class itself provides an explanation for the deviation. I hope to have shown that in neither version can the theory be sustained.

8 Material interests, class compromise, and the transition to socialism*

Adam Przeworski

This essay examines the conflict between capitalists and wage-earners over the realization of material interests in advanced capitalist societies. The central question is whether wage-earners' pursuit of their material interests will necessarily lead them to opt for socialism.

This is an old question and the responses to it are familiar, emphatic, and confused. One response is attributed to Marx and is, in fact, found in some of his writings, particularly in *Wage Labour and Capital*. There Marx maintained that since the national product generated by the capitalist sector of the economy is divided into a part appropriated by capital as profit and a part paid in exchange for labour power as wages, the shares of capital and labour are inversely related. That much is obviously true, since the product is by definition constant at any instant of time. But Marx went much farther. He claimed that even when accumulation is viewed in dynamic terms, in fact, even when workers' conditions are improving, the conflict over distribution retains an essentially zero-sum character. For Marx this conflict is irreconcilable within the confines of the capitalist society.

The political conclusion Marx and most of his followers drew from this analysis is that workers' pursuit of material interest must lead them to realize that these interests can be advanced if and only if the entire system of wage labour is abolished. As Luxemburg put it in 1900, 'as a result of its trade-union and parliamentary struggles, the proletariat becomes convinced of the impossibility of accomplishing a fundamental social change through such activity and arrives at the understanding that the conquest of political power is unavoidable' (1970:30). From the 'objective conflict of material interests' one can proceed to the political, equally objective, 'fundamental interest in socialism' by means of a syllogism.

This response found a mirror image among those defenders of capitalism who claim that the capitalist system is essentially cooperative, that it constitutes a 'non-zero-sum game', and that workers are better off when they

* This essay originally appeared in *Politics and Society*, vol. 10, no. 1, 1980. Reprinted with permission.

cooperate with capitalists to increase the size of the pie rather than fight over relative shares. Marx is said to have been blinded to see only the seamy side of history, the grim side of conflict rather than the radiant promise of cooperation (Boulding, 1970: Chapter 5). The deradicalization of working-class movements constitutes in the eyes of anti-Marxist proponents of economic determinism a sufficient proof that in the course of economic development workers have themselves discovered the advantages of compromise and abandoned all thought of transformation.

The issue is ideological, which is to say important, and it would be naive to expect that we can reach a consensus. Nevertheless, I will show immediately that its present formulation is muddled and that if we can agree to some assumptions we will arrive at unambiguous answers. I will, therefore, proceed deductively, from assumptions to their logical consequences.

The problem defined

I will approach the issue in its narrowest possible formulation since it is in such a narrow formulation that the question has been traditionally posed. Specifically, I will assume that workers under capitalism have an interest in improving their material welfare, and I will base the entire analysis of their political preferences and strategies on this narrow assumption.

Note that it might be true that workers are, in fact, endowed under capitalism with some needs that transcend this system and that by definition can be realized only under socialism, for example, 'an eternal striving for freedom and justice' (Fromm, 1961). This kind of an assumption, however, would reduce the question of workers' preference for socialism to an immediate tautology. The question here is not whether human kind is endowed as a species with some kind of a transcendental need for socialism but only whether the needs that workers seek to satisfy under capitalism would necessarily lead them to opt for socialism as a better system for satisfying these needs.

Secondly, even under capitalism workers may have many needs: a need for autonomy in the work place, for free time, for sex, or for beauty. The quest for satisfaction of these needs may lead workers to reject capitalism. I will return to such eventualities, but for the moment the analysis will be limited to material interests, that is, those needs that can be satisfied through the consumption or use of objectifications of socially organized activities of transformation of nature, which, under capitalism, are commodities. Again, the question is not whether under capitalism workers experience any need that would lead them to opt for socialism but only whether those needs that in principle can be satisfied as the result of the socially organized process of production would inevitably lead them to opt for a socialist organization of this process.

Furthermore, not all material needs become organized as interests. Following Heller (1974), I will treat as interests such needs that can be satisfied by consuming or using commodities and for which the barriers to satisfaction are (in a particular society) external to the needs of a particular individual. If I cannot consume more cake and wine because I want to be beautiful, that is, if the only barrier to satisfying a need consists of my other needs, then this need is not a referent of interest. Hence, needs that can be satisfied by objectifications turn into interests under conditions of scarcity.

I assume, therefore, that workers under capitalism have an interest in improving their material conditions. The question is whether the pursuit of this interest, and only of this interest, would necessarily lead workers to opt for socialism as a superior system for satisfying material needs. Writing at the turn of the century, a leader of the United Mine Workers posed the following choice for organized workers: 'Trade unionism is not irrevocably committed to the maintenance of the wage system, nor is it irrevocably committed to its abolition. It demands the constant improvement of the conditions of the workingmen, if possible, by the maintenance of the present wage system, if not possible, by its ultimate abolition.'[1] The question is whether the demand for 'the constant improvement of the conditions of the workingmen' would necessarily lead workers to opt for the ultimate abolition of the wage system as a whole.

Imagine a situation in which capitalists appropriate profit and consume it entirely. Under such conditions workers would certainly be better off – immediately or at some time in the future – if they did not consent to the private appropriation of profit. They would be better off immediately if they were the ones who consumed this part of the product; alternatively, they would be better off in the future if they withheld this part from current consumption and invested it. Or suppose, more realistically and in the spirit of Marx's analysis, that capitalists do invest some part of profits they withhold and that they themselves consume the remaining part of the increment that resulted from past investment. In this situation the process of accumulation would continue, but workers would not at any time be the beneficiaries of it. Hence, although the game would no longer be a zero-sum one, workers would perpetually be as badly off as they could physically be. Under these conditions workers would again be better off if they did not tolerate the private

[1] John Mitchell, president of the United Mine Workers, cited by Sombart (1976:19).

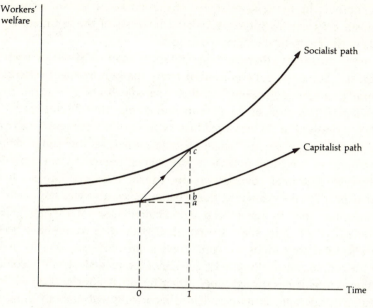

Fig. 8.1

appropriation of profit but instead kept the entire product and either consumed it or invested it for their own future consumption. That the game is not zero-sum does not yet imply that it is a cooperative one: a point always missed by Marx's critics.

These conditions, however, are still too restrictive. All that is needed for workers to rationally opt for socialism out of their material interest are two conditions: that socialism be more efficient in satisfying material needs than capitalism and that moving toward socialism would, immediately and continually improve workers' material conditions. It does not matter whether workers' conditions are deteriorating or improving under capitalism as long as the move in a socialist direction is always immediately and permanently superior for workers' welfare. These conditions are portrayed in Figure 8.1. Even if the situation of workers would have improved under capitalism from level *a* to level *b*, workers would be better off by the amount *c*-minus-*b* if they had taken the socialist path at time $t = 0$. Hence, even if their material conditions were improving under capitalism, rational workers would opt for socialism as a necessary consequence of the pursuit of their material well-being. In this situation, it is indeed true that 'even the most favorable situation for the working class, the most rapid possible growth of capital, however much it may improve the material existence of the worker, does not remove the antagonism between his interests and the interests of the bourgeoisie, the interests of the capitalists' (Marx, 1952:37).

The very possibility that such a situation may exist is sufficient to demonstrate that empirical studies that relate the improvement of workers' conditions ('embourgeoisement') to their 'deradicalization' rest on invalid epistemological premises, as do all empirical studies that do not specify the possible alternatives to the observed history. Even if it were empirically true that workers' organizations became deradicalized at the same time as improvements of their material welfare occurred, one could not draw from this observed historical covariation any causal inferences unless it was possible to prove at the same time that a better alternative was not available.[2] If workers are said to have been deradicalized *because* their conditions improved, then one must admit the possibility that they would have become more radical if these conditions would have improved even more by making a step toward socialism. Empiricist epistemology is intrinsically ideological since it implicitly denies the existence of any historical alternatives: while the proposition that deradicalization coincided historically with embourgeoisement is capable of being judged true or false, the proposition that workers became deradicalized *because* their material conditions improved is not subject to such a test unless the other possibilities are explicitly denied. The observation that workers' conditions improved in the course of the history of capitalism is not sufficient in itself to draw any inferences about their preference for a particular form of social organization. For, if Marx was right, workers are always better off by moving in the direction of socialism.

Before going any further, it might be useful to clarify what moving toward socialism means here and what other options we have. As a first approximation, suppose that workers have three options. One, they can claim the entire capital stock ('means of production') from capitalists and reorganize the system of production in such a way that the directions of investment and the decision to withhold from current consumption would be made by all citizens rather than by owners of capital or their delegates. Investment funds would thus be deducted directly from the gross product, profits being abolished as a juridical and as an economic category. This claim for reorganizing the process of accumulation I consider to be a step toward socialism.

Two, workers can claim the entire current product or even a part of the capital stock without reorganizing the process of withholding from current consumption. This is a purely economicist strategy.

[2] See Przeworski (1980a) for evidence that it is not true that workers became deradicalized as their material conditions improved.

Three, they can claim less than the entire product, thus leaving a part in the hands of capitalists as profit. This strategy opens room for class compromise and cooperation with capitalists.

The hypothesis that material interests lead necessarily to an interest in socialism asserts that *if* workers are interested in a continual improvement of their material conditions and *if* they are rational, they must opt for socialism. This hypothesis would be false if its premises are true and one or both of the following could be shown to be also true: socialism is inferior to capitalism in efficiently allocating resources to socially preferred uses (uses to be chosen by all citizens through some reasonable balloting system), à la von Mises and his followers, and/or conditions exist under which a move in the socialist direction makes workers worse off than a move along the capitalist direction.

I will immediately reject the first possibility and will assume throughout that as a system of organization of production socialism would not be inferior to capitalism in satisfying material needs. Let me only note that this assumption does not refer to the historically realized performance of either system, about which there has been a fair amount of discussion, but to the potential capacity inherent in both systems, again a subject of recurrent debates. In particular, it would be a mistake to compare the historical record of capitalism with the potential envisioned in socialism, since such an approach would imply that workers are at all times as well off as they possibly could be at these times under capitalism. Hence, this procedure would exclude the possibility that capitalism could be reformed to improve workers' welfare.

Suppose, therefore, that socialism is superior to capitalism. The crux of the problem is whether this superiority is sufficient for workers to opt for socialism. If it can be shown that conditions exist under which a move in the socialist direction would be inferior to a move along the path of capitalism, then one could no longer deduce workers' socialist orientation from their material interests.

Let us first imagine what such conditions would be like and only then inquire about their existence. Suppose that socialism is potentially superior to capitalism at any moment of capitalist development (or at least after some threshold, if one believes that conditions must be 'ripe') but that immediate steps toward socialism leave workers worse off than they would have been had they advanced along the capitalist path.[3] The equivalent of Figure 8.1 would then look like Figure 8.2. Under these stipulated conditions, moving from the full potential capitalist path to the full potential socialist path

---

[3] This is true whether this path is upwardly or downwardly sloped. Even if workers' conditions are deteriorating under capitalism, the transition path may still deepen the crisis.

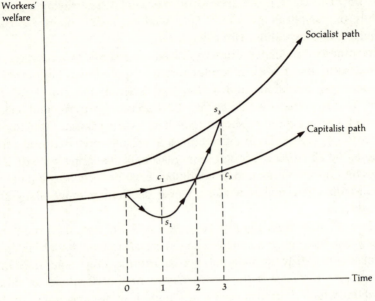

Fig. 8.2

involves a temporary deterioration of workers' welfare. During the period $t = 0$ to $t = 1$, the conditions of workers deteriorate below their past level and below the level that they would have attained under capitalism, c_1, and only then they begin to improve. Although the level of welfare eventually attained on the socialist path, s_3, is higher than the level workers would have reached along the capitalist path, c_3, during the entire period until $t = 2$, these workers would have been better off following the capitalist path. Between the capitalist path and the socialist one there is a valley that must be traversed if workers move at any time toward socialism. If such conditions indeed exist and if workers are interested in a continual improvement of their material welfare, then this descent will not be undertaken or, if it is undertaken, will not be completed by workers under democratic conditions.

At any time workers would thus face a choice between climbing upward toward the best situation they could obtain under capitalism and a temporary deterioration of their conditions on the road to socialism. At a fixed moment of time, we could portray this structure of choices as in Figure 8.3. As long as their current state is above the indifference level corresponding to the bottom of the transitional valley, any move in the socialist direction involves a temporary deterioration of workers' welfare.

Now, if the transition to socialism involves a deterioration of workers'

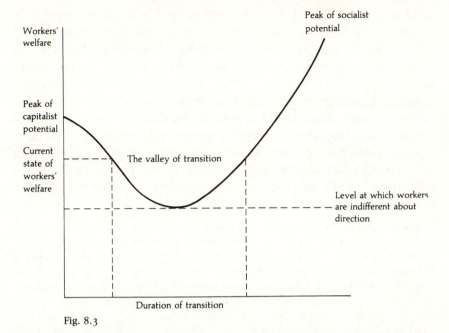

Fig. 8.3

welfare and if workers have an option of improving their material conditions by cooperating with capitalists, then the socialist orientation cannot be deduced from the material interests of workers. I will now demonstrate that this is indeed the case.

The form of class compromise

Thus far we have only defined the issue. The question now is whether conditions for class compromise do in fact exist under capitalism. This is a twofold question. Can workers improve their material welfare by cooperating with capitalists, and does a step toward socialism necessarily involve a temporary deterioration of workers' welfare? Before we answer this question, however, it is necessary to understand what class compromise would look like under capitalism.

In a capitalist society profit is a necessary condition of investment, and investment is a necessary condition of continued production, consumption, and employment.[4] As Chancellor Schmidt put it, 'the profits of enterprises today are the investments of tomorrow, and the investments of tomorrow are the employment of the day after', and in place of 'employment' he might as

---

[4] See Przeworski (1980b) for a more extended discussion.

well have said 'production' or 'consumption' (*Le Monde*, July 6, 1976, p. 5). In any society some part of the product must be withheld from current consumption if production is to continue and consumption is to increase, but the distinguishing characteristic of capitalism is that most of the investment occurs out of profits, that part of the product that is withheld from the immediate producers. Hence under capitalism private profit is the necessary condition for the improvement of material conditions of any group in the society. Unless capitalists appropriate profits, the capital stock becomes depleted, production falls, and employment and consumption fall with it. In fact, capitalists increasingly justify the very institution of profit exactly in these terms, as the following paid advertisement by Mobil Oil Company beautifully illustrates:

Corporate earnings have to rise to levels substantially above those of recent years if our country is not to get into even deeper trouble. [If this does not occur] every group will begin fighting for a larger piece of that static pie. Women, blacks, and other racial minorities, and young people of all backgrounds will be hardest hit. College graduates will find job hunting even tougher. More and more of them will have to take jobs lower in the economic scale. This will further squeeze every minority and everybody else. Economic growth is the last, best hope for the poor and for all the rest of us. Sheer redistribution of income cannot do the job. We must create a steadily larger income pie. This can be done only through economic growth. And only profitable private businesses can make the capital investments that produce economic growth and jobs and tax revenues (*New York Times*, May 6, 1976, p. 17).

This dependence of accumulation upon profit can be formally described in many ways, among which I will choose a very simple macroeconomic model of the form:

$$Y(t+1) = (1 + s/c)P(t) + W(t),$$

where $Y(t)$ stands for the net national product, $P(t)$ for net profit, $W(t)$ for wages, s for the rate of saving out of profit, and c for the capital/output ratio, and where the rate of saving out of wages is assumed to be negligible. At any time t the part s of profits $P(t)$ is saved and invested into an economy in which c units of capital are needed to produce one unit of output. The rate of growth of such an economy depends upon the rate of profit and the rate of saving out of profit:

$$\Delta Y(t)/Y(t) = sP(t)/cY(t) = sP(t)/K(t) = sp(t),$$

where $\Delta Y(t)$ stands for the increase of the product between time t and $(t+1)$, $K(t) = cY(t)$ for the accumulated capital stock, and $p(t) = p(t)/K(t)$ for the rate of profit. Hence the rate of growth varies proportionately to the rate of profit and the rate of saving out of profit. The rate of saving, s, characterizes the behaviour of capitalists, since, given the share of profit in the national product, their decisions to invest and thus to save determine the rate of growth of the economy.

While profit is a necessary condition of development, it is not a sufficient condition for the improvement of material conditions of any particular group. First, capitalists may not invest the profits to increase productivity: despite constraints they may instead consume profits, invest them unproductively, hoard them, or export them elsewhere. Second, even if capitalists do invest profits to increase productivity, no particular group can be in any way assured that it will be the beneficiary of this investment. Capitalists may themselves retain the increment, or they may enter into a number of alternative political alliances. Their market relation with workers ends as the cycle of production is completed and the wages are paid, and there is nothing in the structure of the capitalist system of production that would guarantee that workers would be the ones to benefit from any part of the product being withheld from them as profit.

These structural conditions delimit any possible compromise between capitalists and workers. Since the appropriation of profits by capitalists is a necessary but not a sufficient condition for an improvement of the material welfare of workers, a class compromise is possible only on the condition that workers have a reasonable certainty that future wages will increase as a function of current profits. Any compromise must have the following form: workers consent to the perpetuation of profit as an institution in exchange for the prospect of improving their material well-being in the future. In terms of such a compromise capitalists retain the capacity to withhold a part of the product because the profit they appropriate is expected by workers to be saved, invested, transformed into productive potential, and partly distributed as gains to workers.

This general logic of cooperation is not always stated explicitly. Indeed, during the early period of the development of the working-class movement this compromise was based only on the right of workers to associate, to bargain collectively, and to strike. Eventually, explicit norms did appear pegging wages to prices, to the competitive position of an industry in the international system, and, especially during the expansionist period between 1950 and 1970, to increases of productivity. Nevertheless, whatever the explicit norm cementing a particular 'social pact', the underlying logic of cooperation must relate future wages to current profits. The only conceivable reason for workers to consent voluntarily not to claim the entire social product is to treat current profits as a form of workers 'delegated' investment.

Hence a class compromise must rest on some norm of the form:

$$\Delta \hat{W}(t) = F[P(t\text{-}i)], \, i = 0, 1, \ldots, k, \ldots,$$

where $\Delta \hat{W}(t)$ stands for the increase of wages between time t and time $(t+1)$ expected under a particular agreement, $P(t\text{-}i)$ for the history of profits, and F for the rule that relates past profits to current wage increases under a particular agreement. For the sake of simplicity, and without much loss of generality, let the rule be simply of the form:

$$\Delta \hat{W}(t) = rP(t)$$

The coefficient r represents, therefore, the proportion of current profits that must be immediately transformed into wage increases in the light of a particular agreement.

Note that a compromise is possible only on the condition that $0 < r < (1+s/c)$. Clearly, r must be larger than zero if this rule is to have any meaning. It may be less obvious why it should be less than $(1+s/c)$ rather than simply 1 if the compromise is to be at all tolerable for capitalists. If $r = 1$, then at time $(t+1)$ capitalists pay as wage increases all of the profits they appropriated at time t. In the meantime, however, they would have invested these profits with the marginal rate of return s/c, and after one period they would still be left with the amount $(s/c)P(t)$. Hence only when $r = 1 + s/c$ are the entire profits confiscated at $(t+1)$. This level of r is thus immediately 'confiscatory' with regard to the reinvested current profits, although it still leaves in the hands of capitalists the accumulated capital stock.

The coefficient r indicates the rate of transformation of profits into wage increases under which workers enter into a specific compromise. This coefficient can be treated, therefore, as representing the economic militancy of organized wage-earners.

An agreement concerning the rate of transformation of profits into wage increases, however, would be still too tenuous from the workers' point of view because it leaves open the question whether capitalists will save and invest enough to make wage increases at all possible. The perennial complaint of working-class movements is that capitalists are too lazy or too inefficient to be entrusted with control over investment. Already in 1910, a French socialist noted the 'timidity', the 'uncertainty', the 'lack of initiative' of capitalists. 'We ask the French employers', he continued, 'to resemble the American employer class...We want a busy, active, humming country, a veritable beehive always awake. In that way our own force will be increased' (Griffuelhes, 1910:331). And again, in 1975, Chiaramonte complained in an official report to the Central Committee of the Italian Communist Party (P.C.I.)

about 'a disconcerting lack of ideas on the economic and industrial future of the country and on the productive prospects for their [capitalists'] own industries. They continue to cling to productive, technical, and organizational policies adopted several dozen years ago...' (Chiaramonte, 1975:31).

Investment cannot be left to the control of capitalists: this is the second condition of a full-fledged compromise. While in the early stages of the development of capital–labour relations the conflict focused narrowly on the right to struggle for wage increases, the essential feature of the social democratic, Keynesian compromise has been the attention of working-class organizations to the actual investments out of profits. Having announced the austerity policy, having repeated that the P.C.I. is 'not aiming at a worsening of the situation...or an aggravation of the crisis', Chiaramonte continued, 'this does not mean that we in any way think it would be sufficient to limit the workers' pay claims and demands for greater control over working conditions to automatically obtain an increase in investment and productive reconversion' (1975:34). What the P.C.I. demands in exchange for 'austerity' is control over investment. Or, as the 1973 Conference of the Irish Trade Union Confederation put it, 'all workers must be guaranteed that their wage restraint will lead to productive and beneficial investment and not towards even further increases in the personal incomes of the privileged section of society...' (cited in Jacobsen, 1980:268).

Given the uncertainty whether and how capitalists would invest profits, any class compromise must consist of the following elements: workers consent to profit as an institution, that is, they behave in such a manner as to make positive rates of profit possible; and capitalists commit themselves to some rate of transformation of profits into wage increases and some rate of investment out of profits.

Conditions of class compromise

Thus far we have only specified what a class compromise would look like if one was to be concluded. We can now proceed to the central question of this essay, namely, whether organized workers pursuing their material interests would opt for such a compromise or choose to struggle for a transformation of the system of production.

How would organized workers rationally make such a decision? Assume that workers seek to maximize the sum of wages they expect to obtain in some foreseeable future. Assume further that they discount the future on the basis of risk. Let W^* be the level of workers' welfare associated with a particular level of economic militancy and a particular rate of saving by capitalists, with the capital/output ratio and the level of uncertainty taken as given. Given this definition, workers will choose the level of economic militancy, r, that would maximize W^*, given the rate of saving by capitalists associated with this level of economic militancy. In other terms, workers will choose a level of militancy that constitutes a compromise if and only if this is the level that maximizes their welfare, given the expected response by capitalists.

The question then is what will be the response of capitalists to a particular level of workers' militancy. Capitalists can be expected to choose the rate of saving, s, that will maximize their own welfare given the level of militancy by workers. Assume that capitalists seek to maximize their own expected future consumption C^*, where $C(t) = (1-s)P(t)$ is the consumption by capitalists at time t. Capitalists will thus choose the rate of saving that maximizes C^*, given the expected response by workers.

Now, the outcome of the conflict between capitalists and workers will be a pair of values of r and s, (r^*, s^*), which are associated with such values of $W^*[r,s]$ and $C^*[s,r]$ that both workers and capitalists would be worse off if they chose any other value of the parameter they respectively control. Suppose, then, that if workers behave in a non-cooperative fashion, with $r \geqslant 1 + s/c$, and capitalists respond in a non-cooperative way, with $s \leqslant 0$, then workers obtain some amount $W^*[g,0]$ and capitalists some amount $C^*[0,g]$. Now, the question is whether both classes can improve their welfare by making some agreement in which $r < 1 + s/c$ and $s > 0$. If workers' welfare associated with the compromise solution is higher than their welfare associated with the conflict-oriented strategy then workers should rationally opt for class compromise, and r^*, s^* will be the terms of this compromise. Our problem, therefore, is to discover whether such a solution exists and whether the relation between r^* and s^* constitutes a compromise in the sense that $r^* < 1 + s^*/c$ for reasonable values of c.

Mathematical analysis, which I will not reproduce here, leads to the following conclusions (Przeworski and Wallerstein, 1982). There exist basically two types of situations depending upon the risk workers face as to whether an agreement will hold. If the risk is high that capitalists will not be able to deliver or will deliberately renege on their wage commitments, workers' welfare is the function of their economic militancy as shown in Figure 8.4. When workers face a fair amount of uncertainty – when the institutionalization of capital–labour relations is limited to the right to organize and the state remains in hostile hands – their strategy depends upon their current level of economic militancy. If workers are not highly militant to begin with, that is, if $r < r_m$, they are better off moving to a relatively low level of militancy, r^* equal to about 10 percent of current profits. Suppose that $r = r_1$.

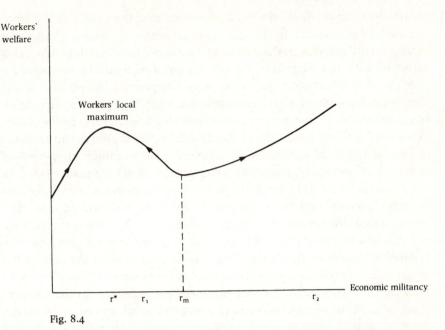

Fig. 8.4

Workers then face a choice of improving their conditions by obtaining from capitalists a commitment to a higher rate of savings in exchange for going down to r^* or of temporarily worsening their situation by moving toward r_m. Clearly, if workers could suddenly jump from their current level of militancy, r_1, to some level, r_2, at which $W^*[r_2]$ is larger than $W^*[r^*]$, they would do so. But increasing militancy requires mobilization, and mobilization is a slow and a costly process that requires organization as well as time and resources. Hence, the threat that workers would suddenly make any compromise conditional upon a high level of r is not very persuasive if workers are not militant at the moment.

If workers are already militant and they face high uncertainty, then they would travel along Luxemburg's road all the way to confiscating profits entirely. This is indeed the case in which organized workers would choose an anticapitalist strategy in pursuit of their material interests. When any compromise would be quite tenuous, once workers pass some threshold of militancy, they are best off making a claim to the means of production.

When the institutional conditions for a relatively certain compromise are developed, workers are better off, however, choosing a low level of militancy and capitalists a high level of saving. The level of workers' certainty that an agreement would hold once concluded depends upon the institutional form of capital–labour relations, the partisan control over the state, and the place of a particular economy in the international economic system. Corporatist arrangements are designed specifically to extend that certainty beyond a particular collective bargain or a particular electoral term: they constitute a form of commitment of the parties to some compromise independent of the short-term fluctuations of both economic and political conditions. In a highly corporatized society, in a system that is insulated from the effects of inflation by wide-spread escalators, in an economy well protected from the fluctuations of the international environment, workers have a rather high level of certainty, or conversely, capitalists' wage commitments are quite rigid.

If we think of workers' certainty in this fashion, it seems very likely that their risk has decreased during the course of the last one hundred years. The history of collective bargaining arrangements is quite different across countries, but at least in some Western European societies the trend is unmistakable. In Sweden, collective agreements began to be concluded at the turn of the century and by 1905 a significant proportion of workers was covered by them. These agreements were not binding, however, until a decision by the Supreme Court in 1916. In 1920 labour courts were established, and by 1926 parties could be sued in these courts for unfair bargaining. In 1938 a system of collective bargaining was centralized country-wide, and this system continues with some modifications to today. This evolution must have increased the binding power of agreements and hence workers' certainty.

This certainty is affected not only by collective-bargaining arrangements in the narrow sense but also by the general organization of conflicts in a society. Extensions of suffrage, reapportionment, public financing of elections, on one hand, and regulation of wages, prices, and profits by the government, on the other hand, all constitute reforms that reduce the uncertainty of distributional outcomes. Their effect is to reduce the power of capitalists to deviate from outcomes specified by a particular compromise, that is, to shift the a priori distribution of wages from one highly biased toward capital and highly indeterminate to one that sharply reduces the variance of this distribution around some norm. Since anecdotes are often more telling than statistics, here is an example of what is considered to be a deviation from class compromise: 'In one important respect a majority of delegates outdid the Eppler Commission. They voted to increase the top rate of income tax – now 53 percent – to 60 percent, while the Commission proposed the rate of 58 percent. This caused Professor Schiller [German Democratic Party minister of the economy at the time] to remark to his cabinet colleagues: "Obviously these people are trying to set quite a different sort of Republic from the one we have"' (*Manchester Guardian*, November 27, 1971, p. 1).

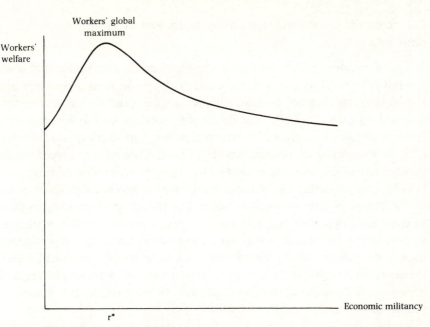

Fig. 8.5

Under such conditions, when workers can be reasonably certain that a compromise would hold, the best strategy of capitalists is to voluntarily offer high rates of saving and the best response of workers is to accept this offer in exchange for a low rate of transformation of profits into wages (see Figure 8.5). Moreover, workers are much better off as they gain certainty and become less militant than they would have been by becoming more militant under the conditions of high risk. Institutionalization of capital–labour relations, coupled with a low degree of economic militancy, is the best situation workers can obtain under capitalism.

This then is the essence of the social democratic compromise. Workers are better off moderating their wage demands in exchange for a higher rate of saving and a higher rate of certainty rather than intensifying their demands and facing a fall of investment. Economic militancy results in lower investment and hence in a deterioration of workers' welfare. Rational, self-interested workers therefore opt for a compromise that, in turn, demobilizes them even further, since, as Habermas observed, 'class compromise weakens the organizational capacity of the latently continuing classes' (1975 :69).

Class compromise, the transition to socialism, and the threat of disinvestment

The entire analysis presented thus far was based on the assumption that while capitalists respond to increased militancy by lowering their investment, the net rate of savings never becomes negative, that is, capitalists always restore the used-up capital stock. In fact, this is not a strategy feasible for capitalists. If the expected rate of profit is zero or negative, capitalists would be better off letting capital stock become depleted, that is, disinvesting. Indeed, under extreme conditions capitalists may find it preferable to disinvest at the highest possible rate, exporting liquid assets and even trying to liquidate fixed assets.

The threat of disinvestment, in turn, has the effect of pushing workers toward a compromise unless they can transform the entire system of economic and political organization almost instantaneously. 'If production does not continue', wrote Kautsky in 1925, 'the entire society will perish, the proletariat included' (1925:273). Let us see, therefore, what should be expected to happen as workers attempt to nationalize the means of production.

Suppose that workers follow a militant strategy, claiming the entire profits and at least a part of the capital stock. The crucial question now is one of political power, specifically, the power to socialize the means of production, abolish profits as a form of withholding from current consumption, and to organize a system in which all persons *qua* citizens could participate in deciding the volume and the direction of investment. At this moment the road sharply bifurcates. If economic militancy is not accompanied by a transformation of economic relations, then capitalists disinvest, an economic crisis emerges almost instantaneously, and workers must be sharply worse off. Moreover, economic militancy not backed by political power opens the threat of political reaction. Varga's warning of 1927 must be remembered: 'If the working class creates conditions in which the profits of the capitalists become impossible but at the same time the bourgeoisie is not defeated politically and the doctrine of the proletariat has not been established, the bourgeoisie, by means of implacable terror, crushes the working class in order to maintain the economic basis of the capitalist system and make possible the exploitation of labour' (cited in Pirker, 1976). Hence a militant pursuit of economic interests is not sufficient to pass smoothly to socialism. Indeed, economic militancy must result in an economic crisis that will leave workers worse off for some time.

Suppose instead that socialist parties win an overwhelming mandate in an election to legislate a society into socialism and that they follow the recipe of Lange, nationalizing a large part of the means of production 'in one stroke' (1964 :125). Both Kautsky and Lange emphasized that nationalization of the means of production must occur without unleashing an economic crisis, and they both thought that this could be accomplished by creating guarantees for those firms that would not be nationalized and by nationalizing the rest 'resolutely' and 'at maximum speed'. Yet Lange himself observed that financial panic would occur even before the election, that is, before the socialist government could nationalize anything. As an Italian industrialist put in on the eve of the elections of 1976, 'we should have stayed and fought but our money is already in Switzerland'. Hence, some disinvestment cannot be avoided, even if a part of the industry is already public. The question is only how much.

Transformation of the relations of production must be accompanied by an economic crisis. While Lenin thought that 'any cook can be taught how to administer a socialist society', in the aftermath of the council movement capitalist production became reorganized in such a manner that immediate producers as a class – and not only as individuals, à la Braverman – lost the capacity to run the system of production on their own. The working class as Marx saw it was characterized not only by its exploitation but at the same time by its capacity to organize, at the social scale, the socialist system of production (Mandel, 1971 :23). But if this was ever true, it is certainly not possible now for the immediate producers to instantaneously assume control over the process of societal production. Nationalization of industries, distribution of land, centralization of credit, and other economic transformations require an organizational and administrative capacity that cannot be acquired overnight. There are no blueprints and experience is limited. Learning by trial and error is inevitable. This is true even when the transformation consists merely of 'capitalist socialization', a replacement of individual capitalists by the state.[5] The transformation of social relations beyond those of property, a 'socialist socialization', is a task for at least a generation. And the dilemma involved in this period is precisely one between continuing the transformation of social relations and continuing the improvement of the conditions of material life, between 'high rate of capitalist growth or low rate of socialist growth', to use the formulation of Chang Chun-Chiao (cited in Tang Tsou, 1977).

Unless, therefore, a dictatorship is established over the proletariat, unless one shares Lenin's unfortunate dictum that 'industry is necessary, democracy is not' (1965, vol. 32 :37), workers will discover that socialist transformation is a costly project for them. Under democratic conditions – and today one

[5] For concepts of 'capitalist' and 'socialist' socialization see Korsch (1975).

cannot envisage any other ones – the support for socialist transformation is likely to be eroded if this support is sought in terms of economic demands and economic promises. One cannot continue to maintain that 'the socioeconomic revolution [will] take place simultaneously with an uninterrupted economic expansion' as did Allende in describing the political model of his government (cited in de Vylder, 1976 :53). The transition to socialism will not begin with 'une augmentation substantielle des salaires et traitement' – the promise of point I.1.1 of French Common Program of the Left of 1972. The rationale for socialism cannot be sought in an immediate improvement of economic conditions. The material interests of workers under capitalism do not lead them to opt for socialism because the process of transition must involve a deterioration of the material conditions of workers.

The threat of disinvestment, and of the resulting economic crisis, is not limited, however, to those rare moments when socialist parties stand at the threshold of power. This threat is permanent: it is a structural feature of the capitalist organization of society. Since profits are private, the decisions of individual firms concerning the volume and the direction of investment condition the actions of all groups and institutions of society, including the state. The state that intervenes in the economy depends upon capitalists for its fiscal resources, for information, for the capacity to elaborate policies, for the capacity to maintain incomes and provide social services, and so on. Moreover, electoral support for any particular government depends upon actions of capitalists. People do not vote exclusively for the public good when they vote for a party: they vote against the incumbent government when their personal income falls or unemployment increases (Kramer, 1971; Stigler, 1973). Hence any party is dependent upon private capital even for its electoral survival in office. Any government in a capitalist society is dependent upon capital. The nature of the political forces that come to office as a result of elections does not affect this dependence, for it is structural, a characteristic of the system and not of the occupants of governmental positions, the winners of elections. Being 'in power' gives little power; parties representing workers are subject to the same structural dependence as any other party.

The social democratic compromise with private capital is thus an expression of the very structure of capitalist society. As the foremost Swedish architect of the social democratic project put it, 'because Social Democracy works for a more equal and more just distribution of property and incomes, it must never forget that one must produce before one has something to distribute' (Ernst Wigforss, cited in Tilton, 1979 :516), and as long as the process of accumulation is private this means that profitability must be protected. The policies pursued by the state in capitalist countries – the policies designed to strengthen and to invigorate the capitalist system of production – are not an expression of some mysterious 'functions' of an autonomous state facing the threat of a revolutionary working class. They are a reflection of a compromise: they express the interests of a class coalition that includes important segments of the working class. These policies tend to reproduce capitalist relations because crises of capitalism are not in the interest of workers, who bear their costs, and because the socialist alternative is a costly one even when capitalists behave simply as profit-motivated, rational individuals. A vigorously developing capitalism in which workers can reasonably expect to benefit from past exploitation is the second best for workers as well as for capitalists. The struggle for the improvement of material conditions under capitalism is precisely that. It is not a struggle for socialism.

Material needs, radical needs, and the transition to socialism

A transition to socialism is unlikely when socialism is treated merely as a superior instrument for satisfying material needs. This assertion can also be formulated differently: transition to a socialism that would be merely a superior instrument for satisfying material needs is not possible under democratic conditions. Under what conditions and to what kind of socialism is transition possible?

I am persuaded that the only honest answer we can give at this moment is that we do not know. Afraid to dream up utopias, pressured by the poverty, repression, and injustice of everyday life, we tend to stake our fortunes on the worsening of each crisis, as if the crises of capitalism would of themselves lead to socialism. Every time capitalism enters a crisis – and it does so often – we claim that it has arrived at the limit of its potential. Every time we are surprised when it rises reformed and healthy from the debris of human suffering, and all we can do is claim that once again the workers' 'true' interests were betrayed by the leaders who sought to protect them from this suffering. Every time a new conflict appears we discover a new mortal contradiction – economic, racial, sexist, ecological, or what not. And we continue to live under capitalism.

All I can do is to sketch, without originality, mainly as a reminder, one way of looking for an answer. With Heller (1974), I will seek what she terms the 'radical needs' in the belief that any answer must satisfy the following requirements. One, it must identify a human need that is shared across class divisions of the capitalist society, that is being generated by capitalism and can be satisfied by the material conditions developed under capitalism, and yet a need that cannot be satisfied under capitalism. Two, the satisfaction of this need must be both a necessary and a sufficient condition for socialism.

Material needs will not do, for they can indeed be satisfied under capitalism. Moreover, their satisfaction is not sufficient for socialism; neither the Soviet dream project of 'council power plus electricity', nor the Social Democratic elusive goal of full employment plus equality, brings us closer to the constitution of a socialist society.

Instead of going on a systematic search for the likely candidates, I will posit immediately that the conditions stated above are satisfied by the need for free time. By free time I mean the time during which anyone is free from labour without any relation whatsoever between this freedom and the capacity to satisfy material needs. Free time is simultaneously the freedom from toil and the freedom from scarcity; it means freedom. Since the issue is important, it will not hurt to be pedantic. I will show below that while the capacity for satisfying this need is generated under capitalism, this need cannot be satisfied unless capitalism is abolished, and that the freedom from toil and scarcity is a necessary and a sufficient condition for socialism. Only then will I examine whether this need is generated under capitalism.

A society in which people are free from labour cannot be a capitalist society. In order to demonstrate the validity of this assertion, it is sufficient to show either that a society free from labour cannot be based on private profit or that, even if such a structure were possible, a capitalist society could never arrive at it. I will use only the second argument.

With Marx, imagine first a society where labour in which a human being does what a machine could do has ceased. All processes of production, maintenance, and distribution are performed by machines unassisted by direct labour. Oil is searched for by sensitive robots, which upon finding it instruct other machines to install self-operating wells and lay pipes to various other machines, some of which transform oil into thread, mix it with automatically grown and picked cotton, and produce neatly packed shirts. Once distributed, these shirts are washed by machines, dried, folded, and reposited in their proper place. Machines are produced by machines according to instructions of meta-machines, which are programmed to produce a basket of goods while minimizing physical resources. Labour time necessary to produce these goods (including machines and meta-machines) is zero. Some human activities ('indirect labour') eventually enter this production process, but they need not occupy us at the moment.

Second, suppose that this process operates in such a way that the output (measured as a vector of physical quantities) can always be strictly larger than it was previously.

Third, all individuals, regardless of particular characteristics, obtain what they need.

Now, the question is whether these three features – automation, accumulation, and independence of need satisfaction from labour – can be jointly generated by a society based on private profit.

Capitalists choose techniques of production that maximize output and minimize cost, whether the cost is machines or living labour. It is a characteristic of capitalism that machines and labour power have a common measure and, albeit not without rigidities, are mutually substitutable. Since under normal circumstances, particularly under wage pressure, it is rational for capitalists to increase productivity per unit of labour rather than increase employment, the general trend is to 'deepen' capital and to reduce dependence upon living labour. As a result, the proportion of the total available labour power that is used as labour falls over time. This does not necessarily imply a secular growth of unemployment as defined for compensation purposes, since labour power freed from the wage relation assumes various forms. Yet under capitalism the opportunity to satisfy material needs ('income') is closely related to employment. The unemployed, partially employed, the aged, and students are typically much worse off materially than those fully employed. Hence under capitalism liberation of labour power becomes unemployment, and as such it constitutes one of the major social problems. In fact, the struggle for 'full employment' is one of the central goals of working-class organizations, to the point that socialism becomes defined as a system that would guarantee everyone a chance to become what used to be called a 'wage slave'. It appears as if the socialist goal of capitalist accumulation would be to find such techniques of production that maximize output by maximizing labour.

Capitalism is seen as an obstacle to this goal, which it is, since as productivity drives wages high, capitalists search for production techniques that use relatively less labour. Government policies designed to bring about full employment are unfeasible for this reason: unemployment is necessary to regulate wages and protect profits.

But if capitalists continue to gradually substitute capital for labour, would it not be true that increasingly more labour time would be liberated and the need for free time would be satisfied under capitalism? Free time is increasingly abundant under capitalism – this much seems to be true. But this is the freedom to sleep under bridges: this freedom is not accompanied by a guaranteed satisfaction of material needs. If time were to be freed under capitalism, it would have to be freed in such a manner that material well-being would be independent of labour. If the capitalist 'double freedom' is to become one, then the freedom not to labour must be simultaneously the freedom to live as well as if one did. Let us thus see what would happen under capitalism if the relation between employment and income disappeared.

Suppose, not at all unreasonably, that workers succeed in making the state intervene in the economy in such a manner that each unit of labour power that is liberated obtains a transfer equal to the wage rates paid for those units that continue to be expended as labour. Note that this case also presupposes some conditions about techniques of production: specifically, it assumes that those techniques are chosen that generate a larger output with less labour. These are the kinds of production techniques that would be necessary to liberate labour power from wage relations without universalizing the status of capitalist unemployment to a socialist virtue. We have seen that capitalists choose these techniques when wages are high and the incomes of people not participating in production are low. But if capitalists were forced to pay for all the labour power not employed as labour they would rush to provide full employment, since labour would then be a constant cost, and maximization of profit would require minimizing the use of machines. If Volkswagen continues to pay compensation for unused labour power, it will eventually return to techniques under which this labour would be marginally productive. The effect of a 'minimal income allowance' or a 'negative income tax' would be the same unless the amounts are so pitiful that they do not cover the costs of training the labour power.

Hence we arrive at the following dilemma: if wage-earners push for full employment, production becomes more capital intensive; if wage-earners push toward liberation of labour power, production becomes more labour intensive. This response is impersonal: it is a response dictated by the logic of the system, not by the intentions of workers, capitalists, or the state.

The dilemma implies that capitalism generates the capacity for liberation of labour power while it cannot provide it. This capacity clearly depends upon the feasibility of finding techniques of production that would satisfy the conditions of a 'socialist socialization' of the means of production, that is, techniques that would increase output while requiring less labour. Such a possibility may be limited. Yet it is clear that techniques of production are not 'given'. They become available as the 'existing' techniques among which capitalists choose because a society, a capitalist society, seeks the particular techniques necessary for liberating labour power: we all know how many people would have been working in the banks today had computers not been invented and introduced. I.B.M. is right: 'Machines should work, people should think.' Yet under capitalism the liberating potential cannot be realized, since the introduction of such techniques is resisted by workers struggling against unemployment and since capitalists have the option of seeking labour intensive techniques when they are forced to pay for liberated labour power.

Socialist accumulation can be accomplished only when it becomes a goal of a society of associated producers. Such a process of accumulation must be based on two principles. First, the forces of production must be organized so as to generate a capacity for an almost instantaneous satisfaction of material needs of everyone while reducing direct labour to a historically possible minimum. Second, besides a minimum of mutual claims no other institutions should exist. Scarcity, labour, and socially organized repression must be abolished. Free time is necessary and sufficient for socialism because it constitutes basic freedom – from want, labour, and socially induced constraint.

Without going into details, let us see what free time implies. First, note that several problems of capitalism become simply irrelevant. 'Unemployment' is no longer the fate of free labour power. Conditions of work lose their importance as work under such conditions disappears. Equality ceases to be a meaningful term: it is an issue only in an unfree society. Freedom from scarcity and labour means that needs become qualitatively heterogeneous, and their satisfaction no longer reducible to a single dimension. Under socialism those people are rich who have rich needs (Heller, 1974). Even democracy is no longer problematic: democratic participation in the making of binding decisions loses its urgency when few decisions made by anyone are binding upon others. A democratic family is a family where all members are equal; a socialist family is one in which they are free. The problem is no longer one of extending democracy from the political to the social realm – the quintessence of social democracy under capitalism – but of reducing mutual constraint. Hence, of the needs and problems of capitalism little if anything remains. 'Free time – which is both idle time and time for higher activity – has *naturally* transformed its possessor into a different subject' (Marx, 1973:712).

Time free from labour is free. While certain ways of dividing activities may emerge as a result of freely formulated choices, this division is no longer an institution. Choices are not only freely made: they are freely formulated. When direct labour is not necessary, places-to-be-occupied in the division of labour no longer exist. We are no longer born, as Sartre put it, in the image of our dead grandfather (1960:15). The choice is no longer 'what will I become', where the 'what' is prior and given as 'a pilot', 'a nurse', or 'a garbage collector'. The 'what' itself becomes the object of individual making; it is continually reinvented by each individual for him- or herself.

These choices may result in specialization of activities, as some people push the frontiers of molecular biology while others push those of tennis. Some people may like to teach others while other people may be captivated by watching trees grow. This freedom obviously poses the question upon which Carr reflected in the seclusion of his Oxford study: would labour (indirect, that is, scientific and direct to the extent to which it is still necessary) happen to be performed as a result of free choice? (1958: Chapter 3). I do not know; we are too far away to speculate.

Free time, from labour and scarcity, also implies that the society, to coin a horror, become 'defunctionalized'. A particular manner of organizing one activity would no longer be necessary for reproducing other activities. Socialist society, to follow Sartre again, would be organized without being institutionalized. 'The family' is no longer an institution: people organize cohabitation as and if they cohabitate. Since functions of the family are no longer given when labour is no longer necessary, sex, nurture, and maintenance need not be associated according to any prior pattern (Mitchell, 1966:40). Sexual repression loses its social basis (Marcuse, 1962).

Needs no longer assume the form of 'interests', that is, the limits of their satisfaction are no longer objectifications of human activity. Their dynamic is driven and restricted only by their internal structure. Objectification occurs if and only if it responds to a need for objectification: I paint or split genes because I like to see painting or the truth of hypotheses. No 'end of history' occurs here, as is sometimes supposed in the argument that Marx was inconsistent when he posited simultaneously that needs are dynamic and that scarcity can be abolished. We must think dialectically: scarcity is abolished because the capacity to satisfy material needs asymptotically converges to their dynamic path.[6] Whether material needs would continue to grow under socialism I again do not know. As long as the satisfaction of needs is externally constrained, we cannot tell what human needs are.

Speaking of the Paris Commune, Marx emphasized that the working class has no ready-made ideals to realize, it has only to set itself free (in McLellan, 1977:545). This statement should not be taken as an injunction against utopian fantasies and even less as one against utopian analyses. All it asserts is that we cannot tell today what a socialist society would be like precisely because we do not know what human beings would want and what they

[6] Differential calculus is only an application of the dialectical method to mathematics – at least this is what Engels said somewhere in *The Anti-Duhring*.

would do if they were free. Socialism is not yet another social order, it is the end of all social orders: this statement should be taken seriously. 'Socialism' in singular is a contradiction in terms, for socialism means freedom and thus variety. It means freedom, not democracy, equality, creativity, or happiness. Socialism is not a new form of coercion to make everyone 'creative'.[7] A free individual may be uncreative; 'realization of human potential' may show that it would have been better if this potential remained dormant. Freedom may turn into universal misery; it may bring forth the truly human sources of repression, if indeed the finite nature of life underlies the aggressive and repressive forces (Brown, 1959). We do not know. Socialism is not a millennium, not a guarantee of happiness. It is a society free of alienation – if this term can still be restored to its meaning rather than be used as a generalized lament – a society in which objective conditions have been abolished, in which people are at every moment free, in which nothing is prior and given, in which life is not an instrument of survival, and things not instruments of power, in which all values are autonomous, in which the relation between a person and oneself is not mediated by things. Abolition of capitalism is a necessity not because such are the laws of history or because socialism is superior to it in any way, neither for reasons of Newton or Kant, but only because capitalism prevents us from becoming whatever we might become when we are free.

Having arrived at an unknown destination we must, unfortunately, return to the very first step. We have seen that capitalism develops the conditions for liberation but it cannot free. We have seen that freedom is necessary and sufficient for socialism. But does capitalism generate the need for freedom, a need that could underlie a political transition toward socialism?

This is not a question to be resolved theoretically. The only way to know is by practice, political practice in the broadest, Greek, sense of the word 'political'. Unity of theory and practice does not have a unique repository in political parties. The need for freedom is integral. Socialist democracy is not something to be found in parliaments, factories, or families: it is not simply a democratization of capitalist institutions. Freedom means de-institutional-ization; it means individual autonomy. Socialism may perhaps become possible, but only on the condition that the movement for socialism regains the integral scope that characterized several of its currents outside the dogmas of the Internationals, only on the condition that this movement ceases to make the socialist project conditional upon the continual improvement of material conditions of the working class. It may become possible when socialism once

[7] See Marcuse's splendid polemic against Fromm in the epilogue to *Eros and Civilization*, pp. 216–51.

again becomes a social movement and not solely an economic one, when it learns from the women's movement, when it reassimilates cultural issues.

The time is not near. There is every reason to expect that capitalism will continue to offer an opportunity to improve material conditions and that it will be defended by force where and when it does not, while conditions for socialism continue to rot. This is why dreams of a utopia cannot be a substitute for the struggle to make capitalism more efficient and more humane. Poverty and oppression are here, and they will not be alleviated by the possibility of a better future. The struggle for improving capitalism is as essential as ever before. But we should not confuse this struggle with the quest for socialism.

Part III
Method

9 'Rational choice' Marxism: some issues of method and substance

John Roemer

I

These comments address some issues of method and some issues of substantive research. With respect to method, I think Marxian economics has much to learn from neoclassical economics. With respect to the substantive research agenda, I think it is the other way around, in many instances.

I do not think there is a specific form of Marxist logic or explanation. Too often, obscurantism protects itself behind a yoga of special terms and privileged logic. The yoga of Marxism is 'dialectics'. Dialectical logic is based on several propositions which may have a certain inductive appeal, but are far from being rules of inference: that things turn into their opposites, and quantity turns into quality. In Marxian social science, dialectics is often used to justify a lazy kind of teleological reasoning. Developments occur because they must in order for history to be played out as it was intended. Thus state actions are explained by their effect of propping up existing regimes; capitalism foments racism and sexism among the working class because those ideologies weaken working-class power and strengthen capitalist power; schools miseducate working-class children in order to maintain bourgeois power. All of these consequences may be true, but they cannot be demonstrated by appealing to the 'historical roles' that must be played by the entities 'state', 'capitalist class', 'working class', 'capital'. For example, an honest Marxist must come to grips with the sceptical argument that competition will eliminate racist discriminatory wage differentials paid by profit-maximizing capitalists, in the usual competitive model; if divide-and-conquer is in fact a capitalist phenomenon, the argument for it must be a good deal subtler.[1] The existence of unemployment cannot be explained by the needs of capital to maintain a pliant working class with a large industrial reserve army, when in a competitive economy there is no agent who looks after the needs of capital.

[1] Roemer (1979) presents a model in which the rational strategy for individual capitalists is to pay discriminatory wages to black and white workers of equal skill levels.

That is: Marxian analysis requires micro-foundations. In broadest strokes, neoclassical and Marxist visions of the capitalist economy differ in that the former sees competition as bringing about an efficient allocation of resources, while the Marxist view has the same invisible hand floundering. Crisis, gross inefficiency, alienation, exploitation, and the like result. The neo-classical model of a competitive economy is not a bad place for Marxists to start their study of idealized capitalism. What Marxists must provide are explanations of *mechanisms*, at the micro level, for the phenomena they claim come about for teleological reasons. In a sense, the problem is parallel to the one bourgeois economics faces in providing micro-foundations for macroeconomics.

There is a more benign (and supportable) interpretation of dialectics. Jon Elster characterizes dialectics as the unintended consequence of rational action, more specifically, the sub-optimal allocations resulting from individual optimizing behaviour.[2] The standard example is the prisoner's dilemma; generally problems of public goods provision and situations characterized by externalities have the property that the invisible hand fails. Elster claims that Marx thought most processes under capitalism were characterized by this sort of problem, and hence the 'dialectical' result that optimizing agents end up in a sub-optimal solution. The famous theory of the falling rate of profit is a case in point: in an attempt to raise their individual profit rates, capitalists introduce technical change which in the new equilibrium lowers all their profit rates. Now Marx's specific reasoning in the theory was wrong, but it exemplifies dialectics as the failure of the invisible hand.

Thus both Marxism and neoclassical reasoning have their respective vices with respect to teleology. Neoclassical economics suffer from a panglossian attitude towards the consequences of individuals' uncoordinated behaviour; Marxism, while not teleological with respect to the consequences of market activity and individual behaviour, asserts that in the big picture, history pushes itself on to more glorious societies, as described in the theory of historical materialism.

In seeking to provide micro-foundations for behaviour which Marxists think are characteristic of capitalism, I think the tools *par excellence* are rational choice models: general equilibrium theory, game theory, and the arsenal of modelling techniques developed by neo-classical economics. This method is a great contribution in the intellectual history of the last century. Against this position the accusation can be levied that the tools were developed to apologize for the rising bourgeois order, to justify capitalism, and hence their use necessarily taints the results with a bourgeois pallor. This argument is a functionalist one of the type I criticized. If Marxists wish to

[2] Elster (1985a), Chapter 1.

impugn the intellectual unbiasedness of rational choice models, they must show precisely where the dirty work is being done. What hypotheses should be changed? In what sense is the characterization of rationality wrong? There are some trenchant criticisms of rational choice models. They are not coming predominantly from the Marxian quarter, but from the cognitive psychologists, who are showing that people do not behave rationally in a variety of ways.[3] When the new cognitive psychology is fully integrated into economic theory, a new microeconomics will emerge, which may look quite different from neoclassical economics.

With rational choice models, Marxian economics has made a good deal of progress in explaining mechanisms which do lie behind otherwise apparently teleological claims. Micro-foundations for the formation of class can be provided by using more or less standard general equilibrium models, and class can be related to exploitation in a way that is quite classical.[4] Mechanisms can be provided which explain why racist pay differentials persist although it is in the interest of any individual greedy capitalist to unravel them, contrary to what the Chicago school of *laissez-faire* would claim. With respect to explaining the persistence of unemployment in capitalist economies, there are a variety of models constructed at the micro level, though credit for them does not go mainly to researchers who call themselves Marxist. The study of technical change and the labour process has been a rich one; and the approach of postulating individual profit-maximizing agents has explained a good deal of the forms of technical change and labour control that might previously have been ascribed to the blind hand of capital.[5]

So I believe the programme of applying neoclassical tools to studying what might be called Marxian questions has been productive. There do remain, of course, some key differences in the use of these models. I would single out, for example, taking agents' preferences as data. Neoclassical economics, being primarily concerned with positive description, usually (though not always) postulates individual preferences as given. I think this postulate is more than methodological: it is ideological and flows from the dictum 'Cogito ergo sum.' Marxism reverses the Cartesian epigram, and asserts that people's preferences are in large part the consequence of social conditioning. This is an important consideration, *if* one intends to use rational choice models for describing welfare, for making normative judgments about the consequences of rational activity. Rational choice models should be used to develop a theory of endogenous preference formation. A materialist psychology is necessary

[3] See the collection of papers reprinted in Kahneman and Tversky (1982).
[4] A summary of this work is given in Roemer, 'New directions', in this volume.
[5] The books by Braverman (1974) and Edwards (1979) are prime examples of this approach.

to derive preferences from endowments and history. This is an example of a specifically Marxian question, which will eventually be solved using standard tools.

For by adopting its usual position of hegemonic individualism (that the individual is taken as given), neoclassical economics tends to confound two diads which should not be joined together: (1) preference versus choice, and (2) choice versus welfare. People do not always choose what they prefer – this distinction, which might seem nonsensical has been made compelling by the work of the psychologists;[6] and people do not always choose or prefer what leads to their welfare because their preferences have been formed under conditions of inadequate opportunity, have been warped, more generally, by capitalist society. Together, (1) and (2) imply that neoclassical welfare economics stands on very weak ground; they imply we cannot easily draw welfare conclusions from observing individual choice. It does not follow that social choice theory, an admirable piece of rational choice architecture, is useless: quite the contrary. It is a theory of how people might or might not be able to design consistent and democratic aggregations of their choices, which is a social engineering problem. It is not, however, *necessarily* a theory of the impossibility of achieving some kind of welfare optimum in a democratic setting. As an alternative to welfare economics, which bases its admittedly weak conclusions on the given preferences of individuals, Marxism proposes what appears to be a more normative concept of exploitation as a measure of the welfare of members of a society.

As to substantive agenda, Marxism makes two great contributions: its theory of the relationship between property rights, technical change, and class struggle (a positive theory), and its claim that capitalism suffers from unnecessary alienation and exploitation (a positive and normative claim). The first of these contributions is summed up in the various theses of historical materialism. The modern reconstruction of historical materialism is a theory of the determination of technical and institutional change.[7] Many gaps must be filled in, and to do the filling, I would call upon rational choice models. One big question is the formation of preferences of the historical actors – in particular, preferences which lead to collective action (class action) which is so important for the theory. A theory of ideology formation is needed.[8] Perhaps ideology is an institution which cuts transaction costs of various

---

[6] See Tversky (1980).

[7] See, for a summary of this approach, Cohen, 'Forces and relations of production', in this volume.

[8] North (1981) presents a theory of ideology. Roemer (1985b) presents a model in which ideology emerges as a rational strategy in a game. Schotter (1984) shows how ideology can also emerge strategically in a game situation.

kinds; or perhaps ideology should be conceived of as a set of satisficing rules which an agent adopts to limit his own feasible set. Another question is to decide precisely where class struggle should be fit into the general equilibrium model: does it determine preferences, or endowments, or is it a bargaining technique in a non-competitive model? There are other possibilities. While the question comes from historical materialism, the solution must be conventional. If class struggle is as important as Marxists say it is, and as I believe it is, there must be a way of putting it properly into an economic model. There is, now, a theory of class formation based on individuals who optimize with given preferences and endowments; the next step is the sociological one of proposing a theory for why members of the same class should overcome the collective action problem in the way they sometimes do, and what effect their concerted action can then have on the equilibrium – does it work by changing prices, endowments, preferences, production functions?

II

In this section I outline an agenda rational choice Marxism can set to answer two important questions to which I have referred which challenge its methodological premises. In rational choice Marxism:

(1) Where is there room for class struggle?
(2) Where is there room for the social formation of ideas, for the formation of the individual by society?

These questions arise as a challenge since the rational choice model assumes the maximization of utility subject to constraint. There are immediately two problems with understanding class struggle. First, class struggle is characterized as breaking constraints; second, class struggle, and collective action more generally, is usually thought to be irrational from the individual's point of view. So it would seem the rational choice paradigm cannot admit class struggle. I argue this is not the case; class struggle is ignored by neo-classical economics because of its emphasis on a particular solution concept, competitive equilibrium. With respect to the second question, it seems clear that the individual must first be defined, his preferences must exist before the analysis starts, for one to be able to use the rational choice method. Hence: where is there room for the social formation of the individual?

To answer these questions, consider a very general description of the historical process, a materialist description. There are two categories of interest. R_t is the full description of technology, institutions, and ownership relations at time t, the conglomeration of the classical Marxian productive forces and economic structure. The second category, P_t, is a list of all the people and their preferences at time t. These people, of course, own things (which are described in R_t), but it is useful to separate the subjective element which is in P from the objective element which is in R. Historical progress is the consequence of two processes, called the *solution process* and the *preference formation process*. At time t, there is constellation $\{R_t, P_t\}$ which gives rise through some solution process, to production and distribution of goods, invention, new institutions, and so on. These come into existence at the next time period, $(t+1)$. Thus we have a process

$$\{R_t, P_t\} \rightarrow R_{t+1}.$$

Neoclassical economics has studied one special case of this solution process: the competitive equilibrium solution, where each agent has negligible power, accepts all signals from the environment as unmalleable by him, and maximizes his utility (given in P_t) subject to the constraints he faces from his property endowment and the given institutions. This process gives rise to an equilibrium allocation which is described in R_{t+1}. But there are other solution processes which can be described.

The second important process is the social formation of preferences: members of a new generation are born each time period (let us say), and their preferences are formed by the state of the world into which they are born. The generation born at time t matures at time $(t+1)$, when it becomes the generation engaging in economic behaviour; its social formation is consequently from the environment R_t existing at t, and the preferences of its parents. This can be schematically represented as:

$$\{P_t, R_t\} \rightarrow P_{t+1}.$$

Very little work has been done to understand the preference formation process.

Thus individuals are formed by society, and these individuals react rationally to their environments to produce tomorrow's environment, which in turn produces individuals who think somewhat differently from before, and react in their environment to bring about yet a new equilibrium.

This is a reasonably general materialist history. It is more general than classical historical materialism, which contains many claims which may or may not follow from the above description – such as, that the social relations of production last only so long as they do not fetter the further development of the productive forces. To analyse that issue, one would have further to articulate R_t. The above model includes historical materialism as a special case.

This model also includes the neo-classical paradigm as a special case.

Neoclassical economics is characterized, in the language of this model, by two special assumptions. First, the solution process studied has been the competitive equilibrium process (until very recently); and second, more importantly, there is no preference formation process. P is taken as constant through time, a constant 'human nature'. There is a certain distribution of preferences in each generation which is essentially unchanged. What changes are the constraints people face, which bring about varying behaviour: but there has been a fundamental antagonism in neoclassical economics to thinking of P itself as formed by R.

If P is taken as constant, then P is seen as the prime mover in history. P sets in motion the sequence of R_t's, and hence our present world R_{1984} is a consequence of the exercise of an unmalleable human nature throughout the ages. Some Marxist interpretations make the opposite error, of underestimating the role of P. Thus, some Marxists say, the preference formation process is more correctly described as

$$R_t \rightarrow P_{t+1}$$

The preferences of this generation are almost wholly a product of their material conditions (or, as I have written above, of their material conditions last year). Were this so, one could eclipse the role of preferences entirely and describe history as a sequence $R_0 \rightarrow R_1 \rightarrow R_2 \rightarrow \ldots$ At each stage there is a micro-process of the formation of preferences; people interact with their environment and bring about a new environment. But we can drop the people and the preferences out of the picture, since they are caused by their environment, and we are left with the evolution of modes of production, with the preferences of agents playing only a passive role. This approach is associated with explaining the evolution of property forms and productive forces without reference to individual decision making. Perhaps with a good enough understanding of the preference formation process, one could indeed represent the evolution of $\{R_t\}$ in this way, with no reference to $\{P_t\}$; but one would miss the *explanation* for why history happened the way it did.

There are, therefore, two hyperbolic positions: the idealist position views history as derived from a constant P, and thinks of the mode of production R at a given time as a consequence only of the minds of people; and the vulgar materialist position thinks of the mode of production evolving independently of minds as preferences P_{t+1} are determined by R_t in the previous state.

Where is rational choice methodology to be used in understanding these two processes? I think in both of them. We have, as I have said, the one major example of a solution concept in the solution process

$$\{R_t, P_t\} \rightarrow R_{t+1}$$

given by neoclassical equilibrium theory. But there are other rational responses people might have to their environment, given their preferences P_t, than to act as price takers and environment takers. They might try to influence their environment, to bargain, they might not accept the terms of trade as given. In fact it is often rational not to do so. The classical case is of a monopolist, who does not take the price as given, but realizes he can change prices and make greater profits. This gives rise to another solution concept, monopolistic competition. Or, if we have monopolistic elements on both sides of the market, there is bilateral monopoly, or bargaining. Now class struggle can be viewed as a kind of bargaining. Class struggle occurs when many agents in the working class, for example, learn to organize and act as one unit, so they can effectively set up a bilateral monopoly against capital. Of course, the situation can be more complicated: there can be all kinds of factions, and so perhaps it is *n*-agent bargaining. The point is class struggle is a method of carrying out bargaining, and bargaining is as good a solution concept as competitive equilibrium – in fact, in many cases, it is much more appropriate, more rational. The question has still to be asked: what makes coalition formation possible? How can workers overcome their individual self-interest, overcome the free rider problem, and engage in class struggle? But I take the answer to this problem also to lie in rational choice analysis. One must understand, at the level of individual preferences, what causes a person to cast his lot with a class despite the possible penalties and costs, when his standing on the sidelines would not weaken the class struggle, and the internal gains to him would be no smaller. We do have some answers to this question, at the level of rational choice theory: for instance, that people derive pleasure from cooperating with others whom they feel are as exploited as they, if together they can win, and indeed, that they would derive less pleasure from 'letting history pass them by'. There is a bond from common oppression which makes people want to fight if they think others too will fight. Class struggle can emerge rationally as part of a solution process. Neoclassical economics has avoided the study of class struggle not because of its rational choice method, but because of its emphasis on the competitive equilibrium solution process, which is not always appropriate. Indeed, there has been an explosion of interest in game theory during the last decade, in which bargaining solution processes are studied in great detail.

I have little to say about the second process in the historical scheme, the preference formation process. There, too, rational choice models will be used to build a theory of the social formation of the individual. It seems studying the question of preference formation requires postulating some apparatus of meta-preferences: a person has a variety of preference profiles he can 'choose' to have, and given the information in his environment, including the constraints he faces, he 'chooses' an appropriate conception of welfare. There will be expectations upon a person by the rest of society, given the place he occupies in R_t, which will direct him to order his options in certain ways. A person born into the Rockefeller family will maximize his satisfaction by choosing to remain a capitalist, by and large. It is more accurate to say that culture chooses a person's preferences for him. But culture can be understood as ideology, and if there are rational foundations for ideology (as I mentioned earlier) then the process of endogenous preference formation can be seen as a rational choice. The social formation of the individual can be explained while at the same time requiring that society be understood as the consequence of many individuals' action.

III

With respect to what might be called welfare economics, Marxism highlights exploitation and also alienation. There has been much recent work on exploitation, and the modern concept looks considerably different from the classical one: for instance, exploitation need not be defined using the concept of labour value, an antiquated tool which does not hold up against modern standards of generality and rigour. Exploitation, rather, should be conceived of as an injustice in the distribution of income resulting from a distribution of endowments which is unjust.[9] To demonstrate the nature of that injustice, political philosophy must be called upon: what Marxian economics can do is work out the allocative consequences in terms of economic variables of an unjust distribution of property (which might include property of various kinds, alienable and inalienable). Here, I think, there is less ground for agreement between Marxists and non-Marxists than in the theory of historical materialism: for the underpinnings of the disagreement are not questions of positive history, but of philosophy concerning what constitutes a desirable or just society. The sharpest form of the political debate on this question is between Marxists and libertarians, on questions of self-ownership, inheritance, and various kinds of rights. It is not at all clear how analytical Marxists will differ from non-Marxist philosophers like Ronald Dworkin, John Rawls, and Amartya Sen, who may be more vigorous in their opposition to utilitarianism and welfarism than are certain Marxists.[10] I mention this simply to indicate

[9] See Roemer, 'Should Marxists be interested in exploitation?' in this volume.
[10] Rawls (1971), Dworkin (1981), Sen (1980) each present theories of justice as equality in which utility is not the concern. Welfarism, a term coined by Sen, is the position that social welfare should be taken to be measured by some function of the utilities of members of the society.

that the lines drawn between contemporary analytical Marxism and contemporary left–liberal political philosophy are fuzzy. This indicates there is a common core, yet to be elucidated.

The Marxist belief – and I call it that, rather than theorem – is that exploitation of important kinds can be overcome by a change in property relations, by socialism. The experience of existing socialism of the last 60 years has forced Marxists to be much more interested in electoral politics and markets under socialism than their counterparts were a generation ago. To what extent can markets be used to implement a regime in which alienation and exploitation are attenuated? Oscar Lange, the Polish Marxist who was perhaps the first economist of the twentieth century to embrace roughly the combination of neoclassical methodology and Marxist research agenda which I have outlined here, was optimistic. The question is very much open. Lange said that Marxist economics is the economics of capitalism, and bourgeois economics is the economics of socialism.

The Marxist ethical view of capitalism comes not from economic models, but from history. In that view all class societies are characterized by the expropriation of a surplus from a large class of direct producers by a small class of property holders. The bourgeois view of history is, in contrast, that each factor earns its appropriate return. Each view represents, I think, a *possible* world, and hence I think consistent models can be constructed to formalize the insights of each view. For that reason, it is not useful to criticize neoclassical economics for its possible inconsistency (which is what the so-called Cambridge controversy was about); the criticism must be, more fundamentally, of the view of history which neoclassical economics models and reenforces. By building axiomatic models, in particular, rational choice models, which represent the Marxian view of history, we do two things: first, we learn more about the mechanisms that may explain history, which is the purpose of any modelling exercise; and secondly, we show that a Marxian view of history is consistent and rigorous as well. If consistent models can be presented to capture two different historical world views, then one must choose between them on the basis of which better describes actual history. But if only one historical world view is studied in a rigorous and axiomatic fashion, there is no contest. In sum, I do not think models are the fountainhead of one's ethics; I think one's view of history implies the models one builds, and if the models are good, they will clarify the ethics whose root lies in the actual history.

IV

According to this outline I can distinguish rational choice Marxism from neoclassical economics in at least these ways. Marxism holds:

(1) a commitment to the malleability of human preferences, to the social formation of the individual;

(2) that the neo-classical theory of welfare economics is weak and misleading, because of the non-autonomous formation of preferences;

(3) a commitment, based on a certain reading of history, to the importance of collective action and power in solution processes; in particular, class power and class action, but more generally nationalist power and perhaps religious power. In competitive equilibrium theory, no one has any power;

(4) a belief in the injustice of capitalism, and the transiency of it, which flows from a historical world view, based on the evolution of forms of property.

What is lost with rational choice Marxism is, principally, teleology. One cannot assert that those things happen which are optimal for the preservation of the capitalist system; or, on the contrary, that the system will destroy itself. Perhaps these events may happen, but the mechanisms at the level of the preference formation and solution processes must be shown to bring them about. The heritage of Marxism, as an idea, is a set of powerful descriptive insights. These descriptions must not be assumed true, but rather shown to emerge as theorems in models whose postulates are elementary and compelling.

10 Further thoughts on Marxism, functionalism and game theory*

Jon Elster

In an earlier article, 'Marxism, functionalism and game theory'[1] I made the following claims. First, Marxist social science has suffered durably from its espousal of functional explanation. Secondly, it has perversely refused to adopt a conceptual tool that would appear to be tailor-made for many of its purposes, viz. game theory. In this essay I shall elaborate on these claims, adducing further examples and suggesting some further conceptual points. I first define and discuss the functionalist mode of explanation and the basic features of game-theoretic analysis. I then single out for discussion five problems that can be and have been discussed in either framework, to show that the game-theoretic one is in most cases superior. Needless to say, this does not mean that game theory can be successfully applied to all problems in Marxism. In particular, I shall argue that often a causal explanation is required.

I. The nature of functional explanation[2]

Functional explanation is a subvariety of the general class of consequence-explanations. These explain social phenomena in terms of their actual consequences, as opposed to explanation by causes (causal explanation) or by intended consequences (intentional explanation). The distinguishing feature of functional explanations is that the explanatory consequences are *beneficial* to someone or something. More specifically, they are usually said to be *optimal* in some respect, which makes for a more testable version of the theory.

An initial puzzle is how the explanans can follow the explanandum in time. It is resolved by pointing out that the explanandum must be a pattern of behaviour, not a one-shot event. We can then explain the pattern by pointing

---

* Many of the points that are made here, in a rather summary fashion, are further elaborated in Elster (1985a).
[1] Elster (1982b).
[2] For discussions of functional explanation in general and in Marxism, see Cohen (1978a), Chs. IX–X and van Parijs (1981).

out how behaviour at one point of time gives rise to consequences that have the effect of maintaining similar behaviour at a later time. I shall take for granted that whenever a functional explanation is proposed, the existence of some such feedback mechanism is assumed.[3] Another question, however, is whether the mechanism must be known for the explanation to be successful. I shall distinguish between four kinds of functionalism, which give different answers to this question.

First, there is the naive variety of functionalism, which tacitly assumes that pointing to beneficial consequences is sufficient for an explanation. This view neglects not only the possibility that the benefits might arise accidentally, but also the possibility that even if non-accidental they might still be non-explanatory. It might be the case, that is, that the explanandum and the benefits are joint effects of a third variable. This naive functionalism is the brand most prominent in Marxist and later Marxist, and will be my main concern here.

Secondly, it has been argued that we may have general knowledge about the kind of mechanism that is operating, even when we are unable to provide the details. This would be analogous to the role of the theory of natural selection in functional explanation in biology.[4] In my opinion this attempt fails because the analogy between social and biological phenomena breaks down at a crucial point. Both social and biological change can be conceived of as *adaptation to a moving target*. In societies, however, the environment to which institutions adapt themselves generally change so rapidly, relative to the speed of adaptation, that an equilibrium is rarely attained or even approximated.[5]

Thirdly, one may cite G. A. Cohen's argument that a functional explanation can be backed by a *consequence law*, just in the way a causal explanation is backed by a causal law.[6] A consequence law is a statement to the effect that whenever the explanandum would tend to produce the explanans, the explanandum is in fact observed. An example could be the statement that social mobility always occurs when the society is such that social mobility would enhance prosperity. If well-established, this law would allow us to

---

[3] For objections to this view, see Cohen (1982a). This article develops the idea, already present in Cohen (1978a), that functional explanation rests on the *propensity* of the explanandum to bring about the consequence. Against this I tend to agree with Ruben (1980).

[4] In one version of this argument, the selection analogy is taken very literally, by assuming that social organizations (such as firms) adapt and evolve by the mechanism of differential survival. For a vigorous rebuttal, see Nelson and Winter (1982). Another version is proposed in Stinchcombe (1974), critically discussed in Elster (1983), pp. 61ff.

[5] Observe the following feature of this adaptation. Since the process is not guided by intentional choice, the moving target cannot be reached by aiming ahead of the place where it will be when the 'arrow of adaptation' reaches it. Instead, the process of adaptation is at all times constrained to move in the direction of the current position of the target.

[6] Cohen (1978a, 1982a).

explain a given case of social mobility by its impact on prosperity, even in the absence of any knowledge about the underlying feedback mechanism.

I have discussed this argument in various places,[7] but without fully doing justice to the subtleties involved. As I presently see the proposal, it is vulnerable to strong pragmatic objections, but on the level of principle it is hard to fault it. Yet in one respect, to be spelled out below, functional explanation remains a second-best mode of analysis, compared to causal explanation.

The pragmatic objections include the following. (i) In many important cases, including those discussed by Cohen in his book, we have far too few instances to sustain a generalization. In particular, this is true for the explanation of the relations of production in terms of their beneficial impact on the productive forces. The rise of capitalism, for example, would seem to be the only instance of the consequence law explaining it. (ii) It is in any case a much better research strategy to search for a mechanism than to search for more confirming instances. (iii) While the idea of 'beneficial' consequences is too vague, that of 'optimal' consequences may be too demanding, in that it may be very difficult to ascertain whether a given pattern is in fact optimal. How, for example, could one determine when the capitalist relations first became optimal for the further development of the productive forces and when they will cease to be optimal?

In principle, however, these objections could be overcome. In that case functional explanation would be almost on a par with causal explanation as regards explanatory power. To see this, some preliminary remarks on the problem of scientific explanation are needed. Generally speaking, an explanation in terms of causal laws or consequence laws is always open to two objections. First, the basis of the law may be correlation, not a genuine explanatory connection.[8] Secondly, even if the law is genuinely explanatory,

---

[7] Elster (1980, 1981, 1983).

[8] The distinction between correlation and causation is familiar. The analogous distinction between (non-explanatory) correlation and functional explanation may be brought out using an example inspired by Veyne (1976). He argues that the subjects in Classical Antiquity accepted their state of submission because of a spontaneous tendency to 'dissonance reduction', not because of manipulation on the part of the rulers. The submission, to be sure, was useful to the rulers, but far from indispensable. If necessary they could have upheld their rule by force. The fact remains, however, that it was useful; moreover, it took place in precisely those circumstances where it would be useful, viz. those characterized by severe social inequality. A moderate degree of inequality would not induce resignation – but nor would it lead to revolt. This allows us to formulate a consequence law to the effect that 'Whenever resignation would be useful to the rulers, resignation occurs', and yet we are not entitled to explain the resignation by these consequences, since there is a 'third variable' – severe social inequality – which explains both the tendency to resignation and the benefits it brought to the rulers.

it may, in any given case, be preempted by some other mechanism.[9] In the case of causal explanation, the best way to reduce the impact of these objections is by shortening the time lag between explanans and explanandum, i.e. by approaching the ideal of a continuous causal chain.[10] I used to think that in the case of functional explanation, the objections could be met only by producing the actual feedback mechanism. In that case, we would have a genuine difference between causal and functional explanation. To improve a causal explanation, we produce another causal explanation. To improve a functional explanation, we must produce a causal explanation.

The error in this view can be brought out by means of an example. Let A stand for upwards social mobility, B for the prosperity of the regime, C for the legitimacy of the regime, D for the desire for upwards social mobility and E for good mobility opportunities. Let us assume, moreover, that these variables are related as follows:

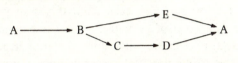

The story, in words, is the following. Upwards social mobility has a favourable effect on the prosperity of the regime, because the 'best brains'[11] of the exploited class move into the exploiting class. The prosperity lends legitimacy to the regime, inducing desires for individual improvement rather than for collective action or revolutionary upheaval. The prosperity, moreover, also creates opportunities for upwards mobility. Desire and opportunity then lead to actual social mobility, closing the feedback loop.

Imagine, now, that only a small part of this story is known. Specifically, imagine that all our knowledge is embodied in the consequence law 'If (if A, then B), then A.' Or: whenever upwards social mobility would enhance the prosperity of the regime, it is actually observed. This consequence law could then be used to explain actual social mobility in a given society, by pointing to the beneficial effect on prosperity. To be sure, however, that we are not dealing with correlation or preemption, we might want to improve the

---

[9] This objection turns upon the distinction between necessitation and explanation. The same example from Veyne serves to show how it applies to functional explanation. Let us assume (contrary to what I believe to be the case) that the rulers could have manipulated the subjects into believing that their rule was just or at least inevitable, and that they did so whenever the subjects thought differently. On this assumption we would be justified in asserting the consequence law stated in the preceding note. Yet in any given case the mechanism underlying the law might be preempted by the spontaneous formation of the same belief, due to dissonance reduction. The consequence law would necessitate this belief, but not always explain its occurrence in any given case.

[10] Elster (1983), p. 29.   [11] Marx (1894), p. 600.

explanation. This might be done by adding to the above consequence law the statements '*B* causes *C* and *E*' and 'If (if *A*, then *C* and *E*), then *A*.' This would be an improved functional explanation. It still does not give the full feedback story, since the link that *C* causes *A* via *D* is not included. This disproves the contention that a functional explanation can only be improved by producing a causal explanation. The functional explanation can be improved and still remain functional if we extend the causal chain *almost* the whole way back to the explanandum. Yet one difference between causal and functional explanation also follows. The limiting case of an improved functional explanation is a causal explanation – if the chain of consequences is extended the whole way back to the explanandum. In this sense functional explanation is, as I said, second-best.

The fourth and final answer to the question we have been discussing is that for a functional explanation to be valid we must indeed provide the full feedback loop. In the light of what has just been said, this response is excessively purist, at least on the level of principle. I remain convinced, however, that for practical purposes it is the only viable research strategy. In any case, it is vastly preferable to the first, naive brand of functionalism. I am not really concerned in this essay with the sophisticated defences of functionalism that have been proposed in recent years, but with the form of Marxist functionalism that has been historically important and that remains central in many quarters.

Some additional remarks on the functionalism of Marx will prove useful later on. First, in Marx and Marxism there is a close link between functional explanation and various other methodological views, such as a speculative philosophy of history, a certain mode of dialectical deduction and the insistence on some form of methodological holism. 'Capital' and 'Humanity' both appear as collective subjects that are somehow prior in the explanatory order to their individual components. In the secular theodicy that Hegel constructed and that Marx took over with some modifications, history is conceived as a process with a given goal, whose realization is somehow guaranteed independently of any knowledge of the individual actions by which it is to be brought about. Secondly, observe that the definition of functional explanation allows for a great deal of juggling with the time perspective, since the chain of consequences can be broken off at one's convenience. It would be too much to say that anything can be shown to work for the benefit of anything by suitable manipulation of the time perspective, but there is no doubt that there is a great deal of leeway, which has led to much laxity in Marxist explanation. Finally, we may note that the objective function – i.e. the maximand which enters into the explanation – is not uniquely determined in Marxism. Sometimes we find that the explanatory benefits accrue to the ruling class, at other times to society in general. The functional explanation of the relations of production, for instance, has the rate of technical change as the maximand – not, as one might expect, the rate of surplus extraction.[12] By contrast, class-specific benefits are central in the explanation of state policies and, more generally, of the politico-ideological superstructure. This ambiguity creates an additional source of laxity in the Marxist explanations.

II. The nature of game-theoretic analysis[13]

Game theory is a branch of decision theory or rational choice theory. It is a tool, in fact *the* tool, for capturing three sets of inter-dependencies that pervade social life. First, the reward of each depends on the reward of all, by altruism, envy, a desire for equality and similar motivations. Next, the reward of each depends on the choice of all, through general social causality. And finally, the choice of each depends on (the anticipation of) the choice of all. The last feature is the most puzzling one, and for centuries baffled those who tried to understand how people can adjust their behaviour to one another without getting into an infinite regress. Game theory short-circuits the regress by the notion of an equilibrium point, i.e. a set of choices that are best-replies to each other. This in turn allows us to define a concept of non-cooperative solution to a game, as the equilibrium point that will emerge through implicit coordination by rational agents. Not all games have solutions in this sense. In particular, some games have several equilibria none of which has the logical or psychological salience that will single it out as the solution. It is also possible to define various solution concepts for cooperative games, in which the agents can explicitly agree to coordinate their choices. Cooperative games, however, are logically secondary to non-cooperative games. This is not an assertion about the motivation of the agents, only a restatement of the principle of methodological individualism.[14]

The following aspects of game theory will prove important later. First, it rests on a symmetry assumption that the agents are equally rational, and moreover that they know each other to be equally rational.[15] This excludes

[12] For this tension, see North (1981).
[13] For an introduction to game theory, see Luce and Raiffa (1957). A discussion of some philosophical problems in rationality theory is in Elster (1984b).
[14] For an assertion of the priority of community, see Taylor (1971).
[15] Harsanyi (1977), Ch. 6.

bluff, manipulation and similar strategies that only make sense if some agents are less rational than others.[16] Since these are important social phenomena, the assumption points to a limitation of the theory. To some extent it may be defended on prudential grounds: even if one may suspect that some other agents are somewhat irrational, it may be more prudent to act on the assumption that they are essentially similar to oneself.[17]

Another point is that games have very different information requirements. Some games are such that the agents can make their choices without anticipating the choice of others. All they need to know is how choices influence outcomes. The Prisoner's Dilemma is one example in this class of degenerate games, in which the interdependence of choices is absent.[18] Other games are such that one must anticipate what others will do before one makes one's own decision. This requires knowledge about the motivation and the information that characterize the other players. An example is the Assurance Game, in which the agents have a conditional preference for cooperation – conditional, that is, on the expected cooperation of others.[19] Frequently, the interdependence of choices in this game is generated by the interdependence of rewards (see section IV below).

Finally, the role of time in game theory should be stressed. Some social interactions are one-shot events, but often the agents know that they also will have to interact in the future. This can make for important differences in the choices, because selfish behaviour that might be rational in a one-shot interaction might not be rational in the longer term, since others might retaliate.[20] Moreover, present choices have implications for future benefits in a direct way, over and above their impact on future choices. The choice today of consumption rather than investment will lead to less consumption later on.

Marxists have tended to be critical of rational choice theory, partly for good reasons, partly for less good. Among the less good are the objection to the subjective character of rational-choice explanation, as opposed to the

---

[16] True, game theory allows bluff in the form of a choice of strategy 'at random', i.e. according to an optimally chosen probability distribution. A rational opponent, however, should be able to determine the distribution from which one is choosing; hence there is no *surprise* as in cases of genuine bluff.

[17] In actual practice many strategic interactions are governed by these two principles. (i) Never hope for a gain that depends on the opponent being less rational than you are. (ii) Never hope for a gain that depends on the opponent being as rational as you are. These maxims can be subsumed under a more general one: always assume that the worst which can happen, will happen. Or again: make your choice in terms of the opponent's capabilities, not his intentions. These maxims, while suitable for military decision-making, are not equally self-evident in the kind of cases discussed in sections III and IV, since here the costs of misjudging intentions are in general much smaller.

[18] Rapoport and Chammah (1965).   [19] Sen (1967).

[20] Axelrod (1984) and Taylor (1976) contain extensive discussions.

materialist explanations favoured by Marxism; the view that the methodo-logical individualism of the theory must go together with an assumption of universal selfishness, and the idea that choice matters little compared to the structural constraints facing the agents. Three more serious objections – of which the first is the one most frequently made by Marxists – are the following.

First, rational choice theory takes the desires and preferences of the agents as given, whereas Marxists want to explain them. One could in fact add a fourth kind of interdependency to the ones mentioned above: the preferences of each depend on the actions of all.[21] Although neither Marxism nor any other social theory has gone very far towards a theory of endogenous preference formation, this is clearly a very important problem.[22] Nevertheless, here as in other cases, the desirability of reduction to deeper levels is not a reason for abstaining from analysis at a less fundamental level. To explain behaviour in terms of the desires of the agents is an important task even if the desires themselves are left unexplained.

Secondly, rational-choice models of behaviour do not yield uniquely determined predictions in all cases.[23] As mentioned earlier, some games do not have non-cooperative solutions.[24] Also, in situations of uncertainty there may be no rational basis for making a choice between the alternatives. More generally, one comes up against the difficulty that there is no way of determining the optimal amount of information that one ought to gather before deciding. The marginal utility of information is not in general a known quantity. Because of these and similar difficulties, rational-choice explanation needs in general a supplement of causal explanation.

Thirdly, people do not always behave rationally. The assumption that they do, is largely a methodological one. One cannot even start to make sense of

---

[21] Values, that is, can be seen as part of the outcome of action, in addition to being a determinant of action. Rational agents might want to take account of this possibility.

[22] Economic theory has made some progress in explaining how the values of one individual change endogenously as the result of his previous choices (Elster, 1984, Ch. II. 6), but to my knowledge there has been virtually no discussion of how the aggregate outcome of many individual actions could include a change of preference in the agents. Sociologists tend to assume that the outcome includes the very same values that went into the choices, but beyond the vague notion of 'social reproduction' no reason is offered why this should be the case.

[23] Elster (1985b) has a survey of the multiple reasons why rational-choice explanations yield less than uniquely determined predictions – partly because of the non-existence of rational choice, partly because of its non-unicity.

[24] A weakness of much of economic theory is the implicit assumption that an equilibrium will be realized even if it can neither be shown to be the convergence point of a dynamic process of adjustment nor the uniquely determined solution to a game. This is notably a weak point in the rational expectations literature. The procedure has some resemblance to functional explanation, since in both cases there is a focus on the desirable consequences of social facts (e.g. a price vector) and a lack of concern for micro-foundations.

people unless one assumes that they are by and large rational.[25] This, however, leaves some scope for irrationality. Impulsive and compulsive behaviour interferes with rationality, as does belief formation by wishful thinking and the like. And one may add that in the case of collective actors, such as trade unions or firms, the decisions may be the outcome of internal bargaining and compromise that does not conform to the canons of rationality.[26] On the level of individual choice there is a presumption in favour of rationality, but many students of politics would argue that there is a presumption against it on the collective level.

III. Explaining technical change

This provides an interesting example where both the functionalist and the game-theoretic approaches fail, so that a causal account is required. I shall consider only the problem of explaining the factor bias of technical change, but similar remarks apply to the explanation of the rate of technical progress.[27]

Consider first the Marxist explanation of the tendency for innovations to be labour-saving in response to a rise in the price of labour relative to that of capital.[28] It is essentially that such innovations are in the interest of capital, since the labour-saving bias will reduce the demand for labour and hence counteract the wage rise. But capital is not a collective actor with eyes that see and hands that move. On the assumption of methodological individualism, capital is only shorthand for the many individual capitalists.[29] True, the capitalists may and do organize themselves in cartels or employers' associations, but it has never been suggested that the factor bias of technical change is deliberately chosen by the capitalist class acting as an organized group. The idea appears to be that the needs of capital tend to be satisfied, by the state, by capitalist collective action or by some other mechanism – and that this tendency is so strong that one does not in fact need to find a mechanism. This of course neglects the many needs of capital that are not satisfied, and does not allow us to distinguish between the cases in which they are satisfied accidentally and those in which the satisfaction has explanatory power.

The traditional non-Marxist story has been a different one. The factor bias

[25] Cp. Davidson (1980) for this view.
[26] See, for instance, Allison (1971).
[27] See Elster (1983), Ch. 4 and Appendix 2 for the arguments as they apply to the explanation of the rate of technical change.
[28] A clear statement of this view is in Offe and Wiesenthal (1980). Marx (1867), p. 638 has a similar argument.
[29] For an explicit denial of this view, see Marx (1857–8), p. 651.

is here explained at the level of the firm, by assuming that it has an incentive to save on labour if wages rise. But twenty years ago W. E. G. Salter pointed out the inadequacy of this account. When wages rise, the firm first has an incentive to substitute capital for labour within the given technique. This being done, it may well have an incentive to find new techniques, but not to find techniques that save more on labour than on capital.[30] An attempt to rescue the traditional view was made by arguing that if firms expected wages to go on rising in the future, they would have an incentive to give their search for innovation a labour-saving bias.[31] But then we must ask why the firms would believe this. If they believe that wages will rise because other firms will not mechanize production, this implies that they believe the other firms to be less rational than themselves, which violates the symmetry postulate of game theory. If this postulate is accepted, the firm will see that it is rational to mechanize if the others do not, but not rational to mechanize if the others do, since there are some costs involved in steering the search in some particular direction. But this means that we are dealing with a game without a non-cooperative solution, so that the behaviour of firms cannot be explained using only rational-choice assumptions.

Various causal explanations could be invoked. Paul David has suggested that factor prices influence factor bias in a roundabout way, arguing that technical change as a local phenomenon is unbiased, but occurs more rapidly in the capital-intensive part of the spectrum of techniques and that firms are induced by substitution to move towards that part of the spectrum.[32] Or firms might form irrational expectations about one another. Or their attention might be directed towards labour-saving because labour, as the factor that has recently become more expensive, has acquired greater saliency.[33]

IV. Class consciousness

Why do people engage in collective action? Why, for instance, would a worker go on strike when he can get the benefits without the costs by keeping on the sidelines? In modern capitalist economies we would invoke picketing or various other social sanctions, but this kind of explanation is of no avail if we address the question of how trade unions came to be formed in the first place.[34]

Marx did not really address the question at the level of the individual worker. He did, however, offer an explanation of the activities of trade

[30] Salter (1960), pp. 43–4. [31] Fellner (1961).
[32] David (1975), Ch. 1. [33] Winter (1981).
[34] Froelich and Oppenheimer (1970). For the general distinction between emergence and stability see van Parijs (1981), Ch. 5.

unions: they serve to enhance the political consciousness of the workers. Let me quote him to that effect:

Trades' Unions originally sprung up from the *spontaneous* attempts of workmen at removing or at least checking [the competition amongst themselves], in order to conquer such terms of contract as might raise them at least above the condition of mere slaves. The immediate object of Trades' Unions was therefore confined to everyday necessities, to expediencies for the obstruction of the incessant encroachments of capital, in one word, to questions of wages and time of labour. This activity of the Trades' Unions is not only legitimate, it is necessary. It cannot be dispensed with so long as the present system of production lasts. On the other hand, unconsciously to themselves, the Trades' Unions were forming *centres of organisation* of the working class, as the medieval municipalities and communes did for the middle class. If the Trades' Unions are required for guerilla fights between capital and labour, they are still more important as *organised agencies for superseding the very system of wages labour and capital rule.*[35]

Now one might deny that this was intended as an explanation of trade-union activity. Marx could simply be read as saying that the economic struggles of the working class are among the necessary conditions for the political revolution that will overthrow capitalism. Yet I believe that for Marx pointing out that something was a necessary condition for the communist revolution, in itself served as an explanation, or at least turned his attention away from the problem of finding one. His speculative philosophy of history made him believe that the advent of communism was inevitable, hence anything that entered among the necessary conditions of that event could be explained or mentally assimilated by that function.

If one takes seriously the problem of finding micro-foundations for collective action and class consciousness, we are inevitably led in the direction of game theory.[36] There appear to be three main approaches. First, observe that as a one-shot event the material reward structure of trade union formation is that of a Prisoner's Dilemma, in which rationally one would not choose to participate. Hence an explanation of the emergence of participation must take one of three possible directions: by emphasizing the repeated aspect of the interaction; by postulating a difference between the material reward structure and what one might call the 'inclusive reward structure' that also takes account of the interdependency of rewards; and by suggesting that the actors do not behave in a fully rational manner.

The first approach rests on the fact that under certain conditions cooperation is rational in an iterated Prisoner's Dilemma. These conditions include uncertainty about when the interaction will end, some concern for long-term gains and full information about the motivation of the other agents. The

[35] Marx (1866a), p. 91. [36] The following draws on Elster (1985c).

advantages of this approach are twofold. Methodologically, the assumption that people are motivated by their material reward is more parsimonious than the idea that the rewards of other people enter into their motivation.[37] Substantively, it allows an explanation not only of working-class behaviour, but also of capitalist collective action, which would be hard to explain on any other assumption than that of selfish motivation.

The second approach rests on the idea that as a result of interacting with one another people come to be concerned about one another, so that there emerges a positive interdependency in the reward structures. If sufficiently strong, this tendency might transform the Prisoner's Dilemma into an Assurance Game, in which the cooperative behaviour would be the solution outcome. This assumes that the actors are informed about one another's motivation, which could be brought about by the very same interaction that changes the motivation. With respect to working-class collective action, this approach would appear to have the advantage of realism. In the light of many studies of the history of the early working class, it is hard to believe that their solidarity was nothing but long-term self-interest. It must be admitted, however, that these are subtle and elusive matters. The ideas of implicit exchange and of conditional cooperation are sufficiently close to each other to generate the same political rhetoric. In principle it should be possible to choose between this approach and the first on empirical grounds, since they rest on different assumptions. For instance, if solidarity could be shown to obtain in interactions with a known terminal date, the first explanation would be discredited.

A third approach, however, is also possible. The agents might be less than fully rational. One should be very hesitant in adopting this assumption, since irrationality in many cases is simply a term for the unexplained residual. To explain participation in elections by saying that people behave 'emotionally', for instance, is not to say anything of substance.[38] Yet some substantive elaborations are available. It appears, for instance, that in very long iterations of the Prisoner's Dilemma people cooperate for a long while even when the terminal date is known[39] – by some kind of cognitive analogy to weakness of will. The distant future simply does not enter into one's calculation in the way it rationally should.[40] Another explanation of participation rests on the

---

[37] Material rewards are first-order benefits that are logically required for the second-order benefits of altruism or sympathy to be possible (Collard, 1978, p. 9).

[38] Olson (1965), p. 108n.

[39] Rapoport and Chammah (1965). For an attempt – in my opinion unsuccessful – to prove the rationality of such behaviour, see Hardin (1982), pp. 145ff.

[40] Note that weakness of will in the ordinary, motivational sense can be modelled as a high time-discount rate, which, rather than favouring collective action, tends to work against it.

idea that the agents confuse causal and diagnostic efficacy.[41] If one believes oneself to be typical or representative of one's class, then one is easily led to believe that by choosing to cooperate one can magically bring it about that others cooperate as well. The idea is familiar from the study of Calvinism[42] and from the conundrum known as Newcomb's Problem.[43]

The problem of collective action is highly instructive from the methodological point of view. Once one has given up the functionalist approach, one has to look for micro-foundations. One must explain, that is, how individuals come to participate in collective action. In trying to construct an explanation one first assumes nothing but selfish motivation and rational behaviour. The first fall-back position is by abandoning the assumption of selfishness while retaining that of rationality. Only as a last resort would one want to question the rationality of the actors.

V. Divide and conquer

Internal divisions within the working class clearly benefit the class of capitalists. Do these benefits explain the divisions? And if so, by what mechanism?

The basic fallacy of a naive functionalist approach to this question can be put in terms of Georg Simmel's distinction between *divide et impera* and *tertius gaudens*.[44] The latter is the fact that bystanders may benefit from struggles in the initiation of which they have no part, neither by omission nor by commission. In *Capital I* Marx quotes the English proverb that 'when thieves fall out, honest men come by their own'.[45] *Divide et impera*, by contrast, presupposes that the party benefiting from the struggle is also responsible for it.[46] An example paralleling the one just given would be a police force deliberately setting up gang warfare. The functionalist fallacy would be the unthinking assumption that the struggle can always be explained in terms of such third-party benefits.

---

[41] Quattrone and Tversky (1985).
[42] Take, for instance, the following passage from a letter circulated by Baptists in 1770: 'Every soul that comes to Christ to be saved...is to be encouraged...The coming soul need not fear that he is not elected, for none but such would be willing to come' (Thompson 1968, p. 38).
[43] Nozick (1969).
[44] Simmel (1908), pp. 82ff.
[45] Marx (1867), p. 675.
[46] One would need to distinguish here between causal and moral responsibility. *Divide et impera* by omission may involve the latter without the former, assuming that one 'could and should' have intervened to prevent the conflict. It is unclear whether this would also constitute an exercise of power. Tentatively, I would agree that it is if it is also true that the agent benefiting from the conflict 'could and would' have set it up had not the two parties done so by themselves. Cp. also note 9 above.

The most important passage by Marx bearing on this question occurs in a letter on 'The Irish question':

The ordinary English worker hates the Irish worker as a competitor who lowers his standard of life. In relation to the Irish worker he feels himself a member of the *ruling nation* and so turns himself into a tool of the aristocrats and capitalists of his country against *Ireland*, thus strengthening their domination over *himself*. He cherishes religious, social and national prejudices against the Irish worker. His attitude towards him is much the same as that of the 'poor whites' to the 'niggers' in the former slave states of the U.S.A. The Irishman pays him back with interest in his own money. He sees in the English worker at once the accomplice and the stupid tool of the *English rule in Ireland*. This antagonism is artificially kept alive and intensified by the press, the pulpit, the comic papers, in short, by all the means at the disposal of the ruling classes. *This antagonism is the secret of the impotence of the English working class*, despite its organisation.[47]

It is not easy to know what to make of this passage. The first part suggests that the prejudices of the English workers arise endogenously.[48] By this I mean that given the domination of the workers by the capitalist and the presence of the Irish, there would be a natural psychological tendency at work to produce prejudice. The frustration or dissonance that comes from being dominated can be eased by the mental operation of drawing the main dividing line in society below rather than above oneself. This would not require any manipulation by the capitalist class, although the prejudices could well be intensified by their action. Towards the end of the passage, however, Marx says that the conflict between English and Irish workers is 'artificially kept alive' by the ruling classes: *divide et impera*, not *tertius gaudens*. In my view, the first explanation is the more plausible one. Ruling classes can exploit prejudices, but not create them.[49]

In other words, the presence of prejudice is better explained by the mental benefits it brought to the English workers than by the material benefits it brought to the capitalists.[50] The overt form of the explanation suggested by Marx invokes intentional manipulation, but I believe that the underlying thought is a functionalist one. Marx simply was not able to believe in the accidental character of the benefits which the prejudices created for the capitalist class: they had to enter into the explanation of the prejudice. This is the crucial step where the analysis goes astray. By comparison, the choice

[47] Marx to Meyer and Vogt, April 9 1870 (in Fernbach, ed. (1974), p. 169).
[48] For a similar analysis of ideology, see Veyne (1976).
[49] Another analysis that seems to neglect this point is Roemer (1979).
[50] This might appear as an instance of blaming the victim, but as observed by Veyne (1976), p. 89 the explanation of ideology in terms of manipulation is not much more flattering. In any case one needs to stress that the external cause of prejudice, viz. the fact of capitalist domination, is as important as the psychological mechanism internal to the worker.

between functional and conspiratorial explanation is of relatively little importance.

There is, however, scope for a game-theoretic analysis of *divide and conquer*. The natural tool here is that of cooperative games, modelling the distribution of income as a result of coalition formation in the set of agents consisting of a capitalist that controls the means of production and the workers who control their labour power.[51] If the workers are unorganized, coalitions can form between the capitalist and some of the workers, excluding other workers. One of the solution concepts for cooperative games ('the Shapley value') then allows us to predict that the rate of exploitation will be much higher than under conditions of perfect competition where the capitalist must negotiate separately with each worker, and *a fortiori* higher than under collective bargaining. This concept rests on the idea that each agent will be rewarded according to his average contribution to all potential coalitions of which he could be a member. Although plausible, the concept lacks behavioural justification, an account of the explicit bargaining mechanism by which the solution could emerge. In fact, cooperative game theory shares some of the weaknesses of functional explanation, in that it takes collective rationality for granted without even attempting to provide micro-foundations.[52]

VI. The theory of the capitalist state

Marx believed that the state in capitalist societies was also a capitalist state. This belief took two forms in his work. Up to 1850 he held it in the direct sense that the state is the tool for the collective interest of the capitalist class, with the two functions of protecting the class against the workers and against short-sighted or free-rider behaviour of the individual capitalists.[53] In his political writings from the 1850s he modified the view so that the relation between class interest and state policy became a more indirect one. He now admitted that the state had some autonomy of action, but added that the autonomy itself could be explained by the benefits it brought to the capitalists. The following passage from the *18th Brumaire* is a statement of this view:

Thus, by now stigmatising as '*socialistic*' what it had previously extolled as '*liberal*', the bourgeoisie confesses that its own interests dictate that it should be delivered from the danger of its *own rule*; that, in order to restore tranquillity in the country, its

---

[51] Shapley and Shubik (1967); see also Telser (1978), Chs. 1.3 and 2.7.

[52] An exception is the Zeuthen–Nash–Harsanyi theory of two-person cooperative games, explaining how the collectively rational outcome can be achieved by a plausible process of stepwise bargaining.

[53] 'The bourgeois state is nothing more than the mutual insurance of the bourgeois class against its individual members as well as against the exploited class' (Marx, 1850a).

bourgeois parliament must, first of all, be laid to rest; that, in order to preserve its social power intact, its political power must be broken; that the individual bourgeois can continue to exploit the other classes and to enjoy undisturbed property, family, religion and order only on condition that their class be condemned along with the other classes to similar political nullity; that, in order to save its purse, it must forfeit the crown, and the sword that is to safeguard it must at the same time be hung over its head as a sword of Damocles.[54]

In a statement written before 1848, Marx comments that to infer from the power of the state to expropriate private property to the conclusion that it is the real owner of all property, is like saying that my watch-dog is the real owner of my house.[55] No doubt he would have said as much after 1850, with the addition that the capitalist class needs protection not only from its individual members but also against its own political rule. The capitalist class abdicates from power out of self-interest, which means that the rulers only have the power as a fief. I would suggest that this perspective is quite wrong, and that another illustration would be more appropriate. To say that the state in a capitalist society must be a capitalist state is like saying that the goose which lays the golden eggs is the real master of the farmer who keeps it alive.

Analogy aside, I believe that the autonomy of the state in capitalist societies is quite substantial and non-derivative. A close reading of Marx's writings on French and English politics shows that he is also committed to this view, even though he attempts to present it as a version of the class interest theory. With respect to England, for instance, he argues that the aristocratic landowners in charge of the government had a real leverage that allowed for some scope for autonomous state policies in their own interests. The capitalist class did not want to take the political power, since this would have the effect of making the two enemies of the working class – capital and government – collapse into one, with an intensification of social conflict as the result. The government, knowing this, could then maximize its own objective function, subject to economic and political constraints. The economic constraint is that the state needs a prosperous capitalist class to ensure its tax base, the political constraint that the capitalists must not be provoked into taking power for themselves.[56]

A further development of this idea calls for game-theoretic analysis.[57] In modern capitalist societies three main collective actors confront one another: organized labour, organized business and the state. Given the existence of

[54] Marx (1852b), p. 143.
[55] Marx (1845–6), p. 355.
[56] See notably Marx's articles on English politics in *The New York Daily Tribune*, 21.8.1852, 25.8.1852, 28.1.1853, 15.11.1853, 1.8.1854 and 9.3.1857. A perspective on the state similar to the one suggested here is found in North (1981), Ch. 3 and *passim*.
[57] The following draws heavily on Przeworski and Wallerstein (1982).

private property, the relation between capital and labour can be modelled as a differential game, in which the workers control the rate of profit and the capitalists the rate of investment out of profit.[58] The strategic choices of the classes depend on their expectations about the future behaviour of the other class. Workers will allow for profits only if they can expect that some investment will take place, leading to increased consumption later on. Capitalists will invest only if they have a guarantee that the fruits of investment will not be entirely confiscated by the workers later on.[59] The role of the state is important in the formation of these expectations, since the state has the power to tax profits and to offer tax reliefs on investment. If the state also has autonomous goals of its own, we are in fact dealing with a non-cooperative game between these three actors. Since the game is not only about distribution, but also about production, it is not zero-sum. All the actors have a shared interest in production, and opposed interests concerning the distribution of the product. The game, moreover, is time-dependent in the double sense discussed earlier, since present choices not only affect future benefits, via the impact on investment, but also future choices, via the impact on retaliatory behaviour. Hence the structure of the interaction is a fairly complex one, too complex probably to be handled analytically in full generality. Simulation studies and partial-equilibrium analysis can, however, bring about real insight into the likely outcomes.

VII. The theory of bourgeois revolutions

Marx wrote – although surprisingly little – about the classical bourgeois revolutions.[60] He also participated actively in the German revolution of 1848. His activities clearly were shaped by his teleological view of history, to the extent of blinding him from certain facts that ought to have been obvious and that are brought to the forefront by game-theoretic analysis.

According to Marx, the English and notably the French revolutions were carried out by the capitalist class with the workers doing their dirty work for them. His teleological view comes out in the statement that when 'the workers opposed the bourgeoisie, as they did in France in 1793 and 1794, they fought only for the attainment of the aims of the bourgeoisie'.[61] In a phrase that he employs in a different context, the workers were 'the unconscious tool of

---

[58] This approach was first suggested by Lancaster (1973).
[59] One can imagine a similar dilemma involving the state, in the relation between local branches of multinational firms and the nation-states serving as host countries.
[60] There are some rambling observations in Marx (1845) on the French Revolution and a somewhat more systematic but equally brief treatment of the English Revolution in Marx (1850b).   [61] Marx, *Neue Rheinische Zeitung*, 15.12.1848.

history',[62] the embodiment of the Ruse of Reason. As in Hegel's analysis in the *Phenomenology*, there was a need to make a clean sweep of the past before the bourgeois order could be constructed, a task that according to Marx fell to the workers.

When the bourgeois revolution belatedly became a possibility in Germany, Marx adopted a different perspective. In *The Communist Manifesto*, written on the eve of the 1848 revolution, Marx and Engels foresaw an active role for the workers in the coming bourgeois revolution, in that they would first help the bourgeoisie to power and then immediately start to fight against the bourgeoisie itself, in a process of permanent revolution.[63] When the revolutionary movement reached Germany, Marx devoted his energy as editor of the *Neue Rheinische Zeitung* to supporting the bourgeoisie, exhorting them to stand fast and not be restrained by constitutional niceties.[64] Yet the German bourgeoisie consistently refused to fulfil their historical mission of overthrowing the feudal rule and prepare the ground for proletarian rule. Instead they just looked after their own interests. In a revealing phrase Marx opposes the parochial and provincial character of the German revolution to the classical bourgeois revolutions. The latter 'reflected the needs of the world at that time rather than the needs of those parts of the world where they occurred, that is England and France'.[65] It is difficult to imagine a more explicit statement of the functional and teleological view of history.

One might argue that such phrases must not be taken literally. Rather they were rhetorical devices that must be understood in a political context. Yet I believe that Marx's own political efforts during 1848 and 1849 show that he was actually guided by the view that events must necessarily evolve towards the rule first of the bourgeoisie and then of the proletariat. Otherwise he would surely have been struck by the idea that the German bourgeoisie was just as capable as him of understanding that to accept the help of the workers might be a poisoned gift. True, he was to some extent aware of this danger. In the words of a later writer, 'the *Neue Rheinische Zeitung* was almost embarrassingly silent on specific proletarian demands',[66] for fear of provoking the bourgeoisie. But if only for prudential reasons Marx ought to have acted on the assumption that the leading members of that class were capable of reading the signs for themselves. In short, Marx's reasoning violated the symmetry postulate that all actors are equally rational.[67] He wrongly believed

---

[62] *New York Daily Tribune*, 25.6.1853.   [63] Marx (1848), p. 519.
[64] *Neue Rheinische Zeitung*, 14.9.1848.   [65] *Ibid.*, 15.12.1848.   [66] Hunt (1974), p. 196.
[67] Similarly, Marx for some time hoped that Russia would intervene against Germany and thus ignite the revolutionary struggle (*Neue Rheinische Zeitung*, 25.6.1848; see also Molnar 1975, pp. 122ff.). Yet 'Russia, fearing revolutionary energy, avoided confrontations' (Felix, 1983, p. 87).

himself capable of manipulating the bourgeoisie by hiding his intentions, just as the Chinese Communist Party believed they could manipulate the Kuomintang until the Shanghai massacre taught them otherwise.

VIII. Conclusion

This survey has not exhausted the varieties of functionalist reasoning in Marx, nor the potential for applied game theory to the problems of Marxism. My concern has been a methodological one. By choosing some cases that can be and have been approached in both manners, it is possible to bring out their strong and weak points. With respect to functionalism, it has been found to be consistently misleading, dangerous in theory as well as in practice.[68] The game-theoretic approach has in most cases been shown to be superior, with some limitations that should be kept in mind. It cannot explain preference change, nor predict behaviour in situations where the notion of rational choice is ill-defined or where people act irrationally. Moreover, the theory of cooperative games, while valuable for purposes of normative analysis,[69] rests on shaky foundations that limit its validity for explanatory purposes.

There is no specifically Marxist form of explanation.[70] Marxism is defined mainly by two other features. First, the belief that alienation and exploitation interfere with the good life for man and that their suppression is not only desirable but feasible. Or at the minimum, the unfeasibility of suppressing them has not been proven. Secondly, Marxism is characterized by a few fundamental theoretical assumptions about the structure and development of societies, with emphasis on the interrelation between property rights, technical change and class struggle. Of these, the first, normative element constitutes the *sine qua non* of Marxism. The second, explanatory element can to some extent be modified and revised without loss of identity. Only to some extent however, since the normative theory itself would have to be given up if it were to be shown that the Marxist proposals are radically unfeasible, either in the sense that communism would not be viable or in the sense that capitalism will never produce a communist revo'ition. By contrast, there is no commitment to any specific methods of analysis, beyond those that characterize good social science generally.

[68] For the disastrous political implications of functionalism in China, see Tsou (1983). The Stalinist notion of 'objective complicity' rests on a similar view.
[69] Roemer (1982a,d).
[70] An exception may be the theory of dialectics, at least in one of its acceptations (Elster, 1978, Chs. 4 and 5).

11 Marxism and functional explanation*

G. A. Cohen

I. Introduction

The Preface to *The Critique of Political Economy* uses a number of explanatory expressions: relations of production *correspond* to productive forces; the legal and political superstructure *rises on* the real foundation; the social, political, and intellectual life process *is conditioned by* the mode of production of material life; consciousness *is determined by* social being. In each case Marx distinguishes two items, the second of which he asserts to be in some way explanatory of the first. He fails to say, here and everywhere else, what kind of explanation he is hypothesizing, and semantic analysis of the italicized phrases would not be a good way of discovering what he meant. My own claim is that the central Marxian explanations are functional, which means, *very roughly*, that the character of what is explained is determined by its effect on what explains it. One reason for so interpreting Marx: if the *direction* of the explanatory tie is as he laid down, then the best account of the *nature* of the tie is that it is a functional one. For production relations profoundly affect productive forces, and superstructures strongly condition foundations. What Marx claims to explain has momentous impact on what he says explains it. Construing his explanations as functional makes for compatibility between the causal power of the explained phenomena and their secondary status in the order of explanation.

Thus to say that an economic structure *corresponds* to the achieved level of the productive forces means: the structure provides maximum scope for the fruitful use and development of the forces, and obtains *because* it provides such scope. To say that being *determines* consciousness means, at least in large part: the character of the leading ideas of a society is explained by their propensity, in virtue of that character, to sustain the structure of economic roles called for by the productive forces.[1]

---

* This essay originally appeared as a chapter in G. A. Cohen, *Karl Marx's Theory of History: A Defence* (Princeton University Press, 1978). Reprinted with permission.

[1] For an extended commentary on 'Social being determines consciousness', see my 1974.

Putting the two theses together, we get such hypotheses as that Protestantism arose when it did because it was a religion suited to stimulating capitalist enterprise and enforcing labour discipline at a time when the capital/labour relation was pre-eminently apt to develop new productive potentials of society. When Marx says that 'Protestantism, by changing almost all the traditional holidays into workdays, plays an important role in the genesis of capital'[2] he is not just assigning a certain effect to the new religion, but proposing a (partial) explanation of its rise in terms of that effect.

While Marx was inexplicit about the structure of the central explanations he hypothesized, there are some hints:

The first 'Statute of Labourers' (23 Edward III, 1349) found its immediate pretext (not its cause, for legislation of this kind lasts centuries after the pretext for it has disappeared) in the great plague that decimated the people.[3]

The Statute cannot be explained by the circumstances of its origin, but only by reference to the persisting effect of legislation of that kind on the developing social structure. We must avoid the error of the 'English, who have a tendency to look upon the earliest form of appearance of a thing as the cause of its existence...'[4]

There is no well-stated alternative to the view that major Marxian explanatory claims are functional in character. The functional construal is nevertheless not popular, for a number of bad reasons, which will shortly be exposed. In practice Marxists advance functional explanations, but they do not theorize their practice accurately. They recoil from the functional construal when it is made explicit, for reasons to be reviewed. They then have recourse to opaque ideas of 'structural causality',[5] to invocation of Engels's unexplained 'determination in the last resort',[6] to the facile suggestion that the priority of the base lies in the fact that it limits the superstructure, as though the converse were not also true;[7] or they effectively abandon the master theses of explanatory priority by interpreting them as merely heuristic.

Marxists regard functional explanation as suspect for a variety of reasons, the most important of which are dealt with in the next two sections.

[2] Marx (1867), p. 276. Protestant reformers themselves stressed that the abolition of saints' days would have a salutary effect on industry. See Hill (1968b), p. 51, and (1974), p. 81.
[3] Marx (1867), p. 272.
[4] *Ibid.*, p. 403, and see also the passages quoted at pp. 232–3 of Cohen (1978a).
[5] Louis Althusser, with whom we may associate this phrase, himself employs functional explanations when he deals with actual social phenomena. See, for example, 'Ideology and the Ideological State Apparatuses', in Althusser (1971).
[6] Engels to Bloch, 21–2 Sept. 1890, in Marx and Engels (1975), p. 394.
[7] See Cohen (1978a), p. 158.

II. Conceptual criticisms of functional explanation

This section is an informal restatement of some of the principal contentions of Chapter IX of Cohen (1978a), in confrontation with a typical critique of functional explanation.

Let us begin with a simple functional explanation. In some industries there is, over a period of time, a marked increase in the mean size of the producing units: small workshops grow into, or are replaced by, large factories. The increased scale reduces the costs of producing a given volume of output. It generates economies of scale. If we find that scale grows just when growth in scale would have that effect, and not otherwise, then it is a plausible explanatory hypothesis that scale grows *because* the growth brings economies. Note that we may be justified in proposing this explanation before we know *how* the fact that enlarged scale induces economies explains large scale. We can know that something operated in favour of large scale, because of its cost effectiveness, without knowing what so operated. We may not know whether the increase was deliberately sought by wise managers, or came about through an economic analogue of chance variation and natural selection. We might be able to claim *that* the change is explained by its consequences without being able to say *how* it is so explained.

Let us now delineate the form of the explanation more carefully. We have a cause, increase of scale, and an effect, economies of scale. It is not proposed that the cause occurred because the effect occurred. Nor even – though this formulation is closer to the truth – that the cause occurred because it caused that effect. Instead, the cause occurred because of its propensity to have that effect: *the increase in scale occurred because the industry was of a sort in which increases in scale yield economies.*

This being the form of functional explanation, a common objection to it is misplaced. We take the objection as it is stated by Percy Cohen. His examples of functional explanation are

that religion exists in order to sustain the moral foundations of society...[and]...that the State exists in order to coordinate the various activities which occur in complex societies. In both these cases a consequence is used to explain a cause; the end conditions of moral order and coordination are used to explain the existence of religion and the State...Critics rightly argue that this type of explanation defies the laws of logic, for one thing cannot be the cause of another if it succeeds it in time.[8]

Now it is true (if not, perhaps, a law of logic) that what comes later does not explain what comes earlier. But it is false that the theses mentioned by Cohen

---

[8] Cohen (1968), pp. 47–8. Cohen's further criticisms of functional explanation are implicitly answered in Chapter IX of Cohen (1978a).

violate that truth. It is a plausible generalization that a society develops and/or sustains a religion when a religion is necessary for (or would contribute to) its stability. The religion of a society might, then, be explained in terms of this feature of the society: it requires a religion to be viable. That feature is not a consequence of having a religion, and there would be no contortion of time order in the explanation.

Now suppose a society requires a religion for stability, and has a religion fulfilling that need. It does not follow that its need for a religion *explains* its having one.[9] The society may indeed require a religion, but it is a further question whether it has one *because* it requires one. It may have one not at all because it needs one, but for other reasons. Imagine ten godless communities, each, because it lacks a religion, teetering on the brink of disintegration. A prophet visits all ten, but only one of them accepts his teaching. The other nine subsequently perish, and the single believing society survives. But they took up religion because they liked the prophet's looks, and not because they needed a religion (though they did need a religion). So the fact that there is a religion, and it is needed, does not show that there is a religion because it is needed. That demands further argument. Perhaps some sociologists mistake the need for further argument as a defect in functional explanation itself.

To say that

(1) *f* occurred

is not to advance an explanation of why *e* occurred.[10] Yet it might be true that

(2) *e* occurred because *f* occurred.

(2) may or may not be true, and if it is true, it is not true simply because (1) is true.

Analogous remarks apply to functional explanation. One does not propose an explanation of the existence of religion by saying that

(3) Religion is required to sustain social order.[11]

Yet it might be true that

(4) Religion exists because it is required to sustain social order.

(4) may or may not be true, and if it is true, it is not true simply because (3) is true.

---

[9] This would follow on C. G. Hempel's theory of explanation: see Cohen (1978a), p. 273.

[10] Unless (1) is offered in response to something like 'Why did *e* occur?', in which case uttering (1) is tantamount to uttering (2).

[11] Again, unless (3) is a response to 'Why is there religion?'

The mere fact that *f* preceded *e* does not guarantee that *f* caused *e*, though it may be true that *f* caused *e*. Similarly, the mere fact that *g*'s propensities are beneficial does not guarantee that *g* is explained by those propensities, but it may be true that it is so explained. The existence of the fallacy *post hoc ergo propter hoc* does not disqualify all causal explanations. Neither does the comparable fallacy of supposing that, if something is functional, it is *explained* by its function(s), rule out all functional explanations.

So Percy Cohen is misled when he rejects a theory of religion solely because it explains religion functionally, and when he impugns Durkheim's account of the division of labour on the ground that it is functional in form.[12] There is nothing in principle wrong with functional explanations, though to identify a function something serves is not necessarily to provide one. Failure to recognize both truths generates confused debate in sociology, for many catch one truth only.

Thus while Cohen mistakenly argues that assigning a function to a phenomenon cannot be explanatory, others suppose that to show that a usage or institution is required or eufunctional is *ipso facto* to explain its existence. Merton's classic paper[13] tends towards the supposition that to establish that an item has functions is automatically to contribute to explaining it. He never satisfactorily distinguishes between explaining something by reference to its function(s) (functional explanation proper), and explaining the function(s) of something.[14] He identifies a function served by the 'Hawthorne experiment',[15] but he fails to note that it is not a function which could contribute to explaining why the experiment took place.[16]

Sociologists often identify interesting functions, but it is always a further question, whose answer needs further evidence and argument, whether what they identify explains why something is so. Sometimes good evidence and argument is forthcoming, but not always.

III. Functionalism, functional explanation, and Marxism

Other objections to the functional explanation of social phenomena spring from the historical association between functional explanation and the theory of *functionalism*. Defects in the latter have affected the reputation of the

12 Cohen (1968), pp. 35–6.
13 'Manifest and Latent Functions', in Merton (1968).
14 For an exposition of that distinction, see Cohen (1978a), p. 252.
15 See *ibid.*, p. 257.
16 It might be claimed, in Merton's defence, that he was concerned only with *identifying* functions of social patterns and institutions, and not with functionally *explaining* them. This is a highly implausible reading. If, however, it is correct, then we may complain that in an article recommending the study of functions Merton neglected their explanatory role.

former. That is regrettable, since, as we shall see, they do not necessarily go together.

By 'functionalism' I mean the trend in anthropology whose chief proponents were Malinowski and Radcliffe-Brown. It affirmed three theses, which were not often clearly distinguished from one another, and which are here listed in ascending order of strength ((3) entails (2) and (2) entails (1)):

(1) All elements of social life are interconnected. They strongly influence one another and in aggregate 'form one inseparable whole'[17] (*Interconnection Thesis*).
(2) All elements of social life support or reinforce one another, and hence too the whole society which in aggregate they constitute (*Functional Interconnection Thesis*).
(3) Each element is as it is *because* of its contribution to the whole, as described in (2) (*Explanatory Functional Interconnection Thesis*).

Thesis (3) embodies a commitment to functional explanation, and it has therefore been criticized on grounds like those discussed and rejected in the last section. But there has also been separate criticism of thesis (2), which proposes no functional *explanations*, but asserts the universal eufunctionality of social elements. It is objected that (2) is falsified by the conflict, strain, and crisis so common in so many societies. How could Malinowski think that 'in every type of civilisation, every custom, material object, idea and belief fulfils some vital function, has some task to accomplish, represents an indispensable part within a working whole'?[18]

(2) is widely thought to be not only false but also viciously conservative in its implications. Marxists have, accordingly, been strong opponents of functionalism, a fact which helps to explain their failure to acknowledge the functional nature of their own explanatory theses.

Whether functionalism is in truth inescapably conservative is a question we need not discuss, though we may note how natural it is to conclude that if everything serves a useful purpose or is, indeed, indispensable, then there is no scope for desirable social change. Radcliffe-Brown's principle of the 'functional consistency of social systems'[19] seems hard to reconcile with the reality of class struggle, and whatever serves to deny the latter is a comfort to conservative convictions.

It should be obvious that a Marxist can assert functional explanations without endorsing any of theses (1) to (3). Functional explanation is compatible with rejection of the doctrine of functionalism, and functional explanation is not necessarily conservative. Functional explanation in

[17] Malinowski (1922), p. 515.   [18] Malinowski (1960).
[19] See Radcliffe-Brown (1957), pp. 124–8, and (1952), p. 43.

historical materialism is, moreover, revolutionary, in two respects: it predicts large-scale social transformations, and it claims that their course is violent.

To say that forms of society rise and fall according as they advance and retard the development of the productive forces is to predict massive transformations of social structure as the productive forces progress. Historical materialism puts the growth of human powers at the centre of the historical process, and it is to this extra-social[20] development that society itself is constrained to adjust. The conservative tendency of functionalism lies in its functionally explaining institutions as sustaining (existing) society. There is no conservatism when institutions, and society itself, are explained as serving a development of power which prevails against forms of society resisting it.

The theory is also revolutionary in that the means whereby society is transformed is class conflict. Transitions do not occur quietly and easily. Society adjusts itself to nature through access to power of a new class. Class struggle is a large part of the answer to the question: *how* does the fact that a new economic structure would benefit the productive forces explain its actualization? We must now consider such 'how-questions' more generally.

IV. Elaborations

I argue in Chapter IX of Cohen, 1978a (pp. 269ff.) that sound functional explanations apply to the development of biological species. The theory of chance variation and natural selection does not displace functional explanation in that domain. Instead, it shows, *inter alia*, why functional explanation is appropriate there. The theory entails that plants and animals have the useful equipment they do because of its usefulness, and specifies in what manner the utility of a feature accounts for its existence.

Now in the absence of such a theory we shall still observe provocative correlations between the requirements of living existence and the actual endowments of living things, correlations fine enough to suggest the thesis that they have those endowments because they minister to those requirements. We can rationally hypothesize functional explanations even when we lack an account which, like Darwin's, shows how the explanations work, or, as I put it in Chapter IX (see p. 271) of Cohen (1978a), even when we lack *elaborations* of the explanations. A satisfying elaboration provides a fuller explanation and locates the functional fact within a longer story which specifies its explanatory role more precisely.

Now the fact that functional explanations may reasonably be proposed, in

[20] In the sense of Chapter IV of Cohen (1978a).

the light of suitable evidence, but in advance of an elaborating theory, is very important for social science and history. For functional explanations in those spheres often carry conviction in the absence of elaborative context. And it would be a mistake to refrain from taking those explanatory steps which are open to us, just because we should prefer to go farther than our current knowledge permits.[21] *If*, for example, the pattern of educational provision in a society evolves in a manner suitable to its changing economy, then it is reasonable to assert that education changes as it does because the changes sustain economic evolution, even when little is known about *how* the fact that an educational change would be economically propitious figures in explaining its occurrence. To be sure, there are grounds for caution pending acquisition of a plausible fuller story, but that is not especially true of functional explanations.

For it is not only explanations of functional cast which, though accepted as explanations, are yet felt to require further elaboration. We are frequently *certain* that *p* explains *q* yet unclear *how* it explains it. Someone ignorant of the contribution of oxygen to combustion may yet have overwhelming evidence that when a match, having been struck, bursts into flame, it bursts into flame *because* it has been struck, for all that his ignorance prevents him from saying how it is that the friction leads to ignition. So similarly, to return to functional explanation, one ignorant of genetics and evolutionary theory, will, when he finds species of insects regularly developing means of resisting pesticides introduced into their environments, naturally conclude that they develop those means because they are protective, although he can say nothing more. Perhaps historians and social scientists never record cases of adaptation as unarguable as the biological ones. But the rest of their explanatory hypothesizing is also based on less impressive evidence than what natural scientists are in a position to demand.

Functional explanations, then, have intellectual validity and value, even if it is said that 'they raise more questions than they answer'. For they answer some questions, and the further ones to which they give rise point research in the right direction.

But now let us examine some ways in which functional explanations may be elaborated.

Consider once again an industry in which average scale of production expands because of the economies large scale brings. We imagined (p. 223) this explanatory judgment being passed without detailed knowledge of a connection between the fact that scale yields economies and the (consequent) fact that scale expanded. Two elaborations readily suggest themselves.

[21] Cp. Plekhanov (1956), p. 330.

First, we can suppose that the industry's decision-makers knew that increased scale would yield economies, and that they enlarged their producing units out of awareness of that functional fact. The functional fact would then play its explanatory role by accounting for formation of the (correct) belief that an increase in scale would be beneficial; that belief, together with a desire for the relevant benefits, being a more proximate cause of the expansion in size. For obvious reasons, I call this a *purposive* elaboration of a functional explanation.

In the above elaboration we neither assert nor deny that the industrial units operate in a competitive environment. The decision makers might be Gosplanners, setting the course of an industry wholly subject to their will. But purposive elaboration can also apply in a competitive setting, in which case among the known benefits to be had from expanding scale might be the very survival of each of the firms in question.

In a competitive economy a purposive elaboration is, as noted, possible, but so is a second imporant form of elaboration. Imagine a competitive economy in which a certain industry would function more efficiently under increased scale, but suppose the managers of the industry's firms are ignorant of the fact. Then if mean scale expands, it is not because anyone seeks the economies increased scale promises. Still, some firms increase the scale of their producing units, perhaps because prestige is attached to size, or because the move is seen as a way of reducing tension between managers; or suppose that there is no intention to increase scale, but, in certain firms, an ungoverned drift in that direction. Then we could not say of any particular firm that its scale grew because of the associated economies. But the functional fact might still explain a change over time in the industry's scale profile, if only those firms which expanded (for whatever reason) would have succeeded, in virtue of having expanded, against the competition. Competition is bound to select in favour of firms whose practice is efficient, regardless of the inspiration of that practice. In the case described, we have what may be called a *Darwinian* elaboration of a functional explanation, for these are its salient elements: chance[22] variation (in scales of production), scarcity (in virtue of finite effective demand), and selection (on the market of those variants which, by chance, had a superior structure).

A third kind of elaboration may be called *Lamarckian*. In Lamarckian biological theory, by contrast with that of Darwin, the species evolves in virtue

---

[22] This designation does not imply that the variation is uncaused or inexplicable. What is meant by 'chance' is that the explanation of the variation is unconnected with the functional value of greater scale. Darwin calls genetic variation *chance* only because it is not controlled by the requirements of the environment.

of evolution within the life history of its specimens, which acquire more adaptive characteristics, and transmit them to offspring.[23] An organ not fully suited to the creature's environment becomes more suited as a result of the struggle to use it in that environment. (An example would be teeth becoming sharper as a result of regular chewing on food best chewed by sharp teeth.) The suggested elaboration is not purposive, because it is not the intention of the organism so to alter its equipment: it is altered as a result of a use which is not intended to alter it, but which reflects the environment's demands. Nor is the elaboration Darwinian. The initial variations, which are then preserved, do not occur by chance relative to the environmental requirements, and there *need* not be any competitive pressure on the organism, expressing itself in differential survival rates as between well- and ill-equipped specimens.

A fourth form of elaboration – really a special case of the first – is appropriate in cases of *self-deception*. By contrast with the second and third forms, the functional fact operates through the minds of agents, but unlike paradigm purposive examples, it does so without the agents' full acknowledgement. An elaboration of this form for the economies of scale case would be quite fanciful, but it is relevant to Marxian theory, as will be seen.

The above classification is not exhaustive, and the types of elaboration reviewed admit of combination with one another: there are often several interlaced routes from the functional fact to the fact it explains. C. Wright Mills contrasted 'drift' and 'thrust' in social development,[24] and it is easy to envisage agglomerations of the two. Thus, returning once again to economies of scale, there could initially be an unplanned drift to greater average size, controlled by competition, and later a perception of the functional relationship, with increasing thrust as a result.

V. Marxian illustrations

Our discussion will be confined to two central topics: the generation and propagation of ideology, and the adaptation of the economic structure to the productive forces.

When Marxists venture functional explanations of ideological and super-

[23] Following Ritterbush ((1964), p. 175), we may distinguish between the *acquisition* of inheritable characteristics and the *inheritance* of acquired characteristics, and it is the former which is of interest here: I am not concerned with the transmission of features from one social entity to another. Lamarck is relevant for his concept of an adaptation to the environment which is not mediated by a prior chance variation. The movement towards the adaptation is from the beginning controlled by the environment's demands.

Lamarck's specification of the mechanism of adaptation, in terms of the 'influx of subtle fluids', is also irrelevant here. What has social application is the concept of plasticity, of organs being able to develop new uses under new constraints.   [24] See Mills (1958).

structural phenomena, they are often accused of espousing a 'conspiracy theory of history'. A Marxist says 'it is no accident that' left-wing commentators receive little space in major American newspapers, or that British trade union leaders end their careers in the House of Lords. He is then criticized for imagining that an omnicompetent elite exercises fine control over these matters. He sometimes tries to forestall the response by disclaiming an assertion of conspiracy, but too commonly he fails to say in what other fashion phenomena like those mentioned are explained by the functions they serve.

Our discussion of non-purposive elaborations of functional claims suggests ways of filling that lacuna, but it is also necessary to point out that Marxists can be too sensitive to the charge that they perceive conspiracies. There is more collective design in history than an inflexible rejection of 'conspiracy theories' would allow, and richer scope for purposive elaboration of Marxian functional theses than that posture recognizes. Thus, while ideologies are not normally invented to fit the purposes they serve, a fairly deliberate and quite concerted effort to maintain and protect an *existing* ideology is not unusual. According to Christopher Hill, nobility and gentry in seventeenth-century England doubted they 'would still be able to control the state without the help of the church', and, therefore, 'rallied to the defence of episcopacy in 1641...for explicitly social reasons'.[25] Ruling class persons with no special devotion to an Anglican God frankly professed that the established church was required to ensure political obedience, and acted on that inspiration. Or, to take another example, when a high state functionary, reflecting on the unequal distribution of information in society, concludes that 'this inequality of knowledge has become necessary for the maintenance of all the social inequalities *which gave rise to it*',[26] he may be expected to see to the persistence of an educational structure which reproduces ignorance in the right places.

Conspiracy is a natural effect when men of like insight into the requirements of continued class domination get together, and such men do get together. But sentences beginning 'The ruling class have decided...' do not entail the convocation of an assembly. Ruling class persons meet and instruct one another in overlapping *milieux* of government, recreation, and practical affairs, and a collective policy emerges even when they were never all in one place at one time.

There are, of course, many shades between the cynical[27] handling of ideology

---

[25] Hill (1968a), pp. 153, 92. Cp. Hill (1974), p. 191.
[26] Jacques Necker, as quoted at Marx (1862–3), p. 307.
[27] What was cynical was not the belief that the existing order ought to be defended, but the use of religion in its defence.

just emphasized and an unhypocritical commitment to it, and a division of labour between lucid and *engagé* defenders of dominant ideas can be quite functional. If awareness of the true name of the game penetrates too far down the elite, it could leak into the strata beneath them. There is always a mix of manipulation, self-deception, and blind conviction in adherence to an ideology, the optimal proportions varying with circumstance.

All classes are receptive to whatever ideas are likely to benefit them, and ruling classes are well placed to propagate ideologies particularly congenial to themselves. But before an ideology is received or broadcast it has to be formed. And on that point there are traces in Marx of a Darwinian mechanism, a notion that thought-systems are produced in comparative independence from social constraint, but persist and gain social life following a filtration process which selects those well adapted for ideological service. Thus it is true but in one respect unimportant that the idea of communism has been projected time and again in history,[28] for only when the idea can assist a viable social purpose, as it can now, by figuring in the liberation of the proletariat, will it achieve social significance. There is a kind of 'ideological pool' which yields elements in different configurations as social requirements change.

Yet it is unlikely that ideas fashioned in disconnection from their possible social use will endorse and reject *exactly* what suits classes receptive to them. Here a Lamarckian element may enter, to make the picture more plausible.[29] In Lamarck's theory the equipment of the individual organism is somewhat plastic, for it changes under environmental challenge when it is put to a novel use. Because of the delicacy of intellectual constructions, sets of ideas enjoy a partly similar plasticity: one change of emphasis, one slurred inference, etc., can alter the import of the whole. Such 'Lamarckian' possibilities are intimated in Marx's review of the numerous uses to which a self-same Christianity is liable,[30] and it is not because 'liberalism' is an ambiguous term that its presumed teaching varies across space and time. And if it is true of revolutionaries that 'just when they seem engaged in revolutionizing themselves and things, in creating something that has never yet existed, precisely in such periods of revolutionary crisis they anxiously conjure up the spirits of the past to their service and borrow from them names, battle cries

[28] Marx and Engels (1846), p. 51.
[29] Plekhanov invoked Lamarck in the service of historical materialism: 'In the same way must also be understood the influence of economic requirements, and of others following from them, on the psychology of a people. Here there takes a slow adaptation by exercise or non-exercise...' (1956), pp. 217–18.
[30] See Marx (1847), p. 82.

and costumes in order to present the new scene of world history in this time-honoured disguise and this borrowed language',[31] then it is perhaps not only for the reason Marx states that they so behave, but also because the only symbols and thought-forms available are those which come from the past, and which they must now adopt and adapt.

In my reading of historical materialism, transformations of economic structure are responses to developments within the productive forces. Production relations reflect the character of productive forces, a character which makes a certain type of structure propitious for their further development. But I do not intend, in offering that formulation, to depreciate the significance of class struggle in history. For class struggle is, in my view, a principal means whereby the forces assert themselves over the relations. To be sure, there are Marxists who would assign an even more basic role to it, but I challenge them to specify what, if not the development of the productive forces, determines the rise and fall of classes.[32]

Classes are permanently poised against one another, and that class tends to prevail whose rule would best meet the demands of production. But how does the fact that production would prosper under a certain class ensure its domination? Part of the answer is that there is a general stake in stable and thriving production, so that the class best placed to deliver it attracts allies from other strata in society. Prospective ruling classes are often able to raise support among the classes subjected to the ruling class they would displace. Contrariwise, classes unsuited to the task of governing society tend to lack the confidence political hegemony requires, and if they do seize power, they tend not to hold it for long.

Sometimes, too, as in the gradual formation of capitalism, the capacity of a new class to administer production expresses itself in nascent forms of the society it will build, which, being more effective than the old forms, tend to supplant them. Purposive and competitive elements mingle as early growths of capitalism encroach upon and defeat feudal institutions that would restrict them. There is also adaptive metamorphosis. For example: a pre-capitalist landed ruling class in an epoch of commercialization requires finance from a not yet industrial bourgeoisie. When landlords cannot meet the commitments engendered by their connections, they lose their holdings, so others, in fear of a similar fate, place their operations on a capitalist basis. Some see what

[31] Marx (1852a), p. 247.
[32] For an exposition of that challenge, see section II of my 'Forces and relations of production', which appears elsewhere in this volume.

is required for survival, and undergo an alteration of class character; others fail to understand the times, or, too attached to an outmoded ideology and way of life, fight against the new order, and disappear.

The ideological and superstructural supports of the old order lose their authority. The sense of oppression and injustice always latent in the underclass becomes more manifest, encouraged by the class whose hour of glory is at hand, and the dominating illusions become pallid. Marx supposed that the ideological defences of existing conditions begin to collapse when those conditions no longer accord with productive growth. Thus

when the illusion about competition as the so-called absolute form of free individuality vanishes, this is evidence that the conditions of competition, i.e. of production founded on capital, are already felt and thought of as *barriers*, and hence already *are* such, and more and more become such.[33]

In similar spirit, Engels opined[34] that ideas of equality and rectification of injustice are perennial, but that they achieve historical power only when and because there is contradiction between the productive forces and the production relations. The class able to take hold of the forces rides up on the resentment of the exploited producers.

[33] Marx (1857–8), p. 652.
[34] Engels (1878), p. 369.

Part IV
Justice

12 The structure of proletarian unfreedom*

G. A. Cohen

I

According to Karl Marx, a member of a social class belongs to it by virtue of his position within social relations of production. In keeping with this formula, Marx defined the proletarian as the producer who has (literally or in effect) nothing to sell but his own labour-power.[1] He inferred that the worker is *forced* to sell his labour-power (on pain of starvation).

In this essay I am not concerned with the adequacy of Marx's definition of working class membership. I propose instead to assess the truth of the consequence he rightly or wrongly inferred from that definition. Is it true that workers are forced to sell their labour-power?

This question is debated in the real world, by non-academic people. Supporters and opponents of the capitalist system tend to disagree about the answer to it. There is a familiar right-wing answer to it which I think has a lot of power. In this essay I argue against leftists who do not see the answer's power and against rightists who do not see the answer's limitations.

II

Some would deny that workers are forced to sell their labour-power, on the ground that they have other choices: the worker can go on the dole, or beg, or simply make no provision for himself and trust to fortune.

It is true that the worker is free to do these other things. The acknowledgment that he is free to starve to death gets its sarcastic power from the fact that he *is* free to starve to death: no one threatens to *make* him stay alive by, for example, force-feeding him. But to infer that he is therefore not forced to sell his labour-power is to employ a false account of what it is to be forced to do

* This essay originally appeared in *Philosophy and Public Affairs*, vol. 12, Winter 1983. Reprinted with permission.
[1] For elaboration of this definition, and a defence of its attribution to Marx, see Cohen (1978a), pp. 63–77, 222–3, 333–6.

something. When I am forced to do something I have no *reasonable* or *acceptable* alternative course. It need not be true that I have no alternative whatsoever. At least usually, when a person says, 'I was forced to do it. I had no other choice', the second part of the statement is elliptical for something like 'I had no other choice worth considering.' For in the most familiar sense of '*X* is forced to do *A*', it is entailed that *X* is forced to *choose* to do *A*, and the claim that the worker is forced to sell his labour-power is intended in that familiar sense. Hence the fact that he is free to starve or beg instead is not a refutation of the mooted claim: the claim entails that there are other (unacceptable) things he is free to do.

III

Robert Nozick might grant that many workers have no acceptable alternative to selling their labour-power, and he recognizes that they need not have no alternative at all in order to count as forced to do so. But he denies that having no acceptable alternative but to do *A* entails being forced to do *A*, no matter how bad *A* is, and no matter how much worse the alternatives are, since he thinks that to have no acceptable alternative means to be forced only when unjust actions help to explain the absence of acceptable alternatives. Property distributions reflecting a history of acquisition and exchange may leave the worker with no other acceptable option, but he is nevertheless not forced to sell his labour-power, if the acquiring and exchanging were free of injustice.

Nozick's objection to the thesis under examination rests upon a moralized account of what it is to be forced to do something. It is a false account, because it has the absurd upshot that if a criminal's imprisonment is morally justified, he is then not forced to be in prison. We may therefore set Nozick's objection aside.[2]

IV

There is, however, an objection to the claim that workers are forced to sell their labour-power which does not depend upon a moralized view of what being forced involves. But before we come to it, in section V, I must explain how I intend the predicate 'is forced to sell his labour-power'. The claim in which it figures here comes from Karl Marx. Now I noted that Marx

---

[2] For Nozick's view, see his (1974), pp. 262–4, which is criticized at p. 151 of Cohen (1978b). For more discussion of false-because-moralized definitions of freedom, see Cohen (1979a), pp. 12–14; Cohen (1981a), pp. 228–9; Cohen (1981b), pp. 10–11. For a partly similar critique of moralized accounts of force and freedom, see Zimmerman (1981), pp. 121–31.

characterized classes by reference to social relations of production, and the claim is intended to satisfy that condition: it purports to say something about the proletarian's position in capitalist relations of production. But relations of production are, for Marxism, *objective*: what relations of production a person is in does not turn on his consciousness. It follows that, if the proletarian is forced to sell his labour-power in the relevant Marxist sense, then this must be because of his objective situation, and not because of his attitude to himself, his level of self-confidence, his cultural attainment, and so on. It is in any case doubtful that limitations in those subjective endowments can be sources of what interests us: unfreedom, as opposed to something similar to it but also rather different: incapacity. But even if diffidence and the like could be said to force a person to sell his labour-power, that would be an irrelevant case here (except, perhaps, where personal subjective limitations are caused by capitalist relations of production, a possibility considered in section XIV below).

To be forced to do *A* by one's objective situation is to do it because of factors other than the subjective ones just mentioned. Many would insist that the proper source of force, and a *a fortiori* of objective force, is action by other people, what they have done, or are doing, or what they would do were one to try to do *A*. I agree with Harry Frankfurt[3] that this insistence is wrong, but I shall accede to it in the present essay, for two reasons. This first is that the mooted restriction makes it harder, and therefore more interesting, to show that workers are forced to sell their labour-power. The second is that, as I shall now argue, where relations of production force people to do things, people force people to do things, so the 'no force without a forcing agent' condition is satisfied here, even if it does not hold generally.

The relations of production of a society may be identified with the powers its differently situated persons have with respect to the society's productive forces, that is, the labour capacities of its producers and the means of production they use.[4] We can distinguish between standard and deviant uses of the stated powers. Let me then propose that a worker is forced to sell his labour-power in the presently required sense if and only if the constraint is a result of standard exercises of the powers constituting relations of production.

If a millionaire is forced by a blackmailer to sell his labour-power, he is not forced to do so in the relevant Marxist sense, since the blackmailer does not

---

[3] Frankfurt points out that natural things and processes operating independently of human action also force people to do things. See his (1973), pp. 83–4. (Note that one can agree with Frankfurt about this while denying that lack of capacity restricts freedom: the question whether internal obstacles restrict it is distinct from the question which kinds of external obstacles do.)

[4] See Cohen (1978a), pp. 31–5, 63–5, 217–25.

use economic power to get him to do so. The relevant constraint must reflect use of economic power, and not, moreover, just any use of it, but a *standard* exercise of it. I cannot offer a satisfying definition of 'standard', but it is not hard to sort out cases in an intuitive way. If, for example, a capitalist forces people to work for him by hiring gunmen to get them to do so, the resulting constraint is due to a nonstandard exercise of economic power. And one can envisage similarly irrelevant cases of relaxation of constraint: a philanthropic capitalist might be willing to transfer large shares in the ownership of his enterprise to workers, on a 'first come first served' basis. That would not be a standard use of capitalist power.

Suppose, however, that economic structural constraint does not, as just proposed, operate through the regular exercise by persons of the powers constituting the economic structure, but in some more *im*personal way, as Althusserians seem to imagine. It might still be said, for a different reason, that if the structure of capitalism leaves the worker no choice but to sell his labour-power, then he is forced to do so by actions of persons. For the structure of capitalism is not in all senses self-sustaining. It is sustained by a great deal of deliberate human action, notably on the part of the state. And if, as I often think, the state functions on behalf of the capitalist class, then any structural constraint by virtue of which the worker must sell his labour-power has enough human will behind it to satisfy the stipulation that where there is force, there are forcing human beings.

The stipulation might be satisfied by doctrine weaker than that which presents the state as an instrument of the capitalist class. Suppose that the state upholds the capitalist order not because it is a *capitalist* order, but because it is the prevailing order, and the state is dedicated to upholding whatever order prevails. Then, too, one might be justified in speaking of human forcing.

V

Under the stated intepretation of 'is forced to sell his labour-power', a serious problem arises for the thesis under examination. For if there are persons whose objective position is identical with that of proletarians but who are not forced to sell their labour-power, then proletarians are not relevantly so forced, and the thesis is false. And there do seem to be such persons.

I have in mind those proletarians who, initially possessed of no greater resources than most, secure positions in the petty bourgeoisie and elsewhere, thereby rising above the proletariat. Striking cases in Britain are members of certain immigrant groups, who arrive penniless, and without good connections, but who propel themselves up the class hierarchy with effort, skill, and luck.

One thinks – it is a contemporary example – of those who are willing to work very long hours in shops bought from native British bourgeois, shops which used to close early. Their initial capital is typically an amalgam of savings, which they accumulated, perhaps painfully, while still in the proletarian condition, and some form of external finance. *Objectively speaking*, most[5] British proletarians are in a position to obtain these. Therefore most British proletarians are not forced to sell their labour-power.

VI

I now refute two predictable objections to the above argument.

The first says that the recently mentioned persons were, *while they were proletarians*, forced to sell their labour-power. Their cases do not show that proletarians are not forced to sell their labour-power. They show something different: that proletarians are not forced to remain proletarians.

This objection embodies a misunderstanding of what Marxists intend when they say that workers are forced to sell their labour-power. But before I say what Marxists intend by that statement, I must defend this general claim about freedom and constraint: *fully explicit attributions of freedom and constraint contain two temporal indices*. To illustrate: I may now be in a position truly to say that I am free to attend a concert tomorrow night, since nothing has occurred, up to now, to prevent my doing so. If so, I am *now* free to attend a concert *tomorrow night*. In similar fashion, the time when I am constrained to perform an action need not be identical with the time of the action: I might *already* be forced to attend a concert *tomorrow night* (since you might already have ensured that, if I do not, I shall suffer some great loss).

Now when Marxists say that proletarians are forced to sell their labour-power, they do not mean: 'X is a proletarian at time t only if X is at t forced to sell his labour-power at t' for that would be compatible with his not being forced to at time $t+n$, no matter how small n is. X might be forced on Tuesday to sell his labour-power on Tuesday, but if he is not forced on Tuesday to sell his labour-power on Wednesday (if, for example, actions open to him on Tuesday would bring it about that on Wednesday he need not do so), then, though still a proletarian on Tuesday, he is not then someone who is forced to sell his labour-power in the relevant Marxist sense. The manifest intent of the Marxist claim is that the proletarian is forced at t to *continue* to sell his labour-power, throughout a period from t to $t+n$, for some considerable n.

---

[5] At least most: it could be argued that *all* British proletarians are in such a position, but I stay with 'most' lest some ingenious person discover objective proletarian circumstances worse than the worst once suffered by now prospering immigrants. But see also footnote 6.

It follows that because there is a route out of the proletariat, which our counterexamples travelled, reaching their destination in, as I would argue, an amount of time less than n,[6] they were, though proletarians, not forced to sell their labour-power in the required Marxist sense.

Proletarians who have the option of class ascent are not forced to sell their labour-power, just because they do have that option. Most proletarians have it as much as our counterexamples did. Therefore most proletarians are not forced to sell their labour-power.

VII

But now I face a second objection. It is that necessarily not more than few proletarians can exercise the option of upward movement. For capitalism requires a substantial hired labour force, which would not exist if more than just a few workers rose.[7] Put differently, there are necessarily only enough petty bourgeois and other nonproletarian positions for a small number of the proletariat to leave their estate.

I agree with the premise, but does it defeat the argument against which it is directed? Does it refute the claim that most proletarians are not forced to sell their labour-power? I think not.

An analogy will indicate why. Ten people are placed in a room the only exit from which is a huge and heavy locked door. At various distances from each lies a single heavy key. Whoever picks up this key – and each is physically able, with varying degrees of effort, to do so – and takes it to the door will find, after considerable self-application, a way to open the door and leave the room. But if he does so he alone will be able to leave it. Photoelectric devices installed by a jailer ensure that it will open only just enough to permit one exit. Then it will close, and no one inside the room will be able to open it again.

It follows that, whatever happens, at least nine people will remain in the room.

---

[6] This might well be challenged, since the size of n is a matter of judgment. I would defend mine by references to the naturalness of saying to a worker that he is not forced to (continue to) sell his labour power, since he can take steps to set himself up as a shopkeeper. Those who judge otherwise might be able, at a pinch, to deny that most proletarians are not forced to sell their labour-power, but they cannot dispose of the counterexamples to the generalization that all are forced to. For our prospective petty bourgeois is a proletarian on the eve of his ascent when, unless, absurdly, we take n as o, he is not forced to sell his labour-power.

[7] 'The truth is this, that in this bourgeois society every workman, if he is an exceedingly clever and shrewd fellow, and gifted with bourgeois instincts and favoured by an exceptional fortune, can possibly convert himself into an *exploiteur du travail d'autrui*. But if there were no *travail* to be *exploité*, there would be no capitalist nor capitalist production' (Marx, 1866, p. 1079). For commentary on similar texts, see Cohen (1978a), p. 243.

Now suppose that not one of the people is inclined to try to obtain the key and leave the room. Perhaps the room is no bad place, and they do not want to leave it. Or perhaps it is pretty bad, but they are too lazy to undertake the effort needed to escape. Or perhaps no one believes he would be able to secure the key in face of the capacity of the others to intervene (though no one would in fact intervene, since, being so diffident, each also believes that he would be unable to remove the key from anyone else). Suppose that, whatever may be their reasons, they are all so indisposed to leave the room that if, counterfactually, one of them were to try to leave, the rest would not interfere. The universal inaction is relevant to my argument, but the explanation of it is not.

Then, whomever we select, it is true of the other nine that not one of them is going to try to get the key. Therefore it is true of the selected person that he is free to obtain the key, and to use it.[8] He is therefore not forced to remain in the room. But all this is true of whomever we select. Therefore it is true of each person that he is not forced to remain in the room, even though necessarily at least nine will remain in the room, and in fact all will.

Consider now a slightly different example, a modified version of the situation just described. In the new case there are two doors and two keys. Again, there are ten people, but this time one of them does try to get out, and succeeds, while the rest behave as before. Now necessarily eight will remain in the room, but it is true of each of the nine who do stay that he or she is free to leave it. The pertinent general feature, present in both cases, is that there is at least one means of egress which none will attempt to use, and which each is free to use, since, *ex hypothesi*, no one would block his way.

By now the application of the analogy may be obvious. The number of exits from the proletariat is, as a matter of objective circumstance, small. But most proletarians are not trying to escape, and, as a result, *it is false that each exit is being actively attempted by some proletarian*. Therefore for most[9] proletarians there exists a means of escape. So even though necessarily most proletarians will remain proletarians, and will sell their labour-power, perhaps none, and at most a minority, are forced to do so.

In reaching this conclusion, which is about the proletariat's *objective* position, I used some facts of consciousness, regarding workers' aspirations

[8] For whatever may be the correct analysis of 'X is free to do A', it is clear that X is free to do A if X would do A if he tried to do A, and that sufficient condition of freedom is all that we need here.

Some have objected that the stated condition is not sufficient: a person, they say, may do something he is not free to do, since he may do something he is not legally, or morally, free to do. Those who agree with that unhelpful remark can take it that I am interested in the non-normative use of 'free', which is distinguished by the sufficient condition just stated.

[9] See footnotes 5 and 6.

and intentions. That is legitimate. For if the workers are objectively forced to sell their labour-power, then they are forced to do so whatever their subjective situation may be. But their actual subjective situation brings it about that they are not forced to sell their labour-power. Hence they are not objectively forced to sell their labour-power.

VIII

One could say, speaking rather broadly, that we have found more freedom in the proletariat's situation than classical Marxism asserts. But if we return to the basis on which we affirmed that most proletarians are not forced to sell their labour-power, we shall arrive at a more refined description of the objective position with respect to force and freedom. What was said will not be withdrawn, but we shall add significantly to it.

That basis was the reasoning originally applied to the case of the people in the locked room. Each is free to seize the key and leave. But note the conditional nature of his freedom. He is free not only *because* none of the others tries to get the key, but *on condition* that they do not (a condition which, in the story, is fulfilled). Then *each is free only on condition that the others do not exercise their similarly conditional freedom*. Not more that one can exercise the liberty they all have. If, moreover, any one were to exercise it, then, because of the structure of the situation, all the others would lose it.

Since the freedom of each is contingent on the others not exercising their similarly contingent freedom, we can say that there is a great deal of unfreedom in their situation. Though each is individually free to leave, he suffers with the rest from what I shall call *collective unfreedom*.

In defence of this description, let us reconsider the question why the people do not try to leave. None of the reasons suggested earlier – lack of desire, laziness, diffidence – go beyond what a person wants and fears for himself alone. But the annals of human motivation show that sometimes people care about the fate of others, and they sometimes have that concern when they share a common oppression. Suppose, then, not so wildly, that there is a sentiment of solidarity in that room. A fourth possible explanation of the absence of attempt to leave now suggests itself. It is that no one will be satisfied with a personal escape which is not part of a general liberation.[10]

---

[10] In a stimulating commentary on the argument of sections VII and VIII, Jon Elster notes that it involves avoidance of two fallacies, that of composition ('What is true of each must be true of all') and that of division ('What is true of all must be true of each'): 'It is true of any individual worker that he is free to leave the class, but not of all workers simultaneously. And the reason why the individual worker is free to leave the class is that the others do not want to leave it; and the reason why the others do not want to leave it is that whatever is

The new supposition does not upset the claim that each is free to leave, for we may assume that it remains true of each person that he would suffer no interference if, counterfactually, he sought to use the key (assume the others would have contempt for him, but not try to stop him). Each remains free to leave. Yet we can envisage members of the group communicating to their jailer a demand for freedom, to which he could hardly reply that they are free already (even though, individually, they are). The hypothesis of solidarity makes the collective unfreedom evident. But unless we say, absurdly, that the solidarity creates the unfreedom to which it is a response, we must say that there is collective unfreedom whether or not solidarity obtains.

Returning to the proletariat, we can conclude, by parity of reasoning, that although most proletarians are free to escape the proletariat, and, indeed, even if every one is, the proletariat is collectively unfree, an imprisoned class.

Marx often maintained that the worker is forced to sell his labour-power not to any particular capitalist, but just to some capitalist or other, and he emphasized the ideological value of this distinction.[11] The present point is that, although, in a collective sense, workers are forced to sell their labour-power, scarcely any particular proletarian is forced to sell himself even to some capitalist or other. And this too has ideological value. It is part of the genius of capitalist exploitation that, by contrast with exploitation which proceeds by 'extra-economic coercion',[12] it does not require the unfreedom of specified individuals. There is an ideologically valuable anonymity on *both* sides of the relationship of exploitation.

IX

It was part of the argument for affirming the freedom to escape of proletarians, taken individually, that not every exit from the proletariat is crowded with would-be escapees. Why should this be so? Here are some of the reasons:

1. Although it is possible to escape, it is not easy, and often people do not attempt what is possible but hard.
2. There is also what Marx called the 'dull compulsion of economic relations'.[13] Long occupancy, for example from birth, of a subordinate class position nurtures the illusion, as important for the stability of the

desirable if it happens to all members simultaneously is not necessarily desirable if it happens to one member separately and exclusively' (Elster, 1979b, p. 63). Elster shows that such structures pervade social life.

[11] See Cohen (1978a), p. 223, for exposition and references.
[12] The phrase comes from Marx (1867), p. 899. See Cohen (1978a), pp. 82–4, for a discussion of different modes of exploitation.   [13] Marx (1867), p. 899.

system as the myth of easy escape, that one's class position is natural and inescapable.

3. Finally, there is the fact that not all workers would like to be petty or transpetty bourgeois. Eugene Debs said, 'I do not want to rise above the working class, I want to rise with them', thereby evincing an attitude like the one lately attributed to the people in the locked room. It is sometimes true of the worker that, in Brecht's words,

> He wants no servants under him
> And no boss over his head.[14]

Those lines envisage a better liberation: not just from the working class, but from class society.

X

In the rest of this essay I consider objections to the arguments of sections VII and VIII, which I shall henceforth call argument 7 and argument 8, after the numbers of the sections in which they were presented. Shorn of explanatory detail, the arguments are as follows:

7: There are more exits from the British proletariat than there are workers trying to leave it. Therefore, British workers are individually free to leave the proletariat.

8: There are very few exits from the British proletariat and there are very many workers in it. Therefore, British workers are collectively unfree to leave the proletariat.

In the useful language of the medieval schoolmen, the workers are not forced to sell their labour-power *in sensu diviso*, but they are forced to *in sensu composito*.

The arguments are consistent with one another. Hillel Steiner has pointed to a potential conflict between them, but it is unlikely to materialize. The potential conflict relates to my attribution to Marxism (see section VI) of the claim that the worker is forced to remain a worker for some considerable amount of time n, a claim which the conclusion of argument 7 is intended to deny. Now, the larger n is, the easier it is to refute the Marxist claim and affirm argument 7's conclusion. But as n grows larger, the number of exits from the proletariat increases, and the conclusion of argument 8 becomes correspondingly less secure. To sustain both arguments without equivocation one must choose an intuitively plausible n under these opposite pressures. But it is not hard to meet that requirement: five years, for example, will do.

Right-wing readers will applaud argument 7, but they will want to resist

[14] From his 'Song of the United Front'.

argument 8. Left-wing readers will have, in each case, the opposite reaction. In the remaining five sections I deal, first, with three right-wing objections to argument 8, and then with two left-wing objections to argument 7. None of the objections to be considered here challenges the premise of either argument. Objections which do so are dealt with in sections of the original article which have been omitted here.

XI

Someone who, unlike Frankfurt, believes that only human action can force people to do things, might object as follows to the derivation of the conclusion of argument 8, that British workers are collectively unfree:

The prisoners in the room are collectively unfree, since the availability of only one exit is a result of a jailer's action. If they had wandered into a cave from which, for peculiar reasons, only one could leave, then, though *unable*, collectively, to leave, they would not have been *unfree* to, since there would have been no one forcing them to stay. It is true that, *in sensu composito*, most proletarians must remain proletarians, but this is due to a numerical relationship which does not reflect human design. It is therefore not correct to speak of the proletariat as collectively *unfree* to leave, as opposed to collectively *unable*. In short, the admitted restrictions on proletarian ascent are not caused by factors which would justify application of the concepts of force and unfreedom.

I have four replies to this objection.

First, what was said about the cave, if it illustrates the thesis that people are forced only when people force them, also shows how unlikely a thesis that is. For it seems false that the hapless wanderers are forced to remain in the cave only if someone put them there, or keeps them there.

It is, moreover, arguable that the (anyhow questionable) requirement of a forcing human agency is met in the cave case. I say that there is collective unfreedom to leave in that as soon as one person left, the rest would be prevented from doing so. And just as there is individual unfreedom when a person's attempt to do A would be blocked by someone else doing it, so there is collective unfreedom when an attempt by more than n to do A would be blocked by that subset of n which succeeded in doing it. This applies to the proletariat, when the number of exits is limited. They are collectively unfree since, were more to try to escape than there are exits, the successful would ensure the imprisonment of those who failed.

But apart from the mutual constraint arising out of the surplus of persons over exits, there is the fact that the adverse numerical relationship reflects the structure of capitalism which, we saw in section IV, is sufficiently connected, in various ways, with human actions to satisfy the un-Frankfurtian scruples motivating the present objection. Proletarians suffer restricted access to means of liberation because the rights of private property are enforced by exercise of capitalist power.

Finally, even if we should have to abandon the claim that workers are collectively unfree to escape and embrace instead the idea that they are collectively unable to, the withdrawal would be only a tactical one. For anyone concerned about human freedom and the prospect of expanding it must also care about structurally induced disability (or whatever he chooses to call it) which he refuses to regard as absence of freedom. Even if he is right that the wanderers are not *forced* to stay in the cave, he surely cannot deny that whoever released them would be *liberating* them.

XII

The objector of section XI doubted that the situation of the proletariat could be described as one of collective freedom, but he did not challenge the very concept of a collective unfreedom distinct from individual unfreedom. I now deal with a differently inspired scepticism. Set aside the question of what causes the restriction on the number of nonproletarian positions. Does the resulting lack of access justify my description of the workers as lacking collective freedom? I argued that there is some sense in which they are not all free to escape, and, since they are free *in sensu diviso*, I called their unfreedom collective unfreedom.

Collective unfreedom can be defined as follows: a group suffers collective unfreedom with respect to a type of action A if and only if performance of A by all members of the group is impossible.[15] Collective unfreedom comes in varying amounts, and it is greater the smaller the ratio of the maximum that could perform A to the total number in the group. Collective unfreedom is particularly interesting when, as in our example, there is more freedom for a set of individuals taken individually than for the same individuals when they are taken as members of a group: collective unfreedom, we might say, is *irreducibly* collective when more can perform A *in sensu diviso* than can perform it *in sensu composito*. And collective unfreedom matters more the smaller the ratio mentioned above is, and the more important or desirable action A is.

A person shares in a collective unfreedom when, to put it roughly, he is among those who are so situated that if enough others exercise the corresponding individual freedom, then they lose their individual freedoms.

[15] That is, if and only if it is not possible that, for all X, X performs A (even if, for all X, it is possible that X performs A).

One might also have to specify the kind of cause that makes it impossible, a complication discussed in section XI and here set aside.

More precisely: X shares in a collective unfreedom with respect to a type of action A if and only if X belongs to a set of *n* persons which is such that:

1. no more than *m* of them (where *m* < *n*) are free (*sensu composito*) to perform A, and
2. no matter which *m* members performed A, the remaining *n* − *m* would then be unfree (*sensu diviso*) to perform A.[16]

Using both expressions as terms of art, one might distinguish between *collective* unfreedom and *group* unfreedom, and I am not here concerned with the latter. In the proffered definition of collective unfreedom the relevant agents are individuals, not a group as such. We are not discussing freedom and the lack of it which groups have *qua* groups, but which individuals have as members of groups. Thus, for example, the freedom or lack of it which the proletariat has to overthrow capitalism falls outside our scope,[17] since no individual proletarian could ever be free to overthrow capitalism, even when the proletariat is free to do so.

Another form of essentially interpersonal freedom is that canonically reported in sentences of the form 'X is free to do A with Y', where Y is another agent, and where, if X does A with Y, then Y does A with X (the last condition is needed to exclude such actions as wiping the floor with Y: 'with' means 'together with' in sentences of the indicated form). This can be called *freedom-to-act-with*, or *relational freedom*.[18] Note that the relevant relation is neither symmetrical nor transitive. If I am free to do A with you, it does not follow that you are free to do A with me, since, for example, doing A might be seeing a film which you would love to see with me but which I do not want to see. And if I am free to make love with you and you are free to make love with him, it does not follow that I am free to make love with him. Freedom-to-act-with figured implicitly in the argument of section VIII, when I hypothesized a sentiment of solidarity which moved each person in the room to regret that (though free to leave) he was not free to leave with the others. But freedom-to-act-with is different from what is here meant by collective freedom: in the case of the latter there need be no reference to another person in the description of the action people are free or unfree to perform.

Now someone might say: since interesting collective unfreedom obtains only when individuals are free, why should it be a source of concern? Why

---

[16] The concept of sharing in a collective unfreedom might be used in an attempt to define the proletariat, for example, as the largest group in a society all members of which share a collective unfreedom with respect to the sale of labour-power. Unlike the definition I described and rejected at p. 25 of Cohen (1979a), this one would have the virtue of keeping Sir Keith Joseph out of the working class.

[17] See Cohen (1978a), pp. 243–5, for remarks on that issue.

[18] Robert Ware brought the important concept of relational freedom to my attention.

should we care about anything other than the freedom of individuals?[19] The question forgets that it is a fact touching each individual in the group, namely, the mutually conditional nature of their freedom, which licenses the idea of collective unfreedom. As soon as enough people exercise the coexisting individual freedoms, collective unfreedom generates individual unfreedoms. If, though free to do A, I share in a collective unfreedom with respect to A, I am less free than I otherwise would be.

But it might be claimed that there are structures manifesting what I defined as collective unfreedom which would not normally be regarded as examples of lack of freedom. Suppose, for instance, that a hotel, at which one hundred tourists are staying, lays on a coach trip for the first forty who apply, since that is the number of seats in the coach. And suppose that only thirty want to go. Then, on my account, each of the hundred is free to go, but their situation displays a collective unfreedom. Yet it seems wrong, the objector says, to speak of unfreedom here.

I do not agree. For suppose all of the tourists did want to go. Then it would seem appropriate to say that they are not all free to go. But in the case of individual freedom, while there is less reason to regret an unfreedom to do what I have no desire to do,[20] I am not less unfree for lacking that desire.[21] Why should the position be different in the case of collective unfreedom? Thwarted desire throws unfreedom into relief, and sometimes thwarted desire is needed to make unfreedom deserving of note, but it is not a necessary condition of unfreedom.

The coach case is a rather special one. For we tend to suppose that the management lay on only one coach because they correctly anticipate that one will be enough to meet the demand. Accordingly, we also suppose that if more had wanted to go, there would have been an appropriately larger number of seats available. If all that is true, then the available amount of collective freedom nonaccidentally accords with the tourists' desires, and though there still is a collective unfreedom, it is, as it were, a purely technical one. But if we assume that there is only one coach in town, and some such assumption

---

[19] One might reply: because there are some things which we may hope groups are free to do which we would not expect, or would not want, individuals to be free to do. But that answer is out of place here, because of the distinction just drawn between group and collective freedom.

[20] Less reason, but not no reason, since the desire for freedom is not reducible to the desire to do what one would be free to do if one had it. I may resent my lack of freedom to do what I have no wish to do: Soviet citizens who dislike restrictions on foreign travel need not want to go abroad. And subtler reasons for valuing the freedom to do what I do not want to do are presented in Elster (1982a), p. 228.

[21] See Berlin (1969), pp. xxxviiiff., 139–40, and Steiner (1974–5), p. 34. But see, too, Elster (1982a), pp. 227–8.

is required for parity with the situation of proletarians, then the tourists' collective unfreedom is more than merely technical.

There are two significantly different variants of the merely technical version of the coach case. In the first the management decide how many coaches to order after first asking each tourist whether or not he wants to go. In that case there is a time at which all are free to go, even *in sensu composito*, though they cease to be after they have declared themselves.[22] But the management might order one coach without consulting the tourists, out of knowledge of the normal distribution of tourist desire. In that case there is no time at which all are free to go, *in sensu composito*, but the collective unfreedom is still purely technical and singularly unregrettable.

Now someone who accepts my concept of collective unfreedom might argue that it is not in general a lamentable thing, and that it need not be lamentable even when the amount of collective unfreedom is not, as above, directly or indirectly causally connected, in a benign way, with people's desires. There is at present (or was when I first wrote this) a shortage of bus conductors in London, so that there is a good deal of individual freedom to become one, but also a large amount of collective unfreedom, since not more than very few of us can be bus conductors. But so what?

The rhetorical question is apposite in this case, but it is out of place when there is unfreedom to abstain from selling one's labour-power to another. As I remarked earlier, the extent to which collective unfreedom with respect to an action matters depends upon the nature of the action. I grant that collective unfreedom with respect to the sale of labour-power is not lamentable merely because it is collective unfreedom, since some collective unfreedom, like some individual unfreedom, is not lamentable. It is what this particular unfreedom forces workers to do which makes it a proper object of regret and protest. They are forced to subordinate themselves to others who thereby gain control over their, the workers', productive existence. The contrast between them and those others is the subject of the next section.

XIII

In an argument which does not challenge the concept of collective unfreedom, Hillel Steiner and Jan Narveson[23] say that if there is a sense in which capitalism renders workers unfree, then it does the same to capitalists. For

[22] That is, there is a time t at which they are all free to go at $t+n$, and a time $t+(n-m)$ at which they are not all free to go at $t+n$, where $n > m > o$. See section VI on the need to refer twice to time in fully explicit specifications of freedom.

[23] In separate personal correspondence.

if having no choice but to sell his labour-power makes the worker unfree, then the capitalist is similarly unfree, since he has no choice but to invest his capital. Sometimes authors sympathetic to Marx say similar things. Thus Gary Young argues that the 'same line of reasoning' which shows that 'the worker is compelled to sell his labor power to some capitalist...shows equally that the capitalist is compelled to obtain labor power from the worker'.[24]

I shall presently question the claim that capitalists are forced to invest their capital. But even if we suppose that they are, the disanalogy between them and workers remains so great that the Steiner/Narveson challenge must be judged rather insensitive.

For the worker is more closely connected with his labour-power than the capitalist is with his capital. When I sell my labour-power, I put *myself* at the disposal of another, and that is not true when I invest my capital. I come with my labour-power, I am part of the deal.[25] That is why some people call wage labour wage slavery, and that is why John Stuart Mill said that 'to work at the bidding and for the profit of another...is not...a satisfactory state to human beings of educated intelligence, who have ceased to think themselves naturally inferior to those whom they serve'.[26] I am sure that many will think it is an irresponsible exaggeration to call wage labour wage slavery. But note that no one would say, even by way of exaggeration, that having to invest one's capital is a form of slavery.

But Steiner and Narveson are not, in any case, entitled to say that capitalists are forced to invest their capital. To begin with, some are so rich that they could devote the rest of their days to spending it on consumer goods. But let us focus on the more modestly situated remainder. When Marxists claim that workers are forced to sell their labour-power, they mean that they have no acceptable alternative, if they want to stay alive. But capitalists, some might say, do have an acceptable alternative to investing their capital: they are free to sell their labour-power instead.[27] Of course, Steiner and Narveson, in order to defend their thesis, might deny that that is an acceptable alternative, and I, for other reasons, might agree. But if they take that line, then they should not have proposed their analogy in the first place. So either the capitalist is not forced to invest his capital, since he could, after all, sell his labour-power;

---

[24] Young (1978), p. 448.

[25] 'The fact that labour and the labourer are inseparable creates certain difficulties', David O'Mahoney declares, but he reassures us that 'analytically labour is no different from any other resource the owners of which contract with the entrepreneur to use it for his purposes' (O'Mahoney, 1979, p. 30).   [26] Mill (1848), p. 766.

[27] We can set aside the special case of a wholly infirm capitalist. If capitalists were in general unable to live except by investing their capital, their bargaining position *vis-à-vis* workers would be rather different.

or, if he is, then that is because of how bad selling one's labour-power is, in comparison with investing one's capital.[28]

It might be said that the capitalist is, *qua* capitalist, forced to invest his capital: insofar as he acts in that capacity, he has no other choice. But even if that is so – and I am not sure that it is – it is irrelevant. For while it is sometimes appropriate to deal with individuals 'only in so far as they are the personifications of economic categories',[29] that form of abstraction is out of place here. We are not here interested in the freedom and bondage of abstract characters, such as the capitalist *qua* capitalist. We are interested in *human* freedom, and hence in the human being who is a capitalist; and if the capitalist *qua* capitalist is forced to invest his capital, it does not follow that the human being who is a capitalist is forced to. It is also irrelevant, if true, that the capitalist is forced to invest his capital as long as he wants to be a capitalist. Note that, in order to confer plausibility on the claim that the worker is forced to sell his labour-power, it is not necessary to stick in such phrases as '*qua* worker' or 'as long as he wants to be a worker'.

Those capitalists who are not dizzily rich are forced to invest their capital or sell their labour-power. So they have an alternative to selling their labour-power which the worker lacks. But they are not gods. Like the worker, they 'enter into relations that are indispensable and independent of their will'.[30] Everyone has to take capitalism as it is. But people have different amounts of choice about where to enter the set of relations it imposes, and capitalists typically have vastly more such choice than workers do.

In the foregoing discussion I did not observe the distinction between the freedom of capitalists *in sensu diviso* and their freedom *in sensu composito*, since the Steiner/Narveson objection is presented without reference to that distinction. We can, however, imagine an objection of the same general style which does make use of it:

The individual capitalist may have more freedom of choice than the individual worker, but your own emphasis is not on the unfreedom of the worker taken as an individual, but on the unfreedom he shares with other members of his class. And if we look at capitalists as a class, we find a similar collective unfreedom. They could not *all* become sellers of labour-power, since for there to be sellers of it there have to be buyers of it. Capitalists consequently suffer from a collective unfreedom parallel to that of workers.

I have three replies to this objection.

---

[28] And not only in comparison with investing capital, but also absolutely, if the account of acceptability in alternatives on p. 258 below is right.

[29] Marx (1867), p. 92. [30] Marx (1859).

Recall, first, that collective unfreedom comes in varying amounts (see p. 248). Then note that even if the objection is otherwise sound, it demonstrates much less collective unfreedom for capitalists than can be attributed to workers, since the members of any group of all but any (say) two or three of the capitalists are not structurally prevented from giving their wealth to those two or three. Mass escape from the proletariat, leaving only two or three workers behind, is, by contrast, structurally impossible.

But one can go further. It is unlikely that capitalists suffer *any* collective unfreedom with respect to becoming wage workers, since if literally all capitalists wanted to do so, so that none of their number was willing to play the role of hirer, it would probably be easy to find workers willing and able to fill it.

Finally, the objection ignores a way in which capitalists could stop being capitalists *without* becoming wage workers: by yielding their wealth not, as above, to particular others, but to society at large. I do not propose this as a new road to socialism, since it is a practical certainty that capitalists will not travel it.[31] My point is that there is no structural barrier against complete self-extinction of the capitalist class, whereas there is a structural barrier to mass exit from the proletariat: the capitalists own the means of production.

XIV

One left-wing objection to the argument of section VII does not question its premise, that there are more exits from the proletariat than there are workers trying to leave it. The objection is that it is unrealistic to infer that the great majority of workers are individually free to leave. For most lack the requisite assets of character and personality: they have no commercial shrewdness, they do not know how to present themselves well, and so on.[32]

To assess this objection, we must distinguish between the freedom to do something and the capacity to do it.

Suppose that the world's best long-distance swimmer has just begun to serve a long prison sentence. Then he has the capacity to swim the English Channel, but he is not free to do so. My situation is the opposite of his. I am free to swim it, but I lack the capacity.

One might suggest, by way of generalization, that a person is unfree to do *A* if and only if, were he to try to do *A*, he would fail to do *A* as a result of the action(s) of one or more other persons; and that a person lacks the

---

[31] 'A proposition is a practical certainty if its probability is so high as to allow us to reason, in *any* decision problem, as if its probability were 1' (Jeffrey, 1970, p. 105).

[32] See the requirements listed by Marx in the passage quoted in footnote 7.

capacity to do A if and only if, were he to try to do A, then, even if circumstances were maximally favourable, he would fail to do A. If a person does A, then he has both the capacity to do it and the freedom to do it (at the time when he does it).[33]

The suggested analysis of '*X* if unfree to do *A*' is both controversial and difficult to interpret. Some would strengthen it by requiring that the freedom-removing action be *intended* to cause removal of freedom. I do not accept that. I think that if you get in my way you make me unfree even if you are there by accident. Others, such as Harry Frankfurt, would defend a weaker *analysans*: for Frankfurt, natural obstacles restrict freedom. I think he is right, but I resolved (see p. 239) to proceed as if he were not.

On the given definitions the left-wing objection, as presented above, fails, since deficiencies of character and personality that make the worker incapable of leaving his class do not therefore make him unfree to leave it. But the definitions, when put together, possess an entailment which might enable the left-wing objection to be presented in a more persuasive form. It follows from the definitions that if one lacks the capacity to do *A* as a result of the action of others, then one is not only incapable of doing *A* but also unfree to do it. To see how this entailment might be used on behalf of the left-wing objection, let us first return to the case of the prisoners in the locked room.

Each is (conditionally) free to escape, and I stipulated that each has the capacity to seize and wield the key, so each, in addition, has the capacity to escape. The stipulation was not required to prove that they are free to escape, but it made the exhibition of their freedom more vivid. Suppose now that some or all lack the capacity to escape, because they cannot pick up the key; and that they cannot pick it up because they are too weak, since the jailer gives them low-grade food, in order to make it difficult or impossible for anyone to escape. Then our definitions entail that those without the capacity to use the key are not free to escape.

Now if workers cannot escape the proletariat because of personal deficiency, then this need not, on the given definitions, detract from their freedom to escape, *but it does if the deficiency is appropriately attributable to human action* (if, for example, it is due to needlessly bad education?). If a worker suffers from an appropriately generated or maintained deficiency of a sufficiently

---

[33] One might say that one is *able* to do *A* if and only if one has both the capacity and the freedom to do *A*.

Some would reject the above definition of incapacity on the ground that it entails that someone who does *A* by fluke has the capacity to do *A*. I reply that if someone does *A* by fluke, then he shows a capacity to do *A*, to wit, by fluke, which other people might not have. Unlike a six-month-old child, I have the capacity to hit the bull's-eye by fluke. For the view I am here opposing, see Kenny (1975), p. 136.

severe kind, then he is not free to escape the proletariat, and he is forced to sell his labour-power. Is he, in addition, forced to sell his labour-power in the required Marxist sense? That depends on whether the causation of the deficiency is suitably connected with the prevailing relations of production (see section V). Positive answers to these questions would upset the argument of section VII. If it is plausible to say that capitalism *makes* most workers incapable of being anything else, then it is false that most workers are free, *in sensu diviso*, not to be proletarians.

XV

Argument 7 says that (most) British workers are not forced to sell their labour-power, since they have the reasonable alternative of setting up as petty bourgeois instead, it being false that all petty bourgeois positions are already occupied. The inference turns on the principle that *a person is not forced to do* A *if he has a reasonable or acceptable alternative course*. The objection of section XIV can be treated as a challenge to that principle. It says that even if an acceptable alternative lies before an agent, he is forced to do A if he is (or, in the improved version of the objection, if he has been made) incapable of seizing it.

A different left-wing objection to the inference of argument 7 is substantially due to Chaim Tannenbaum. Tannenbaum accepts the italicized principle. That is, he agrees that a person is not forced to do A if he has an acceptable alternative course; and he also does not deny that petty bourgeois existence is relevantly superior to proletarian.[34] His objection is that for most workers the existence of petty bourgeois exits does not, as I have supposed, generate an acceptable alternative course to remaining a worker. For one must consider, as I did not, the risk attached to the attempt to occupy a petty bourgeois position, which, to judge by the rate at which fledgling enterprises fail, is very high; and also the costs of failure, since often a worker who has tried and failed to become a petty bourgeois is worse off than if he had not tried at all. The Tannenbaum objection does not challenge the premise of argument 7. The exits may exist but, so the objection goes, it is difficult to know where they are, and the price of fruitless search for them is considerable.

[34] Unlike some leftists, who resist the inference of argument 7 by urging that petty bourgeois life is no better than proletarian, because of its long hours, short holidays, financial risk, and so on. I reply (1) that the petty bourgeois, being 'his own boss', has an autonomy leftists are ill-placed to disparage, since they so strongly emphasize the losses of it entailed by 'proletarianization'; and (2) that it is in any case possible to base the conclusion of argument 7 on the availability of higher grade, not-so-petty, bourgeois positions, into which workers also from time to time rise.

Accordingly, the expected utility[35] of attempting the petty bourgeois alternative is normally too low to justify the statement that most workers are not forced to sell their labour-power.

Attention to expected utility also illuminates the case of the immigrant petty bourgeois (section V), on whom argument 7 was founded. For their lot within the working class is usually worse than that of native proletarians, who are not victims of racism and who are consequently less prone to superexploitation. Hence a smaller probability of success is required to make immigrant attempts at escape rational. The disproportionately high number of immigrants in the petty bourgeoisie is therefore less due to differences in expertise and attitude and more due to objective circumstances than seems at first to be the case.

To assess the soundness of the Tannenbaum argument, let us state it as it would apply to one whom we shall think of as a typical worker, and whom I shall call *W*:

1. The expected utility to *W* of trying the petty bourgeois course is less than the expected utility of remaining a worker (even if the utility of becoming and remaining a petty bourgeois is greater than that of remaining a worker).
2. An alternative to a given course is acceptable in the relevant sense if and only if it has at least as much expected utility as the given course. (The relevant sense of acceptability is that in which a person is forced to do *A* if he has no acceptable alternative to doing *A*.) Therefore,
3. The existence of petty bourgeois exits does not show that *W* has an acceptable alternative course. Therefore,
4. The existence of petty bourgeois exits does not show that *W* is not forced to sell his labour-power. Therefore,
5. The conclusion of argument 7 does not follow from its premise.

The first premise is a (more or less) factual claim, and the second is conceptual. In assessing the truth of the factual premise, we must discount that part of the probability of failure in attempts at petty bourgeois enterprise which is due to *purely* personal deficiencies: see section XIV. Even if we could carry out the needed discounting, it would remain extremely difficult to tell whether the factual premise is true, since the answer would involve many matters of judgment, and also information which is not a matter of judgment but which happens to be unavailable: the frequency with which enterprises founded by ex-workers succeed in the United Kingdom is not given in the bankruptcy statistics, which do not distinguish those new enterprises from other ones. I shall, however, assume that the factual premise is true, in order to focus on the conceptual claim embodied in premise 2.

If a person is forced to do *A* if he has no acceptable alternative, then what

---

[35] The expected utility of a course of action is the sum of the products of the utility and probability of each of its possible outcomes.

makes for acceptability in the required sense? Suppose I am doing *A*, and doing *B* is an alternative to that. In order to see whether it is an acceptable one, do I consider only the utility of the best possible outcome of *B*, or do I take into account all its possible outcomes, summing the products of the utility and probability of each, so that I can compare the result with the expected utility of doing *A*, and thereby obtain an answer?

It seems clear that the best possible outcome of doing *B* cannot be all that counts since, if it were, then I would not be forced to hand over my money at gunpoint where there was a minute probability that the gun would misfire. People are regularly forced to do things to which there are alternatives with low probabilities of very high rewards.

So it appears that expected utility must figure in the calculus of constraint. But I think it figures in a more complex way than premise 2 of the Tannenbaum objection allows. An alternative to a given course can be acceptable even if it has less expected utility than the given course. Illustration: 'You're not forced to go to Brighton, since you can go to Margate, though you're less likely to have a good time there.'

Premise 2 of the Tannenbaum objection is false, but something similar to it may be true. Reflection on the intuitive data leads me to propose the following characterization of acceptability, at any rate as a first approximation:

> *B* is not an acceptable alternative to *A* iff
>> EITHER *A* is particularly bad
>>> and *B* is worse than *A*
>> OR   *A* is not particularly bad
>>> but *B* is,

which simplifies to:

> *B* is not an acceptable alternative to *A* iff
>> *B* is worse than *A* and *B* is
>>> particularly bad.

Expected utility is the standard for judging courses good and bad here, and in order to apply the analysis one has to make not only relative judgments of courses of action but also ones which are absolute *in some sense* (I shall not try to specify it): that is how I intend 'particularly bad'. If we were allowed only relative judgments, we would risk concluding that whenever someone does what is unambiguously the best thing for him to do, he is forced to do that thing. Unflaggingly rational people are not perpetually constrained.

Some consequences of the definition are worth mentioning.

First, even if *A* is an extremely desirable course, one might be forced to take it, since all the alternatives to it are so bad. You could be forced to go to the superb restaurant because all the others are awful. It would then be unlikely that you are going to it (only) *because* you are forced to, but that is another matter. It is not true that you do everything you are forced to do *because* you are forced to do it.

Secondly, all the alternatives to *A* might be absolutely terrible, and no better than *A*, and yet one might still not be forced to do *A*, since some of the alternatives might be no worse than *A*. To be sure, there would be constraint in such a situation. One would be forced to do *A* or *B* or *C*... But one would not be forced to do any given one of them.

Thirdly, the extreme difficulty of assessing probabilities and utilities in real life means that it will often be intractably moot whether or not someone is forced to do something. But that is not an objection to this account, since the matter often is intractably moot.

We supposed that the expected utility of trying the petty bourgeois course is less than that of remaining a worker. Then if my account of acceptability in alternatives is correct, the substance of the Tannenbaum objection is saved if and only if trying the petty bourgeois alternative is a particularly bad thing to do.

I cannot say whether or not it is, because the facts are hard to get at and hard to organize in an informative way, and also because of an indeterminacy in the ordinary concept of constraint, on which I have relied: when estimating the goodness and badness of courses of action with a view to judging whether or not an agent is forced to do something, should we consider his preferences only, or apply more objective criteria? The ordinary concept appears to let us judge either way. It seems to have the defect that neither party to the following exchange is misusing it:

'I'm forced to go to the Indian restaurant, since I hate Chinese food.'

'Since there's nothing wrong with Chinese food, you're not forced to go to the Indian restaurant.'

13 Should Marxists be interested in exploitation?

*John Roemer**

> To work at the bidding and for the profit of another...is not...a satisfactory state to human beings of educated intelligence, who have ceased to think themselves naturally inferior to those whom they serve.
>
> J. S. Mill

> The capitalist mode of production...rests on the fact that the material conditions of production are in the hands of non-workers in the form of property in capital and land, while the masses are only owners of the personal conditions of production, of labour power. If the elements of production are so distributed, then the present-day distribution of the means of consumption results automatically.
>
> Karl Marx[1]

1. Motivations for exploitation theory

Marxian exploitation is defined as the unequal exchange of labour for goods: the exchange is unequal when the amount of labour embodied in the goods which the worker can purchase with his income (which usually consists only of wage income) is less than the amount of labour he expended to earn that income. Exploiters are agents who can command with their income more labour embodied in goods than the labour they performed; for exploited agents, the reverse is true. If the concept of 'embodied labour' is defined so that the total labour performed by a population in a certain time period is equal to the labour embodied in the goods comprising the net national product (NNP), and if the NNP is parcelled out to the members of the population in some way, then there will be (essentially) two groups: the exploiters and the

* I am indebted to the following individuals for many discussions, comments and disagreements: G. A. Cohen, Jon Elster, Joseph Ostroy, Amartya Sen, Philippe Van Parijs, Erik Wright; and to participants in seminars where these ideas were presented, at the University of Oslo, the University of Copenhagen, Yale University, the University of Chicago, the 1983 Maison des Sciences de l'Homme Colloquium in London, and the 1984 Colloque Marx in Paris organized by the Ecole des Hautes Etudes en Sciences Sociales. This is an abridged version of an article in *Philosophy and Public Affairs*, vol. 14, Winter 1985.
[1] Mill (1965), p. 766, and Marx–Engels (1962), p. 25.

exploited, as defined above.[2] Thus, exploitation theory views goods as vessels of labour, and calculates labour accounts for people by comparing the 'live' labour they expend in production with the 'dead' labour they get back in the vessels. Exploitation is an aspect of the pattern of redistribution of labour which occurs through the process of agents 'exchanging' their current productive labour for social labour congealed in goods received. It may not always be easy or even possible to *define* the content of dead labour in the vessels, as when labour is heterogeneous or joint production of many goods from the same production process exists. There is a large literature on these questions, which shall not concern me here. For this essay, I assume labour is homogeneous.

It is important to note that exploitation is not defined relationally. The statement '*A* exploits *B*' is not defined, but rather '*A* is an exploiter' and '*B* is exploited.' Exploitation, as I conceive of it, refers to the relationship between a person and society as a whole as measured by the transfer of the person's labour to the society, and the reverse transfer of society's labour to the person, as embodied in goods the person claims.

What are the uses of exploitation theory? Why is it considered the cornerstone of Marxian social science by many writers? More directly: What positive or normative conclusions might we draw about capitalism from observing that workers are exploited under capitalism? I can identify four main uses or justifications of exploitation theory:

(1) the accumulation theory: exploitation of workers explains profits and accumulation under capitalism; it is the secret of capitalist expansion.

(2) the domination theory: exploitation is intimately linked to the domination of workers by capitalists, especially at the point of production, and domination is an evil.

(3) the alienation theory: exploitation is a measure of the degree to which people are alienated under capitalism. The root of alienation is the separation of one's labour from oneself. If one's labour is put into goods which are produced for exchange (not for use by oneself or one's community) that constitutes alienation. Exploitation occurs because some people alienate more labour than others. It is differential alienation.

(4) the inequality theory: exploitation is a measure and consequence of the underlying inequality in the ownership of the means of production, an inequality which is unjustified.

There is another theory which is, I think, a special case of (4), and so will be numbered:

[2] For a discussion of the grey area of agents, who are neither exploited nor exploiting, see Roemer (1982a), Chapter 4.

(4′) the expropriation theory: exploitation is a measure of expropriation, of one agent owning part of the product which should rightfully belong to another agent.

These four (or five) proposed explanations for our interest in exploitation theory are usually confounded. They should not be, because they constitute different claims. Adherents to exploitation theory tend to emphasize some of (1) through (4) when others of the list become subjected to embarrassments or counterexamples. I will argue that in the general case none of (1) through (4) can be sustained; there is, in general, no reason to be interested in exploitation theory, that is, in tallying the surplus value accounts of labour performed versus labour commanded in goods purchased. My arguments against (1) through (4) are, briefly, these: (1) all commodities are exploited under capitalism, not only labour-power, and so the exploitation of labour does not explain profits; concerning (2), domination is an important issue under capitalism, but exploitation is not germane to its study; concerning (3), differential alienation can be measured using surplus value accounts, but I do not think such alienation is interesting unless it is a consequence of unequal ownership of the means of production. We are thus led to (4) which, I think, is the closest explanation for Marxists' interest in exploitation; but in the general case, I will show inequality in ownership of the means of production, even when ethically indefensible, is not properly measured by exploitation. In particular, it can in theory happen that those who own very little of the means of production are exploiters and those who own a lot are exploited. Hence exploitation (the transfer of surplus value) is not a proper reflection of inequality in underlying property relations.

There is an apparent similarity between this iconoclastic posture toward exploitation theory, and the attacks on the labour theory of value which have accelerated in the past decade.[3] In the final section, I evaluate this similarity, and claim it is quite shallow. While the labour theory of value almost always gives incorrect insights, exploitation theory in many cases coincides with a deeper ethical position – although on its own terms it does not provide a justification for that position. My verdict will be that exploitation theory is a domicile that we need no longer maintain: it has provided a home for raising a vigorous family, who now must move on.

The reader should bear in mind that throughout the essay 'exploit' has a technical meaning, the unequal exchange of labour. When I claim that exploitation theory is without foundation, I do not mean capitalism is just. I believe capitalism is unjust (or ethically *exploitative*) because of sharply

[3] See, for example, Robinson (1966); Morishima (1973); Steedman (1977); Roemer (1981); Samuelson (1971); Elster (1985a).

unequal ownership of the means of production. What I show in section 5 is that this inequality is not necessarily coextensive with the transfer of surplus value from workers to capitalists, and therefore it is inappropriate to base an equality-based morality on the technical measure of exploitation. If I occasionally use 'exploitation' in its ethical as opposed to technical sense, the word will be italicized as above.

2. Definition of terms: a simple model

I have outlined above an identification problem with respect to the motivation for our interest in exploitation. In this section, this identification problem will be posed as starkly and schematically as possible, by exhibiting a simple model in which exploitation emerges simultaneously with accumulation, domination, differential alienation, and inequality in ownership of the means of production. This section, therefore, serves to define terms and to pose the problem more precisely.

Imagine an economy with 1,000 persons and two goods: corn and leisure. There are two technologies for producing corn, called the Farm and the Factory. The Farm is a labour-intensive technology in which no seed capital is required, but corn is produced from pure labour (perhaps by cultivating wild corn). The Factory technology produces corn with labour plus capital – the capital is seed corn. The technologies are given by:

> Farm: 3 days' labour → 1 corn output
> Factory: 1 day's labour + 1 seed corn → 2 corn output

Corn takes a week to grow (so the seed is tied up in the ground for that long). The total stock of seed corn in this society is 500 corn, and each agent owns $\frac{1}{2}$ corn. The agents have identical preferences which are these: each wants to consume 1 corn *net* output per week. After consuming his one corn, the agent will consume leisure. If he can get more than one corn for no more labour, he will be even happier: but preferences are lexicographic in that each wishes to minimize labour expended subject to earning enough to be able to consume one corn per week, and not to run down his stock of capital.

There is an obvious equilibrium in this economy. The typical agent works up his $\frac{1}{2}$ corn in the Factory in $\frac{1}{2}$ day, which will bring him 1 corn at the end of the week. Having fully employed his seed capital, he must produce another $\frac{1}{2}$ corn somewhere, to replace his capital stock: this he does by working in the Farm technology for $1\frac{1}{2}$ days. Thus he works 2 days and produces 1 corn net output. Every agent does this. Indeed 2 days is the labour time socially necessary to produce a unit of corn, given that this society must produce

1,000 corn net each week. It is the labour embodied in a unit of corn. At this equilibrium there is no exploitation, since labour expended by each agent equals labour embodied in his share of the net output. Nor is there accumulation, for society has the same endowments at the beginning of next week; nor is there domination at the point of production, since no one works for anyone else; nor is there differential alienation of labour, since there is not even trade; and, of course, there is equality in initial assets.

Now change the initial distribution of assets, so that each of five agents owns 100 seed corn, and the other 995 own nothing but their labour power (or, to be consistent with our former terminology, nothing but their leisure). Preferences remain as before. What is the competitive equilibrium? One possibility is that each of the 995 asset-less agents works 3 days on the Farm, and each of the 5 wealthy ones works 1 day in the Factory. But this is not an equilibrium, since there is a lot of excess capital sitting around which can be put to productive use. In particular, the wealthy ones can offer to hire the asset-less to work in the Factory on their capital stock. Suppose the 'capitalists' offer a corn wage of one corn for two days' labour. Then each capitalist can employ 50 workers, each for two days, on his 100 seed corn capital. Each worker produces four corn in the Factory with two days' labour. Thus each capitalist has corn revenues of 200 corn: of that, 100 corn replaces the seed used up, 50 is paid in wages, and 50 remains as profits. Capital is now fully employed. But this may or may not be an equilibrium wage: only $5 \times 50 = 250$ workers have been employed, and perhaps the other 745 peasants would prefer to work in the Factory for a real wage of $\frac{1}{2}$ corn per day instead of slaving on the Farm at a real wage of $\frac{1}{3}$ corn per day. If so, the real wage in the Factory will be bid down until the asset-less agents are indifferent between doing unalienated, undominated labour on the Farm, and alienated, dominated labour in the Factory. Let us say, for the sake of simplicity, this equilibrating real wage is one corn for 2.5 days' Factory labour. (In the absence of a preference for Farm life over Factory life, the real wage will equilibrate at one corn for three days' labour, that is, at the peasant's labour opportunity cost of corn, since in this economy there is a scarcity of capital relative to the labour which it could efficiently employ.) Now we have *accumulation* (or at least much more production than before, which I assume is not all eaten by the capitalists), since each capitalist gets a profit of $200 - 100 - 40 = 60$ corn net, and each worker or peasant gets, as in the first economy, one corn net. Hence total net product is $995 + (5 \times 60) = 1{,}295$ corn, instead of 1,000 corn as before. We also have *domination* since some agents are employed by others, and by hypothesis, this gives rise to domination at the point of production. *Differential alienation* has emerged, since some agents (the workers) alienate a large part of their labour to the capitalists, while the capitalists and the peasants alienate no labour (although they work different amounts of time). *Exploitation* has emerged since the workers and peasants all expend more labour than is 'embodied' in the corn they get, while the five capitalists work zero days and each gets 60 corn. Hence, the four phenomena in question emerge simultaneously with exploitation, in the passage from the 'egalitarian' economy to the 'capitalist' economy. With respect to expropriation, we might also say that it has emerged in the second economy.

3. The accumulation theory

The unique positive (as opposed to normative) claim among (1) through (4) is the claim that our interest in exploitation is because surplus labour is the source of accumulation and profits. Explanation (1) uses 'exploit' in the sense of 'to turn a natural resource to economic account; to utilize', while theories (2), (3) and (4) use 'exploit' in the sense of 'to make use of meanly or unjustly for one's own advantage or profit'.[4] A current in Marxism maintains that exploitation is not intended as a normative concept, but as an explanation of the *modus operandi* of capitalism; the production of profits in a system of voluntary exchange and labour transfers is the riddle which must be explained, and which Marx posed in *Capital*, volume I. The discovery that exploitation of labour is the source of profits answers the riddle. (Even though all commodities exchange 'at their values', a surplus systematically emerges at one point, in the labour process. For the value which labour produces is greater than what labour power is worth, and hence what it is paid.) Indeed, the claim that exploitation theory should not be construed as normative theory has its source in Marx, as Allen Wood points out.[5]

The formal theorem supporting position (1) was first presented by Okishio and Morishima,[6] and the latter coined it the Fundamental Marxian Theorem (FMT). It demonstrates that in quite general economic models, exploitation of labour exists if and only if profits are positive. The FMT is robust; the error lies in the inference that its veracity implies that profits are *explained* by the exploitation of labour. For, as many writers have now observed, *every* commodity (not just labour-power) is exploited under capitalism. Oil, for example, can be chosen to be the value numeraire, and embodied oil values of all commodities can be calculated. One can prove that profits are positive if and only if oil is exploited, in the sense that the amount of oil embodied

---

[4] Definitions of exploitation are from *Webster's Dictionary* (1966).
[5] Allen Wood (1981), Chapter 9.
[6] Morishima (1973). Many authors have since studied and generalized the Fundamental Marxian Theorem.

in producing one unit of oil is less than one unit of oil – so oil gives up into production more than it requires back.[7] Thus the exploitation of labour is not the explanation for profits and accumulation any more than is the exploitation of oil or corn or iron. The motivation for the privileged choice of labour as the exploitation numeraire must lie elsewhere, as I have argued elsewhere.[8] In trying to locate the specialness of labour which would justify its choice as the exploitation numeraire, one is inexorably led into arguments that labour is the unique commodity which can be 'dominated' or 'alienated' – the terrain of argument shifts to a defence of theories like (2) and (3).

I conclude position (1) cannot be supported as the reason for our interest in exploitation theory.[9] Despite his avowed lack of interest in normative justification of exploitation theory, the Marxist who argues for position (1) can only rescue exploitation theory from the jaws of the Generalized Commodity Exploitation Theorem by appealing to a special claim labour has on wearing the exploitation mantle, a claim that seems only to be defensible on grounds of the unfairness or unjustness or nastiness of the conditions of labour's utilization. As G. A. Cohen writes, 'Marxists do not often talk about justice, and when they do they tend to deny its relevance, or they say that the idea of justice is an illusion. But I think justice occupies a central place in revolutionary Marxist belief. Its presence is betrayed by particular judgments Marxists make, and by the strength of feeling with which they make them.'[10] And I would add, it is only by appealing to conceptions of justice that exploitation theory can be defended as interesting.

4. The domination theory

For the remainder of this essay, my concern will be to investigate the possibility of defending an interest in exploitation theory for the light it sheds on the three issues of domination, differential alienation, and inequality in ownership of the means of production. My interest in these three issues is normative. If, for example, exploitation can be shown to imply domination of workers by capitalists, and if we argue independently that domination is unjust, then exploitation theory provides at least a partial theory of the

---

[7] This Generalized Commodity Exploitation Theorem has been proved and/or observed by many authors, including Vegara (1979); Bowles and Gintis (1981); Wolff (1981); Roemer (1982a), Appendix 6.1; Samuelson (1982).

[8] See Roemer (1983c) and Roemer (1982b).

[9] R. P. Wolff (1981), while recognizing that the exploitation of labour cannot explain profits, offers a reason other than domination and alienation to be interested in exploitation; as I have argued against his proposal elsewhere (Roemer, 1983c), I will not repeat that discussion.

[10] Cohen (1981b). For an opposite point of view see A. Wood (1981).

injustice of capitalism. (Only a partial theory, since other practices besides domination might be unjust, which exploitation theory would not diagnose.) Identifying the main evil of capitalism as domination, and even extra-economic domination, is a theme of some contemporary Marxist work.[11] It is not my purpose to evaluate this claim (with which I disagree), but rather to postulate an ethical interest in domination, and ask whether that justifies an interest in exploitation theory.

It is necessary to distinguish two types of domination by capitalists over workers, domination in the maintenance and enforcement of private property in the means of production, and domination at the point of production (the hierarchical and autocratic structure of work). The line between the two cannot be sharply drawn, but let us superscript the two types domination[1] and domination[2], respectively. I will argue that each of domination[1] and domination[2] implies exploitation, but not conversely. Hence if our interest is in domination, there is no reason to invoke exploitation theory, for the direction of entailment runs the wrong way. Domination may be a bad thing, but there is no reason to run the circuitous route of exploitation theory to make the point. In certain situations, exploitation requires domination[1], but since we cannot know these cases by analysing the exploitation accounts alone, there is no reason to invoke exploitation if, indeed, our interest in exploitation is only as a barometer of domination[1]. Furthermore, our interest in domination[1] is essentially an interest in the inequality of ownership of the means of production, for the purpose of domination[1] is to enforce that ownership pattern. I maintain if it is domination[1] one claims an interest in, it is really inequality (however defined) in the ownership of the means of production which is the issue. Thus, an ethical interest in domination[1] shifts the discussion to the validity of position (4), while an interest in domination[2] has as its source the moral sentiments reflected in the head-quotation from J. S. Mill, in the analogy implied by the term wage slavery. In this section, I therefore discuss the relationship between exploitation and domination[2].

Domination[2] does not involve the protection or creation of value in capitalist property, but rather the hierarchical, non-democratic relations in capitalist workplaces. Of course, this hierarchy presumably creates (additional) profits, and therefore leads to an increased valuation of capitalist property, and hence is similar to the role of domination[1]; but in discussing domination[2] I am specifically concerned with the domination of the self of the worker, the relation of subordination he enters into with the capitalist when he enters the workplace. While our moral opposition to domination[1] shares its foundation

[11] Ellen Wood (1981); Bowles and Gintis (1981); Wright (1982).

with our moral opposition to feudalism, our opposition to domination[2] shares its foundation with our opposition to slavery. (The analogy is inexact, since many feudal practices involved domination[2] over the selves of serfs; for the sake of the analogy, I envisage 'pure feudalism' as a system where feudal dues are paid because of extra-economic coercion, but the serf never sees or interacts personally with the lord.)

Although domination[2] can create the conditions for profitability and therefore exploitation of labour, the converse is in general not the case. Exploitation does not imply the existence of domination[2]. I showed in my book that the class and exploitation relations of a capitalist economy using labour markets can be precisely replicated with a capitalist economy using credit markets,[12] where domination[2] does not exist. In Labour Market Capitalism, agents optimize, given their endowments of property, and end up choosing either to sell labour-power, to hire labour-power, or to produce for the market using their own labour-power on their own account. Agents segregate themselves into five classes, based on the particular ways they relate to the labour market. The Class Exploitation Correspondence Principle demonstrates that everyone who optimizes by selling labour-power is exploited, and everyone who optimizes by hiring labour is an exploiter. It was assumed, in that analysis, that agents make the decision to sell labour entirely on economic grounds; they do not calculate as part of their objective the disutility associated with being dominated[2], with working under a boss. In Credit Market Capitalism, there is no labour market, but a market for lending capital at an interest rate. At the equilibrium, some agents will lend capital, some will borrow capital, some will use their own capital for production. Again, agents segregate themselves into five classes defined by the particular ways they relate to the credit market. Again, the Class Exploitation Correspondence Principle holds: any agent who optimizes by lending capital will be an exploiter, and any agent who optimizes by borrowing capital will turn out to be exploited. Moreover, the Isomorphism Theorem states that these two hypothetical capitalisms are identical in so far as class and exploitation properties are concerned. An agent who, under Labour Market Capitalism, was a member of a labour-selling class, and was therefore exploited, will be a member of a capital-borrowing class in Credit Market Capitalism, and will be exploited. This result replays the Wicksell–Samuelson theme that it is irrelevant, for the distribution of income, whether capital hires labour or labour hires capital; the mild sin of omission of these writers was not to point out that propertyless agents are exploited in either case, whether they be the

---

[12] For a detailed presentation of this material, see Roemer (1982a), Parts I and II. For a summary, see 'New directions', in this volume.

hirers or sellers of the factor. In Labour Market Capitalism there is domination[2], but in Credit Market Capitalism, there is not.[13]

Moreover, an even sharper example may be constructed of an economy possessing no labour or credit market, but only markets for produced commodities which are traded among individual producers. In such an economy exploitation will result at equilibrium, in general, if there is initial inequality in the ownership of means of production. But in this exchange and production economy, there are no relations of domination[2] of any kind; the exploitation can be accomplished through 'invisible trade'. It is possible to argue that there is exploitation without class in this economy, since all producers enjoy the same relation to the means of production: they work only on their own.[14] Indeed, this example may be taken as the archetype of exploitation, or unequal exchange, between countries where neither labour nor capital flows across borders. Differential initial endowments of countries will give rise to exploitation in trade, even when no relations of domination[2] through international labour migration or capital lending take place.[15]

The previous paragraphs claim to demonstrate that the existence of exploitation does not imply the existence of domination[2], and hence our putative interest in exploitation theory cannot be justified on grounds of a more basic interest in domination[2]. Here I follow Marx, in modelling capitalism as a system where there are no market frictions, but where goods exchange competitively at their market-determined prices. In particular, it seems appropriate, for this thought experiment, to assume all contracts are costlessly enforceable and can be perfectly delineated. For Marx wished to show the economic viability of capitalism in the absence of cheating: and that means contracts are well-defined and observed by all. Now the principal reason domination[2] exists is that the labour contract is not costlessly enforceable, nor can it be perfectly delineated. This point is usually put more graphically, when Marxists speak of the problems of extracting the labour from the labour-power. Indeed, the contemporary labour process literature addresses itself to the methods capitalism (and perhaps socialism) has developed to solve this problem.[16] But for our thought experiment, we are entitled to assume the delivery of *labour* (not simply labour-power) for the wage is as simple and enforceable a transaction as the delivery of an apple for a dime. In such a world, exploitation continues to exist, but domination[2]

[13] I am speaking of a pure form of Credit Market Capitalism; in actual credit markets, lenders often supervise debtors if sufficient collateral is not available, or if there would be problems in enforcing collection of collateral.
[14] For the details of this economy see Roemer (1982a), Chapter 1; for a simple example, see Roemer (1983a).   [15] See Roemer (1983b).
[16] For example, see Braverman (1974) and Edwards (1979).

does not. And I claim Marxists would be almost as critical of such a perfect capitalism as they are of existing capitalism, replete as the real thing is with domination^2 due to the contract enforcement problem. Indeed, Marxists consider sharecroppers and borrowers to be *exploited* (unjustly so, that is), even when domination^2 is absent from those contracts. The Isomorphism Theorem I quoted was an attempt to develop this point formally, that in a world absenting deleterious domination^2 effects, the exploitation observed in labour markets would be indistinguishable from that observed in credit or share-cropping arrangements.[17]

It is therefore difficult to justify an interest in exploitation if our real concern is domination^2, for two reasons. First, domination^2 is directly observable (simply look at who hires whom) and exploitation is not. Hence, calculating whether an agent is exploited (a difficult calculation, necessitating all sorts of technological information to compute socially necessary labour times) would be a strangely circuitous route to concluding he is dominated^2. Secondly, it is not true that an exploited agent is necessarily dominated or that an exploiter is necessarily dominating; the Exploitation-Domination Correspondence states the converse. Exploited (exploiting) agents who are not dominated (dominating) would have a confused ethical status if our judgment about them is made on the basis of exploitation but our interest in exploitation is as a proxy for domination. The hard-working shopkeeper or sharecropper would have our ethical sympathy on grounds of exploitation but not domination^2. This does not help us provide independent reason for an interest in exploitation theory, of course, which is the task at hand. Thus exploitation is a poor statistic for domination^2, on several counts.

My conclusions concerning domination^2 are: (i) our interest in exploitation theory cannot be justified on grounds that it is indicative of or a proxy for domination^2, either logically, or on pragmatic grounds; (ii) although domination^2 is prevalent in existing capitalism, it is arguably a phenomenon of second-order in a *Marxist* condemnation of capitalism, being associated with the imperfections in writing and enforcing contracts, while Marxist arguments should apply to a capitalism with frictionless contracts. In addition, although not argued here (as my concern is not with the evils of domination^2 but with the evils of exploitation), I think the analogy between domination^2 and slavery is ill-founded. It is arguable that the life of the small independent producer is not so marvellous compared to that of the factory worker, that the transition from poor peasant to urban proletarian is one made willingly, even gladly, and with reasonably good information, where the erstwhile independent producer is knowledgeable about the trade-offs. I say

[17] Further discussion of some of these issues can be found in Roemer (1982c).

arguable, not obvious: but it is more than arguable that no population ever voluntarily committed itself to slavery willingly and gladly.

5. The alienation theory

To discuss properly a possible justification of an interest in exploitation theory on grounds that it is indicative of different degrees of alienation, we must separate alienation from, on the one hand, domination and on the other hand differential ownership of the means of production, as those issues are discussed separately under (2) and (4). An interest in differential alienation must be defended *per se*, even in the absence of domination and differential ownership of the means of production. Perhaps the most graphic vision of exploitation is as the extraction of surplus labour from the worker: the extraction, that is, of more labour from him than he receives back as social labour in what he consumes or can purchase with his wages. His labour is alienated from him not because he performs it for another (under conditions of domination[2]) but because it is labour performed to produce goods for exchange, not for use. More precisely, the goods produced are traded to an anonymous final recipient on a market, and in this way labour becomes alienated in a way it would not have been were there a social division of labour but the final disposition of goods was in one's 'community'. (See B. Traven's marvellous story 'Assembly Line' for a discussion of alienation.[18]) Now if everyone started off with the same endowment of means of production and had the same skills and preferences, but all agents produced goods for a market, there would be alienation of labour in this sense, but not differential alienation, since it can be shown everyone would receive back as much social labour in goods as he alienated in production for the market. Exploitation can be said to exist in a market economy when some people alienate more labour than they receive from others, and some alienate less labour than they receive back. Why might alienation be a bad thing? Perhaps because one's time is the only really valuable asset one has, and production for the market is considered to be a waste of time. Perhaps because productive labour for oneself or one's community is what constitutes the good life, but the use of labour to earn revenues solely to survive, not to produce for others directly, is a prostitution of a deep aspect of the self. Thus alienation might be bad, and differential alienation might be unjust or *exploitative*. (There are certainly other forms of alienation in Marx, but this kind of differential alienation appears to be the only kind for which exploitation as the unequal exchange of labour is an indicator.)

[18] Traven (1973).

Any ethical condemnation of differential alienation cannot be a welfarist one, in the sense of Amartya Sen,[19] based only on the preferences of individuals. For I will outline a situation where agents with different preferences start with equal endowments of resources and voluntarily enter into relations of differential alienation (i.e., exploitation) as the way to maximize their utilities. Consider two agents, Adam and Karl who each start off with the same amount of corn, which is the only good in the economy, and can be used both as capital (seed corn) and as the consumption good. We have the same technological possibilities as in the model of section 2.

> Farm: 3 days' labour produces 1 bushel corn
> Factory: 1 day's labour plus 1 bushel seed corn produces 2 bushels corn

Adam and Karl each start with $\frac{1}{2}$ bushel of corn, and each will live and must consume for many weeks. (Recall, a week is the time period required in each case to bring corn to fruition, although the amount of labour expended during the week differs in the two processes.) Karl is highly averse to performing work in the present: he desires only to consume one bushel of corn per week, subject to the requirement that he not run down his seed stock. In the first week, he therefore works $\frac{1}{2}$ day in the Factory (fully utilizing his seed corn) and $1\frac{1}{2}$ days on the Farm, producing a total of $1\frac{1}{2}$ bushels, one of which he consumes at harvest time, leaving him with $\frac{1}{2}$ bushel to start with in week 2. Adam accumulates; he works $\frac{1}{2}$ day in the Factory, utilizing his seed, and $4\frac{1}{2}$ days on the Farm, producing $2\frac{1}{2}$ bushels gross. After consuming one bushel, he has $1\frac{1}{2}$ bushels left to start week 2. In week 2, Karl works up his own seed stock in $\frac{1}{2}$ day in the Factory producing 1 bushel; then, instead of going to the Farm, Karl borrows or rents Adam's $1\frac{1}{2}$ bushels of seed and works it up in the Factory. This takes Karl precisely $1\frac{1}{2}$ days, and he produces 3 bushels gross in the factory. Of the 3 bushels he keeps $\frac{1}{2}$ bushel, and returns $2\frac{1}{2}$ bushels to Adam (Adam's principal of $1\frac{1}{2}$ bushels plus interest of 1 bushel). Indeed, Karl is quite content with this arrangement, for he has worked for a total of two days and received $1\frac{1}{2}$ bushels, just as in week 1, when he had to use the inferior Farm technology. Adam, on the other hand, receives a profit of 1 bushel from Karl's labour, which he consumes, and is left again to begin week 3 with $1\frac{1}{2}$ bushels. He has not worked at all in week 2. This arrangement can continue forever, with Karl working 2 days each week and consuming 1 bushel, and Adam working 5 days during the first week, and zero days thereafter. Clearly there is exploitation in the sense of differential alienation in this story, in all weeks after the first, but its genesis is in the differential preferences Karl and Adam have for the consumption of corn and leisure over their lives. Thus exploitation

---

[19] See, for a definition of welfarism, Sen (1979a).

cannot be blamed, in this story, on differential initial ownership of the means of production, nor can the situation be condemned on Paretian grounds, as no other arrangement would suit Karl and Adam more. They chose this path of consumption/leisure streams. Indeed during any week Karl could decide to work on the Farm and accumulate more seed corn, thus enabling him to cut his working hours in future weeks. (I am assuming he is *able* to do so; if he is not, then Karl is handicapped, and the ethical verdict is certainly more complicated.) But he does not.

So if we are to conclude that differential alienation is *exploitative*, in the sense of ethically condemnable, that verdict cannot be arrived at on Paretian grounds. Indeed, the above example enables us to speak of 'the impossibility of being a differential-alienation-condemning Paretian' in exactly the sense of 'the impossibility of being a Paretian liberal'.[20] For, as the last several paragraphs demonstrate, to avoid alienation Karl must produce only for himself (using both the Farm and the Factory), which will require Adam to work each week for himself. But in the example this is not a Pareto optimal allocation of labour. Only by engaging in differentially alienated labour can Karl and Adam take full advantage of the efficient Factory technology. Thus even the mild welfarist requirement of Pareto efficiency comes into conflict with exploitation-as-differential-alienation. There may still be grounds for calling such differential alienation *exploitative*, but it appears such grounds must be based on *rights*, not welfare outcomes as the agents see them.

We are led to ask, then, whether a person has *right* not to perform more alienated labour than another person. We might be able to argue that one has a right not to be *forced* to perform more alienated labour than another: but that will lead straight into a discussion of differential ownership of the means of production, which is not the issue here.[21] For in our story Karl chooses to perform more alienated labour than Adam from a position of equality of resources and opportunity. Nobody forces him, unless we slide further down the slippery slope of defining the 'resources' available to the person and argue that Karl was forced because he had no choice of the personal characteristics that gave rise to his *carpe diem* preferences. I cannot see a compelling argument for declaiming such a right, in part because I cannot see a compelling argument against the performance of alienated labour, let alone differential alienation. I think moral intuitions on this matter must take their cue from history. It is far from clear that people, in historical reality, have had an aversion to performing alienated labour. Indeed, many (including Marxists) argue that production for the market has been a

---

[20] On the impossibility of being a Paretian liberal, see, for instance, Sen (1979b).

[21] For a discussion of why proletarians can be thought of as forced to alienate their labour, even in a world of voluntary wage contracts, see G. A. Cohen, 'The structure of proletarian unfreedom', in this volume.

liberating process for many populations, a process which they enter into willingly. (Recall, we are not concerned here with domination, of choosing to work for others, but only with alienation, of producing for a market.)

The possibility remains that even though non-differentially-alienated outcomes cannot be defended on Paretian grounds, nor on grounds of rights, perhaps they can be defended for perfectionist reasons. I will not attempt here to defend my position against a perfectionist attack, except to say that my defence would amplify on the point of the two previous paragraphs. It seems that differential alienation of labour, from an initial position of equal opportunity and fair division of assets, can vastly increase the welfare and life-quality of people, and so a perfectionist defence of non-alienation seems remote.

6. Differential ownership of productive assets

The fourth reason to be interested in exploitation is as an index of the inequality in ownership of productive assets. This approach is represented, for example, in the head quotation from Marx. The Marxist position that socialist revolution entails redistribution or nationalization of the means of production to eliminate exploitation traces to this conception of exploitation. (In contrast, the emphasis of exploitation as domination[2] gives rise to industrial democracy as the key aspect of socialist transformation.) In my recent book and in other articles I have claimed that this is the most compelling reason to be interested in exploitation, by showing in a series of models that the existence of exploitation is equivalent to inequality in distribution of initial assets, and that the rich exploit the poor. Hence exploitation theory can be justified if we accept a presumption that initial inequality in the wealth of agents is unjust, for exploitation (in these models) is essentially equivalent to initial inequality of assets. Nevertheless this may appear to weaken the argument for being interested in exploitation (defined as I have done throughout this essay), for it is probably easier to observe inequality in ownership of assets than it is to calculate exploitation accounts.

Still, according to this description of the results, exploitation may be thought of as an *innocuous* appendix to our true ethical concerns: innocuous because although unnecessary, surplus value accounts correspond to underlying inequality in ownership of assets in the proper way. I now go further, and claim that in the general case, exploitation theory leads to results which may conflict directly with the inequality-of-productive-assets theory. And therefore, finding no other reasons to be interested in exploitation accounts, I must say exploitation theory, in the general case, is misconceived. It does not provide a proper model or account of Marxian moral sentiments; the proper Marxian claim, I think, is for equality in the distribution of productive assets, not for the elimination of exploitation.

The 'general case' in which exploitation accounts and inequality accounts diverge occurs when general preferences for agents are admitted. In particular, if preferences for income verses leisure differ across agents, the divergence can occur. Indeed, the two theories can diverge even for cases when preferences are identical for all agents as I will show. In my book, I assumed preferences of all agents were the same, and of certain special forms: either all agents wanted to accumulate as much as possible, or they wanted just to subsist, two preference profiles that appear to be polar opposites. Indeed, there may be a strong case that the assumption of one of these profiles of preferences is not a bad one, historically, in which case exploitation theory might correspond empirically to Marxian ethical conceptions. But I am concerned here with the logical foundations of exploitation theory, and for that purpose general and abstract formulations with respect to admissible preference profiles are essential.

If the preferences of agents do not satisfy a certain condition, then it can happen that the asset-rich are exploited by the asset-poor: the flow of surplus value goes the 'wrong way'. This can occur even when all agents have identical preference maps for income and leisure – but what is critical is that the agents' preference for leisure must change rather substantially, and in a particular way, as their wealth changes. Once this is demonstrated, one can no longer claim that exploitation is a significant index of inequality of initial assets which measures the flow from the asset-poor to the asset-rich.

For concreteness sake, here is a simple example illustrating the divergence between exploitation and inequality of assets. It does not matter, for this example, whether the different amounts of labour which Karl and Adam supply are a consequence of different preferences or the same preferences. All that matters is that given their different initial wealths, they optimize by supplying labour in the pattern indicated. I postulate the same Farm and Factory technologies as before. This time, however, Karl has an initial endowment of 1 corn and Adam of 3 corn. Denote a bundle of corn and labour as (C,L). Thus $(1,1)$ represents the consumption of 1 corn and the provision of 1 day's labour. I assume, as before, that each agent is not willing to run down his initial stock of corn (because he might die at any time, and he wishes, at least, not to deprive his one child of the same endowment that his parent passed down to him). Suppose we know at least this about Adam's and Karl's preferences:

$$(\tfrac{2}{3},0) \succ_K (1,1)$$

$$(3\tfrac{1}{3},4) \succ_A (3,3)$$

(To translate, the first line says Karl would strictly prefer to consume $\frac{2}{3}$ bushel of corn and not to work at all than to work 1 day and consume 1 bushel.) Now note that Karl can achieve $(1,1)$ by working up his 1 corn in the Factory in 1 day; he consumes one of the bushels produced, and starts week 2 with his initial 1 bushel. Likewise, Adam can achieve $(3,3)$ by working up his three bushels in the Factory with 3 days' labour; he consumes 3 of the 6 bushels produced, and replaces his initial stock for week 2. But this solution is not Pareto optimal. For now suppose Karl lends his 1 bushel to Adam. Adam works up the total of 4 bushels in 4 days in the Factory, producing 8 bushels, and pays back Karl his original bushel plus $\frac{2}{3}$ bushel as interest for the loan. This leaves Adam with $3\frac{1}{3}$ bushels, after replacing his 3 bushels of initial stock. Thus Karl can consume $\frac{2}{3}$ bushel and work not at all, which he prefers to $(1,1)$, and Adam consumes the bundle $(3\frac{1}{3},4)$ which he prefers to $(3,3)$. We have a strict Pareto improvement. (The interest rate charged is the competitive one; for if Adam, instead of borrowing from Karl, worked on the Farm for an extra day he would make precisely $\frac{1}{3}$ bushel of corn.) This arrangement may continue forever: Karl never works and lives off the interest from Adam's labour. According to the unequal exchange definition of exploitation, there is no shadow of a doubt that Karl exploits Adam. However, Adam is richer than Karl. On what basis can we condemn this exploitation? Not on the basis of domination or alienation (we have decided), and surely not on the basis of differential ownership of the means of production, since the exploitation is going the 'wrong way'. Indeed, eliminating inequality in the ownership of the means of production should improve the lot of the exploited at the expense of the exploiters. (That is the property relations definition I formalized in other work.[22]) But in this case an equalization of the initial assets at 2 bushels of corn for each renders the exploiter (Karl) better off, and the exploited (Adam) worse off![23]

It should be remarked that the preferences postulated in this example for Karl and Adam are not perverse, in the sense that they can be embedded in a full preference relation which has convex indifference curves of the usual sort, in corn–leisure space. This is the case even when Karl and Adam possess the same (convex) preferences.

This example is a special case of a general condition under which surplus value flows from the rich to the poor. The general condition on preferences for which this perversity occurs is when the cross-sectional labour supply curve is elastic with respect to wealth. If a 1 percent increase in wealth

[22] Roemer (1982d).
[23] Actually, even if there is a unique equilibrium there are some perverse cases in general equilibrium models when an agent can improve his final welfare by giving away some of his initial endowment. This is not such a case.

increases an agent's labour supply by more than 1 percent, then exploitation correlates incorrectly with wealth.

If we have reason for calling unjust the postulated inequality in the original distribution of seed corn assets, then it is Karl who is suffering an injustice in the previous example, and not Adam; but according to exploitation theory, Karl exploits Adam. As I have said, I think the most consistent Marxian ethical position is against inequality in the initial distribution of productive assets; when exploitation accounts reflect the unequal distribution of productive assets in the proper way (that the rich exploit the poor), that is what makes exploitation theory attractive. But if that correlation can fail, as it has, then no foundation remains for a justification of exploitation theory.

It might still be maintained that two injustices are involved when productive assets are unjustly distributed: the injustice of that distribution of stocks, and the injustice of the flows arising from them.[24] Exploitation is a statement concerning the injustice of flows, but I have invoked it only as a proxy for the underlying injustice (more precisely, inequality) of stocks. There remains the necessity for some judgment of the injustice of flows emanating from an unjust distribution of stocks: my point is that flows of labour are an imperfect proxy for that. In the Karl–Adam example, I say that Adam is unjustly gaining from the flows between him and Karl, if the initial distribution of stocks is unjust against Karl, despite the formal exploitation of Adam by Karl. In cases where exploitation does render the correct judgment on the injustice of flows, then perhaps the degree or rate of exploitation is useful in assessing the degree of injustice in the flow. But in the general case counterexamples can be supplied against this claim as well – situations where A is exploited more than B but we would agree B is more unjustly treated. It is beyond my scope here to inquire into a robust measure of the injustice of flows emanating from an unjust stock.

A fifth explanation of our interest in exploitation theory, which I have enumerated (4') as I consider it to be convincing only when it paraphrases the inequality theory, might be called the expropriation theory. The expropriation theory is summarized, for example, by G. A. Cohen,[25] as follows:

(i) The labourer is the only person who creates the product, that which has value.
(ii) The capitalist receives some of the value of the product. Therefore:
(iii) The labourer receives less value than the value of what he creates, and
(iv) The capitalist receives some of the value of what the labourer creates. Therefore:
(v) The labourer is exploited by the capitalist.

The expropriation theory (which Cohen calls the Plain Marxian Argument) does not claim an injustice on grounds of alienation or domination, but on

[24] I thank G. A. Cohen for pressing this point.   [25] Cohen (1979b).

grounds of rightful ownership of what one has made. I think the argument is ethically defensible only when it coincides with the inequality-of-resources theory, that is, when the expropriation takes place because the labourer does not have access to the means of production he is entitled to. To see the unreasonableness of the expropriation theory in the general case, substitute 'Karl' for 'the capitalist' and 'Adam' for 'the labourer' in the above argument (i)–(v) where Karl and Adam are the *dramatis personae* of the last example. Statements (ii) through (iv) remain unobjectionable and perhaps statement (i) does as well; but statement (v) certainly does not follow as an *ethically* convincing statement (although *formal* exploitation exists). If we respect the ownership pattern of assets and the preferences of the agents (which, to repeat, can even be uniform preferences) I see no good reason to give exclusive ownership rights of a product to the person who has made the product. Only on grounds of alienation (which I have said is unconvincing) does it seem one's labour could confer special ownership rights over the product. Justly acquired initial resources, which the direct producer might borrow from another, must count as well in ascribing ownership of the final product. What power the expropriation theory appears to have comes from another assumption, not stated, that the capitalist starts out with a monopoly on the ownership of the means of production, unjustly acquired; it is the injustice of that monopoly which leads us to believe he has no just claim to the product of the labourer. As Cohen says, in his own criticism of the expropriation theory: 'If it is morally all right that capitalists do and workers do not own the means of production, then capitalist profit is not the fruit of exploitation; and if the pre-contractual distributive position is morally wrong, then the case for exploitation is made.'[26]

7. Mollifying the verdict

Many writers have shown the indefensibility of the labour theory of *value*, the claim that Marxian analysis gains special insight from deducing a relationship between embodied labour values and prices.[27] There is no theory of price formation, special to Marxism, with a rigorous foundation. With the demise of the labour theory of value, various writers in the Marxian tradition have shown that the theory of exploitation can be reconstructed on a foundation which does not utilize the labour theory of value.[28] (Marx's logic derived the theory of exploitation from the labour theory of price formation.)

[26] Cohen (1983c).
[27] For a summary of the criticism of the labour theory of value see Elster (1985a), Chapter 3.
[28] Cohen (1979b); Roemer (1981 and 1982a); Morishima (1973).

I have now argued there is no logically compelling reason to be interested in exploitation theory. This claim is not so destructive as might appear to the Marxian enterprise, however, for I think the reasons Marxists have been interested in exploitation theory are important and, to a large extent, distinguish Marxism from other kinds of social science: it is just that these reasons do not justify an interest in exploitation theory which is an unnecessary detour to the other concerns. First, within ethics, Marxism lays emphasis on the importance of equal access to the means of production. It regards with suspicion any large inequality in access to the means of production, while its foil in social science tends to justify such inequality on grounds of differential rates of time preference, skill, or even luck.[29] Having said that equality in the ownership of means of production is desirable as an initial condition, much is left to elaborate concerning inheritance, handicaps and needs. Libertarian theorists view inheritance as a just means of acquiring resources;[30] Ronald Dworkin, in recent work on equality of resources, does not discuss inheritance;[31] Bruce Ackerman in recent work does attack that problem;[32] I imagine a Marxian theory of inheritance, when elaborated, will circumscribe inheritance rights quite sharply.[33] Secondly, Marxism calls attention to domination; domination is of interest on its own, even though it provides no reason to be interested in exploitation. Interest in domination has given rise to an important literature on the labour process and technical change under capitalism, which demonstrates how a specifically Marxian question, perhaps motivated by normative concerns, can give rise to new analysis of a positive type. Another example of positive analysis related to domination and exploitation is class theory. Class position is easily observable, and class may be an excellent indicator of alliances in struggles within capitalism, for reasons closer to domination than exploitation.[34] Thirdly, the

---

[29] Robert Nozick (1974), for example, considers luck to be a just method for acquiring assets.
[30] Nozick (1974).
[31] Dworkin (1981), footnote 9, p. 313.   [32] Ackerman (1980).
[33] For some very tentative indications, see Roemer (1983a).
[34] I have not considered in this essay a sixth possible reason to be interested in exploitation: as an explanation of class struggle, insofar as the exploited struggle against the exploiters. I think that if the exploited struggle against the exploiters, that is because the former are dominated, are alienated, or suffer from an unfair allocation in the distribution of assets. The unequal exchange of labour cannot be the cause of class struggle: rather, that unequal exchange must be the symptom of what must cause class struggle. (People do not calculate surplus value accounts; in fact, one of the classical Marxian points is that the surplus value accounts are masked and veiled by the market, and so the exploited do not see the true nature of the unequal exchange from which they are suffering.) But I have shown, now, that exploitation is not a useful proxy for the various injustices which may, indeed, be at the root of class struggle. Hence, exploitation as defined in this essay cannot cause class struggle.
    In his essay in this volume, Wright shows that exploitation is a good proxy for class consciousness, which in turn may determine class struggle. But, it must be noted, the

concern with alienation is related to the interest Marxists have had in the emergence of market economies and the proletarianization of labour forces, both in the past and the present, an interest which again leads to the posing of questions which would not otherwise have been asked. Fourthly, the concern with accumulation has given Marxists a view of capitalism as guided by a pursuit of profits which in a deep sense is anarchic and collectively irrational, while the predominant opposing view (neoclassical economics) pictures capitalism as collectively rational, as the price system harnesses profit motives to serve the needs of people.[35] While Marxists have not developed a theory of crisis and disequilibrium which is as well-founded and intellectually convincing as neoclassical equilibrium theory, one suspects the Marxian questions will eventually lead to a rigorous theory of uneven development and crisis.

Unlike the labour theory of value, the reasons for a purported interest in exploitation theory have given rise to provocative social theory. There have, on the other hand, been costs to the adherence to exploitation theory, chiefly associated with what might be called the fetishism of labour. The costs are often associated with the inappropriate application of exploitation theory in cases where some underlying deeper phenomenon, which usually coincides with exploitation, ceases to coincide with it. For example, socialist countries have exhibited a reluctant history to use material incentives and decentralizing markets. To some extent, this may result from a confusion concerning the permissibility of 'exploitation' when the initial distribution of ownership or control of the means of production is just. A second cost has been the equation claimed by some Marxists between socialism and industrial democracy, the belief that hierarchical forms of production are necessarily non-socialist. A third example, associated with an overriding concern with alienation, views the final social goal as a moneyless economy, perhaps with no detailed division of labour, in which, somehow, all of society becomes one community.[36] Strictly speaking, the last two examples do not impugn exploitation theory, but rather domination and alienation; but exploitation theory has formalized the concern with labour which reinforces this sort of misapplication.

It should be reiterated that the failure of exploitation to mirror properly the unequal distribution of the means of production is a logical one; as I noted,

exploitation which Wright shows is determining of class consciousness is based on the unequal distribution of various kinds of property, not on surplus value accounts. So his empirical claims can only reinforce the point of this note.

[35] It is this collective irrationality of capitalism which Elster (1985a) sees as the main contribution of Marxian 'dialectics'.

[36] A fine discussion of the costs which dogmatic Marxism has imposed on developing socialist societies is in Nove (1983).

in what are perhaps the most important actual historical cases, preferences of agents are such that the unequal-exchange-of-labour theory coincides with the inequality-of-productive-assets theory, and so exploitation theory pronounces the 'right' ethical verdict.[37]

In parallel to my view on the usefulness of exploitation theory as a proxy for inequality in the ownership of the means of production is George Stigler's observation concerning David Ricardo's use of the labour theory of value. Stigler writes:[38]

I can find no basis for the belief that Ricardo had an *analytical* labor theory of value, for quantities of labor are *not* the only determinants of relative values...On the other hand, there is no doubt that he held what may be called an *empirical* labor theory of value, that is, a theory that the relative quantitites of labor required in production are the dominant determinants of relative values. Such an empirical proposition cannot be interpreted as an analytical theory...

Stigler concludes with a statement which applies to my argument concerning exploitation:

The failure to distinguish between analytical and empirical propositions has been a source of much misunderstanding in economics. An analytical statement concerns functional relationships; an empirical statement takes account of the quantitative significance of the relationships.

Unlike Stigler's Ricardo, I think the labour theory of value is not a useful empirical theory. While the errors in the labour theory of value are Ptolemaic, the defects in exploitation theory are Newtonian. As an empirical statement, surplus value accounts mirror inequality in ownership of the means of production pretty well, if it is true that cross-sectional wealth-elastic labour supply behaviour is as empirically inconsequential as the precession in the perihelion of the orbit of Mercury. But for the sake of clarity and consistency, I think exploitation conceived of as the unequal exchange of labour should be replaced with exploitation conceived of as the distributional consequences of an unjust inequality in the distribution of productive assets and resources. This property relations alternative to exploitation is explained briefly elsewhere in this book.[39]

The central ethical question, which exploitation theory is imperfectly

---

[37] A striking example which suggests that labour supply may be elastic with respect to wealth, and therefore that exploitation theory is even historically wrong in some cases, is presented by Bardhan (1982), p. 78. In India, as the wealth of middle-peasant families increases, poor relations come and join the family. Viewing this extended family as the unit, it appears that labour supply increases with wealth. It is not obvious that the family labour supply increases elastically with wealth, but Bardhan's example shows, at least, there is a range of wealths for which labour supply has positive elasticity.

[38] Stigler (1958), p. 361 and p. 366.　　　　　[39] See Roemer, 'New directions' in this volume.

equipped to answer is: what distribution of assets is morally all right? Exploitation, I have claimed, is a useful measure when, and in so far, as it correlates properly with unequal ownership of alienable productive assets. However, the appropriate correlation does not always hold. When we admit that people have different talents and preferences, then the jurisdiction of a Marxian egalitarianism must be extended to inalienable resources as well. Exploitation, the unequal exchange of labour, becomes in this case an even less appropriate measure of morally indefensible inequality.[40] Precisely what distribution of transferable assets (or of income) provides proper compensation for differential inalienable endowments and needs is the deep question for which exploitation theory provided an approximate and historically appropriate answer for the capitalist era.

[40] For discussion of these issues, see Roemer (1983a) and Roemer (1985a).

14 Marx and equality*

Allen Wood

A capitalist society for Marx is essentially a class society, a society whose fundamental dynamics are determined by the oppression of one class by another. And of course Marx was always an uncompromising foe of oppression in any form. The fundamental mission of the proletariat as Marx sees it is to abolish class oppression, by abolishing class differences which make it possible. The division of society into classes, however, and especially the oppression of one class by another, always involves striking social inequalities, of wealth and opportunity, of power and prestige, of freedom and self-actualization, of fulfilment and happiness. A classless society, by contrast, would seem to be above all a society of equals, where all share equally in the burdens and benefits of social life. Fighters against oppression in many forms have often viewed their fight as a fight for social equality. They have framed their demands in terms of ideals or principles of equality, whether it be equality of formal legal rights or of their *de facto* recognition by society, or equal opportunity for education and achievement, or an equal share of wealth or well-being.

This might lead us to suppose that Marx is also an egalitarian, a fighter for equality and a believer in classless society because he is a believer in a society of equals. But there are, as far as I know, no explicit and unequivocal endorsements of the notion of equality in Marx's writings. In the writings of Engels, particularly in his accounts of earlier radical movements such as the sixteenth-century peasant revolt in Germany, there are statements which appear sympathetic to egalitarian demands of various kinds. But in the writings of both men there are quite explicit disavowals of egalitarianism, and criticisms of it. There are statements to the effect that 'equality' is fundamentally a *bourgeois* idea, having no place in the statement of working class demands or objectives. On the basis of the texts, I think we must regard Marx as an opponent of the ideal of equality, despite the fact that he is also and not any the less an opponent of all forms of social privilege and

* This essay originally appeared in *Issues in Marxist Philosophy*, vol. 4, edited by John Mepham and David Hillel Rubin, Brighton: Harvester Press, 1981. Reprinted with permission.

oppression. In fact, as we shall see, Marx rejects the idea of equality because he views it in practice as a pretext for class oppression. I believe Marx's views on these matters are worth investigating. Since we are so strongly tempted to think that Marx must be an egalitarian, it may teach us something if we find out why he is not.

'Equality' is a rather unclear notion. To begin with, it may be viewed either as a right or as a social goal. Egalitarians may hold that people have a right to be treated equally in certain respects, or a right to equal portions of certain social goods. Or again, egalitarians may desire or favour a society in which people are equal or receive equal amounts of something without holding that people have a right to equal treatment or equal shares, and even irrespective of the system of rights through which the desired distribution of equal status might be brought about. Egalitarians often confuse these two ways of viewing equality, or mistakenly suppose them to be the same in practice. A system of equal rights might lead to a very unequal distribution of wealth, power and well-being. Conversely, it might turn out that the only way of securing an equal wealth or power in society is to accord people very unequal rights to make use of their talents and opportunities to acquire wealth and power.

We ought to distinguish Marx's attitude toward equality as a right from his attitude toward equality as a goal. Toward equality as a goal, I believe Marx's attitude is one of indifference. We find in his writings no specific criticisms of the attempt to achieve equality in people's status, wealth or well-being. Yet I think it can be shown that Marx does not frame his own conception of a classless society in terms of any goal of equality. Further, I think it is at best highly doubtful that Marx regards social equality as something good or desirable for its own sake.

By contrast, Marx's attitude towards the ideal of equal rights is highly critical. One of the main reasons Marx attacks the notion of equality is its close association in people's minds with the notions of right and justice. If someone says that equality ought to prevail in society, this generally goes along with saying that individuals have a *right* to be treated as equals or a *right* to equal shares of some good. It goes along with saying that to treat individuals unequally or to give them unequal shares is *wrong* or *unjust*. As I have argued elsewhere, Marx does not criticize capitalist society for any sort of injustice or for the violation of anyone's rights. In fact, Marx does not think that capitalist distribution involves wrongs or injustices.[1] Consequently, we should not expect to find him attacking capitalism on the ground that it violates anyone's 'equal right' to anything. Marx does believe that capital exploits and oppresses the workers, but he does not attack exploitation or

[1] See Wood (1972, 1979, 1981).

oppression on the grounds of right or justice. Because Marx does not view the abolition of class society as the rectification of injustice or the vindication of rights, he does not conceive of it as the vindication of equal rights. It is no accident that Marx's most extensive and penetrating discussion of equality is his critique of the Gotha Program's demand that the 'proceeds of labour' should be distributed 'with equal right to all members of society' (Marx and Engels, 1968, p. 319).

Whether conceived as a right or as a goal, equality is not a single social ideal but many different and often incompatible ideals. There are any number of different respects in which people might be treated equally by society, and many sorts of things of which they may receive equal shares. The consequence of taking equality in one of these respects may be very different from those of taking it in another. Bourgeois society, for instance, is a society of equals in that it recognizes no privileges due to birth or caste, but treats people as equals insofar as they have an equal right to dispose of themselves and their property. Marx even insists that the market place, where the buying and selling of labour-power goes on, is a realm of equality, 'because each enters into relation with the other, as with a simple owner of commodities, and they exchange equivalent for equivalent' (Marx, 1967, p. 176). The labour market does treat capitalist and worker as equals insofar as they are owners and traders of commodities. Marx's theory in volume 1 of *Capital* even postulates that the worker is paid an equivalent value for labour-power, that is, the worker's wages represent the amount of labour time socially necessary to reproduce the labour-power sold.

Of course Marx's statement that the labour market is a realm of equality is intended ironically. The wage bargain as Marx sees it is highly coercive, and the cumulative result of such bargains is that society is divided into an oppressing class of capitalists and an oppressed class of workers. But we miss the point if we suppose that Marx's ironical intent means that he does not really believe the labour market is a realm of equality, or that he believes its equality is only a sham equality. The relation between capitalists and workers *is* one of equality, in a way in which the relations between masters and slaves, lords and serfs, guild masters and journeymen, are not. The irony is that this equality, far from protecting workers from oppression, is precisely the means by which the oppression of wage labour is carried out. The conclusion to be drawn is not that some other sort of equality is to be preferred to bourgeois equality, but that the fight against working class oppression ought not to be carried on in the name of equality.

Some passages in the writings of Engels appear not to support this conclusion. Engels occasionally draws a distinction between 'political equality' or 'equality of rights' and 'social equality' or 'equality of property' (see Marx and Engels, 1975, 3:393–4, 6:5–7, 28–9, 10:414). The distinction can also be found in Marx's writings (Marx and Engels, 1975, 3:79, 163). On one occasion, Engels describes communism as 'real equality' (Marx and Engels, 1975, 3:393). On another, he attacks property qualifications for voting, saying that in them 'equality is set aside again by restricting it to a mere "equality before the law", which means equality in spite of the inequality of rich and poor – equality within the limits of the chief inequality existing – which means, in short, nothing else but giving *inequality* the name of equality' (Marx and Engels, 1975, 6:28–9). Marx, however, maintains that equality is always essentially a political notion (Marx and Engels, 1975, 3:313). Hence he says that 'real civil equality' is already found in bourgeois society (Marx and Engels, 1975, 10:590). *The German Ideology* says that equality is essentially a bourgeois idea, not a proletarian one (Marx and Engels, 1975, 5:60).

Since equality is not one idea but many, it may seem pointless to argue that it is essentially bourgeois or essentially proletarian. Some conceptions of equality, such as the formal equality of property owners in the market place, can be seen as bourgeois. Others, such as the demand for equal distribution of wealth, might be proletarian. But I think Marx's point is to claim that the idea of equality, as it has served and will serve as an ideological vehicle for historically potent social movements, is the *bourgeois* idea of equality. Proletarians may formulate notions of equality more favourable to themselves, but in Marx's view the idea of equality is outmoded, unhelpful and obfuscatory when used by the working class movement.

Since Engels appears to endorse the notion of equality, it is interesting that the most explicit account of its obsolescence as a proletarian demand is to be found in his writings. Consider this well-known passage from *Anti-Dühring*:

The demand for equality in the mouth of the proletariat has therefore a double meaning. It is either – as was the case especially at the very start, for example in the Peasant War – the spontaneous reaction against the crying social inequalities, against the contrast between rich and poor, the feudal lords and their serfs, the surfeiters and the starving; as such it is simply an expression of the revolutionary instinct, and finds its justification in that and in that only. Or, on the other hand, this demand has arisen as a reaction against the bourgeois demand for equality, drawing more or less correct and more far-reaching demands from this bourgeois demand, and serving as an agitational means in order to stir up the workers against the capitalists with the aid of the capitalists' own assertions; and in this case it stands or falls with bourgeois equality itself. In both cases the real content of the proletarian demand for equality is the demand for the *abolition of classes*. Any demand for equality which goes beyond that of necessity passes into absurdity. (Engels, 1962, p. 143)

If we do not read this passage carefully, we may think that it provides some genuine place for egalitarian demands within the proletarian movement. Engels does appear to be interpreting those demands, and even to be finding some sort of justification for them. But a closer examination shows that this impression is mistaken. The proletarian demand for equality, says Engels, has a double meaning. First, it is a 'spontaneous reaction against crying social inequalities' and as such 'simply an expression of the revolutionary instinct'. We may grant that Engels is favourable toward 'the revolutionary instinct' and sees a place for it in the proletarian movement. But it does not follow that he sees such a place for every idea through which this instinct has found expression. It is quite possible that the revolutionary instinct has found expression through confused ideas which are now outmoded and no longer serve a useful purpose in the movement. As we shall see in a moment, this is just the sort of idea Engels thinks equality is. The fact that Engels sees the revolutionary *instinct* as the only justification for such egalitarian demands suggests that there is no justification for these demands to be drawn from the ideal of equality itself considered as a moral or theoretical notion.

Second, Engels says that the proletarian demand for equality arises when agitators attempt to stir up the workers using the capitalists' own assertions. Presumably these are assertions to the effect that bourgeois equality, equality before the law, equality in the eyes of the state, equality in the market place, is a human right or in some other way a good thing. Hence Engels is understandably cautious about how far genuine proletarian demands could be correctly inferred from these assertions (such inferences, he says, may be 'more or less correct' and are certainly 'more far-reaching'). It is by no means clear that Engels approves of the strategy of stirring up the workers using capitalists' assertions. There may of course be some point to *ad hominem* arguments against capitalist apologists, but not if they are based on invalid inferences from what capitalists say. And Engels surely does not think that bourgeois values and bourgeois assertions should be used uncritically to formulate the goals of the proletarian movement. Thus he is quick to add that when the proletarian demand for equality is derived from bourgeois demands, 'it stands or falls with bourgeois equality itself'. This means that Engels can be taken to endorse the proletarian demand for equality only insofar as he can be taken to endorse the bourgeois notion of equality. But only a few paragraphs earlier, Engels has told us that this notion is derived 'from the economic conditions of bourgeois society', and serves essentially as an ideological defence of those conditions (Engels, 1962, p. 145). Hence there is little reason to suppose that he puts much stock in proletarian demands for equality based on the bourgeois notion.

The real meaning of the proletarian demand for equality, however it is taken, is the demand for the abolition of classes. This, for Engels, is the true and rational content of all such demands. The demand for the abolition of classes, however, is not a demand for equality: the notion of equality is not used to formulate this demand. Instead, it is a demand formulated in terms of the Marxian concept of class. Engels' view is that the demand for equality is a confused and outmoded demand, because it is a demand framed in terms of concepts which have been superseded by the more scientific and realistic ones of Marxian social theory. Before this theory existed, and especially during the time when the bourgeoisie was the most progressive social class, the concept of equality may have been the best one available for the purpose of attacking oppressive social relations (especially feudal ones). But now there is no longer any place in the proletarian movement for the notion of equality or for demands framed in terms of it.

Engels says all this almost in so many words, commenting in a letter to August Bebel on the Gotha Program's demands for 'social and political equality':

'The elimination of all social and political inequality' is also a very questionable phrase in place of 'the abolition of all class distinctions'...The idea of socialist society as the realm of *equality* is a one-sided French idea resting upon the old 'liberty, equality, fraternity' – an idea which was justified as a *stage of development* in its own time and place but which, like all the one-sided ideas of earlier socialist schools, should now be overcome, for it only produces confusion in people's heads and more precise modes of presentation of the matter have been found. (Marx and Engels, 1968, pp. 339–40)

Marx's most interesting discussion of equality is also found in his *Critique of the Gotha Program*, in an often quoted (but often misunderstood) attack on the Program's demand for a 'distribution of the proceeds of labour to all members of society with equal right'. This demand was made in the Program's first paragraph, but Marx postpones his discussion of it until his remarks on the third paragraph, demanding a 'just' or 'fair' [*gerecht*] distribution of the proceeds of labour. He does so because his most basic criticism of the Program's demands for distributive equality is an attack on the notion of distributive justice as a basis for working class demands.

Marx holds that the justice of a system of distribution depends on the functional relation of that system to the mode of production of which it is a part. Specifically it is a function of the social relations of effective control over the means of production. As Marx says in his concluding remarks on paragraph three of the Program:

Any distribution whatever of the means of consumption is only a consequence of the distribution of the conditions of production themselves. The latter distribution, however, is a feature of the mode of production itself...If the elements of production are [distributed as they are under the capitalist mode of production], then the present-day distribution of the means of consumption results automatically. (Marx and Engels, 1968, p. 325)

Further, this distribution is just, since as Marx says in *Capital*, the justice of transactions between agents of production depends on the 'correspondence' or 'adequacy' of those transactions to the prevailing mode of production (Marx, 1967, 3:339). That present day distribution is just, is made explicit by Marx in his opening comments on the Gotha Program's demand for a 'just' or 'fair' distribution:

Do not the bourgeois assert that the present distribution is 'fair'? And is it not, in fact, the only 'fair' distribution on the basis of the present day mode of production? Are economic relations regulated by legal conceptions [*Rechtsbegriffe*], or do not, on the contrary, legal relations arise from economic ones? (Marx and Engels, 1968, pp. 321–2)[2]

After making this point, Marx goes on to criticize the vagueness and confusion in the Gotha Program's phrase 'undiminished proceeds of labour'. '"Proceeds of labour" is a loose notion which Lassalle has put in the place of definite economic conceptions.' Further, no communist society could distribute the whole of the 'proceeds of labour' to individual workers. There would have to be funds 'for replacement of means of production...for expansion of production...and reserve or insurance funds to provide against accidents...These deductions...are an economic necessity and their magnitude is...in no way calculable by equity'. In addition, funds would have to be provided to cover 'costs of administration', for 'the common satisfaction of needs, such as schools, health services, etc.', and 'funds for those unable to work'. In this way, says Marx, 'the "undiminished proceeds of labour"... become converted into the "diminished" proceeds' (Marx and Engels, 1968, pp. 321–3).

Marx's chief target in his comments on paragraph three of the Program is the distributive orientation of 'vulgar socialists', such as the Lassalleans who drew up the Program's demands. Marx criticizes this orientation by considering how means of consumption (the 'diminished proceeds of labour') will probably be distributed in future communist society. In reading Marx's description of communist distribution, it is important to keep in mind his overall purpose in this discussion. Many who have failed to do this have consequently read these descriptions out of context, and supposed that Marx is presenting them as proletarian demands, or (worse yet) as 'principles of distributive justice' against which capitalist distribution is to be measured. But a careful consideration of the context shows that Marx proposes his account

[2] See Wood (1981), pp. 136–8.

of communist distribution precisely in order to point up its *defects*. His point is that since the system of distribution under socialism will change (and should change) as society's mode of production develops, the workers' movement is misguided if it treats any particular distributive scheme as an end in itself or as one of the long-term goals of the movement. The general purpose of the description of communist distribution is to reject the distributive orientation as a whole.

We can see this clearly if we look at the concluding paragraphs of Marx's comment on paragraph three of the Program:

I have dealt more at length with the 'undiminished proceeds of labour' on the one hand, and with 'equal right' and 'fair distribution' on the other, in order to show what a crime it is to attempt, on the one hand, to force on our party again, as dogmas, ideas which in a certain period had some meaning but have now become obsolete verbal rubbish, while again perverting, on the other hand, the realistic outlook which it has cost so much effort to instill into the Party...by means of ideological nonsense about right and other trash. (Marx and Engels, 1968, p. 325)

Keeping this in mind, let us now turn to Marx's account of distribution in the 'first phase of communist society'. 'What we have to do with here', Marx begins, 'is a communist society, not as it has *developed* on its own foundations, but, on the contrary, just as it *emerges* from capitalist society' (Marx and Engels, 1968, p. 323). We are not dealing, in other words, with an ideal scheme of distribution (much less with a conception of 'distributive justice') which we intend the workers to impose on communist society. Rather, we are trying to *predict* in a general and tentative way what will be the consequences, for the distribution of means of consumption, of collective ownership of means of production, in the earliest phases of this collective ownership.

Marx suggests that in 'a co-operative society based on common ownership of the means of production' the distribution of means of consumption will be proportional to each worker's labour contribution:

The individual producer receives back from society – after the deductions have been made – exactly what he gives to it. What he has given to it is his individual quantum of labour...He receives a certificate from society that he has furnished such and such an amount of labour (after deducting his labour for the common funds), and with this certificate he draws from the social stock of means of consumption as much as costs the same amount of labour. (Marx and Engels, 1968, p. 323)

Marx seems to agree with the Gotha Program that first phase communist distribution will be one in accordance with 'equal right'. Specifically, this system of distribution will give each an equal right to means of consumption for equal labour contribution. Its distributive principle could be stated as: equal right for equal labour. Further, Marx's account of first phase communist distribution has in common with the Gotha Program's demands the property of being too vague and nebulous to serve as a helpful guide to any future social planners. Marx indicates that distribution will be made according to each worker's 'quantum of labour'. But he does not tell us how a 'quantum of labour' is to be measured. Marx does intimate that both 'intensity' and 'duration' must be taken into consideration, but he provides no way of weighing the two factors against each other. And he gives us no indication at all how skilled or trained labour will be compared with unskilled labour. It is clear that the way these matters are handled will be decisive both for the meaning of 'equal right for equal labour' and for the workability of any scheme of distribution which follows this principle. Marx has not given us anything beyond the barest sketch of a distributive system, and he has not addressed himself to the most basic questions which would have to be faced by anyone who tried to put his scheme into practice. I think those who endorse Marx's description of first phase communist distribution as a 'principle of distributive justice' not only misunderstood Marx's intent in offering it, but also show poor taste in their choice of ideal proposals concerning economic justice.

The vagueness of Marx's description does not, however, prevent it from serving his own purpose in *Critique of the Gotha Program*. For this purpose is to show that, vague though it is, the system of equal right for equal labour is already defective from the standpoint of social equality. However its details are worked out, this system, though unavoidable in the early phase of communism, can be and should be replaced in later and higher phases. Further, Marx's point is that the system is defective precisely *because* it is a system of distribution according to 'equal right'. This system shares with bourgeois distribution the feature that 'equal right' leads to unequal distribution. As Marx's comment on paragraph three of the Gotha Program is an attack on socialist uses of the notions of right and distributive justice, so accordingly his discussion of communist distribution is an attack on the socialist uses of the ideal of distribution according to 'equal right'.

Marx argues that first phase communist distribution would be defective, and defective precisely from an egalitarian standpoint. Under this system, 'the right of the producers is proportional to the labour they supply; the equality consists in the fact that measurement is made with an equal standard, labour' (Marx and Engels, 1968, p. 324). Yet because 'one man is superior to another physically or mentally and so supplies more labour in the same time, or can labour for a longer time', this 'equal right is an unequal right for unequal labour'. Distribution in first phase communism will inevitably be an unequal distribution, and will be so precisely because it is a distribution according to equal right. But even if workers did not differ in labouring ability, this system of distribution would still be defective from an egalitarian point of view, and once again it would be so precisely because it is a distribution according to equal right. 'One worker is married, another not, one has more children than another, and so on and so forth. Thus [even] with an equal performance of labour, one will be richer than another. To avoid all these defects, right instead of being equal would have to be unequal.' Workers differ in their needs and responsibilities. Equal right for equal labour, even when conjoined with equal labour contribution, will produce unequal satisfaction of needs, unequal well-being.

Some of the judgments made by Marx here are controversial. Marx holds that the system of distribution he is describing is defective on account of the inequalities of wealth and need satisfaction which would result from it. Some people would no doubt disagree with this. They would regard the principle of equal right for equal labour as no more or less than justice demands, and be untroubled by the unequal distribution of wealth and satisfaction which result from it. I think Marx feels entitled to assume that the unequal results of this distribution are defects because he supposes himself to be addressing thoroughgoing egalitarians, who ought to be disturbed by inequalities of any kind. Of course, one cannot consistently be an egalitarian about everything. If people have unequal needs, then one cannot expect them to have both equal wealth and equal need satisfaction. Because of the order in which Marx presents his criticisms, I am inclined to think that he is more deeply disturbed by unequal need satisfaction, and that he would not consider unequal wealth a defect if no one's needs were left unsatisfied. But it is probably a mistake to draw any firm conclusions about this, since Marx seems to be arguing *ad hominem* against the egalitarians, and assumes that any sort of inequality is enough to trouble them. This assumption on his part appears rather naive.

The chief point of Marx's criticism of first phase communist society, however, is that its unequal results are due precisely to the fact that it is a distribution according to equal right. He even presents a general argument in favour of this paradoxical claim:

Right by its very nature can consist only in the application of an equal standard; but unequal individuals (and they would not be different individuals if they were not unequal) are measurable only by an equal standard insofar as they are brought under an equal point of view, are taken from one *definite* side only, for instance, in the present case, are regarded *only as workers* and nothing else is seen in them, everything else being ignored...It is therefore a right of inequality in its content, like every right. (Marx and Engels, 1968, p. 324)

Just as the equal right prevailing in the bourgeois market place leads systematically to inequality, so equal right under communism will also lead to undesirable inequalities. Marx seems to believe that this is due to the very nature of equal right, that every distributive system based on rights of any sort must have similar defects.

This conclusion is surely exaggerated. Even granted the rather Leibnizian assumption that different individuals must be unequal in some respect, it does not follow that a given system of equal right must have unequal results, because it might happen that the equal rights might be based on respects in which individuals are not unequal. Whether any system of equal rights could be devised which does not have unequal results seems to be a factual question, and not decidable by an abstract argument of the sort Marx gives. On the other hand, what Marx's argument does make evident is that there can be no guarantee that a distribution according to equal rights will be an equal distribution in any respect other than that specified by the equal rights themselves. A distributive scheme may give each person an equal right for equal labour, or even an equal share in the means of consumption at society's disposal. But it cannot guarantee equal satisfaction or equal well-being.

Egalitarians may remain unconvinced. Why, they will ask, must equal right be 'one sided'? Why may we not devise our conception of equal right with all aspects of the situation in mind? Marx himself, they may argue, has already done this. For he seems to prefer a principle of equal wealth to one of equal right for equal labour, and a principle of equal need satisfaction to one of equal wealth. He disagrees not with the notion of equal right, but only with a certain conception of what is to be made equal.

This reply, I think, is mistaken. To begin with, Marx's social theory, taken together with his views about what distribution will be like under the first phase of communism, give him good reasons to deny that we are free to impose principles of equal wealth or equal satisfaction on communist society in its first phase. The principle of distribution Marx favours for this society is apparently the one dictated by the level of its economic development. Distribution is a function of the social relations through which production is organized. Marx conjectures that in first phase communism, this will be equal right for equal labour. Defective though this distribution may be, it is the system society must adopt:

These defects are inevitable in the first phase of communist society as it is when it has just emerged after prolonged birth pangs from capitalist society. Right can never be higher than the economic structure of society and its cultural development conditions thereby. (Marx and Engels, 1968, p. 324)

Quite apart from Marx's social theory, I think he is on firm ground when he claims that 'equal right' is 'always a right of inequality in its content', at least if this means that equal rights, whatever their nature, are always in principle rights to unequal shares of need satisfaction or well-being. When I have a right to a certain share of means of consumption, I have a claim on this share against others which, within very broad limits, I may enforce irrespective of the consequences to others of my so doing. This is part of what it means to have a right. In particular, if I have a right to a certain share of these means (as determined, say, by the rules of commodity exchange, or by my labour contribution to society, or by some scheme dividing the means equally among all members of society) then it cannot be the case that my claim to this portion could be defeated or overridden by the fact that, as circumstances fall out, this share of means of consumption provides me with more need satisfaction or well-being than the share others have. By its very nature, any system of distributive rights interacts with other circumstances (such as the different – and hence probably unequal – endowments, needs and fortunes of individuals). The end result of this interaction, the comparative wealth or satisfaction or well-being of individuals, must always be a result not only of the rights they have, but also of the way they choose to exercise their rights and of the other circumstances in which the situation of one individual differs from that of another. No system of rights can by itself guarantee an equal distribution of satisfaction or well-being. If it could, then the rights belonging to the system (rights to a certain share of wealth or means of consumption) would have to be overridden whenever their exercise would disturb such an equal distribution, and the fact of this disturbance would have to count as a sufficient reason for overriding them. But rights which could be overridden merely on these grounds would not be rights at all.

Of course no right is absolutely unconditional. If the consequences of my exercising my right are bad enough for others, then it becomes plausible to argue that I no longer have this right. I have a right to dig as I please on my own property, but not if it turns out that to do so will release a large quantity of poisonous gas into the air others need to breathe. But I think exceptions of this sort are plausible only in the case of consequences which are both disastrous and unusual. It is not plausible to say that I cease to have a right I would otherwise have to a share of social wealth simply on the ground that as things turn out this share comes to more than others have, or that it yields me a greater amount of satisfaction or well-being than their share yields them. A right which could be so easily nullified or overridden would not be a right at all.

But surely, it will be objected, one can say that every person has a right to an equal share of happiness or satisfaction or well-being, and that no one has a right to a greater share of one of these goods than others have. Yes, one can *say* things like this. The question is whether they mean anything.

People can have rights to certain shares of things like money and consumption goods. They can even be entitled to equal shares, as with a gang of thieves who agree to an equal division of the loot. But satisfaction and well-being, even if they can be measured, cannot be doled out directly. The portion of these things one has depends on the portion of the means to them one has, plus other factors (one's needs and desires, how one uses the means at one's disposal, and so on). A true right to an equal share of satisfaction or well-being would have to be a right to exactly that share of means to these goods which in fact led to equal satisfaction or well-being. To suppose such a right is to suppose a case where there would be no way of determining what one has a right to apart from the end result of the distribution of means, that is, the actual comparative satisfaction or well-being people have. There would be no way of knowing whether one had enjoyed one's right, or exceeded it, or had it violated, apart from a detailed examination of the results of a certain distribution of means to satisfaction or well-being. Even if one found a scheme of distribution which had the desired results, it could not be a scheme of distributive *rights* simply because no individual could press the right to the share allotted under the scheme unless the scheme did happen to continue producing the correct distribution of satisfaction or well-being. But the scheme of distribution could never by itself guarantee that it would do this.

When people say such things as that every person has a right to an equal share of satisfaction or well-being, I think what they really do is to express the pious wish that some system of distribution might be found which would always in fact yield equal shares of the relevant goods for everyone. But it is a factual question whether the circumstances of human life will ever permit such a system to be possible. I think when Marx says that every equal right is a right of inequality in its content, he is denying the practical possibility of such a system.

Those who wish to read Marx as an egalitarian may reply at this point that although Marx argues against equality as a right, since he does so on the ground that equal rights lead to unequal distribution of satisfaction, he thereby shows himself to favour equality as a goal. Specifically, he shows that he desires a society in which the distribution of satisfaction is equal.

This conclusion, however, is false, and the inference which leads to it is invalid. We have seen that Marx may be arguing *ad hominem* against egalitarians when he regards unequal satisfaction as a defect of distribution according to equal right. But even if (as is plausible) he believes this himself, it does not follow that he must conceive of the remedy to this defect in egalitarian terms. It may be a bad sign that satisfaction is unequal. It does not follow that the thing to do is to make it equal.[3]

[3] See Sen (1980).

The notion of equality appears nowhere in Marx's bold vision of the 'higher phase' of communist society:

In a higher phase of communist society, after the enslaving subordination of the individual to the division of labour...has vanished; after labour has become not only a means of life but life's prime want; after the productive forces have also increased with the all-round development of the individual, and all the springs of co-operative wealth flow more abundantly – only then can the narrow horizon of bourgeois right be crossed in its entirety and society inscribe on its banners: From each according to his ability, to each according to his needs! (Marx and Engels, 1968, pp. 324–5)

Marx chooses Louis Blanc's slogan 'From each according to his ability, to each according to his needs!' precisely because it is *not* an egalitarian slogan. It does not treat people equally from any point of view, but instead considers people individually, each with a different set of needs and abilities. It might be said that the slogan at least implies that people's needs will be *equally* satisfied. But I think this is false, unless it means merely that all people's needs will indeed *be* satisfied. One might as well say that the Grim Reaper is an egalitarian on the ground that once we die, we are all *equally* dead.

Talk about 'equal satisfaction' is most appropriate when what we really mean is equal *dis*satisfaction. Egalitarians have often thought of equal distribution as a fair or humane way of dealing with scarcity, with situations where there are not enough resources to satisfy everyone. The idea is that if scarcity is spread evenly among people, no one will be harmed too greatly by it. This is not Marx's idea in the *Critique of the Gotha Program*, or anywhere else as far as I know. For Marx, the problem with bourgeois society is not that scarcity is unevenly distributed, but that there is scarcity where there need be none, and that there is a surfeiting class which benefits from a system which subjects the majority to an artificial and unnecessary poverty. It seems clear from the *Critique of the Gotha Program* that Marx believes there will be 'defects' and 'inequalities' in distribution even under communism, until the day when 'the springs of co-operative wealth flow abundantly' enough to permit everyone's needs to be fully satisfied. After that day, of course, equality as a device for distributing scarce resources will no longer be needed, since resources will not be scarce.

I think it is clear that Marx does not consider social equality as something good for its own sake. His critique of 'equal right' implies that he sees nothing inherently 'just' or intrinsically good about any scheme of equal rights, however it is framed. Marx favours an equal distribution for equal labour under the first phase of communism, but not because this is an ideal distributive scheme, but because he believes it is the distribution which will result from collective ownership of the means of production, in its early phases. Communist society will be a classless society, but he regards 'equality' as a confusing and outmoded way of representing the goal of abolishing class distinctions. Further, Marx does not tell us that he favours the abolition of class society because he regards a classless society as intrinsically good. It seems to me more in tune with the general spirit of Marx's thought to suppose that he favours the abolition of classes because he thinks it will lead to other things he values, such as increased human freedom, well-being, community, and individual development or self-actualization.

Marx is very critical of the 'envious' desire of 'crude communism' to impose a uniform standard of life on everyone, 'the urge to reduce things to a common level...levelling down proceeding from the *preconceived* minimum'. This brand of communism, he says, 'has not only failed to go beyond private property, but has not yet even reached it' (Marx and Engels, 1975, 3 :295; cp. 10 :429). No doubt part of what bothers Marx here is that the 'preconceived' standard of life poses an obstacle to human progress. But it seems plain that for him the social equality favoured by 'crude communism' is not any sort of redeeming virtue of its proposals.

I think Marx has little use for the idea of equality largely because in his view struggles carried on in the name of equality have little role to play in emancipating the working class. The particular sort of equality demanded – and largely achieved – by the bourgeoisie against feudal institutions, far from aiding working class emancipation, is one of the primary means of its oppression. Formal inequalities, moreover, play no major role in maintaining this oppression. If wage labourers are treated as inferior to wealthier or more educated classes and made the objects of prejudice or discrimination as compared with them, this is not the basic cause of working class oppression, but only a by-product of the materially and spiritually impoverished mode of life to which the workers' economic position consigns them. The achievement of formal equalities, equality before the law, equality in the eyes of the state, even equal treatment in the market place, will not do much to improve the lot of the workers. What is needed, rather, is working class organization for the purpose of improving the workers' bargaining power, and eventually of wresting control of the means of production from the capitalists. Legal and political measures favourable to workers are not, in Marx's view, generally egalitarian in nature. They consist instead in restricting the ways the capitalist class may exploit labour power and in making it more difficult for the bourgeoisie to profit from this exploitation.

Whether Marx is right about the causes of working class oppression, and about the remedies for it, may be a matter of controversy. Less controversial, I think, is the claim that struggles carried out in the name of equality, even of equal rights, have had some considerable success in combatting other forms of social oppression, such as racial and sexual oppression. Non-whites in both Britain and the United States have yet to attain full equality in the eyes of the state, and they are still in need of legal protection against racist discrimination in such matters as education, housing and employment. Women are not yet recognized as equal to men in the eyes of the law; they are systematically discriminated against in many ways, prominently in matters relating to employment. They are systematically excluded from certain kinds of high-prestige and well-paying jobs, and they are paid systematically less for doing work of equal worth. Much has been done in the name of equality to improve the position both of non-whites and women in these respects, and much more remains to be done. It would of course be unrealistic to think that racial or sexual oppression would end if these inequalities were removed. But it is not unreasonable for the struggle against racial and sexual oppression to place their removal high on its agenda.

I think Marx can be faulted in his estimate of the idea of equality for paying too exclusive attention to working class oppression. He does so because he believes class oppression generally is the key to historical change, and that the struggle between bourgeoisie and proletariat is the key to the historical dynamics of the present age: 'The class struggle is the proximate driving power of history, and especially the class struggle between bourgeoisie and proletariat as the great lever of modern social revolution' (Marx and Engels, 1961–66, 39:407). Further Marx often tries to explain national or racist oppression in terms of its function in capitalist society. Colonialism serves as a means for concentrating wealth in the hands of the European ruling classes, and thus of making capital possible (see Marx, 1967, I:750, 754). National and religious prejudice of English workers against the Irish divides the working class; thus 'the English bourgeoisie has not only exploited Irish poverty to keep down the working class in England by *forced immigration* of poor Irishmen, but it has also divided the proletariat into two hostile camps' (Marx and Engels, 1972, p. 162). Some Marxists quite plausibly offer an analogous explanation of the function of white racism in today's capitalism. Engels even attempts a class-based explanation of the primeval origins of sexual oppression (Marx and Engels, 1968, pp. 494–6).

Even if we grant all these doctrines, however, it still does not follow that sexual, racial or national oppression are merely forms of class oppression. Perhaps the doctrines imply that the abolition of class oppression will make it easier to abolish the other forms, by removing some of their economic support. Even so, it does not follow that the struggle against sexual, racial or national oppression would be unnecessary in the early phases of communist society, which still bears the moral and intellectual birthmarks of the old society. Nor does it follow that there is no need for a concerted struggle against these forms of oppression in bourgeois society, distinct from – if allied with – the working class struggle. And if there is a need for such a struggle, then there might be a place in it for certain ideas (such as equality) which have little or no place in the working class movement considered by itself.

Marx's estimate of equality does need, I think, to be supplemented by the recognition that the working class struggle is not the only progressive social movement and that the notion of equality may have a positive role to play in struggles against oppression which fall outside the working class movement narrowly conceived. To recognize these points would be to supplement or extend the views of Marx and Engels. But it would not be to correct or revise them; it would not necessarily be to abandon any of Marx's positive doctrines. Moreover, it would be to supplement or extend Marx's views in a way which is consistent with the spirit of Marxism itself.

Yet if a place is to be made for the notion of equality within Marxism, care must be taken not to import moral doctrines concerning right and justice which Marx explicitly repudiates. We must not suppose that equality before the law, equal status in the eyes of the state, or equal treatment in the market place are things to be pursued because they are intrinsically good or inherently just. If they are worth pursuing that is because their pursuit at a certain historical juncture advances the interests of oppressed social groups. Nor should we fall under the illusion that the abolition of inequalities is identical with the abolition of oppression. Marx is acutely aware that bourgeois oppression of the proletariat flourishes on bourgeois justice and the equality it involves. Marx believes that no formal or procedural equality, no guarantees of equal treatment and equal status, no system of equal rights, can by itself insure people against the systematic subordination in practice of the interests of some to the interest of others. This is because equal right is always implicitly a right of inequality; equality in form is potentially always inequality in content.

This means that if it is a good thing to strive for the social equality of whites and non-whites or of men and women, then this is because that helps to end specific forms of oppression. And it is only a good thing as long as it tends to have that effect. The ideal of equality is not to be valued as an end in itself or a principle of justice. It recommends itself only as part of the strategy for achieving progressive social change.

No doubt many will reject so exclusively consequentialist a rationale for the pursuit of social equality. But there is quite a bit to be said for such a rationale. The oppression of women and non-whites still persists despite the abolition of many inequalities which once aided it. If we value social equality only insofar as it tends to make things difficult for oppressors and oppressive social relations, then we will see no reason to be more content with oppression because it has survived the abolition of inequalities which supported it. On the other hand, if we value equality for its own sake, then we open the way to those who would use egalitarian arguments to impede the struggle against oppression.

Consider, for example, the policy of preferential hiring (or so-called 'reverse discrimination'). This policy is now widely advocated, and to a much lesser extent practised in a few places. The policy is to give preference in hiring on certain kinds of jobs (such as academic ones) to members of oppressed groups (such as non-whites and women) who have traditionally been under-represented in these jobs due to discrimination or other reasons. Opponents of the policy often argue against it on egalitarian grounds, alleging that it violates the traditional egalitarian principle that there should be no formal constraints of a racial or sexual nature on hiring decisions, that people who apply for jobs should be considered on their merits simply as individuals, and not as examples of their race or sex. To prefer people on racial or sexual grounds, they argue, is just what is wrong with practices discriminating against women and non-whites. 'Reverse discrimination', therefore, amounts to the same infringements of equality.

Well-intentioned defenders of preferential hiring attempt to defend the policy by showing that it is consistent with, even demanded by, the ideal of equality, when this ideal is conceived in a less rigid and individualistic way. Since 'equality' can mean so many different things, there is surely some sense in which this defence will succeed. On the other hand, opponents of preferential hiring are clearly correct in holding that this policy violates one widely accepted egalitarian principle, which has been used in the past to condemn discrimination against women and non-whites. Of course the demonstrable result of following this principle is to perpetuate patterns of employment which are instrumental to the oppression of women and non-whites. Oppression, as Marx tells us, may thrive on formal equality.

The best justification of preferential hiring, however, is exactly the same as the justification for prohibiting discrimination against oppressed groups: for both measures, the justification is that they are timely and practicable ways of promoting progressive social change. If we are unable to convince opponents of preferential hiring on this point, we are unlikely to convince them to accept any egalitarian principles which might justify it.

Also misguided, I think, are those who defend preferential hiring as a form of reparation or compensation to oppressed groups for 'past injustices' to them. As opponents of preferential hiring are quick to point out, this policy is not a felicitous way of distributing either the burdens or the benefits of such compensation. The beneficiaries of preferential hiring tend to be among the least disadvantaged members of the oppressed group, while the burdens of compensation tend to fall almost exclusively on people who have benefited least from 'past injustice'.[4] These arguments, of course, rest once again on a rather individualistic conception of compensatory justice, and might be rejected by some on this account. But it still seems to me that the most candid thing to do is to say simply that preferential hiring is a good policy because it is the most effective way of bringing about urgently needed social change. Once again, if we cannot convince the policy's opponents of this, we are unlikely to convince them to accept any principles of collective compensatory justice.

Marx is a foe of all forms of social oppression. Some will say that some ideal of social equality is implicit either in the notion of oppression itself or in Marx's opposition to it. How can we decide who is oppressed and who is not except by appealing to some principle of equality or justice? And what can Marx find wrong with oppression if not that it violates a principle of social equality?

Perhaps to some people 'social equality' just *means* the absence of social oppression. And 'equality' is a vague enough term that it would be arbitrary to insist that it cannot bear such a meaning. On the other hand, we have seen that Marx and Engels do not regard the notion of equality as useful in identifying what is wrong with class oppression. Oppression for Marx is a feature of social relations by which they systematically subordinate the interests of one group to those of another. To say that the bourgeoisie oppresses the proletariat is to make judgments about what the interests of these groups are and about the systematic effects of certain social relations (e.g. the private ownership of means of production, the relation of capital to wage labour) on these interests. Some of these judgments may be controversial (though in the case of bourgeois oppression of the proletariat, Marx does not think they need be). Some of these judgments may even raise deep or difficult questions about social theory, social explanation or the nature of people's interests. But prima facie at least they do not raise any questions about principles of social equality or justice.

Marx never gives any direct and explicit account of his reasons for attacking social oppression and the class distinctions on which it rests. Certainly he himself never cites 'inequality' as one of these reasons. It betrays a lack of imagination to think that Marx must have hated oppression because he loved equality. I conjecture that Marx is a foe of social oppression because he

[4] See Sher (1975).

believes that as a matter of fact at this stage in human history oppressive societies always squander their potentialities for human fulfilment. Oppression is to be attacked because it stands in the way of the self-development of the human species. I think Marx sympathizes with the ancients who, he says, 'excused the slavery of one on the ground that it was a means to the full development of another' (Marx, 1967, 1 :408). At least, I think Marx does regard oppression as historically justified to the extent that it is necessary for the development of the human species and its powers. In this vein, he calls the development of the social forces of production the 'historical justification of capital' (Marx, 1967, 3 : 34). For these reasons, I think Marx's support of movements opposing social oppression is based on judgments about the historical meaning of oppression in the present epoch, and not on any general principles of liberty, justice or equality.

But it may appear difficult to reconcile this opinion with the fact that Marx shows great sympathy for movements to emancipate the oppressed at all stages of history, and not only when he believes such movements will develop the productive forces. If Marx regards oppression as justified whenever it serves the interests of economic and technological progress, then we ought to expect him to side with the bourgeoisie against the proletariat in the early stages of capitalism. Yet no one who has read *Capital*'s account of the rise of capitalism could suspect him of doing this. As everyone knows, Marx's hero is Spartacus, who is hardly a symbol of economic development. If we hold that Marx's enthusiasm for movements in behalf of the oppressed is due only to his belief that these movements are economically progressive, then how do we explain his sympathy with such movements in all ages, even when they may have stood in the path of economic development?

Of course Marx favours the working class movement not only because it is economically progressive, but also because he believes that along with economic progress it will enhance the freedom, community and humanity of future society. But even apart from this, it is simplistic to suppose that when Marx turns his attention to past historical struggles, his sympathies must necessarily lie with those whose achievements he regards as historically justified by the progressive tendencies in human affairs. There may be some people who view history as a single battle between Good and Evil, Freedom and Tyranny, Equality and Oppression. But Marx is not such a person. Marx's feelings toward a great historical movement such as capitalism, for instance, are deeply ambivalent and unresolved. They are a mixture of awe at capitalism's colossal accomplishments in behalf of human development and horror at the human cost which has had to be paid for these accomplishments. If we ask Marx whether the whole history of capitalism was a 'good' or 'bad' thing, whether this history 'ought' to have occurred, then the only reply we should expect from him is a rejection of our questions as shallow, pointless and inane. Capitalism has been a terrible thing, but also a necessary thing. It has caused monstrous human suffering and human waste, but it has also created unprecedented potentialities for human freedom and fulfilment. The 'good' side of capitalism cannot be separated from its 'bad' side. The important thing now is to seize on the opportunities capitalism has created, which lie beyond capitalism itself. To that end, our sympathies must lie with that historical movement which has the power to realize fully the potentialities of our historical situation. This movement is, of course, the movement of the revolutionary proletariat. Our task is to join with this movement, to mould it and be moulded by it, to breathe the air it breathes, to let its action be our action, its history our history.

Marx sympathizes with the struggles of the oppressed in all times and places not because they possess the same historical justification as the working class movement, but rather because they claim kinship with it. If we are to be revolutionary proletarians, we must recognize this kinship and be loyal to it. In Spartacus and his comrades, Marx sees the same ruthless courage in the face of oppression as he does in the nineteenth-century working class. In the sixteenth-century German peasants, the Levellers, the Babeufists, Marx sees the dawn of the same aspirations which the modern working class treasures (so he thinks) with better prospects of success. Marx does not hesitate to acknowledge this kinship even in the case of earlier socialists whose utopian, moralistic or egalitarian ideas he rejects as outmoded phases of the movement. Marx sympathizes with earlier movements in behalf of the oppressed not because he accepts their ideologies but because for him they constitute a heritage to be revered, preserved and carried to victory. Marx sides with all struggles against oppression because like any self-conscious historical agent, he chooses himself by choosing his ancestors.

Bibliography

Aaronowitz, Stanley, 1981. *The Crisis of Historical Materialism*, New York: Praeger

Ackerman, Bruce, 1980. *Social Justice in the Liberal State*, New Haven: Yale University Press

Albert, Robin and Hahnel, Michael, 1978. *Unorthodox Marxism*, Boston: South End Press

1981. *Marxism and Socialist Theory*, Boston: South End Press

Allison, G., 1971. *The Essence of Decision*, Boston: Little, Brown

Althusser, L., 1971. *Lenin and Philosophy*, London

Axelrod, R., 1984. *The Evolution of Cooperation*, New York: Basic Books

Baran, P., 1957. *The Political Economy of Growth*, New York: Monthly Review Press

Bardhan, P., 1980. Interlocking factor markets and agrarian development: A review of issues. *Oxford Economic Papers*, March

1982. Agrarian class formation in India. *Journal of Peasant Studies* 10, no. 1

1983. Labour tying in a poor agrarian economy: A theoretical and empirical analysis. *Quarterly Journal of Economics*, August

1984a. *Land, Labour and Rural Poverty: Essays in Development Economics*, New York: Columbia University Press

1984b. *The Political Economy of Development in India*, Oxford: Basil Blackwell

Berlin, I., 1969. *Four Essays on Liberty*, Oxford

Bhaduri, A., 1983. *The Economic Structure of Backward Agriculture*, London: Academic Press

Bois, G., 1978. Against the neo-Malthusian orthodoxy. *Past and Present* 79, 60–9

Boserup, E., 1965. *The Conditions of Agricultural Growth: The Economics of Agrarian Change under Population Pressure*, New York: Aldine Publishers

Boulding, Kenneth, 1970. *A Primer on Social Dynamics: History as Dialectics and Development*, New York: Free Press

Bourdieu, P., 1979. *La Distinction*, Paris: Editions de Minuit

Bowles, S. and Gintis, H., 1978. The Marxian theory of value and heterogeneous labor. *Cambridge Journal of Economics* 1, 173–92

1981. Structure and practice in the labor theory of value. *Review of Radical Political Economics* 12, no. 4, Winter, 1–26

Bowles, S., Gordon, D. and Weisskopf, T. E., 1984. *Beyond the Wasteland*, New York: Anchor Press

Braverman, Harry, 1974. *Labor and Monopoly Capital*, New York: Monthly Review Press

Brenner, R., 1976. Agrarian class structure and economic development in pre-industrial Europe. *Past and Present* 70, 30–70

1977. The origins of capitalist development: a critique of Neo-Smithian Marxism. *New Left Review*, July–August

1982. The agrarian origins of European capitalism. *Past and Present* 97, 16–113

1985. Marx's two theories of transition to capitalism (Part One) in *Actes du Colloque Marx*, Editions de l'Ecole des Hautes Etudes en Sciences Sociales, Paris

Brown, Norman O., 1959. *Life against Death: The Psychoanalytic Meaning of History*, New York: Vintage Books

Brunt, P., 1971. *Social Conflicts in the Roman Republic*, London: Methuen

Carchedi, G., 1977. *On the Economic Identification of the Middle Classes*, London: Routledge and Kegan Paul

Cardoso, F. H., 1977. The originality of the copy: ECLA and the idea of development. *CEPAL Review*

Carr, Edward H., 1958. *The New Society*, Oxford University Press

Charamonte, Gerardo, 1975. Report to the Central Committee of the Italian Communist Party, October 29–30. *The Italian Communist* 57, 69–93

Cohen, G. A., 1974. Being, consciousness and roles, in C. Abramsky (ed.), *Essays in Honour of E. H. Carr*, London

1978a. *Karl Marx's Theory of History: A Defence*, Princeton University Press

1978b. Robert Nozick and Wilt Chamberlain, in John Arthur and William Shaw (eds.), *Justice and Economic Distribution*, Englewood Cliffs, N.J.

1979a. Capitalism, freedom and the proletariat, in Alan Ryan (ed.), *The Idea of Freedom*, Oxford

1979b. The labor theory of value and the concept of exploitation. *Philosophy and Public Affairs* 8, no. 4, 338–60

1981a. Illusions about private property and freedom, in John Mepham and David Ruben (eds.), *Issues in Marxist Philosophy*, vol. IV, Hassocks, Sussex

1981b. Freedom, justice and capitalism. *New Left Review*, 125

1981c. Review of Rader. *Clio* 10, no. 2, 219–23

1981d. The labor theory of value and the concept of exploitation, in Ian Steedman et al., *The Value Controversy*, London: New Left Books

1982a. Functional explanation, consequence explanation and Marxism. *Inquiry* 25, 27–56

1982b. Reply to Elster on 'Marxism, functionalism, and game theory'. *Theory and Society* 11, no. 4, 483–97

1983a. The structure of proletarian unfreedom. *Philosophy and Public Affairs* 12, 3–33

1983b. Reconsidering historical materialism. *Nomos* 26, 226–51

1983c. More on exploitation and the labor theory of value. *Inquiry* 26, 309–31

Cohen, J., 1980. Review of Cohen. *Journal of Philosophy* 79, 253–73

Cohen, Jean, 1982. *Class and Civil Society*, Amherst: University of Massachusetts Press

Cohen, P., 1968. *Modern Social Theory*, London

Cole, G. D. H., 1955. *Studies in Class Structure*, London: Routledge and Kegan Paul

Coleman, J., 1974. *Power and the Structure of Society*, New York: Norton

Collard, D., 1978 *Altruism and Economy*, Oxford: Martin Robertson

Dahrendorf, Ralph, 1959. *Class and Class Conflict in Industrial Society*, Palo Alto: Stanford University Press

David, P., 1975. *Technical Choice, Innovation and Economic Growth*, Cambridge University Press

Davidson, D., 1980. *Essays on Actions and Events*, Oxford University Press

de Janvry, A., 1978. Social structure and biased technical change in Argentine agriculture, in H. P. Binswanger and V. W. Ruttan (eds.), *Induced Innovation: Technology, Institutions and Development*, Baltimore: Johns Hopkins Press

de Vylder, Stefan, 1976. *Allende's Chile: The Political Economy of the Rise and Fall of the Unidad Popular*, Cambridge University Press

Dobb, M., 1960. *An Essay on Economic Growth and Planning*, London: Routledge and Kegan Paul

Dworkin, Ronald, 1981. What is equality? Parts 1 and 2. *Philosophy and Public Affairs* 10, nos. 3 and 4, Summer and Fall

Edwards, Richard, 1979. *Contested Terrain*, New York: Basic Books

Ehrenreich, Barbara and Ehrenreich, John, 1977. The professional-managerial class. *Radical America* 11, no. 2

Elster, J., 1978. *Logic and Society*, Chichester: Wiley

1979a. *Ulysses and the Sirens: Studies in Rationality and Irrationality*, Cambridge University Press

1979b. *Freedom and Power*, Oslo. (Unpublished mimeo)

1980. Review of Cohen (1978). *Political Studies* 28, 121–8

1981. Review of Cohen (1978). *Annales* 36, 745–57

1982a. Sour grapes, in A. Sen and B. Williams (eds.), *Utilitarianism and Beyond*, Cambridge University Press

1982b. Marxism, functionalism and game theory. *Theory and Society* 11, 453–82

1983. *Explaining Technical Change*, Cambridge University Press

1984a. The contradictions of modern societies (review article of Olson 1982). *Government and Society* 19

1984b. *Ulysses and the Sirens*, rev. edn, Cambridge University Press

1985a. *Making Sense of Marx*, Cambridge University Press

1985b. The scope and nature of rational-choice explanation. Forthcoming in the *Proceedings of the Israel Colloquium for the History, Philosophy and Sociology of Science*

1985c. Rationality, morality and collective action. Forthcoming in *Ethics*

Emmanuel, A., 1972. *Unequal Exchange*, New York: Monthly Review Press

Engels, F., 1878. *Anti-Dühring*, Moscow (1954)

Evans, P., 1982. Reinventing the bourgeoisie: state entrepreneurship and class formation in the context of dependent capitalist development. *American Journal of Sociology*, Supplement

Fel'dman, G. A., 1928. On the theory of growth rates of national income, translated in N. Spulber (ed.), *Foundations of Society Strategy for Economic Growth*, Bloomington: Indiana University Press (1964)

Felix, D., 1983. *Marx as Politician*, Carbondale and Edwardsville: Southern Illinois University Press

Fellner, W., 1961. Two propositions in the theory of induced innovations. *Economic Journal* 71, 305–8

Fernbach, D. (ed.), 1974. *Karl Marx: The First International and After*, New York: Vintage Books

Finley, M. I., 1973. *The Ancient Economy*, London: Chatto and Windus

1981. *Economy and Society in Ancient Greece*, London: Chatto and Windus

Frankfurt, H., 1973. Coercion and moral responsibility, in T. Honderick (ed.), *Essays on Freedom of Action*, London

Friedrich, C. J., 1950. *Constitutional Government and Democracy*, Boston: Ginn

Froelich, N. and Oppenheimer, J. A., 1970. I get by with a little help from my friends. *World Politics* 23, 104–20

Fromm, Erik, 1961. *Marx's Concept of Man*, New York: Frederick Ungar

Geertz, C., 1963. *Agricultural Innovation: The Process of Ecological Change in Indonesia*, Berkeley: University of California Press

Gerschenkron, A., 1962. *Economic Backwardness in Historical Perspective*, Cambridge, Mass.: Harvard University Press

Gouldner, Alvin, 1979. *The Future of Intellectuals on the Road to Class Power*, New York: Harcourt, Brace and Jovanovich

Griffuelhes, Victor, 1910. L'infériorite des capitalistes français. *Movement Socialiste* 226

Habermas, Jurgen, 1975. *Legitimation Crisis*, Boston: Beacon Press

Hardin, R., 1982. *Collective Action*, Baltimore: John Hopkins University Press

Harsanyi, J., 1977. *Rational Behavior and Bargaining Equilibrium in Games and Social Situations*, Cambridge University Press

Heller, Agnes, 1974. *The Theory of Need in Marx*, London: Allison and Busby

Hill, C., 1968a. *Reformation to Industrial Revolution*, London

    1968b. *Puritanism and Revolution*, London

    1974. *Change and Continuity in Seventeenth Century England*, London

Hirschman, A. 1981. *Essays in Trespassing: Economics to Politics and Beyond*, Cambridge University Press

Hunt, R., 1974. *The Political Ideas of Marx and Engels*, vol. 1, University of Pittsburgh Press

Jacobsen, John K., 1980. Chasing progress. Ph.D. diss., University of Chicago

Jeffrey, R. C., 1970. Statistical explanation vs. statistical inference, in N. Rescher *et al.* (eds.), *Essays in Honor of C. G. Hempel*, Dordrecht

Kahneman, Daniel and Tversky, Amos, 1982. *Judgment under Uncertainty: Heuristics and Biases*, Cambridge University Press

Kautsky, Karl, 1925. *La Revolution Proletarienne et Son Programme*, Bruxelles: L'Englatine

Keni-Paz, B., 1977. *The Social and Political Thought of Leon Trotsky*, Oxford University Press

Kenny, A., 1975. *Will, Freedom and Power*, Oxford

Korsch, Karl, 1975. What is socialization? *New German Critique* 6, 60–82

Kramer, Gerald, 1971. Short term fluctuations in U.S. voting behavior, 1896–1964. *American Political Science Review* 65, 131–43

Lakatos, Imre, 1976. *Proofs and Refutations*, Cambridge University Press

Lancaster, K., 1973. The dynamic inefficiency of capitalism. *Journal of Political Economy* 81, 1092–109

Lange, Oskar, 1938. *On the Economic Theory of Socialism* (B. E. Lippincott, ed.), Minneapolis: University of Minnesota

Lenin, V. I., 1965. *Sochinenya* 32, Moscow

Levine, A. and Wright, E. O., 1980. Rationality and class struggle. *New Left Review*, 123, 47–68

Lipset, S. M., 1968. Social stratification: social class, in E. Shils (ed.), *International Encyclopedia of the Social Sciences*, vol. 15, New York: Macmillian, 296–316

Luce, R. D. and Raiffa, H., 1957. *Games and Decisions*, New York: Wiley

Lustig, N., 1980. Underconsumption in Latin American economic thought: some considerations. *Review of Radical Political Economics*, Spring

Luxemburg, Rosa, 1970. *Reform or Revolution*, New York: Pathfinder Press

Mahalanobis, P. C., 1953. Some observations on the process of growth of national income. *Sankhya*, September

Malinowski, B., 1922. *Argonauts of the West Pacific*, London
    1960. *A Scientific Theory of Culture*, London

Mallet, Serge, 1963. *La Nouvelle Classe Ouvriére*, Paris: Seuil

Mandel, Ernest, 1971. *The Formation of Economic Thought of Karl Marx*, New York: Monthly Review Press

Mao Zedong, 1964. Analysis of class in the Chinese countryside. *Selected Readings of Mao Tse-Tung*, Peking: Foreign Languages Press

Marcuse, Herbert, 1962. *Eros and Civilization*, New York: Vintage Books

Marglin, S., 1967. The rate of interest and value of capital with unlimited supplies of labour, in K. Shell (ed.), *Essays on the Theory of Optimal Economic Growth*, Cambridge, Mass.: M.I.T. Press

Marx, Karl, 1845. *The Holy Family*, in Marx and Engels, *Collected Works*, vol. 4, London: Lawrence and Wishart (1966)
    1845–6. *The German Ideology*, in Marx and Engels, *Collected Works*, vol. 5, London: Lawrence and Wishart (1966)
    1847. The Communism of the paper *Rheinischer Beobachter*, in Marx and Engels, *On Religion*, Moscow (1957)
    1847a. *The Poverty of Philosophy*, in Marx and Engels, *Collected Works*, vol. 6, London: Lawrence and Wishart (1966)
    1847b. *Moralising Criticism and Critical Morality*, in Marx and Engels, *Collected Works*, vol. 6, London: Lawrence and Wishart (1966)
    1850. *The Class Struggles in France*, in Marx and Engels, *Collected Works*, vol. 10, London: Lawrence and Wishart
    1850a. Review of Girardin, *Le Socialisme et l'Impot*, in Marx and Engels, *Collected Works*, vol. 10, London: Lawrence and Wishart
    1850b. Review of Guizot, *Pourquoi la Revolution d'Angleterre a-t-elle reussi?* in Marx and Engels, *Collected Works*, vol. 10, London: Lawrence and Wishart
    1851. Reflections, in Marx and Engels, *Collected Works*, vol. 10, London: Lawrence and Wishart
    1852a. The eighteenth Brumaire of Louis Bonaparte, in Marx–Engels, *Selected Works*, vol. I, Moscow (1958)
    1852b. *The Eighteenth Brumaire of Louis Bonaparte*, in Marx and Engels, *Collected Works*, vol. 10/11, London: Lawrence and Wishart
    1857–8. *Grundrisse*, Harmondsworth: Pelican
    1859. *A Contribution to the Critique of Political Economy*, Moscow: Progress Publishers
    1860. *Herr Vogt*, in Marx and Engels, *Collected Works*, vol. 17, London: Lawrence and Wishart

1861–2. *Zur Kritik der politischen Okonomie* (Manuskript 1861–3) in MEGA II.3. Berlin: Dietz (1976)

1862–3. *Theories of Surplus Value*, vol. I, Moscow (1969)

1865. Results of the immediate process of production. Reprinted as an Appendix to *Capital* I, New York: Vintage Books (1977)

1866. Results of the immediate process of production. Appendix in *Capital*, vol. I, Harmondsworth, Middlesex (1976)

1866a.Instructions for delegates to the Geneva Congress, in D. Fernbach (ed.) (1974)

1867. *Capital* I, New York: International Publishers

1869. Preface to 2nd edn of Marx (1852). In *Marx–Engels Werke*, vol. 16, Berlin: Dietz

1880. *Briefwechsel mit Vera Sasulich*, in *Marx–Engels Werke*, vol. 19, Berlin: Dietz

1894. *Capital* III, New York: International Publishers

1905–10. *Theories of Surplus Value*, London: Lawrence and Wishart (1969)

1952. *Wage Labour and Capital*, Moscow: Progress Publishers

1973. *Grundrisse*, New York: Vintage Books

1977. *The Civil War in France*, in David McLellan (ed.), *Karl Marx: Selected Writings*, Oxford University Press

Marx, Karl and Engels, Friedrich, 1846. *The German Ideology*, New York (1965)

1848, *The Communist Manifesto*, in Marx and Engels, *Collected Works*, vol. 6, London: Lawrence and Wishart (1966)

1961–6. *Werke*, Berlin: Dietz

1962. *Marx/Engels Selected Works in Two Volumes*, vol. II, Moscow

1968. *Selected Works*, New York: International Publishers

1972. *Ireland and the Irish Question*, New York

1975. *Selected Correspondence*, Moscow

1975–. *Collected Works*, New York: International Publishers

McLellan, David (ed.), 1977. *Karl Marx: Selected Writings*, Oxford University Press

Merton, R. L., 1968. *Social Theory and Social Structure*, New York

Mill, J. S., 1848. *Principles of Political Economy*, University of Toronto Press (1965)

Miller, R., 1981. Productive forces and the forces of change. *Philosophical Review* 40, no. 1, 91–117

1984. Producing change: Work, technology and power in Marx's theory of history, in T. Ball and J. Farr (eds.), *After Marx*, Cambridge University Press

Mills, C. W., 1958. *The Causes of World War Three*, New York

Mitchell, Juliet, 1966. Women: The longest revolution. *New Left Review* 40

Molnar, M., 1975. *Marx, Engels, et la Politique Internationale*, Paris: Gallimard

Morishima, Michio, 1973. *Marx's Economics*, Cambridge University Press

1974. Marx in the light of modern economic theory. *Econometrica* 42, 611–32

Nelson, R. and Winter, S., 1982. *An Evolutionary Theory of Economic Change*, Cambridge, Mass.: Harvard University Press

Newberry, D. and Stiglitz, J., 1979. Sharecropping, risk-sharing and the importance of imperfect information, in J. A Roumasset, *et al.* (eds.), *Risk, Uncertainty and Agricultural Development*, North-Holland

Norman, R., 1980. Review of Cohen (1978), *The London Review of Books*, Feb. 21, p. 6.

North, Douglass, 1981. *Structure and Change in Economic History*, New York: Norton

North, Douglass and Thomas, R., 1973. *The Rise of Western Civilization*, Cambridge University Press

Nove, Alec, 1983. *The Economics of Feasible Socialism*, London: George Allen and Unwin

Nozick, Robert, 1969. Newcomb's problem and two principles of choice. In N. Rescher (ed.), *Essays in Honor of Carl Hempel*, Dordrecht: Leiden, 114–46

 1974. *Anarchy, State, and Utopia*, New York: Basic Books

O'Mahoney, D., 1979. Labour management and the market economy. *Irish Journal of Business and Administrative Research*, pp. 16–41

Offe, C. and Wiesenthal, H., 1980. Two logics of collective action. *Political Power and Social Theory* 1, 67–115

Okun, A. M., 1981. *Prices and Quantities: A Macroeconomic Analysis*, Washington D.C.: Brookings Institution

Olson, M., 1965. *The Logic of Collective Action*, Cambridge, Mass.: Harvard University Press

 1982. *The Rise and Decline of Nations: Economic Growth, Stagflation, and Social Rigidities*, New Haven: Yale University Press

Palma, G., 1978. Dependency: a formal theory of underdevelopment or a methodology for the analysis of concrete situations of underdevelopment? *World Development*

Papaionnou, K., 1983. *De Marx et du Marxisme*, Paris: Gallimard

Parkin, F., 1979. *Marxism and Class Theory*, London: Tavistock

Pirenne, H., 1937. *Economic and Social History of Medieval Europe*, New York

Pirker, Theo (ed.), 1976. *Komintern und Faschismus*, Stuttgart: Deutsche Verlags-Anstalt

Plekhanov, G. V., 1956. *The Development of the Monist View of History*, Moscow

Poulantzas, Nicos, 1975. *Classes in Contemporary Capitalism*, London: New Left Books

Preobrazhensky, E., 1926. *The New Economics*, English translation, Oxford: Clarendon Press (1965)

Przeworski, Adam, 1977. From Proleteriat into Class: the process of class formation from Kautsky's *The Class Struggle* to recent contributions. *Politics and Society* 7, no. 4

 1980a. Social democracy as a historical phenomenon. *New Left Review* 122, July–August

 1980b. Material bases of consent: Politics and economics in a hegemonic system. *Political Power and Social Theory* 1, 23–68

 1981. Material interests, class compromise and the transition to socialism. *Politics and Society*, 10, no. 2 (also Essay 8, this volume)

Przeworski, Adam and Wallerstein, Michael, 1980. The structure of class conflict in advanced capitalist societies. Paper presented at Annual Meetings of the American Political Science Association, Washington, D.C.

 1982. The structure of class conflict in democratic capitalist societies. *American Political Science Review* 76, 215–38

Quattrone, G. and Tversky, A., 1985. Self-deception and the voter's illusion, in J. Elster (ed.), *The Multiple Self*, forthcoming from Cambridge University Press

Radcliffe-Brown, A. R., 1952. *Structure and Function in Primitive Society*, London

 1957. *A Natural Science of Society*, Glencoe, Ill.

Rader, M., 1979. *Marx's Interpretation of History*, New York

Rapoport, A. and Chammah, A., 1965. *Prisoner's Dilemma*, Ann Arbor: University of Michigan Press

Rawls, John, 1971. *A Theory of Justice*, Cambridge, Mass.: Belknap

Ritterbush, P. C., 1964. *Overtures to Biology*, New Haven, Connecticut

Robinson, Joan, 1966. *An Essay on Marxian Economics*, New York: St Martin's Press

Roemer, John E., 1979. Divide and conquer: microfoundations of the Marxian theory of discrimination. *Bell Journal of Economics* 10, no. 2, Autumn, 695–705

    1981. *Analytical Foundations of Marxian Economic Theory*, Cambridge University Press

    1982a. *A General Theory of Exploitation and Class*, Cambridge, Mass.: Harvard University Press

    1982b. Why labor classes? Department of Economics Working Paper no. 195, University of California, Davis

    1982c. Reply. *Politics and Society* 11, no. 3, 375–94

    1982d. Property relations vs. surplus value in Marxian exploitation. *Philosophy and Public Affairs* 11, no. 4, 281–313

    1982e. Exploitation, alternatives, and socialism. *Economic Journal* 92, 87–107

    1982f. Methodological individualism and deductive Marxism. *Theory and Society*, July, 513–20

    1982g. Origins of exploitation and class: Value theory of precapitalist economy. *Econometrica* 50, 163–92

    1982h. New directions in the Marxian theory of exploitation and class. *Politics and Society* 11, no. 3, 253–87

    1983a. Are socialist ethics consistent with efficiency? *Philosophical Forum* XIV, nos. 3–4, 369–88

    1983b. Unequal exchange, labor migration and international capital flows: a theoretical synthesis, in Padma Desai (ed.), *Marxism, the Soviet Economy and Central Planning: Essays in Honor of Alexander Erlich*, Cambridge, Mass.: M.I.T. Press

    1983c. R. P. Wolff's reinterpretation of Marx's labor theory of value: comment. *Philosophy and Public Affairs* 12, no. 1, 70–83

    1985a. Equality of talent. *Economics and Philosophy* 1

    1985b. Rationalizing revolutionary ideology, *Econometrica* 53, 85–108

Ruben, D., 1980. Review of Cohen (1978). *British Journal of Political Science* 11, 227–34

Sah, R. K. and Stiglitz, J. E., 1984. The economics of price scissors. *American Economic Review*, March

Salter, W. G., 1960. *Productivity and Technical Change*, Cambridge University Press

Samuelson, Paul A., 1971. Understanding the Marxian notion of exploitation: a summary of the so-called transformation problem between Marxian values and competitive prices. *Journal of Economic Literature* 9, 339–431

    1982. The normative and positivistic inferiority of Marx's values paradigm. *Southern Economic Journal* 49, no. 1, 11–18

Sartre, Jean-Paul, 1960. Foreword to Andre Gorz, *The Traitor*, London: Calder

Schotter, Andrew, 1984. *Free Market Economics: A Critical Appraisal*, New York: St Martin's Press

Schumpeter, J., 1961. *Capitalism, Socialism and Democracy*, London: Allen and Unwin

Sen, Amartya K., 1960. *Choice of Techniques*, Oxford: Basil Blackwell

    1961. On optimizing the rate of saving. *Economic Journal*

    1967. Isolation, assurance and the social rate of discount. *Quarterly Journal of Economics* 80, 112–24

1979a. Utilitarianism and welfarism. *Journal of Philosophy* 76, no. 9, 463–89

1979b. *Collective Choice and Social Welfare*, New York: North Holland

1980. Equality of what?, in S. McMurrin (ed.), *Tanner Lectures on Human Values*, Cambridge University Press

Shapley, L. and Shubik, M., 1967. Ownership and the production function. *Quarterly Journal of Economics* 80, 88–111

Sher, George, 1975. Justifying reverse discrimination in employment. *Philosophy and Public Affairs* 4

Shubik, M., 1982. *Game Theory in the Social Sciences*, Cambridge, Mass.: M.I.T. Press

Simmel, G., 1908. *Soziologie*, Berlin: Duncker und Humblot

Siriani, Carmen, 1982. *Workers Control and Socialist Democracy*, London: New Left Books

Smith, Adam, 1776. *The Wealth of Nations*, ed. E. Cannan, New York, 1937

Sombart, Werner, 1976. *Why is There No Socialism in the United States?* White Plains: M. E. Sharpe

Ste Croix, G. E. M. de, 1981. *The Class Struggle in the Ancient Greek World*, London: Duckworth

Steedman, Ian, 1977. *Marx after Sraffa*, London: New Left Books

Steiner, H., 1974–5. Individual liberty. *Proceedings of the Aristotelian Society*, pp. 33–50

Stigler, George, 1958. Ricardo and the 93% labor theory of value. *American Economic Review* 48, June

  1973. General economic conditions and national elections. *American Economic Review* 33, 160–7

Stinchcombe, A., 1974. Merton's theory of social structure, in L. Coser (ed.), *The Idea of Social Structure: Papers in Honor of Robert Merton*, 11–33, New York: Harcourt, Brace and World

Sweezy, P., 1950. A critique, in R. H. Hilton (ed.), *The Transition from Feudalism to Capitalism*, London (1976)

Tang Tsou, 1977. Mao Tse-Tung: The last struggle for succession, and the post-Mao era. Paper prepared for the Conference on 'What is Communism', University of Chicago, April 7–9

  1983. Back from the brink of revolutionary-'feudal' totalitarianism, in V. Nee and D. Mozingo (eds.), *State and Society in Contemporary China*, 53–88, Ithaca, N.Y.: Cornell University Press

Taylor, C., 1971. Interpretation and the sciences of man. *Review of Metaphysics* 25, 3–51

Taylor, M., 1976. *Anarchy and Cooperation*, Chichester: Wiley

Telser, L., 1978. *Economic Theory and the Core*, Chicago University Press

Thompson, E. P., 1968. *The Making of the English Working Class*, Harmondsworth: Penguin

Tilton, Timothy, 1979. A Swedish road to socialism: Ernst Wigforss and the ideological foundation of Swedish Social Democracy. *American Political Science Review* 73

Traven, B., 1973. *The Night Visitor and Other Stories*, New York: Hill and Wang

Trotsky, L., 1969. *The Permanent Revolution* and *Results and Prospects*, New York: Pathfinder Press

  1977. *The History of the Russian Revolution*, London: Pluto Press

Tversky, Amos, 1980. Choice versus preference: some psychological observations. Stanford University, mimeo van Parijs, P., 1981. *Evolution Explanation in the Social Sciences*, Totowa, N.J.: Rowman and Littlefield

Varian, Hal, 1978. *Microeconomic Analysis*, New York: W. W. Norton

Veblen, T., 1915. *Imperial Germany and the Industrial Revolution*, London: Macmillan

Vegara, Josep Ma., 1979. *Economia Politica y Modelos Multisectoriales*, Madrid: Editorial Tecnos

Veyne, P., 1976. *Le Pain et le Cirque*, Paris: Le Seuil

Weber, M., 1968. *Economy and Society*, New York: Bedminster Press

Winter, N., 1981. Attention allocation and input proportions. *Journal of Economic Behavior and Organization* 2, 31–46

Wolff, Robert P., 1981. A critique and reinterpretation of Marx's labor theory of value. *Philosophy and Public Affairs* 10, no. 2, 89–120

Wood, Allen, 1972. The Marxian critique of justice. *Philosophy and Public Affairs* 1

    1979. Marx on right and justice: A reply to Husami. *Philosophy and Public Affairs* 8

    1981. *Karl Marx*, London: Routledge and Kegan Paul

Wood, Ellen Meiksins, 1981. The separation of the economic and political in capitalism. *New Left Review* 127, May–June

Wright, Erik Olin, 1976. Class boundaries in advanced capitalist societies. *New Left Review* 98

    1978. *Class, Crisis and the State*, London: New Left Books

    1979. *Class Structure and Income Determination*, New York: Academic Press

    1980. Varieties of Marxist conceptions of class structure. *Politics and Society* 9, no. 3

    1982. The status of the political in the concept of class structure. *Politics and Society* 11, no. 3, 321–42

    1983a. Capitalism's futures. *Socialist Review* 68, March–April, 77–126

    1983b. Giddens' critique of Marxism. *New Left Review* 138, March–April

    1985. *Classes*, London: New Left Books

Wright, Erik Olin, Costello, Cynthia, Hachen, David, and Sprague, Joey, 1982. The American class structure. *The American Sociological Review*, December

Young, G., 1978. Justice and capitalist production. *Canadian Journal of Philosophy*, pp. 421–55

Zimmerman, D., 1981. Coercive wage offers. *Philosophy and Public Affairs*, pp. 121–45.